PELHAM
GRENVILLE
WODEHOUSE

"Plum's Literary Heroes"

PAUL KENT

Praise for Paul Kent's *Pelham Grenville Wodehouse Trilogy*

"This is a magnificent book. Kent's erudition, scholarship and easy turn of phrase makes it a must read for Wodehouse fans young and old. By placing the man, his character and his writing so effortlessly and brilliantly into the context of his times he gets to the nub of his greatness in a way others haven't. Reading this book was an utter joy."
David Cazalet, PGW's great grandson

"Paul's books are extraordinarily well researched, detailed, sometimes complex - and extremely readable, so I could review [Volume 3] in six words: 'Engaging, engrossing, entertaining - and hugely important'".
Wooster Sauce, Journal of the P G Wodehouse Society (UK)

"Despite Wodehouse's antipathy towards critics, Kent's first volume demonstrates just how much the thick-skinned of us have to explore in his work. It is therefore excellent news that we await two more volumes of his work that can help us to unpick that poetry and try to better understand the source of that "sunlit perfection".
Eliza Easton in the Times Literary Supplement (TLS)

"I have been enthralled while reading it . . . [Kent's] accounts of Plum himself, and so many of his major characters, are consistently masterful and compelling, bringing time and again new and fascinating insights into their backgrounds, characters and motivations. The book is indeed a masterpiece".
Sir Edward Cazalet, PGW's grandson

"Kent displays an encyclopaedic knowledge of the minutiae of Wodehouse's oeuvre and presents his arguments in a lively and engaging prose style that treads a delicate balance between academic rigour and readability. We read Wodehouse because he was a master of words. We can read Kent for the same reason".
Stewart Ferris, *Wooster Sauce*, Journal of the P G Wodehouse Society (UK)

"[A] whole new perspective on Wodehouse".
Peter van Nieuwenhuizen, The Netherlands Wodehouse Society

"Brilliant. The breadth of Wodehouse and wider references [Kent brings] in is staggering. And again, it's about the writing: hooray! Kent is forging the new path in the way I hope writing about Wodehouse will go".
Tim Andrew, Chairman, The P G Wodehouse Society (UK)

"Some fascinating insights into Plum's work. Tends to make you think about Wodehouse; what you have read and what you think/thought you know/knew. As Abbie Hoffman said: "Steal this book"".
Ken Clevenger, Fans of PG Wodehouse Facebook site

"Vol. 2, which I have just finished has really blown me away. It gave me a warm glow of happiness".
David Salter, The P G Wodehouse Society (UK) member

PELHAM GRENVILLE WODEHOUSE

"Plum's Literary Heroes"

PAUL KENT

TSB
London and New York

P E L H A M
GRENVILLE
WODEHOUSE

P.G. WODEHOUSE 1881-1975
HUMOURIST
NOVELIST
LYRICIST
PLAYWRIGHT

So reads the simple inscription on the memorial stone unveiled in London's Westminster Abbey in 2019, honouring the greatest comic writer of the 20th century. Sir Pelham Grenville Wodehouse KBE was all these things, writing more than 70 novels, 300 short stories, over 200 song lyrics and more than 20 plays in a career spanning eight decades. Over 40 years after his death, Wodehouse is not just surviving but thriving all over the world, so far being translated into 33 languages from Azerbaijani to Ukrainian via Hebrew, Italian, Swedish and Chinese. There are also established Wodehouse societies in the UK, the USA, Belgium, Holland and Russia. His books are demonstrating the staying power of true classics, and are all currently in print, making him as relevant – and funny – as he ever was.

PAUL
KENT

ABOUT THE AUTHOR

Vice-Chairman of the P G Wodehouse Society (UK), Paul Kent began reading Wodehouse at the age of 12 and is now much older than that. He has compiled works on Montaigne, Voltaire and Shakespeare, and a guide to creative writing *How Writers Write*. From 2019-23 he published the highly-acclaimed literary biography *Pelham Grenville Wodehouse*, followed in 2024 by *What Ho!* – a series of ten short pamphlets on Wodehousean themes including *Love*, *Sport* and *Food*. He is currently working on a major, full-length account of Plum's theatrical career entitled *Showbiz Wodehouse*.

Cover design: James Shannon
Typesetting: James Shannon
Index: Madison Melby

Printed and bound in the United Kingdom
ISBN: 978-1-911673-25-5
British Library Cataloguing in Publication Data
A catalogue record for this book is available from the British Library

Library of Congress Cataloging-in-Publication Data
A catalog record for this book is available from the Library of Congress

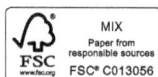

MIX
Paper from
responsible sources
FSC FSC® C013056

The Forest Stewardship Council® is an international non-governmental organisation that promotes environmentally appropriate, socially beneficial, and economically viable management of the world's forests. To learn more visit www.fsc.org

We make every effort to make sure our products are safe for the purpose for which they are intended. For more information see our website or contact our EU Authorised Representative, EAS Project OU, Mustamäe tee 50, 10621,Tallinn, Estonia, gpsr.requests@easproject.com

To my parents, Betty and Fred.

A POTTED LIFE OF P.G. WODEHOUSE

1881	October 15	Birth of Pelham Grenville Wodehouse at 1 Vale Place, Guildford, Surrey
1894		PGW first attends Dulwich College, London
1900		Receives his first payment for writing: from *Public School Magazine* for an article entitled 'Some Aspects of Game-Captaincy'
1900	September	Starts work at the Hong Kong and Shanghai Bank, London
1901	July	First real short story published in *Public School Magazine*, entitled 'The Prize Poem'
1901	August 16	First contribution to *Globe* newspaper
1902	September 9	Resigns from the HS Bank
1902	September 17	First article for *Punch* magazine, entitled 'An Unfinished Collection'
1902	September 19	First book published, *The Pothunters*
1904	April 16	First visit to the USA
1904	August	Appointed Editor of the 'By The Way' column at the *Globe*
1904	December 10	First published lyric, 'Put Me In My Little Cell', sung in *Sergeant Brue* at the Strand Theatre, London
1906	March 6	Employed by Seymour Hicks as the resident lyricist at the Aldwych Theatre
1906	March 19	First meets future collaborator Jerome Kern
1906	August	First novel for adults, *Love Among the Chickens*, published
1907	December 6	Joins Gaiety Theatre as lyricist
1909		Second visit to USA, where he sells short stories to *Collier's* and *Cosmopolitan*
1911	August 24	First play, *A Gentleman of Leisure*, opens in New York
1913	April 8	First play in London, *Brother Alfred*, flops
1914	August 2	Returns to New York
1914	August 3	Meets Ethel Rowley, née Newton, an English widow, at a New York party
1914	September 30	Marries Ethel Rowley and inherits her daughter Leonora
1915	March	Appointed drama critic of [US] *Vanity Fair*
1915	June 26	First appearance of Lord Emsworth and Blandings Castle in the serialisation of *Something New* (*Something Fresh* is U.K. title) in *Saturday Evening Post*
1915	September 18	Jeeves makes his first appearance, in the story 'Extricating Young Gussie' published in *Saturday Evening Post*
1916	September 25	First Bolton, Wodehouse & Kern musical comedy, *Miss Springtime* debuts in New York and is moderately successful
1919	June 7	First Oldest Member story, 'A Woman is Only a Woman', published in *Saturday Evening Post*
1923	April	First Ukridge short story, 'Ukridge's Dog College', appears in *Cosmopolitan*

1926		PGW elected a Fellow of the Royal Society of Literature
1926	July	First Mr Mulliner story, 'The Truth About George', appears in *Strand* magazine
1930	June 1	Starts first contract with MGM in Hollywood
1933	August	First instalment of the first Jeeves and Bertie Wooster novel, *Thank You, Jeeves*, published in *Strand*
1934	January 19	Successfully challenges in court the U.K. Inland Revenue's attempts to claim more income tax on his earnings
1934	June	Settles in Le Touquet, France
1935	June 3	Buys Low Wood in Le Touquet
1936	June 26	Awarded medallion by International Mark Twain Society
1939	June 2	Invested as D. Litt at Oxford University
1939	September 3	Britain declares war on Germany
1940	May 21	PGW, Ethel and animals try to leave Le Touquet in the light of the German advance, but their car twice breaks down
1940	July 21	Start of PGW internment by Germans in camps successively at Loos Prison (Lille), Liege, Huy and Tost (Upper Silesia)
1941	June 21	PGW released from internment and taken to Berlin
1941	June 26	PGW makes the first of five radio broadcasts for fans in neutral USA
1941	July 15	'Cassandra's' BBC radio broadcast of a vituperative attack on PGW, calling him a traitor
1943	September 11	PGW transferred to Paris
1944	May 16	Death of PGW's step-daughter Leonora
1947	April 27	PGW and Ethel arrive in US on SS America
1952	March	Ethel buys a house in Basket Neck Lane, Remsenburg, Long Island, New York, close to Guy Bolton's home
1955	December 16	PGW becomes an American citizen
1960	January 27	PGW elected to the *Punch* table
1961	July 15	BBC broadcasts 'An Act of Homage and Reparation' by Evelyn Waugh
1965	May 27	BBC TV series *The World of Wooster* begins transmission
1967	February 16	BBC TV series *Blandings Castle* begins transmission
1974	November	PGW's last complete novel, *Aunts Aren't Gentlemen*, published in the U.K.
1975	January 1	PGW knighted by Queen Elizabeth II, his wife Ethel taking the title Lady Wodehouse
1975	February 14	PGW dies in hospital

CONTENTS

There is no surer foundation for a beautiful friendship than a mutual taste in literature.
('*Strychnine in the Soup*')

Introduction:
Wodehouse, Reading
and Influence

Wodehouse's writing does feed joyfully on his reading.
Richard Usborne

I find there is nothing in this world I really want to do
except read.
PGW, Letter to Bill Townend, 12 April 1921

Westbrook asks me if reading some English literature
did me any good. I say, "Well, I suppose it was like meat
going into the sausage mills. It will come out in the form
of sausages some time."
PGW, Phrases and Notes

"Ooh, what a lot of g'ate big booful books!"
Bill the Conqueror

In the January 1902 edition of *Public School Magazine*, a new, young, fresh
talent announced itself in English schoolboy fiction:

> "Where have I seen that face before?" said a voice. Tony
> Graham looked up from the bag in which he was rum-
> maging.
> "Hullo, Allen," he said, "what the dickens are you up here
> for?"
> "I was rather thinking of doing a little boxing. If you've no
> objection, of course."
> "But you ought to be on a bed of sickness, and that sort of
> thing. I heard you'd crocked yourself."
> "So I did. Nothing much, though. Trod on myself during
> a game of fives, and twisted my ankle a bit."
> "In for the middles, of course?"
> "Yes."
> "So am I."
> "Yes, so I saw in the *Sportsman*. It says you weigh elev-
> en-three."
> "Bit more, really, I believe. Shan't be able to have any

lunch probably, or I shall have to go in for the heavies. What are you?"

"Just eleven. Well, let's hope we meet in the final."

"Rather," said Tony.

It was at Aldershot – to be more exact, in the dressing-room of the Queen's Road Gymnasium at Aldershot – that the conversation took place. From East and West, and North and South, from Dan even unto Beersheba, the representatives of the Public Schools had assembled to box, fence, and perform gymnastic prodigies for fame and silver medals. The room was full of all sorts and sizes of them, heavy-weights looking ponderous and muscular, feather-weights diminutive but wiry, light-weights, middle-weights, fencers, and gymnasts in scores, some wearing the unmistakable air of the veteran, for whom Aldershot has no mysteries, others nervous, and wishing themselves back again at school.

The Pothunters, of which this is the opening, was P. G. ('Plum') Wodehouse's very first stab at a full-length serial. It would eventually appear as a novel nine months later, and at well over a century's remove it's perhaps difficult to grasp why it's remarkable. Only it is – and here are a few reasons why.

Right from the start, the more alert of his young readers would recognize this new writer, whoever he was, seemed to be taking considerable pains to demonstrate he was one of *them* – which, at least in theory, wasn't that difficult, as Plum had only left Dulwich College a little over twelve months before, aged 18. An avid consumer of school stories, he instinctively knew his priority right from the start would be to do what many of his rivals were *not* doing: he would need to construct credible communities of schoolboys with which his readers could identify, getting in among them and holding a true mirror up to their lives. Only then would they learn to trust him and keep coming back for more. And so, in those 250 opening words, Wodehouse cannily creates a vibrant gathering of young athletes of all shapes and sizes, from the nervous neophyte to the experienced veteran, all milling about in eager anticipation of some sporting action.

As any of his contemporary readers would have known, the Aldershot championships in boxing, fencing and gymnastics was an annual event hosted by the Army Physical Training Corps in late March, drawing entries from around 40 schools. For many competitors, it was the climax of their academic year, one Plum had described wearing his journalist's hat in an article for *Public School Magazine* the previous year entitled 'The Schools of Aldershot.' Plum's fiction immediately rang true, from his casual mention of schoolboy bible *The Sportsman* to the boxers' weights and divisions.

Yet this opening flurry of intel is not conveyed from on high by an omniscient narrator but artfully woven into a breezy conversation between two aspiring boxers, Tony Graham and Allen Thomson. By making them cousins, Plum cunningly enables the boys to banter informally from the off; yet attending different schools, they still have to bring one another (and, of course, us) up to speed with what is happening. Inherited from drama (Shakespeare does it a lot), this is a time-honoured means of imparting what an audience needs to know upfront without a stilted, formal introduction ("Our story begins . . ."). Starting with dialogue, Plum can also show off his uniquely attuned ear for English public-school speech, a feature of his style that would further cement that bond of authenticity with his audience. The conversation ends by neatly throwing forward to the chapter's close, when talk gives way to action and the cousins *do* meet in the bruising middleweight final.

As the third-person narrator takes over ("It was at Aldershot . . ."), he addresses his audience using an informal tone almost identical to that employed by Graham and Thomson, talking *to* his readers, not *at* them. Note also the two elided Bible quotes he deftly slips in: ("From East to West . . ." is from the Book of Psalms and "from Dan . . ." can be found in 1 Samuel). This uncredited material (whose provenance Plum could be reasonably confident his readers would recognize if not accurately place) lends additional colour and sonority to what is already well-polished prose. And we might also remark in closing this short summary how Plum begins his tale *in medias res*, giving himself plenty of leisure to establish what he would often call the crucial "atmosphere" of his story before introducing the main plot-driver (the theft of two silver sports trophies) in the following chapter.

First time out of the traps, Wodehouse is already displaying quite a bit of behind-the-scenes literary nous. There's not an ounce of 'fat' here, Plum instinctively understanding that if a writer didn't grab his readers' attention as quickly as he could, he would risk losing them to rival authors or other forms of entertainment.

Fortunately, he wouldn't. The novelized version of *The Pothunters* sold a respectable if not earth-shattering 396 copies in its first three months, enough to justify his publisher's investment in further volumes; and a contemporary review praised the story's "insight and humour" as well as its "easy, attractive style." Wodehouse was on his way, and whether or not you are drawn to his schoolboy fiction, it quickly becomes clear that the *technical* quality of his early writing set it apart from much of the competition. Soon, it would be judged "hard to surpass."

But where, we might ask, did Plum learn these tricks of his trade, and so early in his career? Although his debut only hints at the glories to come, the fact that he instinctively got so much *right* reveals the massive debt he already owed not just to his reading, but to his ability to sort the wheat from the chaff, take what he needed, and make it his own. That masterful appropriation is, in a nutshell, what this book's about: how quietly and over the first few decades of his career, Wodehouse would make himself as notable a literary synthesist as his lifelong fan T. S. Eliot, but – unlike his acolyte – with no great show he'd sweated over his homework. En route, I will argue that Plum's fiction was among the most elegant manifestations of Eliot's well-known maxim (sometimes attributed elsewhere) that while second rate writers can only *imitate*, great writers *steal* anything they can.

This principle has been misunderstood so often, here's the whole thing in context:

> Immature poets imitate; mature poets steal; bad poets de-face what they take, and good poets make it into something better, or at least something different. The good poet welds his theft into a whole of feeling which is unique, utterly different from that from which it was torn; the bad poet throws it into something which has no cohesion.
>
> ('Philip Massinger,' 1920)

And it's not just poets. Those writers who know their onions don't simply nick stuff and produce inferior knockoffs; they seamlessly alchemize wonderful, fresh, *original* stuff from the pilfered goods – a putting in as well as a drawing out, as an obnoxicated Gussie Fink-Nottle doesn't quite put it in *Right Ho, Jeeves*. In their very different ways, Eliot and Wodehouse were generous givers as well as promiscuous takers, and in this book's first section (Chapters 1-7) we'll be rummaging around in Plum's swag bag, taking a good look at what he swiped.

Which was a lot, for Wodehouse was rarely without his nose in a book. Aged 6, he had already ploughed through Alexander Pope's grandiloquent 18th-century translation of Homer's *Iliad*; and the final time his grandson Edward Cazalet saw him alive he was busy devouring *Smokescreen*, a 1972 thriller by Dick Francis. During the intervening 80-odd years, thousands of books of all kinds must have passed beneath his gaze, as evidenced in his correspondence, records of his copious library borrowings, the contents of his bookshelves and of course, the countless references in his fiction and journalism. His very first published short story ('The Prize Poem' from 1901) not only takes literature – and borrowing from literature – as its subject, but starts as he means to go on by puckishly plagiarizing some dodgy verse his older brother Armine had composed for one such award in 1894, a description of Dulwich College styled after a 17th-century English 'country house' poem of the kind popularized by Ben Jonson in 'To Penshurst':

Imposing pile, reared up 'midst pleasant grounds,
The scene of many a battle, lost or won,
At cricket or at football; whose red walls
Full many a sun has kissed ere day is done.

Plum the magpie would steal from anywhere or anyone – even family. In *The Pothunters* alone, copious allusions to schoolboy favourites from *Great Expectations* to Sherlock Holmes nestle among quotes or references snaffled from Shakespeare (x8), William Wordsworth, W. S. Gilbert, G. A. Henty, Bret Harte, Rabbie Burns, Barry Pain, Lewis Carroll, Wilkie Collins, Rudyard Kipling, Ambrose Bierce, Ovid, the lyrics of several music-hall songs and well over a dozen lifts from the Bible. It's a heady cocktail for a young man of just 20.

In the introduction to the autobiographical *Performing Flea*, Wodehouse's Dulwich study mate and lifelong friend Bill Townend remembered what bliss it had been in that dawn to be alive, lounging in a two-man study with Plum, "evening after evening, when we should have been preparing the next day's work, in reading and in conversation":

We talked incessantly, about books and writing. Plum's talk was exhilarating. I had never known such talk. Even at the age of seventeen he could discuss lucidly writers of whom I had never heard. I was impressed by his knowledge. He was an omnivorous reader [...] [b]ut it is impossible to say who were his favourite authors. He liked so many and all kinds. And from the first time I met him, he had decided to write. He never swerved.

From his schooldays until his death, Wodehouse loved to discuss his packed reading schedule with his correspondents, and we know from letters written during the summer vacation of 1899 that he was reading the novels of Victorian social satirist William Makepeace Thackeray, specifically *The History of Henry Esmond* and *Pendennis*, considering them "[r]attling good books" (he would doubtlessly have bonded with the latter's hero who, when young, "devoured all the novels, plays, and poetry on which he could lay his hands.") He also had a stab at Robert Browning's notoriously tricky poetry, which he doesn't comment on, except to say he prefers Tennyson. The following month Browning is still on the menu, being compared favourably with the "obscure [...] rot" of minor Victorian versifier William Ernest Henley. From out of left field comes news he has finished John Dryden's 18th-century Chaucer's adaptation *Palamon and Arcite* ("3000 lines if it's an inch!") which he judges "rather a good poem full of blud and luv."

Highbrow or lowbrow didn't seem to matter. In an article written for *Public School Magazine* in December 1900, Wodehouse sticks up for popular literature while staging a battle for a typical schoolboy's soul between a very suave Mephistopheles, who is encouraging the lad (Smith) to skip his prep and read a novel; and the boy's Conscience, telling him to knuckle down to some Thucydides. At one stage the demon runs his eye over Smith's bookshelves:

> **Mephistopheles**: Hullo, you've got a decent lot of books, pommy word you have. *Rodney Stone*, *Vice Versa*. *Many Cargoes*. Ripping. Ever read *Many Cargoes*? ...
> **Smith**: Never. Only got it to-day. Good?
> **Mephistopheles**: Simply ripping. All short stories. Make you yell.

The demon singles out three books of Wodehouse's acquaintance, respectively: a boxing novel by Arthur Conan Doyle from 1896; an 1882 body swap drama by F. Anstey whose central premise Plum would fess up to borrowing many years later for his own *Laughing Gas*; and a collection of light-hearted nautical stories by one of his lifetime favourites W. W. Jacobs, also published in 1896. Quite a trove of popular fiction, far more fun to read than boring old "Thick-sides." And in 'Bradshaw's Little Story' from 1902, we learn how the rip-snorting adventures of H. Rider Haggard (*King Solomon's Mines*, *She*) might easily trump Euripides in a schoolboy's affections.

Plum would never stop exploring, weighing each writer for their pound or ounce of pleasure or edification, many not meeting his exacting standards. One of my favourite Wodehouse letters, written to Bill Townend in 1929, casually demands:

> How are you on the Elizabethan dramatists? My opinion, now that I have read them all, is that they are a shade better than Restoration dramatists, but as you rightly remark, that is not saying much.

"Now that I have read them all" is evidence that even as he approached 50, Plum was still boning up on his literary heritage – probably on the lookout for plots – yet he refused to be awed by its antiquity or the veneration in which it was held. Books existed to be enjoyed, not worshipped as cultural artefacts; and the same went for libraries. In *Bill the Conqueror* he creates Cooley Paradene, a fanatical bibliophile whose hoard of literature is his pride and joy:

> The library of Mr. Cooley Paradene at his house at Westbury, Long Island, was a room which caused bibliophiles on entering it to run round in ecstatic circles, prying and sniffing and uttering short, excited, whining noises like dogs suddenly plunged into the middle of a hundred entrancing smells. Its fame, one might say, was international, for articles describing it had appeared in such widely separated periodicals as the Atlantic Monthly, the Quarterly Review and the Mercure de France. On each wall were shelves, and on each shelf volume after volume of oddly ill-assorted sizes – here a massive tome, there next to it a squat dwarf of a book; yonder a thing that looked like a book, but was really a box containing a book. The mere sight of these affected those who appreciated that sort of thing like some powerful drug. Bill, not being a bibliophile, bore the spectacle with more calm.

Plum was more a Bill than a Cooley. When he moved into his plush new residence in Norfolk Street, Mayfair in 1927, his wife Ethel fitted out a "magnificent library" for her husband, who wasn't over-impressed with its floor-to-ceiling shelves. As he confessed to Bill Townend, it looked "a bit too much like 'Mr Wodehouse among his books.'" It swallowed his own collection, and if you looked carefully you could see it had been padded out with "old encyclopaedias etc, bunged in to act as background." To think, he comments, "that I, who always swore that I would never have a book in the house which was not one of my favourites, should have sunk to this!"

It wouldn't be long before he started keeping his true favourites upstairs in his bedroom. These didn't include the works of writers who taxed their readers' patience by piling on the gloom, particularly those like Thomas Hardy or the Great Russians who were also cruel to their characters. George Gissing was eschewed for his default setting of greyness, and Modernists were pilloried for deliberately making their work obscure and difficult to read. Anthony Trollope, who Plum only got round to reading in his 60s, was enjoyable but "too slow." Gustave Flaubert, with his uncanny skill for finding *le mot juste* was a late-flowering favourite, as were English social chronicler Anthony Powell and farcical humourist Tom Sharpe. But for much of the time Plum would settle down and relax with his regular favourites Evelyn Waugh, Barry Pain, Sinclair Lewis, Jerome K. Jerome, Tennyson, and Shakespeare, whose plays he re-read regularly. As his wife Ethel commented in an interview with the *Daily Express* in 1934:

> He reads very few modern novels, but he revels in detective stories, and Thackeray and some of the older writers he will read over and over again […] and never tire of them.

What better preparation could there have been for his own writing? Wodehouse's full-on engagement with every style of literature is inevitably reflected in his carnival of characters: there's usually someone with a book on the boil somewhere in his stories, whether they're reading, writing or discussing it. Gally Threepwood busily compiles his scurrilous memoirs, Percy Gorringe composes modernist nonsense, Officer Garroway takes poetry lessons, Rosie M. Banks crafts her bestselling romances, and Ashe Marson writes for the pulps. Prose and poetry from Shelley to Schopenhauer are regularly quoted, read or recommended. Monday night is Book Night at the Angler's Rest, the fiefdom of Mr. Mulliner, who tells us "[t]here is no surer foundation for a beautiful friendship than a mutual taste in literature." In all, there are over 120 characters in Wodehouse's stories who have written one thing or another, and an even greater number of readers reading them.

Which conveniently brings us to what you can expect from *this* book. Although creative alchemy rarely bares all (and then only grudgingly), I would hope that by the time we part company at least some light will have been shed on how Wodehouse spent three-quarters of a century transforming a glorious cornucopia of influences from his Literary Heroes into comedy gold.

In Chapter 1 we'll begin by surveying the deepest foundations of Plum's writing through what he read while at an impressionable age and how he took it all in – the psychology behind his early reading, if you will. Since Plum rarely wrote about his youth in any detail, we'll be recruiting the services of Rudyard Kipling, Wodehouse's friend and Literary Hero who wrote brilliantly about the significance of teenage reading to future writers, and whose youthful experiences with books bore a marked similarity to Plum's. Chapter 2 will survey the literary market of Plum's childhood and early career, from the penny dreadfuls to sanctimonious sermons, while Chapter 3 will introduce those long-forgotten journeymen of late Victorian and Edwardian letters whose influence helped him develop his unique narrative style.

Chapter 4 will then spool way, way back to Classical and then Biblical times, exposing some of the most fundamental and instinctive elements in Wodehouse's prose. Majoring in the classics at Dulwich, Plum learned to translate Ancient Greek and Latin texts into English, and the other way round. Although something of a slog, it was a discipline that furnished him with an excellent grounding in the complexities of English grammar and syntax; widened his already extensive vocabulary; and familiarized him with the timbre, tone, modulation and rhythms of the words he used – one of the many reasons his writing reads so effortlessly. This sixth sense – what we might call the 'musicality' of his language – also owed a considerable debt to the timeless resonance of the 1611 King James Bible, a resource he mercilessly plundered. Throughout Plum's work there are begattings and smitings, lions' dens and fiery furnaces, lilies of the fields and flesh that is as grass, scales falling from eyes and spirits moving, good fights fought and fatted calves killed. The Book of Isaiah was his most regular supplier, followed closely by St. Matthew's Gospel; but does anyone remember the Books of Joel, Titus, and Nahum? Wodehouse does, a writer for whom "Pleasant words [were] as an honeycomb, sweet to the soul, and health to the bones" (Proverbs 16:24).

Chapter 5 opens in New York at the dawn of the 20th century where Wodehouse, aged 22, fell in love with the sound of the American vernacular and its lively, multicultural slang. His early explorations were greatly assisted by author and playwright George Ade; but this would only be the start of a lifelong affair, Plum clipping examples of language he found amusing out of American newspapers well into his 80s. Which clearly paid off: there aren't many British writers who can invent six varieties of Stateside-sounding hangover, including the "gremlin boogie" and the "cement mixer," as Plum does in *The Mating Season*.

Closing Part One, I'll be devoting a chapter apiece to two literary genres that stand out as Wodehouse's regular favourites, beginning with the romance. Most of his mature plots contain a love story at one point or another, although – as we'll see in Chapter 6 – it may come as a surprise to learn just how widely he read within a genre he relentlessly parodies. But then again, not really, for Plum could never wholly dismiss writing that was commercially successful. Among his contemporaries were many romance writers who sold by the million yet are now largely forgotten, and it has been both a pleasure and a revelation to discover that many are far better than their current obscurity might lead us to believe. He certainly learned a lot from bestselling page-turners like Ethel M. Dell, Ruby M. Ayres and Edith M. Hull, way beyond his insertion of that middle 'M' in Rosie M. Banks. After all, his made-up romance titles *Only a Factory Girl*, *All for Love*, *A Red, Red Summer Rose* and even the racy *Furnace of Sin* often beat these writers at their own game.

But when it came to Plum's rambles through popular literature, none were more keenly anticipated than those featuring a corpse and a cunning detective. All his life, Wodehouse devoured crime novels, mysteries and thrillers from Sherlock Holmes to Mignon G. Eberhart and all points in between, embracing the massively popular adventures of Agatha Christie, Dorothy L. Sayers, Rex Stout and Edgar Wallace. And, as with every other genre of literature he loved, Plum was apt to mock it even though some of those big names would become friends and correspondents who paid him the ultimate compliment of styling their writing after his. Chapter 7 reveals more puttings-in and drawings-out, along with a further set of matchless parody titles like *Gore By the Gallon*, *Death Takes the Cure* and *Madeline Monk, Murderess*.

But this book isn't simply going to be a treasure hunt (or turkey shoot) of the hundreds of writers who play hide-and-seek in Wodehouse's stories. In Part Two, we'll be looking at a second set of Literary Heroes who fundamentally influenced not just his style, but the way he conceived of his calling and the workings of his profession. Chapter 8 features a variety of authors whose lives and works helped Plum get his ideas straight on how to sync up that fundamental three-way relationship between author, text, and reader central to any meaningful experience of fiction. His friend Arthur Conan Doyle was a model he would look up to; less so Hall Caine (author of *The Woman Thou Gavest Me*) and Marie Corelli (*The Sorrows of Satan*), two writers who stretch this book's definition of 'Hero' by being heroically *bad*, offering the young Wodehouse salutary instruction in how not to write and comport himself in public.

But of all the many writers Plum read and enjoyed, there would always be The Big Three, those giants who bestrid his literary sensibility like colossi and who would not simply entertain him throughout his long life but teach him plenty about the ins and outs of his job. Chapters 9 to 11 are individual case studies in how Plum brought his own critical faculties to bear on their lives and works:

- His regular reading of Shakespeare didn't allow him to visualize his #1 writer as a god in some far-off Parnassus awaiting a capricious muse, but a put-upon, self-made craftsman (a bit like himself?) whose measure of success was not literary immortality but bums on seats and box

office returns.
- From the genius of Alfred, Lord Tennyson Plum would learn how great writing need not be incompatible with mass appeal.
- And the career of W. S. Gilbert taught him winning ways with different varieties of humour, while providing salutary lessons in picking his literary battles carefully.

To close the book, it's the turn of the literary Modernists to get the Wodehouse treatment, prompting a general reflection on why Plum, unlike James Joyce or T. S. Eliot, is rarely credited as the major literary alchemist he so evidently is.

So that's the menu; but before the starter arrives, there's four brief items of housekeeping:

Firstly, 'influence' is a many-splendoured and at times slippery thing. Simply because Plum read, referenced, or regularly quoted a particular writer or body of work doesn't necessarily imply he was under their influence. For example, throughout *Leave it to Psmith* Plum shamelessly thieves from Gertrude Jekyll's 1904 book *Some English Gardens*, most notably in re. the flora at Blandings:

> A writer, describing Blandings Castle in a magazine article, had once said: 'Tiny mosses have grown in the cavities of the stones, until, viewed near at hand, the place seems shaggy with vegetation.'

Now here's the uncredited Jekyll's original, referring to the real-life Berkeley Castle in Gloucestershire:

> Tiny mosses have grown in their cavities […] until, viewed near at hand, the mighty walls and sustaining buttresses are seen to be shaggy with vegetation.

It's a fair collar. But Jekyll hasn't influenced Wodehouse; he's simply read her book and nicked some bits he needed. The ever-vigilant David Landman has also spotted extensive and almost verbatim lifts from the *New York Sun* of October 9, 1926, which flesh out the origins of the hog-call "Pig-hoo-o-o-o-ey!"; and Norman Murphy has noticed numerous thefts from the writer Charles Brookfield, who unwittingly contributed the card game Persian Monarchs ('The Smile That Wins') and Archibald Mulliner's show-stopping imitation of a hen laying an egg ('The Reverent Wooing of Archibald' and elsewhere). Articles have been written and speeches delivered on the inspiration allegedly supplied by crime novelist Lord Dunsany, of whom Plum wrote "I never get tired of his stories"; and even Lewis Carroll, whose work pops up around 20 times.

But do these larcenies strictly constitute *influence*? The compendious and well-indexed *Familiar Quotations* by John Bartlett was Plum's constant companion, so there's no guarantee he had actually delved into a particular writer's oeuvre at all but simply looked them up. In an unperformed playscript from 1948, he admits as much:

> **Vincent:** Want some words of wisdom from the Classics? Quote: "Of all the paths that lead to a woman's love, pity's the straightest." Unquote. Seventeenth century.
> **Doctor:** You read the old English authors?
> **Vincent:** No, I read *Bartlett's Book of Familiar Quotations.*

And then there's that lengthy canter in *Over Seventy* which had me pondering whether John Bartlett, in a book calling itself *Plum's Literary Heroes*, should be given a chapter to himself:

> I wonder if Bartlett has been as good a friend to other writers as he has been to me. I don't know where I would have been all these years without him. It so happens that I am not very bright and find it hard to think up anything really clever off my own bat, but give me my Bartlett and I will slay you.

BTW, that uncredited quote about "woman's love" a few lines back arrived courtesy of Francis Beaumont and John Fletcher's drama *The Knight of Malta*. Plum probably *did* look that one up (it's in Bartlett), although one wouldn't put it past him to have read the work of those cruelly neglected 17th century playwrights for pleasure or instruction.

Then there's the issue of careless attribution that passes into myth. To give but one example: the internet is awash with the theory (routinely copied and pasted) that early in his career, Wodehouse fell beneath the spell of Hector Hugh Munro (*alias* 'Saki'), a theory Plum played along with, probably in the belief it might pique the interest of Munro's many fans in his own writing. Unfortunately, the claim is absolute bunk; besides their shared facility for minting pithy epigrams (which clearly owed something to Oscar Wilde), even the most cursory examination of Plum and Saki's writing reveals they are alike as chalk and cheese, the lightness of Wodehouse World dissolving on contact with Saki's cruel, cynical, and absurdist muse. There are no murderous ferrets or terrorist bombs to be found in Plum's fiction, and although both writers are regularly (and correctly) cited as key influences on Evelyn Waugh, the connection, IMHO, ends there.

Third: in my *Pelham Grenville Wodehouse* trilogy, I have already examined Plum's debt to medieval romance in his love stories (*cf.* Volume 2, Chapter 3); and the frequent echoes of Juvenal and Horace's classical satires in his journalism (*cf.* the Introduction to Volume 3) – so I'll not reprise those observations here.

And finally: the influence of theatrical performance on Plum's sensibility is such a massive subject that it demands (and will be getting) a volume of its own, which means it will only be sporadically touched on in this book, despite the star billing of both Gilbert and Shakespeare. So if you're surprised and disappointed you can't find the plays of Terence, J. M. Barrie, or Oscar Wilde in here, don't worry – they'll be in the next one.

In among all this, I mustn't forget *my* Literary Heroes whose painstaking work has made the writing of this book exponentially easier. Among many others, I owe a huge debt of gratitude to – in alphabetical order – Fr. Rob Bovendeaard, Marilyn MacGregor, Neil Midkiff, Norman Murphy, Tony Ring, Arthur Robinson, Diego Seguí, and Karen Shotting who must have spent countless hours rooting out Plum's thousands of borrowings so I didn't have to; to Ananth Kaitharam, the prime mover behind the *Madame Eulalie* website, an invaluable resource of Wodehouseana I visit daily; to Tad Boehmer, the expert cataloguer of Plum's New York book loans; Calista Lucy, Keeper of the Archive at Dulwich College for her invaluable support with Plum's schoolboy reading; and as always, Sir Edward Cazalet, the Cazalet family, Pauline Grant and the Trustees of the Wodehouse Estate for their permission and assistance in conducting such joyful research into Plum's legacy. And to my publisher, Tobias Steed, who not only puts up with me, but runs the Gold Bats, the P G Wodehouse Society (UK)'s cricket team.

Paul Kent, London, May 2025

PART ONE: WODEHOUSE AMONG HIS BOOKS

Chapter 1:
'Old Pop' Kipling and the Young Writer's Imagination

No-one, the owner least of all, can explain what is in a
growing boy's mind.
Rudyard Kipling, Stalky and Co.

Childhood is the time when one reads almost anything:
one has only to read any autobiography of a man or
woman born before, say, 1890 to realise this.
**Philip Larkin (writing as 'Brunette Coleman'),
'What are we writing for?'**

As soon as the boys had turned into Clonliffe Road together they began to speak about books and writers, saying
what books they were reading and how many books there
were in their fathers' bookcases at home.
James Joyce, Portrait of the Artist as a Young Man

One of the poets, whose name I cannot recall, has a passage, which I am unable at the moment to remember, in
one of his works, which for the time being has slipped my
mind, which hits off admirably this age-old situation.
The Long Hole

[Lord Emsworth] was reminded of a Kipling poem the
curate had recited at a village entertainment his sister Constance had once made him attend – something about if
you can something something and never something something, you'll be a man, my son, or words to that effect.
Galahad at Blandings

In the 'Compulsory Preface' to the spoof history textbook *1066 and All
That* by W. C. Sellar and R. J. Yeatman, we find the following proposition:

History is not what you thought. It is what you can remember. All other history defeats itself.

Written in 1930, this remains an eternal truth: after all, if history isn't memorable, it carries the seeds of its own redundancy. But all those things we *can* remember, reliant on our imperfect memories, can often be eccentrically random and/or downright undependable. What we half-learned in school on the occasions we were paying attention gets mixed up with all kinds of other stuff haphazardly hoovered up down the years to create an enormous dog's breakfast that isn't much practical use to anyone.

Except perhaps a writer.

In his poem 'The Circus Animals' Desertion,' W. B. Yeats (very possibly a distant relative of Plum's through his Uncle Hugh) pondered where the raw materials of his art came from:

> Those masterful images because complete
> Grew in pure mind but out of what began?
> A mound of refuse or the sweepings of a street,
> Old kettles, old bottles, and a broken can,
> Old iron, old bones, old rags.

Everything and anything in the writer's memory is grist to the mill, and Yeats proceeds to demonstrate how "old" unpromising cast-offs mysteriously appear and are magically transformed into glitzy "circus animals" ready for their debut in the literary Big Top. Which lends the act of writing a glorious serendipity tantalisingly beyond the author's control.

Because of this involuntariness, most writers can't stop themselves musing on what they do and how they do it, and Wodehouse was no exception – after all, writing occupied most of his waking life. Nowadays this makes him something of a 'postmodernist' or 'metatextualist,' self-important names for someone who writes about writing. It all sounds dreadfully brainy, but when Plum did it he was simply having fun, taking the rise out of his profession, his fellow scribes, and often himself. Which is one of the many reasons Bertie Wooster exists, to offer a jokey, sideways commentary on the act of authorship with all its glories and frustrations. But although a seasoned autobiographer with 11 novels and 39 short stories under his belt, Bertie has never been much cop at remembering anything, particularly other writers' quotations, which makes the act of corralling *his* circus animals more akin to herding cats.

The rot started early: in *Jeeves and the Feudal Spirit*, he recalls how he "practically always fluffed my lines" when Ma Wooster insisted he parrot Tennyson's 'The Charge of the Light Brigade' to entertain her friends:

> "Tum tiddle umpty-pum
> Tum tiddle umpty-pum
> Tum tiddle umpty-pum"
> And this brought you to the snaperoo or pay-off which was:
> "Someone had blundered."

From there he proceeds to crucify Shakespeare, his most regular victim when some literary reminiscence pops into his head which he either misquotes, isn't able to finish, misattributes or can't quite place:

> One of the first poems I ever learned – I don't know who
> wrote it, probably Shakespeare – ran
> I love little pussy; her coat is so warm;
> And if I don't hurt her, she'll do me no harm
> and that is how I have been all my life.
> *(Aunts Aren't Gentlemen)*

Confusing Shakespeare with a nursery rhyme is all in a day's work for Bertie; or, indeed, with the writings of Rudyard Kipling (also in *Aunts Aren't Gentlemen*), the philosopher Edmund Burke and American poet Oliver Wendell Holmes (*Much Obliged, Jeeves*) and even the Ancient Greek polymath Archimedes (*The Code of the Woosters*). So it's fortunate that Jeeves, who "is never happier than when curled up with his Shakespeare," can put him straight when these *faux pas* occur. So well-read does his valet appear, Bertie sometimes thinks Jeeves *is* Shakespeare, as when he unwittingly presses *Hamlet* into service to describe the angry disposition of Roderick Spode:

> His face was flushed, his eyes were bulging, and one had
> the odd illusion that his hair was standing on end – like
> quills upon the fretful porpentine, as Jeeves once put it.
> *(The Code of the Woosters)*

But before dismissing Bertie's powers of recall entirely, it's important to recalibrate the argument somewhat. As he tells us in 1922's 'The Hero's Reward,' his involvement with Nietzsche-loving Honoria Glossop had witnessed her attempting to "mould" his mind through an intensive course of study, such that "I had read solid literature till my eyes bubbled." And this, as things prove, didn't turn out to be a complete waste of time, for while not always able to place their authors, he freely quotes from William Wordsworth, Longfellow, Pope, Keats, the Lords Byron and Tennyson, Jack London, Robert Louis Stevenson, Pliny the

Elder, and even the bestselling Spanish novelist Vicente Blasco Ibáñez, to name but a few. Moreover, we must remember that even Jeeves *very* occasionally gets things wrong. In 'The Inferiority Complex of Old Sippy,' we find the following exchange:

> "What is it Shakespeare calls sleep, Jeeves?"
> "Tired Nature's sweet restorer, sir."
> "Exactly. Well, there you are, then."

Jeeves is referring to the guilty rant in Act 2, Scene 2, in which Macbeth, having killed King Duncan, comes up with several metaphors for the sleep he has "murder'd" – but not this one, which is to be found in Edward Young's rambling 18th-century gloomfest, *Night Thoughts*. Oops.

So this habit of imperfectly remembered borrowing isn't Bertie's sole copyright. Only a few pages into his debut novel *The Pothunters*, Wodehouse has his narrator stumble over a particular saying ("Like somebody's something it is both grateful and comforting") which turns out not to be a lofty literary allusion but real-life advertising copy for an Epps's Powdered Cocoa campaign that debuted in 1855. We soon appreciate what Yeats meant about rag and bone shops in a chapter entitled 'A Literary Banquet' in which all kinds of references are bandied about, often uncredited: a quote from *Macbeth* rubs shoulders with the lyric of a music-hall song by Albert Chevalier entitled 'Our 'Armonics Club'; Wordsworth ('We Are Seven') and Mozart ('Away with Melancholy') are referenced in the same paragraph. Then comes a mention of the versatile prosodist Barry Pain, quotes from two psalms, and the chapter is rounded off with an allusion to *The Tempest* which itself is immediately followed by a snatch of the 1893 popular song 'Private Tommy Atkins.' This is probably the sort of sophisticated gallimaufry Bertie would love to write but doesn't have sufficient knowledge or recall to pull off unaided.

But his creator clearly could, and from an early age. For example, that 'Tommy Atkins' reference was one he likely encountered in his schoolboy reading of Rudyard Kipling's hugely popular 1890 poem, 'Tommy.' And yet the version he quotes is a slightly misremembered rendering of Henry Hamilton's 1893 song lyric 'Private Tommy Atkins,' which he might have seen in his mid-teens at London's Prince of Wales Theatre as part of the smash hit 'A Gaiety Girl.' Some years later, Plum himself would resurrect the Tommy Atkins character in a series of spoof lyrics on the plight of a low-ranking soldier published in *Punch*, *Vanity Fair* and the *Daily Express* between 1903 and 1907. Wheels within wheels, as Monty Bodkin might say – but that's how writers' memories tend to work, and what they read while young unavoidably influences how and what they will write as adults. Obvious, yes, but particularly noteworthy in Wodehouse's case.

As he acknowledged in 1903's *A Prefect's Uncle*, everybody involved in writing is constantly cribbing or being cribbed off. No-one, however exalted, can be wholly original even if they want to be:

> [The] best poets borrowed. Virgil did it. Tennyson did it. Even Homer – we have it on the authority of Mr Kipling – when he smote his blooming lyre went and stole what he thought he might require.

To press his point home, Plum has paraphrased a verse that prefaces Kipling's 1896 'Barrack Room Ballads':

> When 'Omer smote 'is bloomin' lyre,
> He'd 'eard men sing by land an' sea;
> An' what he thought 'e might require,
> 'E went an' took – the same as me!

To illustrate his point about borrowing, Plum has appropriately borrowed a poem about borrowing. And he was perfectly sanguine about it, with no scruples whatever. Writing to Bill Townend in May 1937, he commented:

> I don't think there is any objection to basing one's stuff on somebody else's, providing you alter it enough. After all, all one wants is motives.

Much of the time, he took little or no care to disguise his thievery. The word-for-word quotation from James Martineau's über-serious *Types of Ethical Theory* in the 1916 story 'Jeeves Takes Charge' arrives uncredited, leaving his less well-read readers, as Elin Woodger Murphy correctly states, "with the false impression that he was himself responsible for those dizzying sentences:"

> The postulate or common understanding involved in speech is certainly co-extensive, in the obligation it carries, with the social organism of which language is the instrument, and the ends of which it is an effort to subserve.

Naturally, Plum never suspected his readers would have even *heard* of James Martineau, let alone read and remembered that particular lift.

But then he never reckoned that 40 years later scholars like Richard Usborne would be going through his work with a fine-tooth comb and grassing him up.

Reading Wodehouse's writing from any period, it quickly becomes apparent he had a formidable Rolodex of such references, literary and otherwise, stored someplace in his brain ready for just about any occasion. Much of the time, I would venture that an apposite word or quote pinged into the forefront of his consciousness bang on cue; and, as he grew older, he had his own oven-ready library he would re-heat time and again. Alternatively, if he couldn't access the *mot* or *expression juste*, he could always rely on the formidably cross-referenced Bartlett's *Familiar Quotations*. Had he read the Preface in his well-thumbed edition (the 11th, I think) he would have found a witty meditation by its editor Christopher Morley on serendipity:

> What makes words memorable? It would be useful if we knew, but I doubt we ever shall. The subtle adhesions of adult memory are unintentional and unconscious [...] We have found (in many a secret surprise) that the images which sink deepest are often those we scarcely knew, at the time, we were noticing at all.

Bertie could never learn 'The Charge of the Light Brigade' by rote, yet something or other in his consciousness chimed with the 'little pussy' rhyme. And most of us have a stock of such words, phrases and passages that mean something to us, even if we can't articulate what that something is or why our brain has bothered to remember it. "Who cares?" Morley blithely comments. "The magic happens."

The sheer range of Wodehouse's footnotable borrowings reveals that just about anything could catch his attention and be stored for future use. Like Sidney Price in his 1907 novel *Not George Washington*, he was:

> a booky sort of person. At home it had been a standing joke that, when a boy, I would sooner spend a penny on *Tit-Bits* than liquorice. And it was true. Not that I disliked liquorice. I liked *Tit-Bits* better, though. So the thing had gone on.

Tit-Bits magazine, which published one of Wodehouse's first pieces of paid-for prose ('Men Who Have Missed Their Own Weddings' in November 1900) and for whom he worked briefly as an agony uncle in 1908, was a digest of entertaining extracts from a wide variety of publications conveniently brought together in one place. And for much of his journalistic life during this early period in his career, Plum would edit the 6-times weekly 'By the Way' column in the *Globe* newspaper, which offered its readers much the same service but with humorous commentary. So he was no stranger to the art of gleaning and editing useful material to suit his own purposes, closely resembling James 'Corky' Corcoran, narrator of the Ukridge short stories, who writes quirky, off-beat articles for *Interesting Bits*.

Until 1905, Plum would jot down random phrases and quotes that caught his eye and ear in a notebook, which in 1906's *Love Among the Chickens* he would describe as an "author's rag bag." One such *aperçu* ran:

> Westbrook asks me if reading some English literature did me any good. I say, "Well, I suppose it was like meat going into the sausage mills. It will come out in the form of sausages some time."

And so it did, prompting Dulwich College archivist Jan Piggott to correctly observe that "No modern writer, except perhaps James Joyce, has such an alert and catholic ear." Whether it's a literary quote, an old saw, snatches of Latin or French, vaudeville cross-talk, distinctive accents, something he'd overheard in the street, or individual animal names he found amusing ('marmoset', 'cassowary', 'codfish' or 'cushat-dove'), into the mill they went with all the other sausage ingredients. He'll even throw in the occasional (usually bad) joke:

> "Ah! I wish you had seen me at the lake-hole. I did it one under par."
> "Was your father playing?"
>
> ('A Woman Is Only a Woman')

Or even:

> "She's a trier," [said Gally].
> "I find her trying." Lord Emsworth retorted, one of the most brilliant things he had ever said.
>
> (*Galahad at Blandings*)

And there's plenty more wherever those came from, including the incident in *Uncle Dynamite* when Constable Harry Potter (!) claims to have been "assaulted by the duck pond," only to be asked by Sir Aylmer Bostock, the presiding magistrate, "How the devil can you be assaulted by a duck pond?"

This magpie sensibility would serve Wodehouse well; yet he never got round to publicly exploring quite *how* this rich mix of material came to inhabit his youthful imagination. It would take one of his literary heroes, Rudyard Kipling, sixteen years his senior (and who has already popped up three times in this narrative) to examine that process in a collection of stories published between 1897 and 1929 that according to George Orwell would have "an immense influence on boys' literature" – *Stalky and Co*. In that book, "Old Pop Kipling" (as Bertie affectionately refers to him) presented the young Wodehouse with some fascinating possibilities for what he could (and shouldn't) do within the rigid formula of the schoolboy novels that would launch his literary career. Even more importantly for *this* book, the older writer would chronicle, with an almost anthropological fascination, the ways schoolboys of Wodehouse's vintage developed ways of talking and writing formed from all the different things they read. In Plum's case, this manner of speaking would slowly evolve into the unique writing style that would underpin the success of his entire career. It's as important as that. So that's where our narrative simply has to begin . . .

In the 1901 novel *Acton's Feud* by Frederick Swainson, one schoolboy comments:

> I wish Kipling would write a book every week. He is the only fellow in England that can write.

Despite his tarnished reputation in our own time, Kipling was something of a god to Plum's generation, and when the grand old poet of Empire died in January 1936, a "stunned" Wodehouse (aged 54) confessed to former study mate Bill Townend that:

> He seems to leave such a gap. I didn't feel the same about [Arthur Conan] Doyle or [Arnold] Bennett or [John] Galsworthy. I suppose it is because he is so associated with one's boyhood. It has made me feel much older all of a sudden.

Plum had quoted the laureate's work in his published writing from the very beginning and was still namechecking Kipling's best-known poem 'If' as late as 1970's *The Girl in Blue*. 'A Good Cigar is a Smoke' was borrowed from 'The Betrothed' for the title of a 1967 story; the versatile punchline "the female of the species is deadlier than the male" (which Bertie abbreviates to "the s. of the f. being more d. than the m." in *Right Ho, Jeeves*) would pop up in Plum's last completed novel *Aunts Aren't Gen-*

tlemen in 1974; and the last of many appearances of "toad beneath the harrow" (the epigraph to Kipling's short story 'Pagett, M. P.') to denote someone in dire straits can also be found there, a phrase Plum had first requisitioned for *The Head of Kay's* as far back as 1905.

For a brief period in the late 1920s and early '30s, the two writers were reasonably well acquainted. Wodehouse had met the great man at Fairlawne, the country estate of his stepdaughter Leonora's future in-laws, the Cazalets. In town, they had bumped into one another at London's Beefsteak Club, of which they were both members, and briefly corresponded. 'Old Pop' had sought advice on how to end his short stories, and even more flatteringly, judged Plum's 1928 tale 'Lord Emsworth and the Girl Friend' to be "one of the most perfect short stories ever written." This must have been music to Plum's ears, for Kipling was not only a consummate short story writer but had been the most popular writer *period* in English from around the 1890s until after the First World War. The first-ever English Nobel laureate and a recipient of honorary degrees from Oxford, Cambridge, and the Sorbonne, he was (as literary scholar Andrew Rutherford has it) "the last English author to appeal to readers of all social classes and all cultural groups." Ever loyal, Plum would remark in 1929:

> It was a great moment for me, meeting Kipling, though I suppose a statement like that would make the nibs purse their lips and raise their eyebrows. It's odd, this latter-day hostility to him. How the intelligentsia do seem to loathe the poor blighter, and how we of the *canaille* [the masses] revel in his stuff. I felt like a novice being introduced to the heavyweight champ. But he was geniality himself and didn't pull rank on me. He treated me quite as an equal.
>
> (*Author! Author!*)

The intelligentsia's loss would prove to be the *canaille*'s gain.

Published in serial form from April 1897 when Wodehouse was 15 and studying at Dulwich College, *Stalky and Co.*'s first run of stories was gathered into a book in 1899 and later supplemented with four new tales between 1917 and 1929. Set in a private boarding establishment in North Devon, this *sui generis*, semi-autobiographical school story chronicles the adventures of three teenagers, Arthur Lionel 'Stalky' Corkran, William 'Turkey' M'Turk and Reginald 'Beetle' Beetle, the last of these a reasonable facsimile of the author himself. As we'll see in a moment, Plum had definitely read the book by the summer of 1901, but it's unlikely he would have waited that long to discover what all the fuss was about. Critics had damned it as cruel and even sadistic, most notably the novelist Robert Buchanan (a Scotsman with a grievance) whose intemperate philippic 'Voice of the Hooligan' appeared in *The Contemporary Review* in 1899:

> It is simply impossible to show by mere quotation the horrible vileness of the book describing these three small fiends in human likeness […] The vulgarity, the brutality, the savagery […] reeks on every page.

Perhaps coincidentally, "fiend in human likeness" (or sometimes "form" or "shape") is one of the regular epithets Bertie uses to describe someone he doesn't like. And Buchanan wasn't alone: later critics would include William Somerset Maugham, H. G. Wells and Edmund Wilson, and *Stalky* was curtly dismissed in the 1942 *Concise Cambridge History of English Literature* as "[a]n unpleasant book about unpleasant boys at an unpleasant school."

The United Services College Kipling attended in his teens, and on which his fictional "Coll" is based, was primarily a feeder school for the armed services and was undoubtedly redder in tooth and claw than Plum's more sophisticated Dulwich. Yet notwithstanding that, something clearly rang a bell, and there are many points of connection between Kipling's school "atmosphere" and Plum's, both writers attempting to distil the truth of their personal experiences even as they spun their fictional stories. "No-one, the owner least of all, can explain what is in a growing boy's mind," Kipling wrote; yet that is precisely what he and Plum set out to do.

Writers with developed ears for dialogue, both men were fascinated by the lore and language of schoolboys and strove hard for accuracy. In 'School Stories,' a lengthy article he wrote for *Public School Magazine* in August 1901, Wodehouse remarks that in matters of schoolboy speech, Kipling was at least aiming for realism despite the squeamishness of the marketplace:

> A time may come when a writer shall arise bold enough and independent enough to retail the speech of school as it really is, but that time is not yet. The cold grey eye of the public-who-holds-the-purse is upon us, and we are dumb. Rudyard Kipling went near to it, a gallant pioneer of the Ideal, but even the conversation of Stalky and Co. leaves something unsaid, not much, it is true, but still a something.

Quite what that 'something' was would have been useful to know, but Plum unfortunately kept schtum. Nevertheless, it's clear he considered accuracy in speech and idiom crucial to the credibility of the fictional public school. And as we read the stories of both Kipling and Wodehouse, so we recognize that a key component of that schoolboy chatter originates in what their respective characters were reading. Stalky is a massive fan of R. S. Surtees whose novels of huntin', shooting' and fishin' (particularly 1843's *Handley Cross*) he can almost quote by heart; M'Turk, the aesthete on the team, favours the compendious work of art critic and social reformer John Ruskin (particularly his *Fors Clavigera*), and that of Thomas de Quincey, author of *Confessions of an English Opium Eater*; Beetle, who will go on to be a professional scribe, is described as a creature of "vast and omnivorous reading." 'Taffy' Howell, a close associate of the core group is something of an expert on the nautical novels of Captain Nicholas Marryat which include *Peter Simple* and *Mr. Midshipman Easy*. These favourite books are not simply read and discarded, but chime with something in their individual personalities; in short, *they become part of them*.

Despite the difference in their creators' ages, there is a distinct overlap in what Kipling and Wodehouse's schoolboy characters read and enjoy. This suggests the intriguing possibility there was a sort of 'core' reading list English public schoolboys had developed independently of one another, whichever school they went to, embracing books they were taught, those they sought out for themselves, or those that, like the Bible, were part of everyday school life. We might call it a sort of alternative national curriculum, since in *Stalky* Kipling references writers and works we know Plum was reading (and probably spouting) some years later at Dulwich, among them W. S. Gilbert (*The Bab Ballads*), Shakespeare (*The Merchant of Venice*), Charles Dickens (*Oliver Twist*) and Robert Browning ('Waring'). Other possible correspondences include James Fenimore Cooper (*The Last of the Mohicans*), Lewis Carroll (*Through the Looking Glass*), Alexandre Dumas *père* (*The Count of Monte Cristo*), Charles Kingsley ('The Last Buccaneer'), Sir Charles Sedley ('Phyllis Is My Only Joy') and so on . . . and on. To which Kipling adds snatches of music hall songs ('Arrah, Patsy, Mind the Baby') and local Devon slang, making his rag and bone shop every bit as catholic as Plum's would later turn out to be.

Also prominent in *Stalky* are those linguistic crazes that flare up when pupils, often during vacation, seize on compelling words and phrases that excite their imaginations. In 'The United Idolaters' Kipling notes how boys tend to collect "odds and ends of speech – theatre, opera, and music-hall gags – from the great holiday world" they can try out on their friends when term begins again:

> Dick Four of the red nose and dramatic instincts [...] loafed up and asked [the boys in study Number Five] "how their symptoms seemed to segashuate." They said nothing at the time, for they knew Dick had a giddy naval uncle who took him to the [London] Pavilion and the Cri[terion theatres], and all would be explained later.

As things turn out, "segashuate" isn't taken from a play Dick has seen with his uncle up West, but *Uncle Remus,* Joel Chandler Harris's first collection of re-told African American folk tales published in 1881 when Kipling was 15. As he explains, this "popular holiday gift-book" featured many mimicable accents and was "full of quotations that one could hurl like javelins." Each boy, to show "he was abreast of the latest movement" had no compunction about "shouting a couplet that pleased him" to help bond with the pack. Like most of the literary references in both Kipling and Wodehouse, the lifts are often uncredited and can pass unnoticed – unless of course you happen to know where they come from. But if you do 'get' them, it's as if you've been quietly co-opted into the cabal of *cognoscenti*; which is a neat trick for a writer to pull off, demonstrating that the principle of shared recognition doesn't just work on schoolboys who collect quotable quotes like bubble gum cards. Thanks to a mutual love of reading, *we* can unwittingly bond with characters with whom we might have little else in common – even inky 19th-century semi-feral schoolboys. Both Wodehouse and Kipling were masters of this literary relationship between writer and reader; but once again it's Kipling who lets the daylight in on the magic of how this relationship first takes root in young minds, as it must have done in Wodehouse's back in the 1890s at Dulwich.

As 'The United Idolaters' proceeds, so *Uncle Remus* references snowball over the Coll's bush telegraph. Beetle, as yet unacquainted with the book, is puzzled when he overhears a lowly fag shout to another, "Turn me loose, or I'll knock the natal stuffin' out of you." This "strange speech" catches his ear, and, discovering its origin, he gets a copy of the book and devours it instantly, reading "a wonderful story of a Tar Baby" out loud to his study mates. Similarly captivated, Stalky wrenches it from Beetle, M'Turk from Stalky, and all three are hooked for life. We are told "[t]here was no prep that night," and Stalky almost instantaneously creates an idiolect for himself, chucking in some Franglais – a form of mangled French – he also seems to favour:

> "My Sacred Hat!" cried Stalky. "Brer Terrapin! Where you catchee? What you make-do *aveck*?" This was Stalky's

notion of how they talked in *Uncle Remus*; and he spoke no
other tongue for weeks.

Stalky picks up the ball and runs with it, giving the raw material his personal imprimatur. Other boys adopt their own "word of the week, so to
say" as choice phrases, epithets and individual words crowd into their
minds, each waiting for the moment they can be put to good, witty use
in order to impress their friends.

Even the masters aren't immune to the lure of *Uncle Remus*. The
school chaplain, the Reverend John Gillett, who, more than any other
member of staff understands the boys and enters their mental world, is
quickly on the case. When asked by 'Potiphar' Mullins, Head of Games,
how he is, the reply comes "Loungin' round and sufferin', my son",
a tidied-up version of the original's "'Lounjun 'roun' en suffer'n',' sez
Brer Tarrypin, sezee." Across and even ahead of the craze's curve, Gillett uses his grownup's awareness of how literature can create a kind of
subversive bond among its readers – even breaking down the barriers
between schoolmasters and schoolboys. He's an honorary (and privileged) member of the gang who knows the code. Not so the irascible
Mr. King, who views the "senseless and childish repetition" of catch-
phrases as a sort of communicable disease, an "epidemic" that infects
"immature minds."

It was opinion he shared with Plum's headmaster Arthur H. Gilkes,
who, in his semi-fictional *A Day at Dulwich* published in 1905, seemed
pained by "a kind of strange semi-smart dialogue of repartee one to the
other" prevalent in schoolboy fiction which was "destitute of serious
thoughts or hopes." But that's what can happen when literature, possessing "some sort of elemental appeal," grabs the teenage imagination
– particularly when it syncs up with the gang's collective inability to take
anything seriously. In *The Pothunters,* Plum invents his own Mr. King in
the person of Mr. Thompson, who longs to be a Gillett but seems to lack
all knowledge of "the inwardness of the Human Boy [...] "expect[ing]
every member of his form [...] to be earnest – which very few members
of a Sixth Form are."

It's at this point things dramatically escalate at the Coll thanks to
an *Uncle Remus* earworm. Within hours of first encountering the book,
Stalky has Brer Rabbit's song from Chapter 23 going round in his head,
prompting him to call out:

> "Ti-yi! Tungalee!
> I eat um pea! I pick um pea!"

His call is answered from a nearby study by Dick Four, who responds with Brer Bullfrog's ditty:

> "Ingle-go-jang, my joy, my joy!
> Ingle-go-jang, my joy!
> *I'm* right at home, my joy, my joy –"

The two chants, though "created for the moment," immediately become part of the lingo. At which point two factions rapidly develop within the school – the 'Ingles' and the 'Tungles.' The schism "developed as quickly as in a new religion" and a form of gang warfare begins. In pretty short order, battles erupt, and "one never knew when a peaceful form-room would flare up in song and slaughter." During one bout of particularly violent hostilities the school nearly burns to the ground and the authorities are forced to step in with a combination of lines, beatings and forfeits of pocket money.

However improbable these events may appear, most actually did happen. Kipling, approaching 60, seems to be taking great nostalgic pleasure in recalling events that he almost certainly experienced nearly half a century before. Indeed, in 1895, before the first Stalky stories appeared, he had corresponded with Joel Chandler Harris himself, asking:

> I wonder if you could realize how Uncle Remus his sayings and the sayings of the noble beasties ran like wild fire through an English public school when I was about fifteen. We used to go to battle (with boots and bolsters and such like) against those whom we did not love, to the tune of *Hi yi! – tungalee: I eat um pea I pick um pea etc.*

Clearly a Tungle, Kipling seems to have played his part in the mayhem, and it's interesting to speculate what Harris might have made of this somewhat offbeat fan latter from a man who would become one of the world's most popular writers.

But *Uncle Remus* isn't the only work of fiction to produce a strong reaction among the schoolboys; indeed, Kipling notes how his fictional College had been "infected with *Uncle Remus* as it had been with *Pinafore* and *Patience*" – which is where Wodehouse once again enters the discussion. Gilbert and Sullivan's smash hit *H.M.S. Pinafore* had swept all before it in 1878, to be followed three years later by *Patience*, the very comic masterpiece that Plum claimed as his Road to Damascus entrée into musical theatre, a work he would end up referencing over 40 times in his fiction right up until 1963's *Stiff Upper Lip, Jeeves*. Printed editions and/or compilations of the G & S operettas were wildly popular in schools, and as if to prove it Stalky deftly inserts one of Plum's favourite *Patience* quotes ("If you're anxious for to shine in the high aesthetic line") into a conversation with M'Turk.

But Plum would go one step beyond simple quotation, later publishing two full-length (and highly competent) parodies of songs from the libretto, preserving many of the verbal ideas and rhythms contained in the originals ('The Road to Success', *Vanity Fair* [UK] magazine January 5, 1905; and 'Sing It!', *Pearson's*, July 1907). Once hooked, he stayed hooked, and what may have caught his attention as part of a schoolboy craze osmosed into something more lasting and valuable within his creative imagination.

And this is the whole point of these teenage literary crushes; far from being here today and gone tomorrow, even those that appear the most trivial and inconsequential can enjoy an unexpectedly long shelf life, even among those who aren't literature junkies or don't go on to be writers. That's how I first came across Wodehouse at my school; and we mustn't forget that prior to radio, TV, gaming and the internet, burying yourself in a book was one of the few ways to profitably pass the time in a boarding establishment, particularly during the long winter nights of Christmas Term. Indeed, the real-life Stalky, L. C. Dunsterville, acknowledges the importance of his own recreational reading in his autobiographical *Stalky's Reminiscences* from 1928, in which he confirms that much of what his friend Kipling wrote checks out, including his own reading habits. In his early days at the United Services College, prior to meeting his future compadres, Dunsterville existed on a diet of pulpy adventure stories:

> Like most boys my fancy ran to rather lurid works of fiction […] My first favourite was *Ned Kelly, The Ironclad Bushranger* [by J. S. Borlase] with a thrill in every chapter. The second favourite was *Jack Harkaway* [by 'Bracebridge Hemyng']. I also read most of Fenimore Cooper's splendid stories of Red Indians, and Captain Marryat's books of adventures at sea. Another author was 'Gustave Aimard,' who wrote of Spanish adventures and vendettas. From his books I learnt a whole set of Spanish oaths and imprecations, *which still linger in my memory*. [italics mine]

Borlase, Bracebridge and Aimard's works were excellent examples of the 'penny dreadfuls' – serialized fiction full of cheap thrills we'll be examining in the following chapter. But it was soon after Dunsterville teamed up with Kipling and G. C. (M'Turk) Beresford that his literary horizons broadened considerably:

> The period of Ned Kelly and Jack Harkaway was succeeded by Ruskin, Carlyle, and Walt Whitman. We did a good deal of reading, hidden away in our hut in the middle of the densest patch of furze-bushes, or in a tiny room we hired from one of the cottagers [...] Reading to ourselves or out loud was our only recreation, and the hatching of plots against people who had 'incurred our odium.' *The Confessions of a Thug* [a bestselling crime novel from 1839 by Philip Meadows Taylor said to be a favourite of Queen Victoria] was one of the books we read aloud, and Walt Whitman we thoroughly enjoyed in the same way. You can't get the real effect out of W. W. in any other way.

To facilitate their research, the fictional Stalky and his friends build an outdoor "place of retreat and meditation," a "palace of delight" where they can read, perform and smoke unmolested. This three-man hideaway is reminiscent of Plum and Bill Townend's Dulwich study in which they wiled away the hours chatting about books while ignoring prep, once again confirming that reading can be a communal and bonding activity, yet one that is ever so slightly subversive.

Finally, we come to the books the schoolboys were taught at the Coll, a subject dealt with in a later Stalky story 'The Propagation of Knowledge' from 1926. To the chagrin of the sarcastic Mr. King, the system of examinations with its short, almost random syllabuses was never designed to promote an understanding of Literature, but a 'bits and pieces' approach that witnessed "the pearls of English Literature [...] [being] wrenched from their settings and cast before young swine rooting for marks." Which was perfectly usual, and still is, but all grist to the mill for a future writer with his sausage machine of a brain.

If the near-absence of English Literature on the Dulwich school curriculum was replicated in other public schools across the country (see Chapter 4 and Appendix 1 for more on this), there must have been a lot of auto-didacts among the future writers of Plum's generation. Dunsterville, who ended up in the military, went on to write several books, including a volume of stories he described as "pure fiction" which make up in entertainment what they lack in literary finesse; and Beresford would also publish his reminiscences (*Schooldays With Kipling*) in 1936, with details of those communal reading sessions appearing in Chapter 2. *Stalky and Co.*'s wise old headmaster, knowing that Beetle/Kipling was not Oxbridge material (and that like Plum, his parents couldn't afford to send him to university) grants the boy privileged access to his personal bookshelves in order to encourage his enthusiasms. Kipling himself had discovered a wealth of literature in his own headmaster's collection, exhaustively catalogued in 'The Last Term' – everything from Hakluyt to Lermontoff via Ossian and Rossetti. It would be fascinating to know what titles the young Wodehouse borrowed from *his* College library; unfortunately, no records survive, but you can bet he was the bane of the duty librarian. He would also pester the news vendor at the near-by West Dulwich railway station, to which he would regularly stroll to "read the weeklies and the magazines" – particularly the *Strand*, which had begun serializing the Sherlock Holmes mysteries in 1891, and in which he would later be publishing his own stories.

Back in the classroom, a sleepy Beetle is about to offer a perfect illustration of the principle that began this chapter – that our lives are the sum of what we unconsciously remember. Pointlessly drilled by Mr. King on the work of Doctor Samuel Johnson, the wretched boy is asked to share with the class "one single fact" connected to the great man "which might at any time have adhered to what [...] must, Mr. King supposed, be called his mind." Beetle dredges the shallows of his knowledge only to come up with the following limerick he remembers from a back number of *Punch*:

De tous ces défunts cockolores [self-important men]
Le moral Fénélon,
Michel Ange et Johnson
(Le Docteur) sont les plus awful bores.

Rather than sending his charges to sleep with Le boring Docteur Johnson's Shakespeare criticism, King reads out the mighty historian Thomas Macaulay's description of the great man: "a grotesque figure with untied shoe-strings, that twitched and grunted, gorged its food, bit its finger-nails, and neglected its ablutions." *That* is Doctor Johnson as he has come down to many of us rather than the god-like scholar and lexicographer; and we mustn't forget that just as Mr. King is entertaining his pupils with this disrespectful portrait, Kipling is also entertaining *us*. It's what *he* remembers of Johnson too, and he's managed to put it to good use. But note in this example that what Beetle and Mr. King jointly produce is not the 'official' picture of the great man, but a cock-eyed version that would be a gift to any humorist.

The unfortunate Beetle is then awarded 100 lines to copy out for sleeping on the job. But he's well prepared; in anticipation of future transgressions, he already has a stock of them ready to submit:

> They covered such English verse as interested him at the moment, and helped to fix the stuff in his memory.

Beetle turns what is intended as a punishment to his advantage, for he seems to *want* to cultivate the facility for pulling quotations from the air so he can insert them in his future writing or conversation. Wodehouse's Charteris, a literary type who appears in several of his earliest stories, also hoards pre-written lines *and* scatters round quotes from the great and the good like confetti in a manner not dissimilar to Beetle's. As we'll see in Chapter 2, they both edit school newspapers. But Beetle's second-finest subversive hour arrives when he discovers the *Curiosities of Literature* (compiled by British Prime Minister Benjamin Disraeli's father Isaac), a set of volumes containing a glorious charivari of offbeat facts and stories, including "personal peculiarities of the great." These "fascinating inutilities" are what engage his imagination, and, as it turns out, help get his mates through their exams.

As at Plum's school (and mine), *King Lear* is on the Coll's syllabus, and Beetle discovers an out-of-the-way passage from the 17th-century diarist and drunken gossip John Aubrey that contradicts a received morsel of Johnsonian wisdom about the character of Poor Tom. Sharing this rare nugget with his study mates, Stalky immediately recognizes they're on to a winner, and commissions Beetle (who is exempt from the exam) to dig out all sorts of other obscure and contentious curiosities about Shakespeare and the other writers they're going to be tested on, knowing that Mr. King – being a more traditional type of scholar – will never have heard of them. It's a job tailor-made for Beetle, who throws himself into the task with gusto. Brownie points are in the offing, and the boys divvy up those of his findings that might prove useful in their essays. Of Jonathan Swift, we learn:

> "Died mad. Two girls. Saw a tree, an' said: 'I shall die at the top.' Oh yes, an' his private amusements were 'ridiculous an' trivial.'"

M'Turk bags that one; at which point Beetle starts on "that *Clarissa* chap" – aka the fabulously successful Samuel Richardson, who almost single-handedly turned the romantic novel into an industry with his *Pamela* and, yes, *Clarissa* – one of the longest and most tedious novels ever written:

> "He was the 'Shakespeare of novelists.'"

"King won't stand that. He says there's only one Shakespeare. Mustn't rot about Shakespeare to King," Howell objected.

"An' he was 'always delighted with his own works,'" Beetle continued [...] "Oh yes, an'" – he consulted some hieroglyphics on a scrap of paper – "the – the impassioned Diderot (dunno who *he* was) broke forth: 'O Richardson, thou singular genius!'"

Howell wins that one, despite fierce competition from Stalky.

For Beetle's benefit, Denis Diderot was a French philosopher, encyclopaedist and Anglophile who, while imprisoned for sedition, annotated a copy of Milton's *Paradise Lost* using a toothpick as a pen, and ink made by scraping slate from the walls and mixing it with wine. This 'believe it or not' kind of fact unfailingly captures the boys' imaginations, and when the resulting essays are handed in, King is genuinely and uncharacteristically impressed by their originality.

It's a trick that bears repetition, and once more there's a Wodehouse connection. In the library, Beetle is reading some Oliver Wendell Holmes (a Plum favourite), gets fed up, and moves a few inches down the alphabetized shelf to *Nathaniel* Holmes, one of the chief propagators of the theory that the plays normally attributed to Shakespeare were actually written by the philosopher and essayist Francis Bacon. As we'll see in Chapter 9, this unlikely attribution was one of Plum's favourite hobby horses, one that he would get a good deal of comic mileage from – as does Beetle. Knowing Mr. King's hatred of such heresies, he reckons the most casual mention will work on his teacher "like a Seidlitz powder" [a popular laxative], which it does. As King starts to fizz, Stalky studiously takes notes which the boys then regurgitate during the *viva voce* test conducted by an outside examiner who, as it happens, is not unsympathetic to the idea that The Man from Stratford was a total fraud. The boys pass the test with flying colours and are praised in the examiner's report for their extra-curricular reading, while King is singled out for encouraging them to question literary orthodoxy. Being a Shakespearean traditionalist, this both angers and puzzles him, and it's only the savvy Gillett who realizes that the boys – and Beetle in particular – have been playing King like a fiddle ("The devil! The young devil!"), but he keeps mum and the story ends with King none the wiser.

Travelling some of the less-familiar byways of male teenage psychology, *Stalky and Co.* proves a far more intriguing and complex work than it is usually given credit for. As one early critic – Christopher Morley – argued, a great teacher of English Literature had been lost in

Kipling, since he had so clearly demonstrated how young students could love their reading while at the same time not take it too seriously. And although Wodehouse didn't have the benefit of reading those two later Stalky stories ('The United Idolaters' and 'The Propagation of Knowledge') before he set out on his own literary journey, he had already *lived* them, gathering up his first garlands of other writers' blooms that he would put to good use in his future career.

But what and who would he be up against? And what could he pilfer from *them*?

Chapter 2:
Of Reckless Eric and Others

"I'm going to school, so, hurrah! hurrah! hurrah!"
Frederic W. Farrar, Eric

"Here we are!" said McTurk. "'Corporal punishment
produced on Eric the worst effects' […] oh, naughty Eric!
Let's get to where he goes in for drink."

Rudyard Kipling, Stalky and Co.

"Are you the Bully, the Pride of the School or the Boy
who is Led Astray and Takes to Drink in Chapter 16?"
PGW, The Lost Lambs

As a child, of course, I read *Eric* and *St. Winifred's* and
the Talbot Baines Reed stories in *The BOP* [Boys' Own
Paper]. I loved them all.
PGW, Letter to Richard Usborne, 1955

In 1905, Wodehouse's respected headmaster Arthur H. Gilkes published a brief monograph entitled *A Day at Dulwich* which opens with
the following remarks:

> It is possible to take exception to the tone of many ac-
> counts of school life given in stories, in which boys are rep-
> resented as continually trying to evade the school rules, as
> subjects by no means in sympathy with the powers that are
> supposed to control them […] These stories are objection-
> able, among other reasons, because they do mischief to
> boys, and because they largely misrepresent both fact and
> nature.

Perhaps he had already twigged that one ex-pupil, whom he had described in a school report as having "the most distorted ideas about wit
and humour," had been making a tidy living writing such defamatory
stories for almost five years and was an acknowledged expert in the field.

Those of us not weaned on public school stories might be at a loss
to understand how tales of the monied and privileged could be a gate-

way drug into reading for many a late Victorian schoolboy, Wodehouse included – but they were. Even into his 70s, Plum continued to read public school fiction for pleasure; of *Graeme and Cyril* which we'll come to later in this chapter, he wrote to Richard Usborne in 1955, "I was re-reading it only the other day and it's great stuff." It had made "an enormous impression on me" despite having "practically no plot," quite simply because "the atmosphere was wonderful."

Nostalgic? Absolutely. But what we need to understand is that when Plum was attending Dulwich College in the 1890s, he was living through a golden era of schoolboy fiction, and exactly the right age and social class to fit its target demographic. Given that there were over 200 public schools in England at around this time, it was a large and lucrative market; one that, as Eton alumnus George Orwell would later remark in his classic essay 'Boys' Weeklies,' was considerably boosted by those who didn't attend public school yet were attracted to what he calls their "glamour." So before we look at the titles that influenced Plum's writing, we might profitably take a quick tour of what else on the bookstands was competing for his attention as he approached man's estate.

First off, we have the so-called "penny-dreadfuls" or "bloods" that started to proliferate in the 1830s and had managed to stay the course for over half a century. At their peak, there were close on a hundred publishers of high-turnover penny-fiction in England, mixing rousing tales of Robin Hood, Dick Turpin, Buffalo Bill, and Jack Harkaway (the real-life Stalky's favourite rogue) with re-workings of late 18th-century Gothic horror. In 1846, Sweeney Todd the Demon Barber of Fleet Street debuted in the serial 'The String of Pearls' (billed as "A Domestic Romance") from which the following is taken:

> Lupin twined his left hand in the hair at the back of the head of the wretched woman, and then he held her head over the wash-hand basin. There was a bright flash of the knife, and then a gushing, gurgling sound, and blood poured into the basin, hot, hissing and frothing.

There was also the diabolic Spring-Heeled Jack and Varney the Vampire, whose *Feast of Blood* isn't far removed from Plum's own imaginary splatterfests *Gore by the Gallon*, *Severed Throats* and *Blood on the Banisters*. Here's an idea of its style:

> "Flora! Flora!" he cried; "Flora, speak!"
> All was still.
> "Good God!" he added; "we must force the door."

"I hear a strange noise within," said the young man, who trembled violently.
"And so do I. What does it sound like?"
"I scarcely know; but it nearest resembles some animal eating, or sucking some liquid."

This and other emetic publications enjoyed massive circulations, some in the hundreds of thousands, and from around the time of the 'Jack the Ripper' murders in 1888 a series of sensational trials had sought to link actual crimes with their widespread consumption.

Turn down the schlock several notches and we arrive at our second format: the ripping schoolboy yarns that appeared in magazines like *Boys of England*, *Chips*, *The Halfpenny Marvel* and *Pluck*. Lumping these together with the more downmarket dreadfuls into one overbrimming cloaca of frightfulness, Gilkesian pedagogues issued regular jeremiads about their harmful effects on young minds. But that didn't mean school libraries – including Dulwich's – were exclusively stocked with wholesome, improving literature, as reflected in the playlet Plum concocted for the July 1901 issue of *Public School Magazine*, in which a "Mere lad" craving some light leisure reading approaches the librarian's desk, staffed by an insouciant prefect who's trying to get some shut-eye:

> **Mere lad** (briskly): "'Sorrows of Barrabbas' [sic], please."
> **Prefect** (drowsily): "Eh?"
> Mere lad repeats request.
> **Prefect** (after a prolonged search, which was obviously hopeless from the start): "It's out, I'm afraid."

Sorrows of Barabbas is a satirical conflation of two titles (*The Sorrows of Satan* and *Barabbas*) by superstar author Marie Corelli, whose melodramatic novels were currently flying off the shelves (see Chapter 8). Disappointed, the lad moves on to more likely territory:

> "Then can I have 'For Philip and Fatherland'?"
> Prefect (in a tone of incredulous horror): "Henty?"
> (Note: When one has cast off childish things and begins to grow a moustache, Henty is Anathema).

For many years, the hugely prolific G. A. Henty had been a market leader in schoolboy fiction, cranking out over 120 tales of derring-do set just about anywhere from Ancient Egypt to the Peninsular War via the

Crusades and Anglo-Saxon England. Typically prefacing his books with a short address to "My Dear Lads," Henty knew his market (males 9-16) and ruthlessly catered to it – hence Plum's remark about moustaches. Indeed, Wodehouse the future writer would have learned much from what he called this "deservedly popular and justly widely-read" novelist's easy familiarity with his loyal army of readers, and that there was absolutely no shame attached to sticking with a winning formula. Titles such as *By Sheer Pluck: A Tale of the Ashanti War*, *Redskin and Cowboy: A Tale of the Western Plains*, and *In the Reign of Terror: The Adventures of a Westminster Boy* had propelled Henty's annual sales to a reported 150,000, around 30 times that of the most popular adult novel of the period. His style would sometimes read like a cross between an adventure and an encyclopaedia entry, as when two English chaps arrive in Lima, Peru in his 1902 serial *The Treasure of the Incas*:

> "The first thing to do, Bertie, is to buy ourselves a couple of good ponchos. You see all the natives are wearing them."
>
> "We certainly want something of the sort, Harry. I thought it was heat that we were going to suffer from, but it seems just the other way. To judge from the temperature we might be in Scotland, and this damp mist chills one to the bone."
>
> "I am not much surprised, for of course I got the subject up as much as I could before starting; and Barnett told me that Lima was altogether an exceptional place, and that while it was bright and warm during the winter months, from May till November on the plains only a few miles away, even in the summer months there was almost always a clammy mist at Lima, and that inside the house as well as outside everything streamed with moisture."

Clunky, yes: but this educational content made the canny Henty a shoo-in for school libraries. At Dulwich, the May 1899 edition of *The Alleynian* exhaustively listed all the new titles that had been added to its shelves – and a very mixed bag they were. Top of the heap was H. Rider Haggard with eight titles, seven from Anthony (*The Prisoner of Zenda*) Hope, four apiece from Henty and the prolific H. Seton Merriman (whose novels included *Dross* and *A Pariah*), then two each from Kipling, H. G. Wells, and historical novelist W. H. Ainsworth. Among the left-field choices was *Helbeck of Bannisdale*, a romance with a lot of added philosophy by Mrs Humphry Ward, *Fisher Lass*, a tale of the Norwegian peasantry by Bjørnstjerne Bjørnson, and Walter Besant's "romance of to-day" *Armorel of Lyonesse.* Bringing up the rear were the military rem-iniscences of old soldier Lord Roberts (who Plum would later pillory in *The Swoop!*), and the Reverend W. H. Fitchett's anthology of *Deeds that Won the Empire.* Unfortunately, we have no record of who borrowed what at Dulwich until 1902, but as in Plum's playlet, it was most likely the adventures that took the biggest hammering.

This was certainly true of the reading habits of Arthur Conan Doyle, one of Plum's ultimate Literary Heroes (see Chapter 8). He too had been a rabid consumer of adventure stories, such that "a special meeting of a library committee was held in my honour, at which a bylaw was passed that no subscriber should be permitted to change his book more than three times a day." He brilliantly described their appeal thus:

> I do not think that life has any joy to offer so complete, so soul-filling as that which come upon the imaginative lad, whose spare time is limited, but who is able to snuggle down into a corner with his book, knowing that the next hour is all his own. And how vivid and fresh it all is! Your very heart and soul are out on the prairies and the oceans with your hero. It is you who act and suffer and enjoy. You carry the long small-bore Kentucky rifle with which such egregious things are done, and you heave out upon the topsail yard, and get jerked by the flap of the sail into the Pacific, where you cling on to the leg of an albatross, and so keep afloat until the comic boatswain turns up with his crew of volunteers to handspike you into safety. What a magic it is, this stirring of the boyish heart and mind! Long ere I came to my teens I had traversed every sea, and knew the Rockies like my own back garden.

So carried away is Doyle by this recollection, it continues for another three pages, concluding that:

> It was all more real than the reality. Since those days I have in very truth shot bears and harpooned whales, but the performance was flat compared to the first time I did it with Mr Ballantyne or Captain Mayne Reid at my elbow.

R. M. Ballantyne was a Scottish writer of juvenile fiction who published over 100 books, while Thomas Mayne Reid hailed from Ireland and spent several years in America, where he briefly served in the army and where several of his stories are set. Among his fans were Anton Chekhoy, Vladimir Nabokov and Theodore Roosevelt. No, really.

Sometimes the boy isn't just the father of the man; he *is* the man. Plum and Doyle were to become fast friends and spent a good deal of time together discussing reading and writing. As inky-fingered and scuff-kneed schoolboys, they may have resembled James Joyce's Joe Dillon, who is similarly hooked on stories of the Wild West and other exotic locations:

> He looked like some kind of an Indian when he capered round the garden, an old tea-cosy on his head, beating a tin with his fist and yelling:
> 'Ya! yaka, yaka, yaka!'
> Everyone was incredulous when it was reported that he had a vocation for the priesthood.

Joyce was only a few weeks younger than Wodehouse, and it is intriguing to speculate whether Plum behaved in a similar fashion. Or whether he was torn off a strip by Gilkes in a manner not dissimilar to Joyce's Father Butler laying into Dillon:

> "What is this rubbish?" he said. "*The Apache Chief*! Is this what you read instead of studying your Roman history? Let me not find any more of this wretched stuff in this college. The man who wrote it, I suppose, was some wretched fellow who writes these things for a drink. I'm surprised that boys like you, educated, reading such stuff!"

To which one can only add that he shouldn't have been; and in the cases of Wodehouse, Doyle and Joyce, this unsanctioned reading would echo through their entire careers.

Sometime in 1893 aged 11 Plum stumbled on an early issue of *Chums* magazine, becoming a loyal devotee who five years later would correspond with its editor asking for tips on how to become a journalist. It was here he had encountered a serialization of *The Iron Pirate* by Max Pemberton, "A Plain Tale of Strange Happenings on the Sea" which pops up in his 1909 novel *Mike*, borrowed from the school library by Shoeblossom, who can't seem to find a quiet enough place to settle down and read it:

> His inability to hit on such a spot was rendered more irritating by the fact that, to judge from the first few chapters (which he had managed to get through during prep. one

night under the eye of a short-sighted master), the book was obviously the last word in hot stuff.

Which it was: here's a short extract featuring a two-man knife-fight on board ship:

> [T]he American had the strength of it, and he forced To-votsky's hand back upon him, stabbing him with his own knife again and again, so that the man's breast was covered with wounds, and he seemed like soon to faint from weakness. It might have been that he would have died where he stood, but by some terrible effort he forced himself free; and with the howl of a wild beast, he thrust his own knife to the hilt in the American's side. It broke at the handle; but the long blade was left embedded in the flesh, and the force of the blow was so overwhelming that Skinner drew himself straight up with death written in his protruding eyes and distorted features.

Many publications that featured such colourful writing were here-to-day-gone-tomorrow, but *Chums* managed to survive several format changes until wartime paper shortages finally did for it in 1941. Back in 1894, the year Plum entered Dulwich, it was joined by the *Union Jack*, brainchild of the crude but undeniably shrewd publisher Alfred Harmsworth, on whom Plum's rascally Lord Tilbury may well be based. As its editor proudly proclaimed:

YOU NEED NOT BE ASHAMED
TO BE SEEN READING THIS!
Parents need not fear when they see their children
reading the Union Jack. There will be nothing of the
'dreadful' type in our stories. No tales of boys rifling their
employers' cash-boxes and making off to foreign lands, or
such-like highly immoral fiction products.

In among stories of the Ashanti and Matabele wars could be found abridgements of works by Charles Dickens, Sir Walter Scott and James Fenimore Cooper that might have allayed parental anxiety as to the quality of literary fare on offer. We also find one of the many iterations of ace amateur detective (and Sherlock Holmes rip-off) Sexton Blake, who comes out with sententious claptrap like this, addressed to a naval officer who has hired him:

"I would rather work for nothing for a naval man like your-self, one of the best protectors of our precious flag, the pride of England, than I would take bank-notes from those who are careless of the honour of old Britain."

It wasn't called the *Union Jack* for nothing. The Harmsworth stable of schoolboy titles gradually compromised their vaunted respectability and led a race if not quite to the bottom, then somewhere not far off, prompting Wodehouse's fair-weather friend A. A. Milne to comment that "Harmsworth killed the penny dreadful by the simple process of producing the 'ha'penny dreadfuller'."

Wodehouse's own school stories wouldn't tread this well-beaten path to literary perdition, being somewhat classier – although he did once spin a yarn along these lines even as his more respectable school tales were doing good business. The only commission he ever got from his beloved *Chums*, *The Luck Stone* began serialization in September 1908, and although the magazine dubbed it "a Story of fun and adventure at School," its author privately described it as a "not so public-schooly" tale with "rather a lurid plot" featuring guns that actually shot people. So un-typical was it that he resorted to the pseudonym 'Basil Windham,' and reading it now, it's difficult to fathom whether Plum is struggling in these new and choppy waters or whether he can't quite keep a straight face:

> "Keep quiet, you worm!" said Tommy. "Reserve your re-marks until this court calls upon you to speak. By Jingo, if you interrupt again, I'll give you a jab in the bazooka, which'll make you see stars for the rest of the night."

And then Plum produces the hardware:

> There was a flash and a crack. A bullet zipped between the two boys. Another flicked up the dust at their feet. Ferris turned and ran on again.
> The two boys redoubled their efforts, but, as they ran, they were aware of a throbbing noise down the road. Ferris heard it, and shouted. An answering shout came from the darkness.
> "It's a motor," gasped Jimmy. "Quick, or he'll get to it."

There follows what must be one of the first ever car chases in print, which ends badly for the villains on a sharp bend:

"The car is smashed all to pieces. They must have been
travelling at over thirty-five miles an hour."
"And –"
"And the men?" said the colonel. "All dead."

This is reminiscent of the less-than-optimal New York gangland sections from *Psmith, Journalist*, in which the baddies are similarly hapless.
Truly, Plum was never cut out for this type of writing, and he probably
knew it: in future, he would tend to lampoon it through comedy villains
such as Chimp Twist, Oily Carlisle and Soapy and Dolly Molloy. Although occasionally armed with shooters, these are small-time crooks
whose repertoire of petty crime includes shoplifting, stealing cultured
pearls, selling dodgy oil shares and, in *Money in the Bank*, beaning Jeff
Miller with a stone tobacco jar. Not contract killing.

Whatever he might have consumed in private, when the time came
for Plum to be published, his early journalism reveals a more serious
side to his nature. In the 'School Stories' article from August 1901 (q.v.),
the 19-year-old Wodehouse shows himself full to bursting with opinions,
both favourable and not, about the school literature he had read while
in the process of being educated. Already a writer himself (his debut
short story had been published only the previous month) the precocious
Plum was already promising his readers the benefits of his considerable
experience. He would tell things as they were, without fear or favour, a
critic who could not be "judged by ordinary standards." "Where I rush
in," he adds, "angels might very well fear to tread"; at which point he
launches into a breathless summary of his likes and dislikes in schoolboy
literature.

His biggest beef with the pulpier school stories was their tendency to crowbar unlikely adventures into an institutional setting. Keen to
avoid offence (and potential lawsuits) by dissing real magazines, he invented fictional titles like "Farthing Bits" and "Snappy Kag-nag," which
were, in his opinion, dreadfuls dressed in public school uniform:

> It is only in the half-penny weeklies that you get the really
> unfettered school-story, where the villain, after his custom-
> ary defeat, goes off to the local "public" [house] and bribes a
> humble friend of the tramp persuasion with sixpence down
> and two goes of rum shrub to murder the hero outright.

Despite such improbabilities, he fulminates, these writers still have the
cheek to market their travesties as "Tales of Public School Life." Writers
of this kind of dreck should look to their sins and repent:

> [I]f you are brazen enough to make your hero fall in love with the Doctor's daughter or experience adventures like unto those of the mediæval swashbuckler, you may do so [...] But can you look me in the face and tell me that you really think you have portrayed school life as it is? No, you shrink abashed, as I knew you would.

Then he turns to questions of commerce. In a throwaway aside that is nevertheless hugely telling, he mentions that "You can't do this sort of thing [write implausible, violent plots] in the circulating libraries" for fear of limiting the audience for your material. Such institutions, a cross between a bookshop and a lending library, were massively popular throughout the 18th and 19th centuries in both Britain and America and were still going strong during the early years of the 20th, allowing a mass audience to rent books they wouldn't otherwise be able to afford. Most had standards as to what they would stock – publications were rated either "Satisfactory", "Doubtful" or "Objectionable" – and by pitching their respectability level too low, writers would jeopardize their access to this massive market of potential readers. Hoping for healthy sales, Plum wasn't going to make *that* textbook error. Erring on the side of caution, he would throw in his lot with the more wholesome purveyors of schoolboy fiction, although here too he would find plenty he wasn't happy with.

In 1879, in response to what it saw as the tsunami of unwholesome fiction available on the open market, the Religious Tract Society had begun publishing *The Boy's Own Paper* which traded in the slightly more sanitized kind of adventure stories and tales of public school life until its demise almost a century later in 1967. Its motto, *Quicquid agunt pueri nostri est farrago libelli* (literally 'Whatever boys do is the mixed cattle fodder for our small book') was not strictly accurate, and its stated mission to raise the bar in schoolboy fiction was by no means a novelty in the publishing industry. But it was one of the most successful titles in its corner of the market, sometimes hitting 200,000 copies an issue. It was certainly the longest-lived magazine of its kind, thanks in no small part to its creator G. A. Hutchison, who deftly steered the paper's original editorial policy towards showing rather than telling its readers how they might become "Manly Men."

In theory at least, Hutchison was aiming for "boys and not their grandmothers," and when fellow members of the Society suggested his organ should carry sermons, Hutchison resisted, saying "we'll have religion, but we'll have it in solution and not *en bloc*." So it was that Christian values were introduced more subtly, although to a modern sensibility still somewhat in-your-face. In the Preface to one schoolboy novel published by the Society, Hutchison decried "that fatal kind of sermonizing which all but inevitably repels those whom it is meant to benefit" while only a few lines later quoting this homily from the pen of theologian Frederick W. Faber:

> God is God, and right is right,
> And truth the day must win;
> To doubt would be disloyalty,
> To falter would be sin.

Which looks pretty *en bloc* to me. But *TBOP*'s longevity was testimony to how well its various editors managed the tricky balancing act of holding its readers' attention while not straying *too* far from the straight and narrow – although its contents sometimes perilously skirted penny-dreadful territory. Among my favourite lines is the wonderfully matter-of-fact "[i]t was the work of a moment to amputate McNab's leg"; or this from an 1888 serial in which the high priestess Morgana, inappropriately garbed in a dress with a plunging neckline, is attempting to hack off a blind man's leg with one hand while pouring out a goblet of poison with the other. The ancient tumulus in which the tussle is taking place subsequently collapses on top of them, prompting one of her acolytes to wearily sigh "It is time for us to become Christians." Not for the squeamish then; nor was the article detailing the ins and outs of taxidermy ("Pull the eyes out of their cavity and fill up their place with wool soaked in arsenical soap.")

The daddy of the 'improving' Victorian yarn was without doubt *Tom Brown's Schooldays* by Thomas Hughes, published in 1857 but held up as a model in Wodehouse's time and still in print today. Some commentators have argued that school stories would have died out long before Plum arrived on the scene had it not been for the long shadow cast by this seminal work, which has apparently influenced everything from Billy Bunter to Harry Potter. But that didn't stop Wodehouse accusing its author of peddling the most monstrous humbug in an article he published in *Public School Magazine* ('The Tom Brown Question') in December 1901, an attack I've already examined at length back in Volume 1 of my trilogy (pp. 68-9), so won't repeat here. Suffice to say, Hughes's brand of righteous preaching was not to our man's taste, and he was clearly no great believer in the rights and privileges accorded to sacred cows. In taking on the biggest beast in his own small field, Plum was going out on something of a limb by contrasting Tom Brown the living and breathing schoolboy of the novel's first half, with Tom Brown the "patent medicine" of its second, who is simply a vehicle for the soupy morality so beloved of the more sententious Victorians.

It would be all too easy to propose a binary opposition in Plum's mind between this queasy sort of morality tale and the equally exploitative adventure yarns we've already looked at and play them off against one another. But his response was more nuanced – or perhaps even confused – than that, seemingly torn between the merits (and de-merits) of the two. Where, he must have asked himself, would he – *could* he – pitch his own work in among all this stuff? In 'School Stories' he quickly establishes the boundaries of the argument as he sees them: at the raw and 'real' end of things is *Stalky and Co.*, while Frederic W. Farrar's *Eric, or, Little by Little* is an example of its polar opposite, a sermon thinly disguised as a schoolboy novel which, published just one year after *Tom Brown*, looked suspiciously like a cash-in.

It was a credible set of bookends, for Kipling had already pilloried *Eric*'s sanctimony within his own story. Beetle even turns the title of Farrar's book into a verb when he escapes punishment for a catalogue of crimes by melodramatically play-acting the wronged innocent in front of his sixth-form accusers ("Didn't I 'Eric' them splendidly?", he asks afterwards). For *Eric* is the story of an implausibly good and virtuous boy who goes to the bad "little by little." Brutalized by his schoolfellows and unjustly punished by the powers that be for wrongs he didn't commit, he then *really* goes to the dogs in a wild orgy of drinking and smoking and ends up dead.

This unlikely tale became a bestseller in mid-Victorian Britain and was still notorious in Kipling's and then Wodehouse's generations. In Plum's 1927 'Portrait of a Disciplinarian,' the somewhat barking 85-year-old Nurse Wilks gifts a copy to George Mulliner, long since qualified as a doctor, imagining him still a child. Similarly, Stalky, aged 16, is sent one by a maiden aunt who no doubt hopes he will read and inwardly digest its cautionary message. M'Turk commands Beetle to immediately take *Eric* down the pawn shop to raise necessary funds for tobacco, only to discover the pawnbroker is already stuffed with copies and will only offer him ninepence, even with another Farrar masterpiece, *St. Winifred's*, thrown in. This invites us to speculate that *Eric* might have been one of the most bought yet least read novels in history. Here's a brief sample of dialogue from the opening of the story:

> "Oh, mother," [Eric] said, "I am so happy. I like to say
> my prayers when you are here."
> "Yes, my boy, and God loves to hear them."
> "Aren't there some who never say prayers, mother?"

"Very many, love, I fear."
"How unhappy they must be! *I* shall *always* love to say my prayers."
"Ah, Eric, God grant that you may."

And although Eric *will* die with God on his lips, he's led a far from exemplary life in the meantime. Or rather he has, but as an example to other schoolboys not to stray from the paths of righteousness. I can't resist including his dying words and the narrator's commentary, as Eric, teetering on the very brink of the hereafter, learns he has managed to outlive both his parents and younger brother Vernon:

> "Yes, mother," he murmured, in broken tones, "forgiven now, for Christ's dear sake. Oh, Thou merciful God! Yes, there they are, and we shall meet again. Verny – oh, happy, happy at last – too happy!"
> The sounds died away, and his head fell back; for a transient moment more the smile and the brightness played over his fair features like a lambent flame. It passed away, and Eric was with those he dearliest loved, in the land where there is no more curse.

Or, presumably, booze and cigarettes. So influential was Farrar's tale, it is apparently credited with the popularity of Eric as a first name in English-speaking countries – although not with Eric Blair, who changed his name to George Orwell to avoid any possible association with the book. Edith Nesbit, author of many seminal children's stories including *The Railway Children*, was similarly dismissive, judging it "impossible to read."

Farrar's *St. Winifred's*, a rather better story despite its use of a similar plot arc, would follow in 1862. Like two medieval pilgrims, Walter Evson and his little brother Charlie do their best to avoid such mortal sins as "eating and drinking forbidden things," playing cards, "organised cribbing," and smoking. True, some of their fellow pupils really are ghastly, and Farrar's handling of the bullying scenes is deft, lively and strangely involving. But a homily is never too far away, as in the following scene when Kenrick catches the no-good Wilton stealing money from his desk:

> "This, then, is the creature whom I have suffered to call me friend!" said Kenrick; "for whom I have given up some of the best friends in the school! And this is your gratitude! Why, you worm, Wilton, what do you take me for? [...]

Faugh! your very touch sickens me! – go!"

A winning combination of sanctimony, good grammar and melodrama of a kind that would never find its way into Plum's school stories, being, as he puts it, "too richly flavoured for ordinary consumption."

Wodehouse the critic goes remarkably easy on Farrar, favourably referencing his books in both his stories and journalism. Perhaps he hadn't read the latter's claim that *Eric* was written "with but one single object – the inculcation of inward purity and moral purpose." Yet he comes down hard on a similar work by the Reverend J. E. C. Welldon who had taught at Dulwich from 1883-85 and published a novel not dissimilar to *Eric* entitled *Gerald Eversley's Friendship* in 1895. Back in the 'School Stories' article, Plum makes great good sport of the book's pervading odour of sanctity:

> At the risk of courting an action for libel, I really must say a word or two about that book, though I cannot do much more than repeat, with variations, the sound remarks of Mr. E. F. Benson, in "The Babe B.A." Gerald is, to quote Mr. Benson, "a little beast aged about thirteen." He spends most of his leisure time forming theories of life and wrestling with spiritual doubts – all this at the age of thirteen.

The Babe B.A., subtitled "Being the Uneventful History of a Young Gentleman at Cambridge University," contains Benson's lengthy take-down of Welldon's book, noting that on several occasions, its author tries his best to convince us his novel is "a study in real life." To which the Babe's friend Reggie responds, "If that is real life, give me fiction."

Plum agrees wholeheartedly: Gerald's fall from grace begins not with anything as sinful as weed or the demon alcohol but by reading novels on Sunday morning. His father (a priggish clergyman) and his wife (Gerald's Dickensian stepmother) both upbraid their charge for this sinful habit:

> "I think, Gerald, a Christian will naturally wish to spend Sunday in reading books of a serious kind, not light, secular literature which perishes in the using, but his Bible and such other books as are profitable to his soul's health."

Next thing we hear, the rebellious Gerald's bunking off church and ditching the formalities of organized religion. But "trying to live the Christian life without Christ" is not a circle he is allowed to square:

Gerald is punished with a tormented soul, and, having left school, by his guiltless fiancée dying on the eve of their wedding. As the narrator almost gleefully informs us:

> There seems to be a tacit assumption among storytellers that every story that is told should issue in happiness. That is the way of stories; it is not the way of life. Life is full of tragedies, often known, oftener unknown, that find no satisfaction in this world.

Right there, Plum may well have resolved that his stories were going to be everything that *Gerald Eversley's Friendship* wasn't.

He would spare Welldon's blushes by omitting to name him. Actually, I'm not sure he ever managed to finish *Gerald Eversley*, since in 'School Stories' he tells us the poor lad dies of a "galloping consumption" at the story's close, which he actually doesn't. Instead, he expires in an undisclosed manner at some unspecified point in the future having spent the intervening period doing good deeds among the poor of northern England. But Wodehouse's biggest beef with novels such as *Eric*, *Gerald Eversley's Friendship* and *Tom Brown* seems not to have been the sanctimonious lecturing but, once again, their sheer far-fetchedness.

For a start, real schoolboys, even those who regularly misbehave, are usually admonished with a few hundred lines of Livy, Saturday detention or whackings with a cane rather than an early grave (Eric) or lifelong spiritual misery (Gerald), punishments that most certainly don't fit the crime. You get the feeling that neither Plum (nor Kipling in *Stalky*) were convinced God and Satan were wrestling for the souls of their young protagonists because of a few minor transgressions. *Schoolboys really weren't that bad*, as Plum goes to great lengths to re-assure us in 1908's 'The Lost Lambs' in the persons of the supposed 'bullies' Stone and Robinson:

> There was, as a matter of fact, nothing much wrong with Stone and Robinson. They were just ordinary raggers of the type found at every public school, small and large. They were absolutely free from brain. They had a certain amount of muscle, and a vast store of animal spirits. They looked on school life purely as a vehicle for ragging […] One's opinion of this type of youth varies according to one's point of view.

Indeed; but Farrar, Welldon and Hughes had made their schoolboys' peccadilloes appear far worse than they actually were in order to hammer home their redemptive message. Stalky also remarks that St. Winifred's pupils implausibly seem to "spen[d] all their spare time stealing [...] when they weren't getting drunk at pubs"; and on another occasion, he even appears somewhat jealous:

> "[F]ellows drinkin' and stealin', an' lettin' fags out of window at night, an' – an' doin' what they please. Golly, what we've missed – not goin' to St. Winifred's!"

In his 1901 article 'The Improbabilities of Fiction,' Plum argues that the 'bad boy' cliché can ruin an otherwise viable story. Most typically, he was little more than a plot device:

> It is in the conduct of the villain, or villains, chiefly, that improbabilities occur. The villain always has too much pocket-money, and he *will* spend it on gin. You can't argue him out of it. "I am a bold, bad scoundrel," he says, "and I can't do anything right. I must and will have gin. Gin and billiards. Oh, yes, and a cigar; and it must be a bad one, too, because the public expects me to be ill after it."

He goes on to complain that such schoolboys "must either drink enough for six men and a boy, or else you must be a total and offensive abstainer." What he calls a "golden mean" is missing – until he suddenly remembers that Stalky, of all people, *is actually it* ("I forgot Stalky for the moment.") Here's what Stalky himself has to say about drinking in the story 'In Ambush,' complete with an exclamation Plum regularly put in the mouth of Stanley Featherstonehaugh Ukridge:

> I never got squiffy but once – that was in the holidays [...] an' it made me horrid sick. 'Pon my sacred Sam, though, it's enough to drive a man to drink, havin' an animal like Hoof for House-master."

For Plum and Kipling, it seems, viewing characters as either 'good' or 'bad' leaned not towards realism but good old-fashioned melodrama, and was something to avoid. So, searching for a similar "golden mean" between the penny dreadful and the sanctimonious sermon, Plum set off to find it as soon as he left his own school. He'd read the books, knew his market, thought things through, and his commercial antennae were already fully functional.

It wasn't sheer luck that most of Plum's early fiction first appeared as serializations in the classier schoolboy magazines. Of his novels up to 1913's *The Little Nugget*, all except the first two (*The Pothunters* and *A Prefect's Uncle*) were published in *The Captain*, a monthly that had first appeared in 1899. Not only was it respectable; it proved an instant smash with its target audience, racking up sales of 500,000 per issue in its first year. Indeed, it was thanks to that journal Plum was inspired to start writing his school stories in the first place, at least if we can trust his memory. For it was there in 1900 he had first encountered Frederick Swainson's *Acton's Feud*, which as we'll see in Chapter 3, gave him plenty of food for thought.

Published by the acknowledged founding father of popular journalism George Newnes (who had cannily circulated a range of so-called "penny-delightfuls" to counter the "dreadfuls"), *The Captain*'s audience of "boys and 'old boys'" fitted Plum's favoured atmosphere like a glove, and if we glance at the magazine's pre-publicity for his 1905 yarn *The Head of Kay's*, it's possible to see just what it was that so appealed to editor, R. S. Warren Bell, writing as 'The Old Fag':

> There is some very clever character-drawing in *The Head of Kay's*, the action is brisk and the whole tale abounds in that happy humour which prevails in everything this rising young writer produces.

Having "won his spurs as a *Captain* serial writer" with *The Gold Bat*, Plum was clearly destined for greater things. Warren Bell was a serial writer himself, and twelve months later in September 1905, *The White Feather* would merit a fuller endorsement:

> Mr. Wodehouse has a keen eye for every side of school life, and he is particularly far-seeing in his summing up of the characters of masters as well as of boys [...] [Having] kept closely in touch with his old school, he is able to write from the standpoint of the boy in a manner which must appeal to all boy readers. Throughout the tale one cannot but chuckle over the gay wit which characterizes all his work, which work, by the way, appears to find favour with the most discriminating gentlemen who at the time of writing are perspiring in editorial chairs. You may with confidence look forward to this new story from his pen.

"Confidence" is the key word here, aimed simultaneously at the boys, their parents and even the paper's editor: if the writer got the balance correct, the boys would be entertained; the parents – who were probably shelling out the pocket money that paid for their sons' reading matter – could sleep soundly knowing their offspring weren't buying violent, seditious rubbish; and the editor needn't concern himself with cancelled subscriptions, getting into public rows with the moral majority or receiving threatening memos from the magazine's owner.

Building this confidence was something Wodehouse took seriously from the off, influencing what he wrote and recommended to his readers. Hence, I suspect, his enthusiasm for the writings of Talbot Baines Reed, one of the big noises in public school literature whose family had strong ties to the Religious Tracts Society; indeed, the *Boy's Own Paper* would be the first-run publisher for almost all his fiction until his untimely death aged 41. Plum introduces him thus:

> The late Talbot Baines Reed was probably the most successful of school-story writers, in that he wrote a great many stories and all of them good, some infinitely better than others, but none weak.

Among the 15 or so he published, Reed's best-known title was *The Fifth Form at Saint Dominic's* (serialized 1881-2, appearing as a book in 1887), although Plum clearly favours the later *Tom, Dick and Harry* (1892-3, 1894) which he describes as "nearly perfect as it is possible for a school-story to be." As if to prove that lavish assertion, he kept a copy in his personal library until his death, and, perhaps by way of tribute, wrote a cricketing story with the same title in 1905. There was also a novel he doesn't mention, *My Friend Smith*, whose narrator befriends an unorthodox, well-dressed, smooth-talking chap at school, after which they both get clerical jobs in the same London business (now which Wodehouse plot does *that* remind you of?) Plum's opinion of Reed's writing echoed that of the *Spectator* magazine's reviewer, who gushed:

> There is no-one who has more insight into the character of the genuine English schoolboy than Mr. Reed; no one who knows better his hatred of meanness, his wonderful impulsiveness, his capacity for mischief, and his too often hasty judgment. There can be no doubt that his reproductions of the quarrels, the hates and jealousies of the public-school boy is by far the most accurate and realistic that anyone has yet penned.

Plum's instincts seem to have been on the money, for over a century later, the literary scholar Isobel Quigley could still write that Reed had "alter[ed] the long-winded, garrulous and moralistic school story into something popular and readable, a convention followed by his successors." One of whom, of course, was Wodehouse.

As we've seen, it was a job that needed doing. But if Plum was planning on using Reed's work as a model, he would have been erring on the side of conservatism, and even, occasionally, dullness. While he avers that none of Baines's output was "weak," his enthusiasm does carry just a whiff of faint praise. Reed's brand of storytelling is clear, orderly and well-written, the dialogue what we might call serviceable, rarely rising to the lively. Take this passage from *The Fifth Form at Saint Dominic's*, which I've edited to highlight the direct speech:

> "What I propose is, that we get up a paper of our own!"
> "Upon my word, it's a splendid idea!"
> "We've as good a right, you know, as they have, and ought to be able to turn out quite as respectable a paper."
> "Rather, if you'll only get the fellows to write."
> "Oh, I'll manage that."
> "Of course you'll have to be editor, Tony."
> "If you like."
> "Well, I call that a splendid idea."

Which doesn't really set the world on fire. Overall, reading Reed can be literally monotonous and above all, *adult*, as if he was constantly aware of the eyes of those parents and editors boring into him, warning him not to stray from the path of instruction even for an instant. He even ventures into *Eric* territory, as the tellingly named Loman slides little by little down the slippery slope:

> from deceit to gambling, from gambling to debt, from debt to more deceit, and so on. How drinking, low company and vicious habits had followed [...] [until] the critical moment came [and] he yielded to the tempter and stole the [exam] paper.

But while openly expressed morality only occasionally breaks the surface of Reed's writing, it remains waiting in the wings in a sort of ecumenical *esprit de corps* that all right-thinking boys in his work seem to possess, focused on the greater good of house and school. Plum would take this on board, promoting it to the plot driver of 1905's *The Head of Kay's* and a motif in several of his other schoolboy novels. Was it also a feature of life at Dulwich? Probably.

This solemnity is the dominant atmosphere in Reed's stories: form positions and being in the "cock [top-rated] house" are the holy grail of his boys, and at what should be the climax of *Tom, Dick and Harry* we are treated to a suspenseful but hardly thrilling recitation of each character's exam results, complete with marks scored. Dialling up the earnestness still further, the story's narrator – a former pupil named Tom Jones – outs himself as an adult, and the distance this opens up between himself and his readers is one from which the book never truly recovers. He reminds us that he and his mates were "stupid [...] young fools" at the time the book's action takes place, and this judgmental perspective can never be quite forgotten, indicating that while Jones clearly understands how schoolboys' minds work, he isn't necessarily 100% in their heads or on their side. Not a mistake Plum would make: his narrators are more like approachable uncles than lofty *patresfamilias*.

Then comes Reed's moral medicine administered straight no chaser. Nasty schoolmaster Jarman (another allegorical name straight out of *Pilgrim's Progress*) manages to set the school buildings on fire with a carelessly discarded cigarette; Jones's younger self is sound asleep and fails to evacuate, forcing flawed good guy Tempest (yes, another allegorical name) to re-enter the burning building and rescue him. Both are badly injured, and as Jones slowly recovers, he receives a visit from his mother:

> She urged me to show my gratitude for my escape, by seeking to follow more closely in the footsteps of that Saviour to whom she had often taught me to look for help and guidance, and at the same time she urged me to pray for the guidance of the Holy Spirit.

Quite how Plum's "nearly perfect" verdict managed to survive this weapons-grade ick is difficult to say, bearing in mind his impatience with *Tom Brown* and *Gerald Eversley*. But at least nobody dies in Reed's best stories, and one of the things I think may have chimed strongly with Plum was the writer's regular theme of rehabilitation, either personal or institutional, that characterizes the best of his own school novels from *The Head of Kay's* to *Mike* by way of *The White Feather*.

'The only way is up' is no bad perspective for a school story, and unlike Farrar and Welldon, Plum doesn't luxuriate in the moral decline of his central figures as they circle the plughole of iniquity before disappearing down it. The generative 'bad' moments in his plots all happen rather quickly and early on when there's still time to set things right, so we don't feel as if we're caught in the pale shadow of an Ancient Greek tragedy where everything is hard-wired to turn out badly:

- In *Mike*, Mike Jackson simply has to move schools to destroy his world and send him into a damaging sulk during which he refuses to do what he's best at – play cricket. But then there's an outbreak of fisticuffs with the cricket captain and he's welcomed back into the fold, recapturing some of his old form.
- In *The White Feather*, R. D. Sheen flees a confrontation with town ruffians and is straightaway sent to Coventry by the rest of the school. So he takes boxing lessons from an old pro, wins at Aldershot and is successfully readopted.
- *The Head of Kay's* sees Kennedy disappointingly transplanted from the best house to the rowdiest at Eckleton School through no fault of his own, but because he might stand a chance of leading it out of the doldrums. Which he does.

Although the uphill road may have twists and turns, it still heads in the general direction of a successful outcome with typical Wodehousean positivity, following a rhythm that would carry over into his mature novels. And no one, of course, dies.

Centring these plots around a sticky problem – and not necessarily a *moral* problem – lends them a focus and coherence lacking in Plum's first three school novels *The Pothunters*, *A Prefect's Uncle* and *The Gold Bat*, which are looser, more episodic affairs. But he (almost) never falls into the trap of feeding his readers a line: plots exist to carry the action forward rather than serving as hooks to hang messages on – something Reed never *quite* manages when his lads are caught in spiritual turbulence. Also largely absent from Reed's formula is Wodehouse's comic perspective that prevents things getting too sweaty and serious; and while Reed proves himself a perfectly able comic writer in the short-form 'Eighteen Hours with a Kid' that Plum so enthuses about in 'School Stories' ("one of the best pieces of work he ever did"), such humour as exists in his other work is unfortunately kept on a tight rein and comes over as somewhat self-conscious.

To my ear at least, Reed is a 'penny plain' prosodist, and it was in the arena of style that Wodehouse would quickly show him a clean pair of heels. More of what Plum would later call "oomph" was necessary to impact on his readers, which would translate into at least four related improvements:

- a greater intimacy between narrator and reader

- a less earnest tone
- sharper humour
- more and better dialogue

No single author he cites in 'School Stories' could provide all four of these desirable ingredients; but there were at least two that could surpass Reed in that final department.

Before we discover who they are, it needs pointing out that when Plum first set professional pen to paper as the new century dawned, there was a pre-existing writing style he could – and would – adapt to suit his own purposes, one that would help him incorporate those more oomphy assets into his writing. Wodehouse scholars Tony Ring and Barry Day have christened Plum's version "Early Ironic," the style of the "gentle satirist," which more than anything else makes his work "still readable today." John Dawson calls it "Socratic irony," as in an amused narrator casting a wry look at mankind's follies. They're all absolutely right, and although it would take over two decades to perfect his take on it, Wodehouse would manage to get that style's distinctive *voice* down pat almost as soon as he hit the ground. Indeed, it's so central to his achievement, there follows a separate chapter on where he got it from.

Chapter 3:
Talk Talk

"Young man, you talk too bloody much [...] That mouth
of yours. Does it shut? It does. Then shut it, blast yer.
Lord-love-a-duck, anyone would think you were one of
those ghastly fellows in Shakespeare that do soliloquies."
Money in the Bank

"I think you must really let Jackson go on with his work,
Smith. There seems to be too much talking."

"My besetting sin," said Psmith sadly.
Psmith in the City

"Don't *talk* so much! I never met a fellow like you for
talking!"
Leave It To Psmith

"Don't talk so much, Uncle Fred!"
Service With a Smile

Wodehouse World is stuffed to the gills with world-class "buzzers" of all
ages – to wit, characters who can talk the hind legs off a donkey. And
we'll begin with one selected almost completely at random from this
embarras de choix, the "always merry and bright" Mike Cardinal from
1948's *Spring Fever*, published when Plum was in his late 60s. Here's one
of many possible examples of him talking that talk, describing a scenario in which he has booted the former burglar Augustus Robb up
the backside for belittling Teresa "Terry" Cobbold, to whom Mike is
addressing his remarks:

> "If we are to be saved from the disruptive forces that
> wrecked Rome and Babylon, we cannot have retired porch
> climbers speaking in this lax manner of girls who are more
> like angels than anything. It strikes at the very root of ev-
> erything that makes for sane and stabilized government."

At which point Terry informs him that he has done Augustus Robb a
great wrong, since said porch climber was Mike's biggest booster and

was urging her to marry him. To which Mike responds:

> "God bless him! To think that foot of mine should have jolted that golden-hearted trouser seat. I will abase myself before him tomorrow. But isn't it extraordinary […] how everyone wants you to marry me? […] It's what the papers call a widespread popular demand. Don't you think you ought to listen to the voice of the People?"

Soon after this torrent of persiflage, Mike formally pops the question ("Terry, you little mutt, will you marry me?") only to be soundly rebuffed. On enquiring why, Terry informs him that he speaks of marriage "as if it were a sort of game." Which, to be fair to Mike, it isn't; it's just that by the way he talks, he makes it *sound* like it is. Unfortunately, he can't help himself, for this is his naturally peppy way of speaking. So why, given the seriousness of the moment, *does* he insist on talking like that? Or feel he *ought* to?

Well, for a start, this is comedy, and saying exactly what you mean in words of one syllable isn't usually the best way to get a laugh. So we find that many of Wodehouse's lead characters are blessed with the gift of the gab and have kissed the Blarney stone several times over, masters of a kind of *performed* speech also regularly discernible in the tone and style of Plum's first and third person narrators. It isn't always as full-on as Mike's, but its presence is a reliable indicator that its speakers and writers are all, to a greater or lesser degree, show-offs. Or, in classic showbiz psychology, the direct opposite. For Mike (and a good many of Plum's other gabbers) the mannered way he talks is the "protective armour" of the frantically over-compensating introverted male. "You think I'm not sincere because I clown," he complains to Terry; but when he needs to "change the record" and come over all serious, he can't stop himself being "flippant."

It's a facet of learned behaviour that will never leave him – just as it never left his creator when he was writing. We can witness its roots as early as Wodehouse's journalism for *The Alleynian* school magazine, in which he reviews one of his own stage performances from 1899:

> Wodehouse then informed the audience kindly but firmly of his irrevocable intention of departing for "for'ing" parts on the morrow. He gave Philadelphia as his probable destination, and held out hopes of returning at some future date. At the repetition of the last verse, the gallery joined in the chorus. The start was quite fair, but the superior

stamina of the many told in the end, and after a gruelling race, the singer was beaten by a bar and two notes.

This performative "Early Ironic" voice I mentioned at the close of the previous chapter is, as we'll be seeing, the *fons et origo* of Bertie Wooster's storytelling skills. Its published ancestry stretches back at least to *The Pothunters*, Plum's first novel from 1902 in which we meet 'Alderman' Charteris, whose fascination with words powers the *Glow Worm*, an alternative school paper. Then there's Marriott in 1903's *A Prefect's Uncle*, who entertainingly describes a schoolboy dust-up thus:

> "[Percy] hits Skinner crisply in the right eyeball, blacking the same as per illustration. The subsequent fight raged gorily for five minutes odd, and then Wilson, who seems to be a professional pugilist in disguise, landed what my informant describes as three corkers on his opponent's proboscis. Skinner's reply was to sit down heavily on the floor, and give him to understand that the fight was over, and that for the next day or two his face would be closed for alterations and repairs […] I have spoken."

Indeed he has. *Mike*'s Clowes and Wyatt can also be added to our list of gabblers, as can Horace Silver from *The Head of Kay's*:

> It was one of his amusements to express himself from time to time in melodramatic fashion, sometimes accompanying his words with suitable gestures.

But these young motormouths are mere showroom dummies compared to a character whose linguistic dexterity easily trounces them all.

Psmith is undoubtedly the king of Plum's early wordpsmiths (sorry, couldn't resist), although we might properly describe him as 'private' rather than 'shy'. He too flirts with journalism (in, er, *Psmith, Journalist*), but his true calling cards are the stream-of-consciousness torrents of verbiage that embellish and then dominate his immediate reality. His high eloquence translates the ordinary into the unconventional, beginning with his choice of sobriquet, converting the commonest surname in England to something quite exotic by the simple addition of an initial plosive that isn't sounded "as in ptarmigan, psalm, and phthisis." I've already written about Psmith at some length in Volume 1 of my trilogy *Pelham Grenville Wodehouse*, so no need to repeat myself here, but here's a brief snatch of his persiflage to refresh our memories, as he calmly requisitions Spiller's study on his very first day at Sedleigh school:

> "What the dickens," inquired the newcomer [Spiller], "are
> you doing here?"
> "We were having a little tea," said Psmith, "to restore our
> tissues after our journey. Come in and join us. We keep
> open house, we Psmiths. Let me introduce you to Com-
> rade Jackson. A stout fellow. Homely in appearance, per-
> haps, but one of us. I am Psmith. Your own name will
> doubtless come up in the course of general chit-chat over
> the tea-cups."
> "My name's Spiller, and this is my study." […]
> "Of all sad words of tongue or pen," said he, "the saddest
> are these: 'It might have been.' Too late! That is the bitter
> cry. If you had torn yourself from the bosom of the Spiller
> family by an earlier train, all might have been well. But
> no. Your father held your hand and said huskily, 'Edwin,
> don't leave us!' Your mother clung to you weeping, and
> said, 'Edwin, stay!' Your sisters –"
> "I want to know what –"
> "Your sisters froze on to your knees like little octopuses (or
> octopi), and screamed, 'Don't go, Edwin!' And so," said
> Psmith, deeply affected by his recital, "you stayed on till
> the later train; and, on arrival, you find strange faces in the
> familiar room, a people that know not Spiller."

Which clocks in at Psmith on 175 words, Spiller a distant second with
20. Suitably tweaked to different characters and narrative circumstances, it would become Wodehouse's default narrative voice, a sort of verbal Swiss Army knife that could deliver all the tones and timbres he
required, barring, of course, high seriousness.

This manner of expression has a long and rich literary lineage dating back to the earliest Classical drama, Italian *commedia dell'arte* and on
through Shakespeare and Restoration Comedy to the present day – anywhere, in fact, we find characters parading their verbal smarts. They
may be braggarts like Plautus's *miles gloriosus* Pyrgopolynices; the fantastical Don Armado from Plum's favourite Shakespeare play *Love's Labour's
Lost* ("I am for whole volumes in folio!"); the extravagant narrator of Alexander Pope's mock-epic *The Rape of the Lock*; or the finicky Lady Lofty
in Thomas Horde's *The Female Pedant*. In seeking to put language through
its paces even when they don't need to or aren't very good at it, these
stylists each develop a distinctive and sometimes extravagant voice or id-

iolect. We know that Plum was familiar with at least some of the works in which they appear, but we can turn to George Orwell's magisterial essay 'Boys' Weeklies' for a further pointer to his more proximate inspirations.

The more satisfactory school stories, Orwell notes, present their readers with a "carefully graded" range of characters, one of whom every boy can identify with. Somewhere among the hearty, the sportsman, the aristocrat, the swot, the sneak and the dare-devil can be found one who doesn't *quite* fit in; not always the loner but certainly the law unto himself who "possesses some special talent" while still holding his own in schoolboy society. In Wodehouse, that special talent is often the facility with words we're currently examining, the ability to use language, written or spoken, as both shield and weapon. One of the first things Psmith utters on his debut is the telling question "Do I look as if I belonged here?", directed square-on at a slightly incredulous Mike Jackson when they first meet at Sedleigh. And no, he doesn't, this etiolated, immaculate, monocle-wearing apparition who can talk his way into or out of anything.

An immediate influence on Wodehouse must have been the unprepossessing, speccy Beetle, that cunning linguist from *Stalky and Co.* Although he edits the official school magazine, he has a darker, subversive side that manipulates spoken and written language to help work through his teenage rebellion, usually under the Coll's social radar. In 1899's 'The Last Term,' his parting *tour de force* involves breaking into the school printer's premises and re-arranging the metal type of the forthcoming Latin prose exam paper, rendering the words gibberish, so when it's printed off and presented to the examinees the questions are unanswerable. Beetle then mischievously suggests that Mr. King must have been "screwed as an owl" when he set the paper. No mean actor himself, he usually leaves the talking to those born performers Stalky and M'Turk, as in the following example in which the former, "assum[ing] the air of a judge" performs a mock arraignment of the long-suffering Mr. King:

> "He has oppressed Beetle, M'Turk and me, *privatim et seriatim*, one by one, as he could catch us. But now he has insulted Number Five [i.e. all three of them] up in the music room and in the presence of these – these ossifers of the Ninety-third, wot look like hairdressers. Binjimin, we must make him cry 'Capivi!'"

Here we find breathless Dickensian speech rhythms and idiosyncratic pronunciation butting up against Latin legalese, all topped off with references from Surtees's *Handley Cross*, from which Stalky carries over a Bertie-esque mistake ("capivi" should read "peccavi" – "I was wrong"). At which point M'Turk takes over:

> "And besides [King's] a Philistine, a basket-hanger. He wears a tartan tie. Ruskin says that any man who wears a tartan tie will, without doubt, be damned everlastingly."

Which is rewarded with a "Bravo!", as if we've just witnessed a stage performance. Whether Ruskin actually did damn patterned neckwear (you can search all 39 volumes of his Collected Works if you'd care to) it's a telling demonstration how just about anything can be pressed into service in these acts of verbal fencing.

Although Beetle & Co often seem to speak interchangeably, Anthony Pembury from Talbot Baines Reed's 1881 novel *The Fifth Form at Saint Dominic's* (q.v.) is more a solo act, standing out from Reed's other generally monochrome schoolboys in his desire to entertain. In the following passage, he's ribbing Stephen Greenfield, who's incredibly green even for a new bug:

> "I'm lame, you see," said Pembury, presently. "You are quite sure you see? Look at my left leg."
> "I see," said Stephen, blushing; "I – I hope it doesn't hurt."
> "Only when I wash my face. But never mind that Vulcan was lame too, but then he never washed. You know who Vulcan was, of course?"
> "No, I don't think so," faltered Stephen, beginning to feel very uneasy and ignorant.
> "Not know Vulcan! My eye! where have you been brought up? Then of course you don't know anything about the Tenth Fiji War? No? I thought not. Dreadful!"

Apart from the lameness Pembury shares with Vulcan, just about everything else is eyewash, as is the "Doctor's examination" he tells Greenfield he'll have to sit the following day. So although Tony, as he's known, "cannot box, [...] he can *talk*," rendering him both popular and mercifully unbullied, possessing "an air of authority about [him]" which others "dared not defy." His father is a newspaper editor, and Tony follows in his footsteps by almost single-handedly writing and publishing the *Dominican*, a subversive broadsheet that pillories the school's senior boys. And like Beetle (and Plum), he ends up being a journalist in adult life.

Another possible influencer was Andrew Home, whose inventory of around a dozen volumes of school stories between 1896-1909 spans Plum's time at Dulwich. Here's our man's verdict:

> Andrew Home is another who rarely fails to do well in school-story writing, whether long or short. His short stories possibly contain his best work, notably one, whose title I forget, which introduced a German master and the Scotch uncle of one of the members of the German master's class. The only part of it that I remember definitely is the sentence "Eh, mon, but ye've a queer accent wi' ye're Eenglish," which, when you come to think of it, is about the best thing one could say to a German master, and is such stuff as catch-phrases are made of.

It seems Plum always kept an ear open for interesting forms of expression, and his own forays into cod-Scotch, courtesy of Sandy McHoots, Angus McAllister and others deserve a monograph of their own. Like Reed, Home was a functional rather than dazzling dialogue writer; and in the splendidly titled novel *From Fag to Monitor* (first serialized in *Chums* in 1895) he creates a schoolboy not unlike Psmith who has fashioned an entire alter ego for himself, which involves talking in a ridiculously over-formal, roundabout way. We first glimpse George Gosling, who has re-invented himself as 'Algernon de Vere,' in a train carriage on his way up to Whitborough school, where he tries out his spiel on the naivest of new boys, the narrator Jack Graham:

> "Going to Whitborough?"
> "Yes," said I. "And you?"
> "That is my present intention."
> (Why can't he say "Yes" and have done with it, thought I.)
> Then, asking a question in my turn, in a free and easy style, which I hoped would impress him:
> "Going to Hobill's?"
> "I am about," said the youth, "to resume my studies at High Cliff House, under the direction of Mr. George Hobill, Bachelor of Arts, the headmaster. May I assume that you are also bound upon the same delightful errand?"
> "Oh, yes, I'm going," I replied, perfectly astounded by the other's eloquence.

Gosling keeps up his jester's role throughout the encounter, inventing a string of cod-Latin words ("in slumbero profundo" for deep sleep, and "suetonius" for suet pudding) that amuse rather than excite belly laughs. He does impressions, too ("He can do Hobill lecturing fit to make you split") and like Pembury with Greenfield fills Graham's innocent head with no end of invented nonsense about the school's manners and mores. But as with Reed's brand of humour, it's all a bit laboured, and it's scarcely a wonder that virtually nothing of Home's writing seems to have stuck in Plum's memory.

Far more influential on Wodehouse was the work of another mystery man, Frederick Swainson. Schooled at Haileybury and receiving his B.A. from Cambridge in 1895, he went on to enjoy a distinguished career in the military, writing a dozen or so stories for *The Captain* and *Strand* between 1899 and 1907. And, errrr . . . that's about all I've been able to find out. What most regularly pops up during otherwise fruitless biographical searches is Plum's assertion that it was Swainson's best-known novel *Acton's Feud* that first inspired him to have a go at fiction. Until that point his *métier* looked likely to be journalism, and he would much later comment to David Jasen that it was "[a]wfully funny how something like that gives you a kick-off."

Acton's Feud began serialization in *The Captain* in March 1900 as Plum was getting ready to leave Dulwich, and was then published as a single volume in 1901. It was the latter version Plum gushingly (and anonymously) reviewed for *Public School Magazine* in its January 1902 issue, judging it "the best story of Public School life that has ever appeared." And he probably meant it, since it satisfies all the criteria of truth to life he demanded. As the central figure, John Acton is neither a goody-goody nor a villain but a convincing amalgam of both who has to work the baser qualities out of his system as the plot progresses. "One's sympathies are with him" as Plum puts it; and, as his own R. D. Sheen would later manage six years later in *The White Feather*, Acton rehabilitates himself in both the form room and the boxing ring, winning the silver medal at the Aldershot tournament. The greater part of Plum's review consists of praise for the dialogue:

> Mr. Swainson has hit off the speech of school-life to perfection. It is in the dialogue that most school-stories fail. Even the best of them are behind the times. Mr. Swainson is up-to-date.

I suspect it wasn't simply the accuracy Wodehouse latched on to, but its vigour and inventiveness, as evidenced in the sizeable (though edited) chunk he quotes, in which Grim, attempting some Latin translation, has come over all poetical and is getting ragged by his mates:

> "Whatever is the good of getting the very word the Beak
> wants, Grimmy? I always translate *Carmen* – a song. Does
> it matter a cherry stone that it sometimes means a charm?
> Think of your friends, Grimmy, do. If I didn't know you
> were a bit cracked, I'd say your performance was undilut-
> ed smugging."
> "Cork that frivol, do," said Grim, "and look over there.
> How beautiful it is!"
> "How beautiful what is?" asked Wilson, astonished.
> "The sunset, you ass!"
> "Matter of fact," said Wilson, elaborately agreeing with
> his friend as a mother might with a sick child, "it is rather
> fine. Not unlike a Zingari blazer; eh?"
> "Zingari blazer!"
> "Exactly like. And that pink on the trees would do for the
> Westminster shirts."
> "Blazers and shirts," cried Grim, in disgust, "Oh! get out."

This is not even the best example of verbal jousting he could have chosen – but there, in just a few lines, is Plum's model for his own schoolboy
speech, dominated not by an individual but spoken, with varying ability,
by several of the boys.

By comparison, Talbot Baines Reed could only summon a fraction
of the energy to be found in these exchanges, adding only the meagrest
dusting of slang; "serene" and "honour bright" (both synonyms for
'Okay') are just about all his knowledge runs to. Swainson, by contrast,
treats us to the full English, as would Plum only months later. To begin
with, we have standard public school lingo: "Beak" [master]; "smug-
ging" [showing off] and "ass." There's a smattering of idiolect ("frivol",
"do") together with some accurate schoolboy intel on the real-life Il
Zingari Cricket Club (whose members don jazzy red, gold and black
blazers to this day); and the sporting colours of Westminster School,
which were referred to as "pinks" whether they were actually pink or
not. And while we're about it, we should also acknowledge Wodehouse's
stated enthusiasm for the novel's opening sentence:

> Shannon, the old Blue had brought down a rattling eleven
> – two internationals among them – to give the school the
> first of its annual soccer [sic] matches.

This, Plum tells us, gratifyingly "plunge[s] straight into the middle of things," wasting no time immersing its readers in the plot (cf. the opening of *The Pothunters* quoted at the start of this book). He also praises Swainson's verbal economy ("the descriptions of the various incidents of interest throughout the book are absolutely without padding, 'and therefore best,' as the advertisement says.") Add all that together, he gushes, and "*Acton's Feud* is a classic. No home will be complete without it." And Plum wasn't alone in his enthusiasm: the *Spectator*'s anonymous reviewer was also enthused by both "the dialogue [and] the schoolboy wit and humour" which he judged both authentic and "represented with no little skill."

Of course, whether schoolboys *actually* spoke anything like that is another question entirely. As Plum acknowledged elsewhere, real-life school life is for the most part pedestrian and boring, with conversation tending towards the functional and uninspired rather than a feast of reason and flow of soul packed with vim and *bons mots*. But that needn't – indeed couldn't – be the case in fiction, which must engage and hold the imagination. Swainson clearly grasped the important principle, as did Plum, that a high ratio of dialogue to narration was the best way of keep his prose's energy levels fully charged. And so another passage that would have appealed to our man occurs in Chapter 8, in which the boys of Biffen's (yes, another Wodehouse borrowing and yes, Swainson invents a pupil whose nickname is "Fruity") choose a song for their in-house concert. With the barest minimum of authorial intrusion, the whole chapter is cast almost entirely as speech or reported speech – nearly six continuous pages in my edition – of which this is a short snatch:

> "I say, you fellows," said Grim, "it's to be a concert, you know, and except for Fruity's epilogue there isn't any music down yet." Cherry groaned to think he'd been let in for a song.
> "What about Thurston?" asked half a dozen of the fags.
> "Right, oh! Now, 'Dicky Bird,' hop up to the front, and trot out your list."
> Thurston wasn't shy, and rather fancied his bleat, so he said, "Oh! I don't mind at all."
> "We thought you wouldn't," said the chairman, winking.
> "What do you say to '*Alice, where art thou*'?"
> "We don't fancy your shouting five minutes for her at all. Next, please."
> "'*Only to see her face again*,' then?"
> "Whose?" said Sharpe, irreverently.

"Why, the girl's the fellow is singing about," said Thurston, hotly.

"Oh! You'll see her the day after to-morrow, Dicky Bird, so don't you fret about that now. Do you know '*My first cigar*'?"

"Do you mean the one that sent you to hospital, Grimmy?"

"No I don't. None of your cheek. I'm chairman. I mean the one Corney Grain used to sing."

"Yes."

"Well, you sing that and you'll make the fellows die with laughing. And mind you illustrate it with plenty of life-like pantomime, do you hear?"

"Carried, nem. con.," shouted all the fags with enthusiasm.

Swainson is practically writing a play here. The Biffen boys run through their repertoire of (actual) popular songs and artists using the kind of quick-fire vaudeville cross-talk Plum would also favour, complete with comic misunderstandings, nicknames, backchat, slang ("P and O" for 'piano'; "key-thumper" – a rollicking song) and even advertising slogans ("cut out and get yours"). Once again, a rich mix that Plum could very likely have learned from.

Acton's Feud remains in print today, and apart from some toe-curling racism placed in the mouths of Acton and Worcester (whose name Plum might also have squirrelled away for future reference) it remains a perfectly serviceable adventure, built around the sort of coming-of-age theme Wodehouse would also employ in his better school novels.

Also featured in Plum's review is a plug for a second school story that seems to have profoundly influenced him, *Graeme and Cyril* from 1893. Despite just about every appearance to the contrary, its writer Barry Pain was not a Farrar with a muscular Christian message to preach: rather he was a jobbing writer who specialized in humorous works with strong, well-delineated first-person narrators of which the *Eliza* sketches are perhaps the best known. Much of his work first appeared in *Punch*, and no fewer than 21 of his books could be found in Plum's personal library. Of Pain himself he remarked in old age:

> "I would guess [he] had as much influence on my writing as anyone. No one, I gather, reads him today, but he was awfully good. He was marvellous at creating character in a few swift strokes."

Which he was, and even though Pain's school output only extended to one novel and two short stories, they were nevertheless "first class and truer to life than anything that anyone has ever written anywhere [...] [t]he atmosphere is just the right atmosphere, the various characters are life like, and, crowning praise of all, there is no bully."

But while Pain gets the Wodehouse uptick for atmosphere and realism, it's difficult to understand why *Graeme and Cyril* pushed any of his buttons at all. Aside from the occasional sparkling dialogue which we'll come to in a moment, its plot is pure *Eric* and profusely littered with the kind of sanctimony Wodehouse would rarely choose to mess with. I mean, how about this for pure humbug?

> [A]lmost the only thing that does one's self real good is self-sacrifice. Self-sacrifice is at the root of all true religion; it is at the root of all true heroism; it is one of the reasons for that enthusiasm which every one feels for a public school with which he has been in any way connected.

Pain was educated at Sedbergh school, and these sentiments give the impression of being genuine. And yes, there's the usual litany of drinking, smoking and gambling that Farrar would have been proud of, complete with a high-profile death at the end of the book.

But all is not what it seems here; lurking beneath the surface are clues that Pain is actually a note-perfect parodist, who had done an excellent job mimicking the preachy type of school story while keeping an absolutely straight face. Only very occasionally does he let the mask slip, as in the following *ex cathedra* comment taken from the book's final chapter:

> [A]t Oxford and Cambridge there is too much preaching [...] Society is never any the better for the best of its prigs.

Had he picked up on this and other similar clues (which include some very wise but utterly unorthodox views on pedagogy), Plum might have concluded he was in the presence of a true craftsman, a master mimic who could turn his hand to any style or subject.

As well as his brief flirtation with the more sententious kind of school story, Pain would try his hand at just about anything, from *The Diary of A Baby*, the comic musings of a particularly precocious one-year-old girl, to science fiction and horror stories involving werewolves that are said to have influenced H. P. Lovecraft. There was also *Nothing Serious*, a title Plum would steal for his 1950 collection of short stories, and 'An Exchange of Souls,' concerning a personality swap between a scientist and his fiancée that ends in bitter tears. But best of all from

Plum's perspective, there's Cyprian Langsdyke aka 'The Celestial,' a "whimsical" character who is a whizz with words and hence – somewhat inevitably by now – editor of the school magazine. And even better, one who prefers "[g]ood, solid, rhymed poetry" to non-rhyming blank verse which, as we'll see in this book's final chapter, was one of Plum's regular bugbears.

Like Psmith in Plum's Mike Jackson plot arc, Langsdyke arrives late to the party, a good two-thirds of the way through the novel, but immediately makes his presence felt. A complete one-off, he comes equipped with a following of acolytes, and is wont to sit on the hot water pipes holding forth on "public affairs" to his small crowd of admirers. A Wildean figure who "very rarely spoke quite seriously," he is prone to come out with *bons mots* and aphorisms such as these:

> "You were always a lazy beast, Fathead [...] You were in the fifth when I was; you're in the fifth now; you'll stick in the fifth until the sea gives up its dead, I believe."
> "Never prepare Livy – that's my motto in life [...] I find that all Livy's divided into two parts. One part you can translate, even if you don't prepare it, and the other part you can't translate even if you do."

In 'School Stories' Plum calls him "the most cleverly-drawn character that can be found in the whole range of school fiction," and by way of tribute has his own character Pillingshot refuse to do his Livy prep. Impossibly self-confident, Langsdyke adjusts Desford School's reality to suit himself, picking and choosing – just like Stalky, Charteris and Psmith – which rules are convenient to obey. "You just do as you like," he advises his pal Smithson, and as long as "[i]t isn't the kind of thing that masters ever think of boys doing" he's in the clear. He has an ongoing project to read the whole of Dickens, an activity he conducts in the early hours, and is partial to midnight feasts. He's also a naturally gifted writer: when he wins the school Essay and Composition prizes, he "did not seem to be in the least moved by his success." In short, he has style, and it's clear that Psmith owes him a considerable debt. So taken is Wodehouse, he writes:

> If, by the time you have finished "Cyril and Graeme," [sic] you are not panting to obtain a further glimpse of the Celestial, I refuse to have anything more to do with you, and I shall instruct my head-footman to refuse you admittance when you call at my address.

Notice how Plum the apprentice journalist is already aping Langsdyke's manner of speech in his writing.

But all good things come to an end, and at 18 or so all these eloquent mis-shapes leave school and proceed to university or get a job. Some like Beetle and Pembury go into journalism, as of course did Wodehouse, taking their facility with language along with them. And it is here that writers like Pain would prove even more influential on Plum, inducting him into the school of so-called 'New' English humour that embraced other professional freelancers including James Payn (who gave Barry Pain his first significant career leg-up), Andrew Lang, J. M. Barrie, F. Anstey, Hilaire Belloc, Jerome K. Jerome, Harold Begbie, George Grossmith, and Bertram Fletcher Robinson – the last three of whom Plum would later get to work with. A cabal of prolific, hard-working scribes who could crank out decent quality gear no matter what they turned their hands to, most have been badly traduced by posterity, their productivity and versatility largely ignored thanks to the disproportionate prominence of one or two of their works (as in Grossmith's *The Diary of a Nobody* and Jerome's *Three Men in a Boat*). Together, and with many other lesser-known writers in humorous magazines like *Punch*, they ensured the 1880s and '90s were a golden age of whimsical comic writing of the kind Plum would have eagerly latched on to.

In 'The Manoeuvres of Charteris,' we catch the eponymous schoolboy enthusiastically recommending one of these writers to Tony Harrison, languishing in double detention with nothing to read:

> "James Payn [...] wrote a hundred books, and they're all simply ripping, and [...] I'm going to borrow a couple and you're going to read them. I know one always bars a book that's recommended to one, but you've got no choice. You're not going to get anything else till you've finished those two."

There's no reason to believe Plum didn't share his character's enthusiasm. Old Etonian James Payn was a workaholic poet, essayist and magazine editor (*Chambers's Journal* and *The Cornhill Magazine*) who also published around 60 novels (but certainly not 100). A misfit in school and life, he pursued his calling with a monomania that rivalled Plum's, and whatever genre he chose to write in, there always appeared an affable lightness in his style that engaged his readers – and kept them reading. In the "Prefatory" to an early novel *Lost Sir Massingberd* (a sort of romance with a touch of Gothic horror) he wrote of his efforts:

In these days, when every man and woman becomes an author upon the least provocation, it is not necessary to make an apology for appearing in print. Perhaps there was always something affected in those prefatorial justifications; although they did disclaim any literary merit, it is probable that the writers would have been indignant enough had the critics taken them at their word; and perhaps the publication was not entirely owing to "the warmly-expressed wishes of numerous friends." But, at all events, we have done with all such excuses now. Not to have written anything for the press, is no small claim to being an Original.

Behind this mask of the unassuming amateur was a writer who knew exactly what he was doing; and if we were to venture a possible role model for the young Wodehouse, it would probably be someone not too dissimilar. From the off, Plum joined the ranks of these versatile professionals and would have been proud of the association; indeed, if we look at the first ten years of his bibliography, we'll see that alongside his school stories, he also managed to produce:

- a fairy tale (*William Tell Told Again*, 1904)
- a comedy romance (*Love Among the Chickens*, 1906)
- a literary satire (*Not George Washington*, 1907)
- song lyrics for musical comedies and revue ('Put Me in My Little Cell,' 'Oh, Mr. Chamberlain!,' 1904 onwards)
- four seasonal pantomimes (1903-1907)
- a near 'penny-dreadful' (*The Luck Stone*, 1908)
- a comedy anthology (*The Globe By the Way Book* – in which could be found an episodic melodrama *Wine, Women and Song!* – 1908)
- a full-length satire (*The Swoop!*, 1909)

And all this in addition to the hundreds of poems, articles, reviews, interviews and humorous "pars" [paragraphs] that would appear in a dizzying variety of newspapers and magazines, most notably *The Globe*, where he edited the six-times-weekly 'By the Way' column from 1904 onwards.

From 1900 until he left England in 1914, Plum was a blooded denizen of London's 'New Grub Street,' the title of George Gissing's 1891 novel about two very different men trying to scrape a precarious living in a crowded, cut-throat market of literary freelancers: one arty, shy and uncompromisingly uncommercial, the other a self-promoting jack-of-all-trades who will write anything for money and fame. Gissing (who Plum would pillory for writing stuff "as grey as a stevedore's undervest" in 1960's *Ice in the Bedroom*) proposed this binary model as if writers could not escape being one or the other.

But why, Plum must have thought at some point early on, couldn't you be both? A writer who produces high-quality work that is popular *and* makes money? Although he had no way of knowing this, the mighty Kipling had always thought of himself as not so much an artist but "first and foremost a good workman." 'Old Pop' wished his brothers in rhyme would forget all that guff peddled by the Romantic Poets about "soul development" and took a dim view of those Aesthetes who had behaved like "irresponsible demi-god[s]," off their heads on opium or absinthe as they tried to contact their capricious muses. No, he averred, great writers went to their desks every morning, sat down and worked – *hard*. Advice, as has been well documented, Plum zealously followed. Yet while there is no difficulty arguing that the quality of what he produced during his journeyman days was hit-and-miss, there can be little doubt that learning on the job against the background of such gifted, versatile and down-to-earth all-rounders would prove no bad thing.

Once again, the 'magpie' principle was the most likely way Plum picked out what he needed. Sticking with Barry Pain for a moment, that writer's short novel *Confessions of Alphonse* from 1917 is the obvious source of Monsieur Anatole, the supreme slinger of roasts and hashes employed by Bingo Little and then Bertie's Aunt Dahlia at Brinkley Manor who is first referenced in 1929's 'The Spot of Art.' Here's a brief snatch of Alphonse's extended dramatic monologue:

> My friends, listen. Make attention a little. I am a man that knows on which side is the buttered toast. If you think you see some greens in my eyes, you do the bloomer. I know my interest. It is that one day I – I who speak to you – shall be the proprietor of the restaurant. Yes!

Alphonse gifted Wodehouse almost verbatim steals like "as cool as some cucumbers" (Plum's version is "so cool as a few cucumbers") and "we must take some roughs with a smooth" ("I can take a few smooths with a rough"). This isn't *quite* cribbing; in fact it's more of a tribute, as we witness Plum, now a mature writer in mid-season form, taking out and putting in, and actually improving on his inspiration. Whereas Pain has to laboriously sustain Alphonse's mock-French accent over 72 pages (in my edition) long after its novelty has worn off, Plum has the good sense to allow Anatole just three paragraphs of direct speech in *Right Ho,*

Jeeves, in which he can set off all his verbal fireworks at once. Here's the second of those paras, when a dozing Anatole is rudely awakened by Gussie Fink-Nottle pulling faces at him through the bedroom window:

> "Wait yet a little. I am not finish. I say I see this type on my window, making a few faces. But what then? Does he buzz off when I shout a cry and leave me peaceable? Not on your life. He remain planted there, not giving any damns, and sit regarding me like a cat watching a duck. He make faces against me and again he make faces against me, and the more I command that he should get to hell out of here, the more he do not get to hell out of here. He cry something towards me, and I demand what is his desire, but he do not explain. Oh, no, that arrives never. He does but shrug his head. What damn silliness! Is this amusing for me? You think I like it? I am not content with such folly. I think the poor mutt's loony. *Je me fiche de ce type infect. C'est idiot de faire comme ça l'oiseau* [...] *Allez-vous-en, louffier* [...] Tell the boob to go away. He is mad as some March hatters."

Neither Plum nor Pain is poking fun at funny Frenchmen with silly accents, but revelling in comedic idiolects that are brilliantly *suorum generum*. At root, both characters are speaking English while retaining French grammatical constructions and vocabulary; toss in some haphazardly acquired slang, mix the odd metaphor, and the recipe is complete. On this occasion Plum takes the opportunity to show off his command of actual French, as he had been living the life of a tax exile across the Channel for some time and was about to move there permanently. But where he scores over Pain is in his dramatic sense of how and when to use such a wonderful resource, having learned a thing or two from his time in the theatre, imagining his character performing his lines rather than narrating his story. Only then can the comedy be turned up to 11 as Anatole stubbornly refuses to be talked down off the ceiling, leaving us eager to hear more from him.

Alphonse would also bequeath the germ of the idea that would become the celebrated opening of *The Luck of the Bodkins*:

> With long experience, I know now when an Englishman is going to say words of French even before he begin; there comes always a look of anxious shame into his eyes. That means he is going to say *omelette aux fines herbes* or something a little like it.

In Plum's hands, it becomes:

> Into the face of the young man who sat on the terrace of the Hotel Magnifique at Cannes there had crept a look of furtive shame, the shifty hangdog look which announces that an Englishman is about to speak French.

At which point Pain signs off with a punchline ("And the worse a Englishman speak French, the more he pay you for understanding and not laughing"); while Plum, recognizing an absolute gift of a comedy cue, conjures a masterful routine between Monty and the French waiter, which the latter concludes with "Right ho, m'sieur," each playing the game and giving as good as he gets.

Alongside Pain, another of *Punch*'s versatile contributors was Thomas Anstey Guthrie whose pen-name 'F. Anstey' regularly graced its pages, such that Plum confessed to being "soaked in Anstey's stuff" at a young age. So soaked in fact, that when the writer's memoirs were published two years after his death in 1934, the *Yorkshire Post*'s reviewer commented that he was "in many respects the P. G. Wodehouse of the last generation." As with Pain, it's Anstey's ear for comic speech that seems to have been Plum's main interest, a facility ruthlessly exploited in Anstey's two-volume *Voces Populi* [The Voices of the People], the first of which appeared in 1890. Over the course of 55 short playlets, he introduces a kaleidoscopic range of social types, each with its own distinctive manner of speaking. Here's a left-wing orator giving a fire-and-brimstone speech not dissimilar in sentiment, delivery and content to the tub thumper in Plum's 'Comrade Bingo':

> "The weather is against us, Feller Republikins, there's no denyin' that. As we were tramping along 'ere, through the mud and in the rain, wet to the skin, I couldn't 'elp remarking to a friend o' mine, that if it had been a pidging-shootin' match at Urlingham, or a Race-meeting at Hascot, things 'ud ha' been diff'rent! Ther'd ha' bin blue sky and sunshine enough *then*. Well, I 'spose hany weather's considered good enough for the likes of hus! Hany weather'll do for pore downtrod slaves to assert their man'ood and their hindependence in! Never you mind – hour turn'll come some day! We sha'n't *halways* be 'eld down, and muzzled, and silenced, and prevented uttering the hindignation we've a right to feel!"

Plum borrowed the book from the New York Society Library (hereafter NYSL) in 1951, no doubt to reacquaint himself with a favourite work he had read half a century before. For over the course of his career, Anstey created literally hundreds of characters, either named individuals or types such as "The Usual Comic Cockney," "Mrs. Flusters," or "A Strict Old Lady," all of which would have been a rich resource for a writer on the lookout for decent comic accents to imitate. But of all Anstey's characters, the one who seems to have caught Plum's ear most comprehensively was Mr. Hurry Bungsho Jabberjee.

Whereas the likes of Stalky, the Celestial and Plum's cast of buzzers tend to know precisely what they mean while gleefully playing with language and expression, Jabberjee has only an imperfect grasp and even less control of what he is saying for much of the time. When we first meet him in 1897's *Baboo Jabberjee, B.A.*, he is touting for a journalist's job and addresses his prospective editor thus:

> VENERABLE AND LUDICROUS SIR. Permit me most respectfully to bring beneath your notice a proposal which I serenely anticipate will turn up trumps under the fructifying sunshine of your esteemed approbation [...] Since my sojourn here, I have accomplished the laborious perusal of your transcendent and tip-top periodical, and, hoity toity! I am like a duck in thunder with admiring wonderment at the drollishness and jocosity with which your paper is ready to burst in its pictorial department. But, alack! when I turn my critical attention to the literary contents, I am met with a lamentable deficiency and no great shakes, for I note there the fly in the ointment and *hiatus valde deflendus* to wit the utter absenteeism of a correct and classical style in English composition.

Again, these are not the words of a comedy foreigner but a complex idiolect that owes much to effusive yet linguistically challenged Shakespearean characters like Dogberry (*Much Ado About Nothing*) and Mistress Quickly (*Henry IV* pts. 1 & 2) by way of Mrs. Malaprop in Sheridan's 1775 stage play *The Rivals*. But Jabberjee, a Bombay law student at large in London, is sufficiently smug to believe his way of writing actually *is* "a correct and classical style in English composition," while that of the local British scribes is "no great shakes." In the follow-up *A Bayard from Bengal*, he sets out to chronicle the adventures of "[a] typically splendid representative of Young India on British soil" (himself), while earnestly hoping "to avoid the shocking solecisms and exaggerations indulged in by ordinary English novelists," of whom he cheekily cites Kipling as a main offender.

As with many of the other books we've come across thus far, Jabberjee's tales were common currency among English schoolboys, and Plum adds the occasional reference in his early stories to show he's on board. In 'The Manoeuvres of Charteris,' he borrows the brilliant description "a beaming simper of indescribable suavity" to denote an insincere smile; but it's in his 1908 "lurid" school story *The Luck Stone* that he attempts a full-blown impersonation in the character of Ram, a small, round boy in gold-rimmed spectacles from Calcutta who is less than enamoured with the food at Marleigh School, as he informs Mr. Spinder, one of the teachers:

> "Hon'ble Spinder," he said, "you are paid by parents to provide poor boys with good, wholesome food, but hoity-toity, what a falling-off is there! Our stomachs groan with beastly pangs. Listen, honourable sir, to the voice of Reason! How can brain work if body is not fed? How can poor boy floor intricacies of Latin grammar without stodgy feed? We are as if to sink with hunger. Do not think me, hon'ble Spinder, a presumptuous for addressing you. I cannot remain hermetically sealed. The mutton," proceeded Ram, descending to details, "is not roasted with sufficiency. Hoity-toity and alackaday, it is of a red colour – not pleasing to look upon, and nauseous to masticate. The porridge is not an appetising. The fowl-eggs are, alackaday, frequently advancing into the sere and yellow of honourable old age.

Not *too* bad, but nowhere near Anstey's standard of inventiveness or fluency. Then there's Plum's favourite borrowing which I think first appeared in 1903's *A Prefect's Uncle*:

> The Bishop, like Mr Hurry Bungsho Jabberjee, B.A., became as silent as the tomb.

The tomb motif would become a regular steal, frequently uncredited, and often used in conjunction with '*sotto voce*,' another Jabberjee tic. It hung on in Jeeves and Bertie stories until their last completed adventure *Aunts Aren't Gentlemen* from 1974, and both Plum's characters, each in his different way, inherits elements of Jabberjee's grandiloquence.

Bertie's is the more obvious debt as he too aims for narrative sophistication while not *quite* managing it: for instance, "An eye like Mars to threaten and command" is indeed a quote from *Hamlet*, and a feather in a writer's cap if used properly. But Bertie reveals he cannot have understood the allusion when, in *The Mating Season*, he asks Jeeves:

> "What's that thing of Shakespeare's about someone having an eye like mother's?"
> "An eye like Mars, to threaten and command, is possibly the expression for which you are groping, sir."

Jabberjee makes the identical error on a date with his girlfriend:

> When I duly turned up, lo and behold! I found she was escorted [...] by her eagle-eyed mother (JESSIMINA herself inherits, in Hamlet's immortal phraseology, "an eye like Ma's, to threaten or command").

This was an age-old joke even when Anstey got hold of it, appearing both in Dickens's 'The Haunted Man' from 1848 and before that in George Daniel's obscure *Merrie England in the Olden Time*, first serialized in 1842. Which once again serves to illustrate how Plum's distinctive humour often has more convoluted roots than even he might have realized. But note what he does with his inheritance. Here we have an aural joke which has to be made to work in print; but whereas Anstey *explains* the gag to us by using "Ma's," Plum avoids this necessity by cunningly putting it in dialogue, preserving the original "Mars." It's a tiny but telling improvement that both smooths the delivery and flatters us when we get the joke for ourselves.

But Jabberjee's influence on Bertie operates at deeper levels than verbal parallels. Here we have two young men, both innocents abroad in London, each "provided with a big education" and keen to show off their "golden verbolatory of diction" in print, creating distinctive comic styles with skill and bravura while punching above their intellectual weight. Add to that both men are "highly chivalrous chap[s] in questions of the fairer sex" yet ambivalent about marriage and it can be argued that along with the Edwardian Knut, Jabberjee may just be the biggest single influence on Bertie's persona and narrative style. Which is praise indeed.

But what of Jeeves? Once again there is verbal parallelism, particularly in Jabberjee's use of the Latin and medieval French he's learned from his legal studies. Jeeves borrows *surgit alimari aliquid* (*Much Obliged, Jeeves*) from him, *ultra vires* (*Thank You, Jeeves*), *amende honorable* (twice in

Thank You, Jeeves) and of course *rem acu tetigisti* (passim, but here in *Joy in the Morning*):

> "Precisely, sir. *Rem acu tetigisti.*"
> "*Rem* – ?"
> "*Acu tetigisti*, sir. A Latin expression. Literally, it means 'You have touched the matter with a needle,' but a more idiomatic rendering would be –"
> "Put my finger on the nub."
> "Exactly, sir."

Plum didn't just throw this stuff together: note how he brilliantly has Bertie putting his finger on the nub even as he's *saying* "Put my finger on the nub." Anyhow, Bertie quickly picks up on the use of the phrase and takes it further in *Aunts Aren't Gentlemen* when he praises Jeeves for having "*tetigisti*-ed the *rem acu.*"

But whereas Jabberjee and Bertie are trying to gussy up their verbals with only a woolly awareness of what they're doing (although Bertie does at times respond well to instruction), Jeeves knows exactly what he's about, being the best-known but by no means exclusive speaker of a register Plum calls "butlerese," a cocktail of verbal traits whose base ingredient is Jabberjee's periphrasis. Jeeves most often uses this manner of speech when translating something Bertie has just said into his own more formal idiom, as in the following excerpt from 'The Great Sermon Handicap':

> "Jeeves [...] it's beastly hot."
> "The weather *is* oppressive, sir."

Or here, at greater length, from 'The Purity of the Turf':

> "Bit of a snob, what?"
> "He is somewhat acutely alive to the existence of class distinctions, sir."

This habit quickly became his trademark, even a reflex, which makes Jabberjee one of Jeeves's unlikeliest yet closest partners in rhetoric.

Anstey wasn't a regular writer of school stories, but he did make one notable contribution to the genre, whose plot driver Plum, by his own admission, "shameless[ly]" cribbed for his 1936 novel *Laughing Gas*. In mitigation, he informed his brother Armine:

> I don't believe the reading public remembers [Anstey's]
> book at all and the theme may seem quite new.

This was wishful thinking: originally published in 1882, Anstey's massively popular *Vice Versa* entered its 59th reprint a few weeks after *Laughing Gas* was published and was regularly re-issued until at least 1962. The original scenario centres on a body swap effected between the pompous and self-regarding Paul Bultitude and his son Dick that compels the father, looking exactly like his son but speaking in the unchanged manner of his adult self, to spend some weeks as an inmate at his son's boarding school. Anstey makes great hay with the contrast between the schoolboys' manner of easy informality and Paul's stuffy and self-important speech, which for most of the novel we must picture coming from the mouth of a ten-year-old. The school's headmaster is similarly perplexed:

> "You've come back this year, sir," said Dr. Grimstone, "with a very odd way of talking of yourself – an exceedingly odd way. Unless I see you abandoning it, and behaving like a reasonable boy again, I shall be forced to conclude you intend some disrespect and open defiance by it."
> "If you would allow me an opportunity of explaining my position, sir," said Paul, "I would undertake to clear your mind directly of such a monstrous idea. I am trying to assert my rights, Dr. Grimstone – my rights as a citizen, as a householder! This is no place for me, and I appeal to you to set me free. If you only knew one tenth –"
> "Let us understand one another, Bultitude," interrupted the Doctor. "You may think it an excellent joke to talk nonsense to me like this. But let me tell you there is a point where a jest becomes an insult."

The very same words can be judged either "nonsense" or perfectly good sense depending on whose mouth they emerge from, Anstey opening yet another vista on the comic use of language – a character speaking in a manner we wouldn't expect him to. Which is essentially what makes Bertie's written work so distinctive, particularly when we learn, often by his own admission, that the writer of such deathless narrative is "mentally negligible" and endowed with "the brains of a peahen."

In the first few tales that feature Bertie, Plum could have no inkling that he would have sufficient legs to be a useful returning character, and if we refer back to the performative energy and élan of The Celestial

and Jabberjee, he still sounds just a little bit limp. Plum must have recognized this deficiency, slightly re-jigging (and greatly improving) four
of the earliest Bertie stories published between 1916-17 for inclusion in
1925's *Carry On, Jeeves*, by which time he'd got the character straight in
his head. Contrast the opening paragraph of 'Leave It to Jeeves' with its
rebooted successor in 'The Artistic Career of Corky' and the differences
are plain as a pikestaff. Here's the first of these registers:

> Jeeves – my man, you know – is really a most extraordinary
> chap. So capable. Honestly, I shouldn't know what to do
> without him. On broader lines he's like those chappies who
> sit peering sadly over the marble battlements at the Penn-
> sylvania Station in the place marked 'Enquiries.' You know
> the Johnnies I mean. You go up to them and say: "When's
> the next train for Melonsquashville, Tennessee?" and they
> reply, without stopping to think, "Two-forty-three, track
> ten, change at San Francisco." And they're right every
> time. Well, Jeeves gives you just the same impression of
> omniscience.

There's a jabberer if ever you heard one, albeit a jabberer with a poetic
turn of phrase ("marble battlements") and a decent vocabulary ("omni-
science"). But that subsequently turns into *this*:

> You will notice, as you flit through these reminiscences of
> mine, that from time to time the scene of action is laid in
> and around the city of New York; and it is just possible
> that this may occasion the puzzled look and the start of
> surprise. 'What,' it is possible that you may ask yourselves,
> 'is Bertram doing so far from his beloved native land?'

> Well, it's a fairly longish story; but, reefing it down a bit
> and turning in for the nonce into a two-reeler, what hap-
> pened was . . .

And off he goes. The jabbering, which grows slightly annoying *en bloc*, is
jettisoned entirely. The writing remains very much performative, but the
great difference is Bertie's voice, which is now altogether more poised,
self-assured, relaxed, and at least for some of the time *in control*. In the
first extract, it's as if he's speaking to fill a vacuum, nervously afraid
his ingenuity will conk out; by the second, he even has the chutzpah to
refer to himself in the third person, and his use of the sailing ("reefing")

and movie ("two-reeler") metaphors separated by a verbal tag ("for the nonce") is absolutely masterful. The better Bertie gets, the greater the discrepancy between his lowly level of intelligence and exceptional writing ability; but after a while we cease to notice and simply revel in his unlikely comic invention.

Having found his distinctive voice and narrative style, Bertie went on to infect his fellow Drones, who would carry that peculiarly Wodehousean idiom into all the other corners of Plum's fictional world. Ultimately, we can asseverate that not just Bertie but Bingo Little, the Freddies Threepwood and Widgeon, Monty Bodkin, Pongo Twistleton, Archibald Mulliner and the rest of Plum's troupe of overgrown schoolboys (which also includes Uncle Fred and Gally) are all variations on a theme that at base owes its existence to those jobbing writers of his youth who each had his take on that "Early Ironic" voice. And even more important than that: almost all Plum's written legacy occupies and exploits that same light tonal range he had been quietly refining from his earliest published writing. A dialled-down version of his male characters' direct speech, suitably tweaked and purged of its idiocies, became *his* default third-person narrative voice too; quietly authoritative yet utterly personable, intellectually lively but not *too* clever, elegantly rhythmical and bursting with seamlessly linked comic ideas, his prose transcended its immediate influences to become a unique phenomenon that invites but ultimately defies imitation.

There are literally hundreds, possibly even thousands of favourite passages I could use by way of illustration, but here's a well-known gobbet, genuinely selected at random, from the 1935 version of 'The Custody of the Pumpkin,' which finds Lord Emsworth focusing the lens of his new telescope on second-son Freddie who is behaving with all the soppy abandon of the loved-up:

> White and shining, he tripped along over the turf like a Theocritan shepherd hastening to keep an appointment with a nymph, and a sudden frown marred the serenity of Lord Emsworth's brow. He generally frowned when he saw Freddie, for with the passage of the years that youth had become more and more of a problem to an anxious father.
>
> Unlike the male codfish, which, suddenly finding itself the parent of three million five hundred thousand little codfish, cheerfully resolves to love them all, the British aristocracy is apt to look with a somewhat jaundiced eye on its younger sons.

Those first three words encourage us to 'see' Freddie in romantic soft-focus as he hastens to his pastoral ("Theocritan") tryst with his future wife Aggie; the subsequent clause alliterative, rhythmical and onomatopoeic ("tripped", "turf") in its description of Freddie's eagerness; the sudden long, mournful vowels ("frown", "brow") alter the mood, introducing his father's disdainful perspective and setting up the codfish zinger, the latter part of which is expressed in elegant Jeevesian periphrasis. And notice how it's "codfish" and not "cod" or "fish" because it scans better within the sentence and is a more interesting word. Now compare those three sentences with the bumptious tone of some of his early journalism from Chapter 2, and it's possible to experience not just the roots of his narrative voice, but just how far Wodehouse had come in adapting his own manner of speaking and writing into a match-winning style that continues to delight more than a century since it was first written.

In a November 2022 edition of the *Spectator*, the bestselling novelist William Boyd opined that "[t]rue comic genius" resided in "the ability to create a unique tone of voice" which he characterized as "deadpan, perfectly timed, self-deprecating, abjuring all whimsy (the British disease) and grandstanding." Such talent he judged to be extremely rare and Wodehouse, in his view, had it in spades. We may wish to finesse individual items in Boyd's *carte du jour*, but there's really nothing fundamental to disagree with. Taken together, the overall effect is one of comic lightness; not the wispy, delicate "soufflé" of the anonymous *Punch* review from the 1950s so often re-quoted on Wodehouse book jackets, but the result of a lot of damned hard work making sure *exactly* the right words appear in *exactly* the right order to produce the *illusion* of effortless writing.

And we might add that some of the key ingredients of this Wodehousean voice, complete with their venerable authority and almost total eschewal of whimsy *should* actively work to negate this lightness; it's just that somehow, as we're about to see, Plum made sure they didn't.

Chapter 4:
Of Classics and the Bible

"So you've won the Scripture-knowledge prize, have you?"
"Sir, yes, sir."
"Yes," said Gussie, "you look just the sort of little tick
who would."
Right Ho, Jeeves

Our bright-eyed lads are taught insane constructions in
Greek and Latin from morning till night.
Work

"You're reading History? A perfectly respectable school.
The very worst is English Literature."

Evelyn Waugh, Brideshead Revisited

She said no contract until I'd got what she called a thorough grounding in English literature [...] English literature, you know what that means – Shakespeare, Milton
and all those."
Pearls, Girls and Monty Bodkin

Given his future vocation, it's surprising just how little English literature Wodehouse was formally taught in class. Reading the twice-yearly 'Form Work' tables for the period Plum attended Dulwich College (see Appendix 1), we find:

- Shakespeare: *Merchant of Venice* [sic] and *King Lear*
- Milton's *Paradise Lost*
- Tennyson's long narrative poem *The Princess*
- "General Papers on English Literature" and "Essays on literary subjects"

And that's it. As we'll discover, both Tennyson and Shakespeare would remain on the list of Wodehouse's lifelong favourites; but the rest of these slim pickings provide little by way of enlightenment if we wish to discover where his vast knowledge of literature came from, and what influenced his writing style.

The truth was that in Wodehouse's schoolboy years, the subject of 'English' (the study of language, grammar, and the critiquing of literary texts) wasn't even offered as an option in many educational establishments. At Dulwich, it was lumped in with History, a practice by no means uncommon in other schools. Almost 20 years after Plum left, the critic Sir Arthur Quiller-Couch would still lament that "the teaching of our language and literature is, after all, a new thing and still experimental." At most, he tells us, a freshman arriving at university might only have been taught "two or three plays of Shakespeare; a few of Bacon's Essays, Milton's early poems, Stopford Brooke's little primer [of literary history], a book of extracts for committal to memory, with perhaps Chaucer's *Prologue* and a Speech of Burke." And sometimes, as with Plum, not even that.

The young Wodehouse had entered Dulwich on "the Classical side," and if you're browsing through Appendix 1 it's immediately apparent that much of the English he was exposed to in the schoolroom was shot through the prism of languages that were far older:

- the *Latin* and *Ancient Greek* translations involved in his classical studies.
- the *Early Modern English* of the King James Bible used in his Divinity lessons and twice-daily school services.

So it is that this chapter falls into two halves, as we examine how Wodehouse's acquaintance with the Classics and the Bible subtly but radically influenced the kind of English he would later write as a professional.

Wodehouse was not a star classicist like his older brother Armine, although he was more than competent, being one of four boys awarded a scholarship of £10 per annum for consistently good form work. This was no small potatoes, being worth around £1K today, but even so he may not have been entirely convinced of the relevance of what he would later call (in *The Girl on the Boat*) an "expensive classical education." One of his earliest pieces, 'The Adventure of the Split Infinitive' from 1902, is a dreadful Sherlock Holmes spoof in which the 'crime' is the grammatical solecism of the title, committed – ironically – by a school headmaster. But there are mitigating circumstances, as the all-knowing Doctor Wotsing suspects:

> "I understand you to say that your English education was
> neglected in favour of Latin and Greek. Am I right?"
> "Absolutely on the bull's-eye."
> "Sir," I said, "I acquit you of all blame. You are more

sinned against than sinning. Run away and reform."

Wotsing implies – as we would today – that a knowledge of English grammar might be the more obvious route to avoiding splitting infinitives than a diet of the classics. But even now, opinion differs. At the time of writing, Dulwich's Head of Classics waxes lyrical on the College's website about a subject that "enriches our own thoughts, ideas and the speech by which we express them." Or, he might have added, get them down on paper. And Plum would also come round to that way of thinking, judging his classical bias "the best form of education I could have had as a writer." But what precisely did he mean by that? And how would knowledge of two 'dead' languages help lay the foundations of his future career writing in English?

Wodehouse's principal activity in the classroom would have been to construe and translate the set texts. If you've never had to do it, the process tends to be mechanical, highly boring and soul-sapping: the scene in *Monty Python's Life of Brian* in which a schoolmasterly Roman centurion violently coerces Brian to correct his faulty Latin graffito *Romanes eunt domus* will give you the idea. Or there's this, from Geoffrey Willans's sublime *Down with Skool!* in which reluctant student Nigel Molesworth is harried by his exasperated Latin teacher [italics – but not spelling – mine]:

> "The gauls – *galli* – subject – go on molesworth *oppugnant* – what does *oppugnant* mean – they are atacking *fossas*. Ditches. What did you say molesworth? Why on earth atack a ditch? Keep your mind on the sentence. The gauls are atacking the ditches [...] *sagittis*. What's *sagittis* molesworth what case come along boy – *sagitta sagitta sagittam* first declension – *with* arows by with or from arows [...] The gauls are attacking the ditches with arows – *telisque* – *telisque*, molesworth?"

And so on for 45 minutes, or 90 in the dreaded 'Double Latin.'

Fortunately, some Latin writers – Virgil for one – yielded their treasures more willingly, as Plum informs us in 'Work' from December 1900:

> A scholar who cannot translate ten lines of the "Aeneid" between the time he is put on and the time he begins to speak is unworthy of pity or consideration.

Livy was another cinch. But then there was the exquisite torture of

Double Greek, which was a whole new world of pain, and in 1903's 'A Shocking Affair' Wodehouse endows Mr. Mellish, the fiendish classics master at St. Austin's, with a masochistic genius

> for picking out absolutely untranslatable passages, and de-
> siring us (in print) to render the same with full notes. This
> term the book had been Thucydides, Book II, with regard
> to which I may echo the words of a certain critic when
> called upon to give his candid opinion of a friend's first
> novel, "I dare not say what I think about that book."

This was the same nightmare text that had melted his own brain in Dulwich's Lower V. Thucydides, he writes, had "made himself a thorough master of the concisest of styles [...] and in so doing became unreadably obscure." Getting your head round the Athenian historian was like "play[ing] billiards with a walking-stick and fives-balls," requiring utterly arcane micro-skills which included the ability "to distinguish $\mu\acute{\eta}$ from $o\mathring{v}$" [two forms of negative] and being familiar with "[t]he various intricacies of $\pi\rho\acute{\iota}v$ ['before']."

By the time Plum reached the VI form, things had grown more difficult still. Navigating through a passage "containing a notorious *crux* [an unsolved textual variant] and seventeen doubtful readings" would have been a daily occurrence, at which point it was necessary to consult what my Greek master called "the Learned German" authorities. These were a bunch of 19th-century classicists who had tirelessly gone through every surviving work in antiquity with a fine-tooth comb, presenting their detailed considerations on textual irregularities at exhaustive length. As Plum laments:

> Culture and "sound scholarship" now begin to show them-
> selves. It is not enough at this stage merely to be able to
> translate the lesson; you must know the notes and be pre-
> pared to give Professor Donnerundblitzendorf's profound
> excursus on line 33, and to describe the feelings of Herr
> Rotterdorp when he read same.
>
> ('Under the Flail', November 1901)

Wodehouse would regularly use a shared loathing of classical translation to bond with his early schoolboy readers (and the present writer), offsetting years of pent-up frustration in *The Pothunters* by inserting a joke only his most alert readers would recognize. Charteris, who we met in the previous chapter, reasons with his mates:

"What does our friend Thucydides remark on the subject?
Conscia mens recti, nec si sinit esse dolorem
Sed revocare gradum.
Very well then."

Sounds good, but it's all wrong – and Charteris knows it. Most obviously, Thucydides has suddenly started writing in Latin, and appears to have cobbled together this plausible-looking quotation from Ovid (the first three words), Virgil (the last three) linked by five from . . . P. G. Wodehouse, who shoehorns in some half-remembered stuff to make it scan. Translated into English, it makes very little sense whatever, but none of those in Charteris's audience seems to get this small but telling pleasantry.

Joking aside, there were plusses in all this slog. However nitpicky and monotonous the process of translation, Dulwich's syllabus introduced students to a wide variety of literary styles – among them prose, poetry, drama, oratory and letters, as well as the full range of classical genres – history, epic, tragedy, comedy, pastoral, satire, lyric, biography, and philosophy. The priority was to inculcate an instinctive understanding of the ways classical texts *worked* such that the boys could turn poetry and prose from Greek and Latin into English – and back again. This latter skill was called "composition," and we learn that at the fictional St Austin's "The Sixth did four compositions a week, two Greek and two Latin." At Dulwich there is a large red leather-bound book into which boys were invited to copy out their best work for the edification of others (I couldn't find anything by Plum, but Armine contributed four entries). This ability to compose Latin verse in elegiac couplets or hexameters was considered the acme of academic achievement, helping nurture (it was thought) an elegant style of spoken and written English while broadening the student's vocabulary, since literally hundreds of thousands of individual words in the domestic vernacular are rooted in Greek and Latin. It was a practice that would continue in many educational establishments until at least the 1950s.

Not that pupils necessarily understood the benefits of this slow, accretive process, as we discover in the revealing 'Treating of Cribs' article Plum anonymously contributed to *Public School Magazine* in January 1902. Making the overstressed student's life easier (aka cheating) was of course rife, and the widespread use of English translations to help with prep was, "[l]ike a false income-tax return [...] expected of you." In the 1904 story 'Homœpathic Treatment,' Liss of Wrykyn school is the proud possessor of the Bohn's Classical Library "crib" of Livy's *History of Rome*, and the annotated renderings of Richard Claverhouse Jebb were also popular. But in the eyes of certain clerical uncles (of whom Plum had four) cribbing was a shoo-in for the eighth deadly sin:

> [H]e will himself inform you without a blush that the only sensible way of preparing a play of Aeschylus is to look up all the words in the dictionary, and disregard the excellent translation which Mr. Bohn has been at so many pains to publish for your benefit.

In 'Ruthless Reginald,' Wodehouse constructs a full-length (possibly autobiographical) story from this same scenario. Beaten by Rigby for an offence that wasn't his fault, Reginald Rankin – Rigby's 'fag' – swears revenge, seeing his chance when the prefect is laid low in the Infirmary and his relatives propose a visit:

> "My uncle and aunt are coming down to-morrow [said Rigby], and they'll want to see my study after they've looked me up here. [...] On the second shelf of my book-case you'll find a crib to the 'Agamemnon.' You'd better cart that away and hide it till they've gone. My uncle's a bishop, and he has views of his own on cribs. Thinks they're deceitful. See? You'll know the book. It's blue, and it's one of Bohn's series."

Only Reginald, being of a devious and vindictive nature, *doesn't* remove the Aeschylus crib in question. Instead, he smuggles in further "deceitful aids to study" and a few more surprises for the uncle to discover, as the subsequent letter from the angry clergyman to his nephew makes clear:

> I found on your shelves such an array of Dr. Bohn's *English Translations of the Classics* as I could not have believed (but for ocular evidence) to have existed at one of our public schools.

At which point the bishop gives Reginald the sovereign he had intended for his nephew.

Of the set texts that might have proved useful in Wodehouse's future career as a humorist, Juvenal's *Saturae* and those of the less bilious Persius would no doubt have been congenial (see the Introduction to Volume 3 of my *Pelham Grenville Wodehouse* for more on Plum's use of classical satire). Also featured were two works by the comic playwright Plautus (*Menaechmi* and *Rudens*) whose use of the 'wise servant/foolish master' motif was an undoubted template for Jeeves and Wooster. The only snag here is that in (much) later life Plum didn't recall having read them. Although there existed

> an obvious similarity of thought between Plautus and me [...] for some reason neither Plautus nor Terence came my way. Why would this be? Because P and T were supposed to be rather low stuff?

But if there had been a bias against Roman comedy at Dulwich (or Plum simply misremembered), it was more than counterweighed by a sizeable glut of Aristophanes, who had five of his raucous farces on the syllabus: *Pax* ('Peace'), *Vespae* ('The Wasps'), *Nephelai* ('The Clouds') *Hippeis* ('The Knights'), and *Ranae* ('The Frogs') – which would indicate that lurking somewhere in the Classics department was a master who enjoyed a scurrilous laugh. Likely candidates include H. F. Hose, a career classicist who would later publish *Dulwich Latin Exercises for Middle Forms* and befriend Plum's fellow Alleynian Raymond Chandler, sending him postcards handwritten in Greek; Philip Hope, a Cambridge graduate known for the theatrical flourish with which he entered the form room; or William Beach Thomas, who would abandon teaching for a career in journalism, giving Plum the crucial leg-up into the *Globe* newspaper that allowed him to become a full-time freelance in 1902. It may have been any or none of these men, but the Aristophanean bias in the classroom was also reflected in the six productions of the playwright's work (in the original Greek) that were staged by the students during Plum's time at Dulwich – a far greater number than any other playwright – with *The Frogs* performed twice in 1895 and 1898. There's a photo of Wodehouse playing a choric character in the latter (he sits at the far right of the image with his frog mask on his knee), and in 'The Ways We Have' (a column for *Public School Magazine* from 1901) he would fondly recall the Founder's Day production of *The Knights* the previous year, at the end of his final Midsummer Term. This, for him, appears to have outshone the other items on the bill:

> The Greek play [has] more of the "knockabout-comedian" style of wit in it than in the other Speeches. It is this that gives the finishing touch to the performance. When an audience sees a prominent member of the Eleven, as Cleon, being hit on the head by an illustrious Prefect, as the Sausage-Seller, with half-a-yard of raw sausages, it naturally feels that the wit of the ancients was not so very far

behind that of Britain's Variety Theatres, after all.

To Plum, performance – and in particular comedic performance – would always prove a welcome antidote to dry scholarship. It no doubt cheered him that the same cock-eyed goings-on he so enjoyed in the 'lower' forms of contemporary theatre had already been a thing for almost two-and-a-half millennia. But had he been paying attention in class, he would have learned there was plenty more to Aristophanes than just slapstick and sausages; stuff he could possibly use, for neither he nor his comic ancestor could resist burlesquing the literature of his time. And *The Frogs* – which is essentially a comedy about the nature of tragedy – might have cast a particular spell over a writer who would later use *Macbeth* and *Hamlet* as regular foils for Bertie's jokes.

First performed in 405 BCE, *The Frogs* raises artistic questions for writers in just about any genre in any age. At its heart is a lengthy knock-about dispute between two of Plum's set dramatists, Aeschylus and Euripides, who arrive on stage childishly trading insults "like two baker's girls":

> EURIPIDES: I saw through him a while back. All that savage grandeur – it's all so uncivilized. No control, no subtlety. Just a tsunami of words full of bombast and superlatives, pumped up with polysyllables.
> AESCHYLUS: Hah! Well that's about the standard of literary criticism I'd expect from a hobbledehoy like you. What are your tragedies but a farrago of clichés, as tatty as the threadbare characters that speak them?

At which point the gossipy, good-natured god of drama (and wine) Dionysus intervenes and tries to bring some order to the proceedings. In a comic inversion worthy of Jeeves and Bertie, he lacks the mental equipment of his servant Xanthias, and rather than being a figure of authority is often the butt of the jokes. Euripides then castigates Aeschylus for the same crime that Plum would jokily level at Shakespeare, that his writing sounded OK but didn't actually mean anything; and as the scenario pans out, Aeschylus's old school style – characterized as over-complex, allusive and patrician – is contrasted with the new breed approach of Euripides, which is described as lighter on its feet, "democratic" and full of things "the audience could understand." Plum might well have been nodding his head throughout the proceedings: as we've recently seen, there was no love lost between him and Aeschylus ("too difficult"), having a somewhat softer spot for Euripides, who "is not difficult compared to some other authors, but [...] does demand a certain amount of preparation."

As rehearsals for *The Frogs* proceeded, the 16-year-old Wodehouse would have realized (if he hadn't already) that as a writer you could poke fun at even the most sacrosanct culture and get away with it. It's no great leap to propose that his more ludicrous wordsmiths like Ralston McTodd and Rodney Spelvin owe something to Aristophanes's pioneering satirical portraits of cultural figures, which may also have incited him to write what Bill Townend remembered as "a series of plays after the pattern of the Greek tragedies, outrageously funny, dealing with boys and masters." Unfortunately, these are missing presumed lost; but from this description they sound less like tragedies and more like *ad hominem* spoofs like those to be found in *The Frogs*. Other Aristophanean themes Plum may have picked up on include the respective merits of formal or colloquial language; where to pitch his tone; matters of concision and exposition; entertainment versus didacticism . . . and so on, for as well as being a knockabout comedy, *The Frogs* also serves as a serious-minded masterclass for the aspiring writer, a checklist of things worth learning or avoiding.

Despite six years of intensive study, Wodehouse rarely acknowledged his debt to the Classics, perhaps because he never fully appreciated how deeply they had penetrated his literary subconscious. Eighteen months after leaving Dulwich, he would write how abandoning his school textbooks felt like a kind of liberation, albeit one tinged with early onset nostalgia:

> I abandoned that section of my library without regret [...] [it] haunted me, and reminded me of all the knowledge I had once possessed, which is now no more, and which, if I know it, will never, never return.

Only it would – because it never left him. Hacking his way through the dense brambles of Greek and Latin texts under his own steam had left its mark, and in 1922's *The Girl on the Boat* we find the 40-year-old Wodehouse almost sentimentally aping the haughty schoolmaster:

> No two males behave in the same way under the spur of female fickleness. *Archilochum*, for instance, according to the Roman writer, *proprio rabies armavit iambo*. It is no good pretending out of politeness that you know what that means, so I will translate. *Rabies*—his grouch—*armavit*—armed— *Archilochum*—Archilochus—*iambo*—with the iambic—*pro-*

prio—his own invention. In other words, when the poet Archilochus was handed his hat by the lady of his affections, he consoled himself by going off and writing satirical verse about her in a new metre which he had thought up immediately after leaving the house. That was the way the thing affected him.

That anonymous Roman writer was Horace, whose *Ars Poetica* Plum had studied in the Remove, and from which that original, beautifully concise five-word Latin sentence is taken. Suddenly we are all Molesworths and Plum our Latin teacher, as he moves between formal and humorous registers in his twin translations – the literal followed by the colloquial – and proving that once you've got it, you never quite lose it.

But although he rarely paraded his classical skills, at least one person recognized their presence in his writing. On receiving his honorary Doctor of Letters from Oxford University in June 1939, Wodehouse was publicly lauded in Latin by Dr. Cyril Bailey, who concluded his address with the following:

> *Hoc quoque, lingua etsi repleat plebeia chartas,*
> *Non incomposito patitur pede currere verba,*
> *Concinnus, Lepidus, puri sermonis amator.*

Which loosely translated alludes to Plum's disciplined (*non incomposito*), everyday language (*lingua plebeia*) that reveals him to be harmonious (*concinnus*), agreeable (*lepidus*) and a lover of perfect speech (*puri sermonis amator*). As elegantly rendered by Dr. Bailey, each one of these is a core classical virtue Wodehouse would have taken away from all that sweaty translation and composition whether he realized it or not.

And now we'll stir some Early Modern English in with the Latin and Greek – because it's time to get Biblical. And while the Bible can't strictly be classed as a 'Literary Hero', it's a hugely significant ingredient of Plum's prose with over 2,300 references thus far identified, cruising ahead of its nearest rival William Shakespeare by a ratio of almost 2:1. Indeed, Wodehouse would loot it so often, it's important to remind ourselves that in matters of religion he was a devout fence-sitter. Though he lacked a rooted faith, the King James translation of 1611 (hereafter the KJB) was a unique and convenient *literary* resource already dinned into his memory. For almost three centuries, it had been the best-known version, and would be until the *New English Bible* (1961-70) expunged much of its poetry and substituted limp, vanilla prose that was almost entirely unmemorable. The KJB, by contrast, *sounds* as if it means business:

it can forcefully instruct and gently persuade, harry as well as charm. And as with the Church of England itself, it's difficult not to feel that Plum had a profound respect for it, even as he used it for his own comic contrivances. He began his borrowings just weeks into his publishing career with "there is no such balm in Gilead" (a slight rewording of Jeremiah 8:22) which appears unattributed in 'Concerning Relations' from March 1901's *Public School Magazine*.

His exposure began at an early age. As we've already noted, no fewer than four of Plum's uncles were Anglican clergymen, and he regularly spent the school holidays with three of them. During these sojourns he would likely have fallen in with the rhythms of the household, hounded out of bed for prayers before breakfast and made to attend Morning Service and Evensong on Sundays. Add to which he was educated at a series of residential institutions where religious observance and instruction were the bedrock of their regimes, and you have a lad whose instinct for self-preservation was best served by mugging up his Bible whether he was a believer or not.

The first of these establishments was The Chalet School in Croydon run by the "very religious" Prince sisters, who once severely chastised Plum for stealing a turnip from a neighbouring field. It was a lesson he'd never forget: in 1963 and well into his 80s, he recalled that as a result, "I can't remember having done any other naughty thing the whole of the three years I was there." A very different experience arrived when, aged about 9 or 10, he was sent to Malvern House Preparatory School near Dover, presided over by the "short-tempered tyrant" Richard Harvey Hammond. Wodehouse scholar Norman Murphy plausibly conjectures this gentleman was the model for the scourge of Bertie Wooster's early school life, the Reverend Aubrey Upjohn M.A., that "prince of stinkers" who, in case there was any doubt about the connection, also teaches at an establishment called Malvern House. Petulant and no mean wielder of the cane, Upjohn has something of the Old Testament prophet about him, standing "about eight feet six in height, with burning eyes, foam-flecked lips and flame coming out of both nostrils." Yet it was under Upjohn's stern tutelage that Bertie won the prize for Scripture Knowledge, as he never tires of telling us.

At Dulwich, the young Wodehouse also had a formidable headmaster in the person of our old friend Arthur H. Gilkes, similarly lofty of stature and possessed of a luxuriant white beard. Resembling, as Mr. Mulliner describes one such preacher, "a sort of blend of Epstein's Genesis and something out of the Book of Revelations [sic]" he was an enthralling orator blessed with a "terrific" dark-brown voice that "scared the pants off" his pupils. If Gilkes was reading the Bible lessons at the twice-daily school prayers you can bet Plum would have been paying attention, probably not to any religious message but the formal beauty of the language and how brilliantly it lent itself to vocal delivery. As the mighty headmaster notes in *A Day at Dulwich* as he coaches the school captain how to read Psalm 147 out loud before the school: "The boys like to listen […] at least they will if you will think about what you are reading, and you must not be ashamed to show it. Don't you see what a beautiful lesson it is?" Once again, there's the instinctual understanding that a reading shouldn't simply be a reading, but a performance, the form and content melding seamlessly if it's presented well.

In the classroom, Plum had been taught selections from the New Testament, including the Acts of the Apostles, the Epistles of St. Paul, and the gospels of St. Mark and St. Matthew. Add to that the Life of St Francis of Assisi and some Biblical history, and that's the sum total of his formal studies in what was called "Divinity" (or "Divs"). But you don't get to quote from the Good Book with the breadth and frequency Wodehouse did unless you know it pretty well yourself – or have a nifty Companion that lists the most apposite words and phrases that help express what you're trying to say. But even allowing that he lived in an age when Bible study and churchgoing was far more prevalent than it is now, his onboard knowledge and/or *ad hoc* research remains impressive. Quite how much he knew (if anything) about the KJB's provenance is an impossible question to answer; but looking at its history reveals some useful hints as to how Plum might have taken in what he was reading (or hearing) and used it in his own work.

The KJB was a co-operative effort of around 47 scholars, a complex tissue of compromises that tried to address no fewer than sixteen different rules laid down by King James I as to how the task should be approached. Its primary aim was to reconcile new and corrective scholarship on the original Hebrew, Greek and Aramaic texts with what clerics would be familiar with from previous English translations, so as not to offend a whole range of warring interest groups from ceremonial traditionalists to the most radical, reforming Puritans. All this had to be rendered into what we now call 'Early Modern English,' a language barely a century old and rapidly evolving. So what emerged, quite understandably, was a massive linguistic patchwork quilt – not that you'd ever guess from the way it reads and sounds.

Adam Nicolson, author of *When God Spoke English*, provides some useful descriptions of the finished result. Citing the formal "civility, learning and eloquence" that underpinned the project, he offers the following masterly summation of the translators' efforts:

> The book they created was consciously poised in its rheto-
> ric between vigour and elegance, plainness and power. It is
> not framed in the language [...] of intellectual display [...]
> it exudes, rather, a shared confidence and authority.

Already that's a lot of balls for a translator to keep in the air: but with
its "grandeur of phrasing and the deep slow music of its rhythms" it
was to prove a compelling package that remains the preferred Biblical
text for many despite the availability of many modernized translations.
Nicolson continues:

> [T]he King James Bible has always given its readers that
> the words are somehow extraordinarily freighted, with
> a richness that few texts have ever equalled. Again and
> again, the Jacobean Translators chose a word not for its
> clarified straightforwardness [...] but for its richness, its
> suggestiveness, its harmonic resonances.

And that little lot is, in sum, what likely appealed to Wodehouse; the
exotic, poetic strangeness of the words coupled with the tonal authority
that underpins the whole thing seems to have been – literally – music
to his ears.

So much for the language. Then there were the stories themselves.
If we examine Bertie's regular reversion to the Bible, he appears attracted by the more melodramatic and fantastical tales from the Old Testament that could rival any penny dreadful in gore and sensationalism.
Among those on which he is an authority are:

- Lot's wife (Genesis 19): "I don't know if the name of Lot's
  wife is familiar to you, and if you were told about her rather remarkable finish. I may not have got the facts right,
  but the story, as I heard it, was that she was advised not to
  look round at something or other or she would turn into a
  pillar of salt, so, naturally imagining that they were simply
  pulling her leg, she looked round, and – bing – a pillar of
  salt." (*Joy in the Morning*, also in *Jeeves and the Feudal Spirit* and
  Much Obliged, Jeeves).
- The mysterious writing on the wall foretelling King Belshazzar of Babylon's of his imminent death (Book of Daniel 5),
  as in the following altercation from *Right Ho, Jeeves*:
  Aunt Dahlia: [Tom] says that Civilization is in the melt-
  ing-pot and that all thinking men can read the writing on

the wall."

Bertie: "What wall?"

Aunt Dahlia: "Old Testament, ass. Belshazzar's feast."

Bertie: "Oh, that, yes. I've often wondered how that gag was worked. With mirrors, I expect."

Plum is also inordinately fond of "weighed in the balance and found wanting" (the gist of that writing on the wall) which appeared in 1902's *The Pothunters* and on at least nine occasions afterwards.

- Job's affliction with boils (Book of Job 2), rehearsed with a self-pitying Aunt Dahlia who reckons she could give the Bible's best-known serial victim a run for his money:

  Aunt Dahlia: "[M]y only daughter, for whom I had dreamed such a wonderful future, is engaged to be married to an inebriated newt fancier. And you talk about boils!" [...]

  Bertie: "I don't absolutely talk about boils. I merely mentioned that Job had them." (*Right Ho, Jeeves*).

Bertie is also aware that the children of Israel were fed by manna from heaven when out wandering in the wilderness (Exodus 16); that Daniel survived a spell in the lion's den (Book of Daniel, 6), as did Shadrach, Meshach and Abednego in a burning fiery furnace (Book of Daniel, 3); that Jonah took up temporary residence in the belly of a whale (Book of Jonah, 1); that Balaam had a troublesome ass (Book of Numbers, 22); that Jezebel was defenestrated, trampled by a horse and eaten by dogs (Second Book of Kings, 9); that a deaf adder once stopped its ears and would not hear the voice of the charmer (Psalm 58); and that some scales fell away from Saul's eyes and he was afterwards known as Paul (Acts of the Apostles, 9). Note how all but one of these are to be found in the blood and guts Old Testament prior to its Christian rebranding in the New.

As Bertie reveals throughout his autobiographies, he is no shallow Biblical scholar: in *Very Good, Jeeves* alone he employs about 30 references taken from 14 books in both Old and New Testaments, literally from Acts to Zechariah:

- "*the lion lying down with the lamb*" – a mix of images from the Book of Isaiah in which the lamb actually takes its rest with a wolf, and the lion turns veggie like the ox.
- "the food was more or less *turning to ashes in my mouth*" – Isaiah again, who warns that he who worships a false idol

"feedeth on ashes."
- "He is one of those kids who *never let the sun go down on their wrath*" – an almost unchanged lift from Paul's Epistle to the Ephesians.
- "The Pyke [...] must be *cast into outer darkness where there is wailing and gnashing of teeth*" – again, an almost perfect quote from the Gospel of St. Matthew.
- "Wanted to extend *the olive-branch*" – from Genesis, when the dove arrived at Noah's ark with an olive branch in its beak, indicating that land was ahoy, the floodwaters were receding, and God's anger had been assuaged.

And this is no flash in the pan, giving the lie to Gussie Fink-Nottle's accusation that Bertie secreted lists of the kings of Judah about his person prior to sitting the Scripture Knowledge exam. He may get off to a slow start in the early stories, but from *Very Good, Jeeves* (1930) onwards his narratives are packed with Biblical references, averaging close to 40 per book and eventually peaking in 1963's *Stiff Upper Lip, Jeeves* with almost 50. And while many of these are regularly recycled, he would have needed fairly capacious pockets to accommodate all *those* scraps of paper.

Wodehouse didn't just plunder the Bible but also the written and cultural heritage of the entire Anglican Communion, including the Book of Common Prayer and the hymns sung at the services he must have attended in his youth. Take for example the outpourings of that unlikely evangelist George Cyril Wellbeloved, the well-oiled pigman to Lord Emsworth and Sir Gregory Parsloe-Parsloe. In *Pigs Have Wings*, he scours his memory for "a smattering of what he had learned in the days when he was trailing clouds of glory" at Sunday School, so as to illustrate how saboteurs from nearby Blandings were seeking to nobble his porcine charge, Queen of Matchingham. In the end, he lights on a well-known Victorian hymn 'Christian! Doth Thou See Them?' (a translation of a poem by St. Andrew of Crete) that Sir Gregory clearly doesn't recognize:

> "See the troops of Midian prowl and prowl around."
> Sir Gregory thought this over.
> "Yes. Yes, I see what you mean. Troops of Midian, yes. Nasty fellers. You did say Midian?"
> "Yes, sir. Midian, troops of. Christian, doth thou hear them on the holy ground? Christian, up and smite them!"

George Cyril's plan of action seems inspired by the grisly revenge the Israelites took on the Midianites in the Book of Judges 6-8. Attack, he avers, is the best form of defence, and he trusts that history will repeat itself in his own, somewhat less Biblical struggle protecting his prize sow.

Some years later in *Galahad at Blandings*, George Cyril has retired, but makes a sentimental journey to visit the Empress, his charge before he defected to Sir Gregory. Only trouble is, the mammoth porker is completely unresponsive to his trilling, and once more the Wellbeloved memory grinds into action, coming up with this wayward exegesis of Psalm 58:

> "She's like the deaf adder in Holy Scripture. I don't know if you're familiar with the deaf adder. It comes in a bit in the Bible I used to learn at Sunday school. Like the deaf adder, it says, what don't pay a ruddy bit of attention to the charmer, though he charms till his eyes bubble."

Which, I'm sure you'll agree, is a fair summary of the original:

> The wicked […] are like the deaf adder that stoppeth her ear; which will not hearken to the voice of charmers, charming never so wisely.

Here, the divine sublime collides head-on with the comic ridiculous, and there's the added fun of hearing the sonorous, allusive language of the KJB being ham-fistedly paraphrased by a son of the soil.

At which point the conversation turns into something of a Biblical quote-fest, with the Eton-educated ninth Earl – ironically the proud possessor of an ultra-rare Gutenberg Bible – failing to grasp the principle of Biblical metaphor. George Cyril fears the Empress has developed swine fever, at which suggestion Lord Emsworth accuses him of being a fool, something to which the veteran pigman naturally takes exception:

> "I suppose you know what happens when you call your brother a fool," he said austerely. "You're in danger of hell fire, that's what you're in danger of. You'll find it in the Good Book. 'If thou sayest to thy brother, Thou fool […]'"

Once again, it's a masterly paraphrase, this time of Matthew 5:22. But sometimes the fatheaded Lord Emsworth can prove remarkably sharp, confronting his former pigman with the undeniable fact "You're not my brother!" while falling into the same trap as those who, in Matthew

12:46, informed Jesus that his family was getting tired of waiting for him as he preached to his followers. Jesus countered, pointing to his audience, "whosoever shall do the will of my Father which is in heaven, the same is my brother, and sister, and mother." George Cyril, clearly understanding this admirably inclusive creed, will have none of his lordship's quibbling:

> "For purposes of argument I am [your brother]. All men are brothers. That's in the Good Book, too."

And so it is, in Matthew 23:8. To which communistic claptrap Lord Emsworth can only respond with "Get out! Get off my property immediately!", having lost the disputation game, set and match.

But Clarence isn't alone in his incomplete knowledge of matters ecclesiastical. His creator was prone to misinterpretation – perhaps mischievously, perhaps not – in his regular use of a quotation from Edward H. Bickersteth Jnr.'s 1875 hymn "Peace, perfect peace, with loved ones far away." In the sense Bickersteth intended the words, being sundered from one's family was a cause for regret, but consolation was possible since "In Jesus' keeping we are safe, and they." By contrast, Eustace Hignett in *The Girl on the Boat* regards family separation as a blissful state to be celebrated with champagne and song, since his mother is one of Wodehouse's many "middle-aged lad[ies] of commanding aspect" who are inclined to high-handedness. And he's by no means alone, since Wodehouse uses the hymn on at least five other occasions to mean exactly the same thing. Perhaps the most touching example arrives at the close of *A Pelican at Blandings* when we eavesdrop on Clarence and brother Gally enjoying a hearty supper having dispatched their domineering sister off to America. Once more masters of their own destiny, the relief is palpable as they proceed to eat what they want, where they want and dress how they want, blissfully unmindful of whether Connie is in Jesus's keeping or not.

But even with the constant mickey-taking, Wodehouse clearly considers the Bible's mellifluous language a force for the good. In 1935's 'Tried in the Furnace' (cf. Psalm 12, v.6, "The words of the Lord are pure words / as silver tried in a furnace of earth, purified seven times"), the lesson read aloud in church brings about a profound change in Barmy Fotheringay ('Fungy') Phipps:

> There is something about evening church in a village in the summer-time that affects the most hard-boiled. They had left the door open, and through it came the scent of lime

trees and wall-flowers and the distant hum of bees fooling about. And gradually there poured over Barmy a wave of sentiment. As he sat and listened to the First Lesson he became a changed man.

"The beauty of the words" working in tandem with the "peace of his surroundings" gently persuades Barmy to do some soul-searching; and having wrestled with his conscience, he charitably decides to renounce his romantic claim on Angelica Briscoe in favour of his love-rival and childhood friend, Pongo Twistleton, even though "[i]t would play the dickens with his heart and probably render the rest of his life a blank." Which proves generous rather than necessary, since it's eventually revealed her affections lie with a third party.

So to Wodehouse as a writer, as well as to his characters, the combination of sound and sense in the Bible's "pure words" could be both powerful and useful. When he quotes from the Good Book there's usually some exotic or unusual word, term or name that seems to have caught his eye or ear, or an intriguing image that has presented itself to his imagination. If stuck, he could always turn to the back of his *Bartlett's Familiar Quotations*, where there were 31 double-columned pages crammed with the more familiar KJB quotes.

But this ready resource by no means accounts for many of Plum's borrowings. To select some of his more esoteric lifts: in Chapter 1 of *Leave it to Psmith*, we get two borrowings for the price of one in Lord Emsworth's description of his gardener Angus McAllister as a "stiff-necked son of Belial," drawing on the books of Exodus and Deuteronomy in a manner not unworthy of an Old Testament prophet cursing the ungodly. The latter is an epithet that Ukridge also favours:

> "Hank Philbrick," said Ukridge without preamble, "is a son of Belial, a leper, and a worm."
> "What's happened now?"
> "He's let me down, the weak-minded Tishbite!"

A Tishbite may denote a resident of Tishbe in Gilead, or (more likely) a word that Wodehouse liked the sound of. Either way, it provides him with twin plosives Ukridge can really spit out as he berates his former friend. Then there's this, from 'Ukridge's Dog College' when Corky, the narrator, receives an anguished communication from his impecunious friend:

> It was the sort of telegram which Job might have sent off after a lengthy session with Bildad the Shuhite.

Bildad makes the cut, but Plum could just as easily have chosen Eliphaz the Temanite or Zophar the Naamathite, another pair of Job's comforters with sonorous names. Or how about the time Sam Shotter instructs Chimp Twist in no uncertain terms to nix the moustache in *Sam the Sudden*?

> "Shave it," said Sam firmly. "Hew it down. Raze it to the soil and sow salt upon the foundations."

Here, Sam conflates passages from Deuteronomy and Judges to add rhetorical weight to his instruction. And a last one for the road; a cheeky reworking of Mark 1:7 in 'The Purification of Rodney Spelvin':

> "Have I asked her to marry me? I, who am not worthy to polish the blade of her niblick!"

Rodney Spelvin clearly knows his New Testament and doesn't care if he messes around with it (the original involves sandals rather than golf clubs and is spoken by John the Baptist, foretelling Christ's coming).

To import such mysteriously "freighted" language from a bygone age lent Plum's prose added novelty and a deeper texture, as well as offering his readers a possible glow of recognition, in like manner with those shared cultural references we examined earlier. Stephen Fry, who plays Jeeves to Hugh Laurie's Bertie in the TV adaptations *Jeeves and Wooster* and is a massive Wodehouse fan, may have borrowed "Moab is my Washpot" as the resonant title for his autobiography from Psalm 60 or 108 in the KJB; but he is equally likely to have found it in *Uncle Dynamite* or *Ice in the Bedroom*, where it is also used to betoken happiness with one's lot in life. Other similar circumlocutions could include:

- "There was in her manner a suggestion of the hart panting for cooling streams when heated in the chase" – a more stylish way of suggesting that Myra Schoonmaker is all hot and bothered about something (Psalm 42: 1, used in *Service with a Smile, Frozen Assets, Much Obliged, Jeeves, Pearls, Girls and Monty Bodkin* and several others).
- "She was animated by the same sentiment which made Samson pull down the temple pillars at Gaza" graphically expresses Dolly Molloy's brand of incandescent and often violent anger (Judges 16: 29-30, from *Pearls, Girls and Monty Bodkin*).
- "The blighter whose head I want on a charger is the bally manager" finds Archie Moffam similarly narked, channel-

ling Herodias's antipathy to John the Baptist which was to result in the prophet's decapitated head being displayed on a tray (Mark 6:27-28 in *Indiscretions of Archie*).

- "Ah, well, all flesh is as grass."

  "No, it isn't. It's nothing of the kind. The two things are entirely different. I've seen flesh and I've seen grass. No resemblance whatever."

  This is a literary/scriptural dispute between Freddie Fitch-Fitch and Sir Aylmer Bastable as to whether the former's chosen epithet is apt to describe the mutability of human existence (Isaiah 40: 6, in 'Romance at Droitgate Spa'; also in 'Tangled Hearts,' *Jeeves in the Offing*, *The Adventures of Sally*, 'Ukridge Sees Her Through' and many others).

- "Wasted my substance. What a lesson this should be to all of us, Phipps, not to waste our substance."

  "Yes, sir."

  "A fool's game, wasting your substance. No percentage in it. If you don't have substance, where are you?"

  In this exchange, Smedley Cork wishes to convey the ennui of a mis-spent life to Phipps, the butler, repeatedly alluding to the parable of the Prodigal Son, "and there wasted his substance with riotous living" (Luke 15:13, *The Old Reliable*).

And so on almost ad infinitum. Plum's borrowings are quoted in full or in part, alluded to in one or two words, used as similes, hinted at or paraphrased, or even merged with other extra-Biblical literary quotes down through history. Very often they are virtually undetectable, and only very rarely might we get the sense that Wodehouse is parading his knowledge for us to admire. Moreover, in societies where Christian instruction is slipping ever lower down the list of educational priorities, future generations of Wodehouse readers might not even recognize these references. But they will sense, if they are paying any degree of attention, those hundreds of lacunae where the register of the language changes, courtesy of Plum's quotes and references from 31 of the 39 books in the Old Testament, and 22 of the 27 in the New.

Has any other fiction writer managed such an impressive scorecard? Gilkes might even have been proud.

Chapter 5:
American, I Like You

Why America? I have often wondered about that.
Over Seventy

"So our talk sort of goes over the top, does it? Well, you'll
learn American soon, if you stick around."
Jill the Reckless

I'm very fond of slang in books.
Author! Author!

I have to take a trip to the States every so often to brush
up my vocabulary. If I'm away a long time it gets rusty.
**Cheerio! American Slang Is Far
Better Than England's;
Mr. Wodehouse, Past Master of It in
His Stories, Says So**

"Plummie loves America," Mrs. W[odehouse] said.
Ethel in the New Yorker, 1960

Almost one year after the Armistice that brought the Great War to an
end, the October 1919 edition of the veterans' magazine *The American
Legion Weekly* carried the following bellyache:

> To the doughboy who shared trench and billet with the
> Tommy and to the gob who chased subs with the Limey,
> the idea of an Americanized Englishman is preposterous.
> Our men found the English good brothers-in-arms, but
> they found them exasperatingly lacking in the ability to
> absorb, assimilate or even understand American expres-
> sions and mannerisms.

The anonymous writer was not the first to propose that Britain and
America were 'two nations divided by a common language,' nor would
he be the last. But his solution to the problem was truly unique: read the
works of that "English Master of Yankee Slang" P. G. Wodehouse, and
you'll learn the lingo by default. In his books and song lyrics, our scribe

gushes, Wodehouse was busy celebrating American English as a vital force in the forward evolution of the mother tongue, and, moreover, wrote it like a native:

> Most Limeys who try their hand at writing American "produce results compatible with the artistic effects of a hod carrier attempting embroidery work," [but] Wodehouse writes for his American audience as though he has been one of us from birth. When he writes American slang he writes it as it is slung, with the ring of sincerity.

Praise indeed. And furthermore, "thousands who read the Wodehouse stories and see the Wodehouse plays do not suspect that he was – still is – a subject of George V, of the House of Guelph."

The author, who implies he has personally discussed the subject with Wodehouse, notes that Plum employed slang as "a short cut to expression"; but there was actually far more to his "bi-slangual ability" than economy alone. For side by side with all the other literary influences he referenced and channelled, American slang and its inventive informality was one of the most important components of his mature writing style. In a letter from 1923, he noted that "all I want to do is to get back and hear the American language again"; and its vital importance to his work is brilliantly summed up by journalist Claud Cockburn in his contribution to the 1973 festschrift *Homage to P. G. Wodehouse*:

> Wodehouse's first serious writing – I do not use the word ironically or facetiously – was done in the United States. An English writer exposed to, immersed in and inspired by the American writing-style and life-style […] must be jolted, or boosted, into an awareness of the English language which a man who had never experienced the creative schizophrenia of the partially expatriated might never acquire.

And it's that same "creative schizophrenia" I'll be looking at in this chapter, as Plum's classically influenced English butted up against the idiomatic, multicultural mish-mash of his second home's second language.

Unfortunately, Wodehouse's first attempt at writing transatlantic argot was chalk-down-a-blackboard bad. Published in *Punch* in September 1903, 'The Prodigal' proposes that Sherlock Holmes, convalescing after his supposedly fatal contretemps with Moriarty at the Reichenbach Falls, cooled his heels in America for a while before making his triumphant comeback. As he tells Doctor Watson on his return to London:

> "I've been in the U-nited States so long now, tracking down
> the toughs there, that I reckon I've *ac*-quired the Amurri-
> can accent some. Say, do you think the public will object?"

In a word, yes – and they'd have every right to. Just get a load of this:

> "Wal, darn my skin if I didn't surmise I'd seen you be-
> fore somewhere. Watson! Crimes, so it is. Oh, this is slick.
> Yes, *Sir*. This is my shout. Liquor up at my ex-pense, if *you*
> please. What's your poison?"

The only way was up – or out of town on a rail. So just how did Wodehouse progress from being a tin-eared torturer of the American idiom
to a celebrant celebrated by the Americans themselves?

A good start was crossing the Atlantic to conduct his research *in
situ*, eventually spending roughly 36 of his 93 years on this planet in the
Land of the Free:

- Plum first visited America aged 22 in 1904, and again in
  1909, that second stay lasting around seven months.
- From 1914 to 1919 he lived full time in America while enjoying massive success as a lyricist in Broadway musical
  comedy, and a journalist with his own theatre column in
  Vanity Fair.
- Between 1919 and 1939, domiciled back in London and
  then France, he was a regular transatlantic commuter,
  spending two lengthy stints in Hollywood as a scriptwriter.
- In 1947, he moved Stateside for good, taking out citizen-
  ship eight years later.

Stepping off the boat into that "land of romance" for the first time
in April 1904, Wodehouse seems to have immediately tapped into the
energy of the place. "To say that New York came up to its advance
billing," he famously wrote later, "would be the baldest of understate-
ments. Being there was like being in heaven, without going to all the
bother and expense of dying." On his debut in 1915, Bertie Wooster
experiences much the same feeling, picking up on

> something in the air, either the ozone or the phosphates
> or something, which makes you sit up and take notice. A

kind of zip, as it were. A sort of bally freedom, if you know what I mean, that gets into your blood and bucks you up, and makes you feel that […] you don't care if you've got odd socks on.

('Extricating Young Gussie')

And those twin senses of freedom and energy were accentuated by the exotic, colourful and urgent language he heard for the 19 or so days he was there. Clearly smitten by America, he stayed smited for the rest of his life, not just by the place but also by what he would later call the "breezy vernacular" spoken and written there.

Quickly realizing he was on to something, the May 1904 entry in his *Money Received for Literary Work* read:

> In New York gathering
> Experience. Worth many
> guineas in the future,
> but none for the moment.

He already sensed that his future – artistically and financially – lay not in one country or the other, but both. His literary heroes W. S. Gilbert and Arthur Conan Doyle had both done excellent business in the States, and he too wanted a piece of the pie. Indeed, it's not particularly fanciful to imagine he spent most of his brief stay in the Big Apple scribbling notes.

Wodehouse's various sporting enthusiasms (specifically boxing) were the proximate cause of that first visit, and on his return to London he lost no time translating his experiences into saleable material, basking in the glory of one who had done something out of the ordinary. In the August 25 issue of *Vanity Fair* (UK), he placed an article that analysed a baseball game, including liberal quotes from a match report that had been published in the *New York Journal* a few days prior to his arrival. In addition to instructing his British audience about the arcane rules of the sport, Plum marvels at his fellow journalist's "breezy, 'git-thar'" ['get there'] description of the New York Highlanders' glorious 8-2 evisceration of the Boston Americans (the "Champeens"), who had won the American League *and* the first-ever World Series the previous season:

> Champeens, hey? Champeens? Huh! Bet when we got through with them they felt like running home and sobbing out the sad story at mother's knee. Champeens, hey? Chanpeens [sic]? It seems very hard to believe it to-night,

dear friend. Why, sized beside a Yankee, a champeen didn't look any bigger than a freckle on a frog's leg yesterday, and there's an affidavit to go with that statement, if necessary.

According to Wodehouse scholar John Dawson, Plum may have embellished this quotation somewhat. But whether or no, this partisan outburst – written in what Dawson calls an "odd admixture of a burbling Brit and a slangy New Yorker" – could hardly be confused with a Test Match report in *The Times*. Plum helpfully glosses for the benefit of his British audience, noting that "Baseball [...] flavours the literature of the country – or that section which is represented by the newspapers" – and this he judges to be a Good Thing. "This is the right stuff" he enthuses. "It stirs. It invigorates. It would thrill a pew-opener. You feel that you want to read on and find out what it is all about." And wouldn't every writer want that? Although the first great baseball novel (Bernard Malamud's *The Natural*) would not appear until 1952, Plum (for a Brit) was way ahead of the curveball in wanting to give this no-holds-barred style of writing a wider currency.

Within weeks of his return to England, Wodehouse would be made editor of the *By the Way* section of the London *Globe* newspaper, but although a humorous column, he could never write stuff as 'out there' as his confrere on the *Journal* without spooking the horses. Almost ten years earlier in 1895, *The British Printer* had highlighted how the English writer was hog-tied by respectability, running an article entitled 'Envious Descriptive Powers!' in which baseball was once again the subject:

> The wealth of playful expression and delicate refinement sometimes displayed by "the great American language," completely puts in the background our methods of forcible description by means of "the Queen's English." Illustrating this, we note that the *Daily News* makes some selections from a report of a baseball match in *The Quincy Herald*, Illinois, which are interesting as betokening the powers of speech indulged in by Quincy journalists: 'Quincy was playing Omaha, a neighbouring city, and had the worst of it.' Hence the wrath of the Quincy critic. 'The glass-armed toy soldiers of this town were fed to the pigs by the cadaverous grave-robbers from Omaha.' Quincy is 'the Gem City,' and her players 'had their shins toasted by the basilisk-eyed cattle-drivers from the West.' These 'grisly yaps' (the Omaha men) 'ran the bases' victoriously. Hickley, the Quincy captain, 'led the rheumatic proces-

sion to the Morgue.' Quincy 'ran bases like pall bearers at a funeral.' They are styled 'geesers' and 'hoodos,' and are said to be 'whangbasted like a glass full of doodlegammon.'

Or, to put it indelicately, the Quincy players felt completely shat on. Twenty years later, that closing nonsense simile had evolved into "Everything was yellow, rocky and whangbasted like stig tossed full of doodlegammon" (*Lincoln* [Nebraska] *Daily News*, June 10, 1915); and so it was that a version of those final few words somehow managed to find its way into the 1916 serialization of Plum's novel *Piccadilly Jim*:

> "Life is peculiar, not to say odd. You never know what is waiting for you around the corner. You start the day with the fairest prospects, and before nightfall everything is as rocky and ding-basted as stig tossed full of doodle-gammon."

Before Karen Shotting's phenomenal feat of research dug out this arcane lineage in 2016, I'd assumed Plum was simply showing off his knowledge of American slang and had gone just a bit too far. But no – he was actually quoting something that had caught his eye.

In the very next issue of *Vanity Fair* (September 1, 1904) following the appearance of Plum's baseball article, we witness our man experimenting with a short fictional piece set in the States, his first with an American narrator. And not just any old narrator, but a former head of state. 'The Pitiable Position of a President,' as with so much of Plum's early output, had been prompted by a newspaper headline, in this case "A man who was caught kissing his wife on the beach at Atlantic City, New Jersey, has been fined £2." In Plum's version the ex-POTUS has been fined a cool $20 million for breaking a law he had himself put on the statute book – the *Anti-Public Affection Bill* – which forbade alfresco osculation. The quality of the slang demonstrates a marked improvement on that Sherlock Holmes piece (how could it not), at least resembling colloquial speech rather than a patchwork of tin-eared music-hall parodies:

> I've told you I have an A1 collection of slap-up natural endowments. Well, I didn't let them rust. I used them. I did my own work and everyone else's. Blarneyed Senators, bullied Congress, fixed up half-a-dozen Black Bills, and smashed Tammany. How? By bribing officials to be incorruptible.

In *Over Seventy*, Plum would facetiously reminisce that "[a]fter that trip to New York I was a man that counted [...] when some intricate aspect of American politics had to be explained to the British public." Well, here's a small shred of evidence that he had done a bit of boning up on transatlantic affairs of state, with that gloriously satirical last line giving Mark Twain a run for his money. A leap forward it may have been, but Plum would take a long while not just to fine-tune his ear to American accents, but to make them fit naturally into his fiction. And, indeed, to find ways of bringing America and England together in his plots. In effect, this important aspect of his apprenticeship was only just beginning.

His second outing as a baseball reporter – 'New York Crowds' (*Vanity Fair*, November 24, 1904) – is a forensic affair, with Plum once again playing the role of a dutiful cultural ambassador rather than joining in the fun. Transcribing the call-and-response bantering of the fans at the Polo Grounds, he introduces us to Dillon, the "Rooter-in-chief" – a sort of leather-lunged chorus-master of the bleachers; and Sam Mertes, *the* big hitter for the New York Giants (and Harpo Marx's favourite baseball player):

> **Dillon** (patiently): "Well, *what's* the matter with Mertes?"
> **The Crowd** (reassuringly): "*He's* all right!"
> **Dillon:** "What?"
> **The Crowd:** "He's all right."
> **Dillon:** "Who?"
> **The Crowd:** "Mertes."
> **Dillon:** "*Who?*"
> **The Crowd:** "*Mer*-tes."
> **Dillon:** "WHO?"
> **The Crowd** (with a glad bellow that nearly brings down the neighbouring skyscrapers with a run): "MERTES. HE'S ALL RIGHT!!!!!"

An interesting bit of social history, with the capitals, italics and hyphens in this passage indicating that Plum was listening carefully not just to the words of the routine but the intonation, emphasis and timing, already revealing himself to be a keen student not just of the words but the music of Americanese. And the memory lingered: he would echo the "He's all right!" response in several future novels and stories, even managing to shoehorn it into a discussion of the work of John Bartlett, compiler of his preferred dictionary of quotations, in *Over Seventy* some 50 years later.

Now it is we arrive at something of a milestone. It was around this time (Summer 1904) that Wodehouse first went public with his adoration of George F. Ade, an American with an English father whose work on both the stage and the page would influence him greatly, and in particular his use of slang. Perhaps he had picked up a copy of 1900's *Fables in Slang*, or the same year's *More Fables*, or even 1901's *Forty Modern Fables* during his first visit to the States; or seen a performance of Ade's *The County Chairman* that was doing great business at Wallack's Theatre during his stay (in 1917 Plum, along with Guy Bolton and Jerome Kern, would successfully adapt Ade's 1904 play *The College Widow* as *Leave it to Jane*). But whenever it was the two became acquainted, Wodehouse was sufficiently smitten to publish a skilful homage to one of Ade's short sketches within weeks of his return home, imitating the author's style and unorthodox capitalizations such that there's no mistaking his source, despite failing to credit him. Here's the second half of the tale, as a Young Man does his best to woo an Accomplished Young Lady who can't seem to make up her mind what she wants in a husband. Seemingly it's brawn, so he dutifully becomes a gym bunny prior to proposing:

> "Nay," said the maiden, "It is true that your biceps is Considerably Enlarged, and you could doubtless, if so disposed, Fell an ox with a Single Blow, but Mere Strength has ceased to appeal to me. What I really dote upon is Ber-rains!"

> So the Young Man went off . . . and set to work to become a Ripe Scholar. He read Shelly [sic] and Browning and Ruskin and Emerson, and after a year of Acute Depression and Incessant Headache, he returned to the maiden, and said: "I should esteem it a Personal Favour if you would allow your Soft and Sagacious Orb to rest upon me for a space. I have followed your instructions, and I flatter myself that in the way of Culture I am now No Small Potatoes." And quoting lightly an Appropriate Passage from *The Ring and the Book*, he embarked upon an eloquent and impassioned eulogy of the Registry Office, to which he proposed to lead her at as early a date as would be convenient.
> (*Punch*, July 20, 1904)

This is less an *hommage*, more an act of grand larceny, such that there's no need to insert a paragraph or two from Ade for purposes of comparison. But although Plum was never again so brazenly plagiaristic with Ade's stuff, his admiration of the American's style was no nine-day wonder.

In October 1905, he was urging his *Globe* readers to check out Ade's work if they wished "to make a study of the American language, by which we mean the language as it is spoken rather than written." Three years later in the same organ, he was pondering how "[t]he greater part of American humour relies on the turning of phrases":

> Mr. George Ade, in one of his fables, speaks of a mild man at a luncheon counter "pronging about forty cents' worth of lunch." Examined closely, there is nothing screamingly funny about saying "pronging" instead of "eating with a fork"; and yet, given out suddenly, as it were, as everything humorous should be, it undoubtedly *is* funny. It seems to make the picture more vivid.

So taken was Plum, he would file the verb 'to prong' away for future use in 1921's *The Adventures of Sally* and 1926's 'Jeeves and the Impending Doom'. As late as 1971's *Much Obliged, Jeeves* he was still purloining the occasional Adean phrase to suit his needs. When Ginger Winship realizes – a little late in the day – that he prefers Magnolia Glendennon as a love prospect to Florence Craye, he comes out with:

> "Where one goes wrong when looking for the ideal girl is in making one's selection before walking the full length of the counter."

Which is not unreminiscent of Ade's title 'The Fable of Eugene Who Walked the Length of the Counter Before Making His Selection,' taken from his 1902 collection *The Girl Proposition*. No surprise, then, that among the first things to catch Herbert Warren Wind's eye when he visited Plum at his home in Remsenburg at the turn of the 1960s were nine volumes of Ade's work neatly arranged on his host's shelves, ready for consultation. As far as I'm aware, Plum's novel *Money for Nothing* wins the prize with five borrowings ("lamps" – cigarettes; "tightwad" – miser; "swozzie" – fathead; "pippin" – young woman, and "knock-out drops"), and there are many more examples dotted through his work. But really, it's not so much the number or frequency of attributions that is important, but what he took away from Ade's *use* of language.

First of all, Ade represented the kind of linguistic freedom – exercised within a tightly formatted story structure – that would become the hallmark of Plum's mature work. As the latter had pointed out in his *Globe* column, the "turning of phrases" was the cornerstone of this kind of humorous writing, not only serving to surprise and delight the reader but to render "the picture more vivid" with the energy given off by the writer's inventiveness. Slang, used consistently and with a clarity of purpose, as Ade had ably demonstrated, could turn into an idiolect – as indeed it would with Plum. Witness the several volumes of Wodehouse 'nifties' that have been published down the years; or even better, log on to Facebook and witness the gleeful exchanges of favourite words and phrases, dozens and dozens a week, among members of Wodehouse fan groups. For many of the participants, English is not their mother tongue, and several admit that learning Wodehouse's version is far more entertaining than any language course. Aside from the knock-on effect on his book sales, I feel Plum would have loved to witness this, for his use of slang embraced a playful, anti-elitist approach to art to which he seems to have subscribed from the word go.

Which brings us to an interesting question: at this early stage in his career, was Plum's creative conscience troubled that the use of slang in literature was still considered infra dig by polite society? Very possibly, for even the mild slang he had used in his school stories had come under fire. In October 1904, an anonymous piece in *The Athenaeum* magazine lamented that parents must "grieve at the sordid slang in which [*The Head of Kay's*] abounds" – a criticism not shared by other reviewers and one that Plum could easily shrug off. But it would have served as a warning that the taste police of the *haut monde* were always on their guard. The more demotic the slang, the less respectable the writing (and the writer): in *The American Scene* published at almost exactly this time, the novelist Henry James had called out short stories written "in one of the slangy dialects promoted by [those] illustrated monthly magazines" of the type that would carry Plum's short stories and serialize his novels for the next 40 years.

Wodehouse addresses this issue in the sort-of autobiographical *Not George Washington* from 1907 when the lead character, James Orlebar Cloyster, contrasts his literary tastes with those of Malim, a conservative north London aesthete:

> Malim was a man of delicate literary skill, a genuine lover of books, a severe critic of modern fiction. Our tastes were in the main identical, though it was always a blow to me that he could see nothing humorous in Mr. George Ade, whose Fables I knew nearly by heart. The more robust type of humour left him cold.

Here, Wodehouse may have been hinting at his own 'low' tastes, openly acknowledging that not everyone was as big a fan of Ade's style as he was. When Ade was attacked by the Scottish poet, novelist and literary critic Andrew Lang, who opined that slang was all well and good in Chicago but would simply not do for the more refined tastes of the mother country, Plum had rushed to his defence in the London *Globe*'s 'Notes of the Day' column of November 1, 1904:

> [T]he golden rule that governs the use of slang is that it should not be overdone. It is a luxury, and must not be indulged in too freely. Within limits it is an excellent thing. The slang of to-day is the classic phrase of to-morrow. Many of the expressions we admire in Shakespeare must have been the rankest of slang in Elizabethan times. To use slang argues a pleasant and genial mind in an author, which is a thing to be commended.

In theory if not always in practice, the young Wodehouse had clearly grasped some of the fundamentals of (a) how slang might be employed to best effect, and (b) its cultural significance. Applied sparingly and judiciously, it connoted that the writer was informal, up-to-date and a "genial" sort, eager to engage with readers from walks of life other than his own. Moreover, slang should not be peremptorily dismissed as transitory or merely vulgar; it was perfectly capable of entering the language, as Shakespeare had ably demonstrated by bequeathing around 1,700 first-use words to English. It's nigh-on impossible to register quite how many words Wodehouse himself coined, but of the 1,750 times he is quoted in the *Oxford English Dictionary*, that peerless reference guide credits him with 143 originations, or words used in a unique sense or sub-sense (that second stat arrives courtesy of Barry Phelps. Tony Ring has calculated the figures as "over 1,600" and 192 respectively). While many of these are not strictly slang, they point us in the direction Plum would himself be following as he gradually approached his mid-season (and mid-Atlantic) form.

Did George Ade kick off this love of the literary off-beat? Probably not – or at least not exclusively. From first to last, Plum was drawn to informality, and those too precious or over-serious about their language and literature served as butts of his humour throughout his career. One of his best-known put-downs, from 1923's 'The Clicking of Cuthbert', describes the gloomy realism of Russian novelist Vladimir Brusiloff:

> Vladimir specialized in grey studies of hopeless misery, where nothing happened till page three hundred and eighty, when the moujik decided to commit suicide.

Compare this with Ade's "Dyspeptic" reader in "The Fable of the Man Who Didn't Care for Story-Books" who loathes "the dull, gray Book [where] nothing happens until Page 150. Then John decides to sell the Cow." Here, Plum picks up Ade's ball and carries it over the touchline, bettering his inspiration – but in 1904, where we recently left him, the time when he could routinely pull off this sort of triumph was still some way in the distance.

A significant way station was reached when 'Kid Brady – Lightweight: How he Made His Debut' was published in the September 1905 issue of *Pearson's*. Plum's first-ever placing in an American magazine, this early curiosity follows the fortunes of a homeless orphan from England's West Country at large on the streets of New York. Six more episodes would follow, creating a sort-of serial made up of discreet, stand-alone stories charting the Kid's rise to US lightweight boxing champion and beyond.

The opener gives Wodehouse the chance to show off a few of the slangy smarts he might have picked up during his American sojourn: "buncoed" (swindled) and no fewer than three synonyms for dollar bills: "greenbacks," the "long green," and "wafers." Then, stirring in a brief tour of the sights and smells of New York's Chinatown and a good deal of Irish-American dialect speech courtesy of Mike Mulroon (later the Kid's manager) and police officer O'Gorman, Plum was clearly aiming to create the most convincing snapshot of working life in the Big Apple he could manage. For those rare occasions he has the Kid talk, Plum wisely includes a get-out clause in case of inauthenticity:

> During his two years at the gymnasium he had observed the speech of the gentlemen who came there, and had pruned his own of the little growth of dialect which had grown on him.

So it is that in the first episode, the Kid speaks more like one of Wodehouse's fictional schoolboys than a ginuwine Dead End Kid straight outta Devon.

Throughout the series, Plum chose to err on the side of caution, using slang carefully and thriftily. If we weed out dialect transliterations like 'bhoy' (boy), 'wan' (one), and 'mate' (meat); specialized insider language ('six to four,' 'pool-joint,' or 'straight-left'); specific cultural references such as 'Delmonico's' (the famous NY restaurant), or Mrs Carrie Nation (the notorious saloon smasher of the Temperance movement), and general exclamations ('say', 'sure'), the pickings really are quite slim, averaging two or three slang terms per story. For the record, here's a selection: 'gazebo' (bloke), 'bully' (good), 'rub' (sucker), 'bounce him! (throw him out!), 'on your way!' (come off it!), 'smoke-wagon,' and 'bubble' (car), 'take to the tall timbers' (escape to somewhere remote), 'strong josher' (big joker), 'gettin' gay' (overly familiar), 'get outside' (eat), 'rag' (newspaper), 'snap-shotter' (camera), 'low dodge' (dirty trick), 'get it good' (get what's coming to him), 'snug' (drunk), 'mongler' (low-grade person) and 'pie' (easy or good). There's just enough and not too much – even if the stories themselves are no more than competent.

There seems to be two related uses of slang in the Kid Brady stories, both of which point forward to Plum's later mastery. The first is scene-setting; Wodehouse is helpfully offering his services as a knowledgeable tour guide, while at the same time letting his American readers know that as a Brit, he had taken time and trouble to understand the culture he was writing about. Although the stories would not be widely available in England for over a hundred years, these intended acts of bridge-building lend Plum's sophomore American writing – and by extension himself – authenticity, in the same way the slang and cultural references he was busy weaving into his school stories were intended to make his target audience of teenage English males know he understood *them*. In short, Wodehouse was consolidating his literary stock with his readers, encouraging them to trust him. The difference between the slang here and that on display in his later work is one of ownership; early on, Plum was busying himself curating other peoples' contemporary slang rather than inventing the timeless argot that would prove one of the hallmarks of his best work. Apropos of which . . .

His second use of slang is less calculating and more playful. Most slang words and phrases are, at root, metaphors; alternative ways of expressing the literal that delight with their inventiveness, mischief, or simply their sound. There is already evidence in these stories, even as Plum erred on the side of caution and respectability, that he too is aware of the way American slang is broadening his syntax, grammar and vocabulary. From the very start, he was blessed with sensitive antennae for words, images and ideas that amused him; and as he grew more confident, the more he would incorporate them into his writing. I have no wish to let the daylight in on magic, but there was clearly something about 'pie' that made it exactly the right word to use as a synonym for 'easy.' And hopefully we too, when we read it, will see what he's getting at:

"See here, it's no pie to be put to sleep by a boy not big enough to look over the side of a ship; but a light-weight champeen's a thing that might happen to any one."

Spoken by a bullying ship's mate who the Kid has just beaten to a pulp (in 'How Kid Brady Took a Sea Voyage') this literally means, "It's less emasculating to be bested in a fight by a champion boxer than a young, weedy boy." And I'm sure there's no arguing with that. It's just that Plum's version sounds better – but nowhere near as sophisticated as his use of slang would later become.

In the meantime, to maximize potential audiences on either side of the Atlantic, there seemed to be nothing for it but to write parallel versions of everything, one English, one American. For example, in the 1911 short story 'Absent Treatment' – the first appearance of Bertie Wooster prototype Reggie Pepper – we are treated to one outing with Reggie as a Brit, and a second version as a Yank. The English rendering appeared in the March 1911 version of *Strand* magazine, the American on August 26 that same year in *Collier's Weekly*. As Wodehouse scholar Neil Midkiff notes, it's impossible to know for certain which of the two was written first and which bits of the 'conversion' were performed by Plum himself, a sub-editor on either magazine, or a combination of all three. In the American story's 5,600 words, there are around 175 separate variations. Here's a few examples:

ENGLISH	AMERICAN
feel pretty well fed up with things	feel like thirty cents (a particular favourite: refusing to allow for inflation, Plum was still using this one into the 1950s)
they aren't half-hearted about it	they are no pikers – they go the limit
nothing happened	it was a case of all quiet along the Potomac
talking	showing a flash of speed

The American versions are almost without exception livelier. Moreover, the flow of some of the American speeches has improved beyond recognition from the 1903 Sherlock Holmes train-wreck. Here's a few lines of US Reggie's narration:

> Have you ever seen that picture, 'The Soul's Awakening'? It represents a blonde well up in the peacherino class rubbering in a startled sort of way into the middle distance with a look in her eyes that seems to say: "Surely, that is George's step I hear on the porch. Can this be love?" Well, Bobbie had a soul's awakening too. I don't suppose he had

ever troubled to think in his life before – not really *think*. But now he was wearing his brain to the bone. He was saying the sort of things to himself that the football coach says to the squad when they're eight points down at the end of the second quarter.

Quite an improvement, BUT . . . the alteration in Reggie's narrative voice in the American version slews his personality somewhat from a timorous, self-conscious English 'silly ass' to a more self-assured and certainly less effete 'wise guy.' What we end up with is two different characters sharing the same body in the same story, as the "dear olds" and "don't you knows" beloved of the Edwardian Knut rub shoulders with "feel like thirty cents" and "I've got the goods now sure." Things don't quite jell; although that said, the American take does contain an Ade-ism Plum would later happily re-visit:

> Alcohol may be a food, as the wise guys tell you, but you can take it from me it's not a brain food

is the clear descendant of Ade's

> Mr. Byrd […] discovered that Alcohol was a Food long before the Medical Journals got onto it ('The Fable of the Regular Customer and the Copper-Lined Entertainer')

. . . and in turn a prototype of Bertie's marginally better

> It was my Uncle George who discovered that alcohol was a food well in advance of modern medical thought ('The Delayed Exit of Claude and Eustace')

Aside from Reggie, further examples of early characters who swap nationalities in different versions of the same story include Jimmy Pitt from 1909's 'The Gem Collector' (in which he's English); *The Intrusion of Jimmy* (in which he's American); *The Intrusions* [plural] *of Jimmy*, and *A Gentleman of Leisure* (English again). This bibliographer's nightmare would be swiftly followed in 1912 by John Maude and Betty Silver from *The Prince and Betty* who are both English or both American depending on which serialization, novel or dramatization you read. But whether or not this conversion process proved artistically convincing (Neil Midkiff rightly judges the English-language variations more "bland"), to have to write two of everything on a regular basis would likely prove a massive, time-wasting chore. So what to do? "Find a mid-Atlantic voice," came the answer in Plum's literary subconscious.

Nowhere is this search more evident than in November 1909's 'In Alcala', in which the failed romance of Rutherford Maxwell (Brit) and Peggy Norton (American) speaks eloquently of the difficulty of blending American English with the mother tongue. Once again, there are at least two published versions of the story, only this time they're not that dissimilar. Rutherford, having emigrated from Britain, is holed up in a New York bank while writing magazine stories in his spare time. He has little opportunity for leisure, still less for socializing or romance. Peggy, a strident yet sensitive chorus girl, tries to coax "the biggest human clam in captivity" out of his shell by editing his language, starting with his name:

> "What did you say your name was?" she asked.
> "Rutherford Maxwell."
> "Gee! That's going some, isn't it! Wants amputation, a name like that. I call it mean to give a poor, defenseless kid a cuss word like – what's it? Rutherford? Haven't you got something else some shorter – Tom, or Charles, or something?"
> "I'm afraid not."
> The round, gray eyes fixed him again.
> "I shall call you George," she decided at last.

So that's the name sorted – still more buttoned-up than her own diminutive Peggy, but a step in the right direction of informality. Next comes the tone and style of George's conversation:

> "Say, you're English, aren't you?"
> "Yes. How did you know?"
> "You're so strong on the gratitude thing. It's 'thanks, thanks,' all the time. Not that I mind it, George."
> "Thanks. Sorry – I should say 'Oh, you Peggy!'"

Well, no, but it would be a start in breaking down that wall of diffident formality and politeness that, in Peggy's experience, characterizes George's fellow countrymen. As the somewhat one-sided conversation progresses, Peggy starts to lose patience with his reticence:

> "Say, you don't mind my putting you on the stand like this, do you? If you do, say so, and I'll cut out the dis-

trict-attorney act and talk about the weather."
"Not a bit, really, I assure you. Please ask as many questions as you like."
"Guess there's no doubt about your being English, George. We don't have time over here to shoot it off like that. If you'd have just said 'Sure!' I'd have got a line on your meanings."

And there we have it. When George is not being a human clam, he uses fifteen words when, in Peggy's lingo, just one will do. "Damn you and your blasted English haw-haw!" she erupts at a future meeting when George lapses back into his taciturn, over-formal ways.

So here it is that we don't have two nations divided by a common language, but two people, obviously attracted to one another, whose respective cultures don't even allow them to conduct a proper conversation. You can practically hear Plum reminding *himself* to be less of a Henry James, punctiliously weighting every phrase for its pound or ounce of respectability, and more of a George Ade who was happy to publish and be damned (and yes, there are at least two Ade-isms in the story – "actorine" (a female actor), and "rube" – both, not surprisingly, courtesy of Peggy).

The two-nation problem didn't go away: the serialization of *Psmith, Journalist,* which debuted at almost exactly the same time as 'In Alcala', sees Psmith's highly stylized English butt up against Pugsy Maloney's Noo Yoik sort-of Irish brogue, with Wyoming-born Billy Windsor caught somewhere in the middle. Here's a slab of Pugsy, telling Billy how he has come to be in possession of a lost cat:

> "Dere was two fellers in de street sickin' a dawg on to her. An' I comes up an' says, 'G'wan! What do youse t'ink you're doin,' fussin' de poor dumb animal?' An' one of de guys, he says, 'G'wan! Who do youse t'ink youse is?' An' I says, 'I'm de guy what's goin' to swat youse one on de coco if youse don't quit fussin' de poor dumb animal.' So wit dat he makes a break at swattin' me one, but I swats him one, an' I swats de odder feller one, an' den I swats dem bote some more, an' I gets de kitty, an' I brings her in here, cos I t'inks maybe youse'll look after her."

Wodehouse chucks everything into Pugsy's maiden speech, including several kitchen sinks, toning it down only slightly for another Irish-American – Spike Mullins – who would pop up in 'The Gem Collector' precisely one month later. Ever our friendly linguistic tour guide, Plum is out to impress us with these verbal pyrotechnics. But his ironic description of Pugsy's monologue as a "Homeric narrative" carries with it a whiff of condescension, relegating Pugsy to a vaudevillian comic turn and emphasizing his role as a foil for Psmith's educated insouciance. As in the case of George and Peggy, there's no coming together of the two cultures, only a temporary acquaintance followed by separation when Psmith and Mike return to Cambridge, their adventure over, never to return.

Richer pickings can be found in 1913's *The Little Nugget*, in which the ghastly American teenager Ogden Ford is shipped over to England, importing his own unique brand of disrespectful slang with him. His first exchange with new tutor Peter Burns would prove way more sulphurous than anything in Wodehouse before or since, turning into a gloves-off slanging match. "Up an alley!" is pretty close to "f*** off" in intent, and just in case Peter doesn't get the message, Ogden elaborates with "Fade away. Take a walk." Peter doesn't, and has his vocabulary broadened by "I should say nix," "swell around," "hot-air merchant," "bet your life," "you want making a head shorter," and "Oh, slush!" Quite the nasty little piece of work is our Ogden, but it's once again a bravura display from Wodehouse. Where can he have heard such language?

By 1915, however, Plum had evidently done a lot of thinking around the subject of slang, broadening the scope of the formal/informal dichotomy into a root-and-branch re-evaluation of the Old and New Worlds, using language and humour as his shop window for an examination of deeper, cultural themes. In a scripted interview he gave the *New York Times* in November of that year (the strangely titled 'War Will Restore England's Sense of Humor'), he had been a full-time resident across the pond for over a year, and clearly felt he was entitled to sound off on a subject close to his heart. His thesis? That formality, aided and abetted by the class system, was holding English humour back; American humorists were racing ahead, and his fellow Brits would do well to take a leaf out of their book. As we might expect, George Ade is first cab off the rank as a shining example of this 'new' approach to humorous writing:

> There is nobody in England today to compare with
> George Ade, for example. George Ade is the greatest
> American humorist, I suppose. What a delight his work is!
> 'In Babel,' 'Archie' – everything he has written!

Spearheaded by his inventive use of slang, Ade's humour broke down social barriers – what Plum calls the "polished conventional sort of thing" favoured by his fellow countrymen. He then proceeds to reel off eight American writers he rates highly, including Ring Lardner, Booth Tarkington and, cannily, George Horace Lorimer, editor of the prestigious and well-paying *Saturday Evening Post*, who had given him a career-changing leg-up earlier that year by serializing the first Blandings novel *Something New* (and who would publish his work uninterrupted for the next 20 years). None of these named writers was too prissy to use the vernacular; indeed some of them – Lardner, for example – traded on it. His work, Plum predicts, would never make it over the Atlantic "due principally to the English prejudice against slang. And this prejudice is so strong that there could never be an English George Ade." Unless, of course, it was him: in this article, he's almost handing in his application form.

Chief among these slangy Americans was Sinclair Lewis, whose writing debuted in the *Post* at almost exactly the same time as Plum's. Wodehouse would follow Lewis's career through his golden years of the 1920s in brilliant novels of skewed social realism like *Main Street, Babbitt, Arrowsmith* and *Elmer Gantry*. It seems to have been an enduring fascination: Plum even namechecked him as late as 1949's *The Mating Season*, twenty years after Lewis had requested a full set of Wodehouse books to read on the sea passage home to America from England. Lewis went public with his admiration in a warm review of *Summer Moonshine* he wrote for *Newsweek* in 1937, in which he enthuses:

> Like The New Yorker magazine, Mr. Wodehouse is a more dangerous Communist propagandist than twenty Daily Workers. For he disposes of the gilded lily and the stuffed bodice not by misunderstanding them and frothing at the mouth, but by understanding them perfectly and smiling till the reader smiles with him, and that, to stuffiness, is deadlier than strychnine.

The first American to win the Nobel Prize for Literature, Lewis would use his acceptance speech to vilify the "clear and cold and pure and very dead" writing beloved of the Jamesian tradition, a view that exactly chimes with Wodehouse's earlier opinions on "stuffiness" as expressed in the *Times* article.

Wodehouse had begun to push back against these strictures by creating the occasional English and American character who seemed comfortable in either country. Psmith had only ever been a tourist, but this new breed would be genuinely cosmopolitan. Arguably the first of these mid-Atlantic types is Tom Garth, an Oxford grad who works as a journalist for the *Manhattan Daily* in 'How Kid Brady Broke Training.'

Jimmy Pitt, who we've already met, is another candidate. Then there's Jimmy Crocker, making the opposite journey from west to east, "cutting [such] a wide swath in dear old London" that he's nicknamed "Piccadilly Jim." But by 1915, we also have future Wodehouse superstar Bertie Wooster, who, when we first meet him in 1915's 'Extricating Young Gussie' has trickled over to the Big Apple to rescue his cousin Augustus Mannering-Phipps from marriage to an American vaudeville performer, and proceeds to spend the next five stories Plum wrote about him (spanning 1916 to 1918) domiciled in Gotham, totally immersing himself in the atmosphere and culture while resolutely remaining himself.

Although neither Bertie nor Gussie tumbles headlong into slang, the latter at least changes his ridiculous double-barrelled name to "George Wilson":

> "[Y]ou try calling yourself Augustus Mannering-Phipps over here, and see how it strikes you. You feel a perfect ass. I don't know what it is about America, but the broad fact is that it's not a place where you can call yourself Augustus Mannering-Phipps."

And that, in its way, seems to be a good thing. At this stage in his development, Bertie didn't have a surname to be encumbered with. But only a few paragraphs into the second story to feature him – 'Leave it to Jeeves' – we belatedly learn the truth, and it's surely not coincidental that there's a Wooster Street in Manhattan just yards away from the Hotel Erle, where Plum holed up on his 1909 visit. The newly monickered B. Wooster gets with the script almost straight away, does his best to acclimate, and positively wallows in the city's cosmopolitanism.

Rather than playing the English toff looking down from a great social height on all the quaint colonials, Bertie seems to joyfully *integrate* with Americans from many walks of life. He even picks up the odd bit of slang: we have the baseball term "pulled the most awful bone" (to make a big mistake), "bunkoed" (swindled), "give it the double-o" (an intense stare), and "bat" (binge). And because Bertie narrates his own story, we recognize there's a bit of cross-cultural osmosis going on *within his character*. Unlike dear old Reggie, there's only one of him, not two. And, like his creator, who had moved to New York in 1914 and wouldn't return home until 1919, he's making like a local.

There's also evidence in this story that Wodehouse was doing some serious research into popular culture by reading the American funnies or comic strips, namechecking the hugely popular *Buster Brown*, *Mutt and Jeff* and their respective creators Richard F. Outcault and Bud Fisher. In the 1919 *American Legion Weekly* sketch that opened this chapter, the writer remarks how Wodehouse is a devotee of the "slang perpetrations" of other widely syndicated cartoon series such as *Judge Rumhauser, Happy Hooligan,* and *Goldberg's Boobs.* Indeed, keeping up to date on how Americans thought and spoke seems to have been a lifetime's occupation: back in England in 1929, Plum commented to Bill Townend that an urgent summons to dance attendance on the legendary impresario Flo Ziegfeld in New York would give him a welcome opportunity to "brush up on my American slang." In the (I think) 1960s scrapbooks preserved by his grandson Edward Cazalet, Plum has neatly cut around several examples of a newspaper column entitled 'Judge Junior's Dictionary,' a glorious alphabetical compendium of dozens of slang terms, ranging from "Ada from Decatur" (point 8 in a crap game) to "Wooden Kimono" (a coffin) via "Hot Sock" (a good dancer), "Knows his Groceries" (he's no fool), and one of Plum's later personal favourites "Half-Pint" (diminutive in stature), as well as several useful synonyms for 'drunk' ("blotto," "boiled," "busted," "fried," "high," "jingled," "on his nose," "potted," "shellaced," "snockered," "snorted," and "tight").

With all this raw data swimming around, Plum's temptation had been to jam it into a story to let his readers know he'd done his homework. But by the time of what I've elsewhere dubbed his "mid-season form" (c. 1920 onwards), his use of slang was starting to subtly evolve. Avoiding the trap of grandstanding it *à la* Pugsy, he preferred to quietly insinuate it into his prose style as background seasoning rather than the dominant flavour. In short, he'd stepped down from his roles as tour guide/social anthropologist and learned to wear his learning lightly, or, as the eminent Wodehouse scholar Norman Murphy rightly puts it, "he simply absorbed the phraseology and popular quotations of England and America and forgot they were peculiar to one country." As an example of this process in action, let's take the term "in the soup" ("in a bad situation: in trouble," according to Merriam-Webster) and see what our man does with it over time.

American in origin and first used at the close of the 19th century, it makes its Wodehousean debut in Plum's 'A Fiscal Pantomime' from 1903, in which "poor Joseph" will be "place[d] [...] in the soup tureen" if certain political manoeuvrings come to pass. By 1908's 'The Lost Lambs,' Psmith has picked up on it ("Without brain, where are we? In the soup, every time"). But then, later in the same serial, he elaborates on the metaphor by specifying which kind of soup he's talking about:

> "I should say that young Lord Antony Trefusis was in the soup already. I seem to see the *consommé* splashing about

his ankles."

Later that same year in 'The New Fold,' our Rupert's at it again:

"I have to a certain extent landed Comrade Bannister in the bouillon."

Then Psmith passes the ladle to Bertie, who sees the bouillon and raises him:

[T]hat poor old Bingo was knee-deep in the bisque was made plain by his mere appearance – which was that of a cat which has just been struck by a half-brick and is expecting another shortly.

Now cut to *Right Ho, Jeeves*:

Not even on the occasion [...] when I had inadvertently become betrothed to Tuppy's frightful Cousin Honoria, had I experienced a deeper sense of being waist high in the gumbo and about to sink without trace.

Now we're presented with a spicier American variant. But it's in *The Mating Season* where Bertie really lets rip with his soup metaphors: in Chapter 11 he's once again "splashing about in the gumbo"; by Chapter 18 things have eased a bit and he's not "so very much deeper in the broth than I was before"; but Chapter 21 sees him going down for the third time, as he informs Jeeves:

"There have been occasions, numerous occasions, when you have beheld Bertram Wooster in the bouillon, but never so deeply immersed in it as now."

These variants span forty-plus years, stretching from 1908 to 1949, during which Plum doesn't once allude to the American provenance of "in the soup," assuming that he knew in the first place. It's slang all right, but he has gradually subsumed it into *his* slang, used, predominantly, by English characters. And while we're on the subject of soup, there's the adjective "soupy," used in 'Honeysuckle Cottage' to describe someone hopelessly romantic ("A soppy, soupy, treacly, drooping girl with a roguish smile"); and the noun "soupiness" ("I am never at my best when the situation seems to call for a certain soupiness" – Bertie again, from *Right*

Ho, Jeeves), which both appear to be uniquely Wodehousean usages. So it is that in *Laughing Gas*, to take a novel completely at random, we are presented with a melange of such American slang as "beasel" (a lively young woman), "red-hot mamma" (ditto), "snootful" (however much alcohol it takes to get drunk), "plug-ugly" (a lout), "beating the gun" (getting advantage over), "Easy Street" (having wealth or comfort), "pix" (motion pictures), and "Roscoe" (a pistol) – all of which rub matey shoulders with an equally eccentric selection from Plum's stock of home-grown slang.

In Wodehouse's mature work, then, England and America don't simply come together as one; they form a third culture, a hybrid that is distinct from its twin origins and peculiar to Wodehouse World. And whether he realized it or not, he was also evolving a transatlantic voice when writing *in propria persona*, which was not a million miles away from his narrative style in his novels and stories. Particularly in his theatre criticism for *Vanity Fair* magazine, mostly written during his extended sojourn in the States from 1914 to 1919, he shows himself busy cultivating the image of the urbane cultural commentator while occasionally letting fly some choice examples of slang he's picked up, often from the sports pages. Speaking of a fellow song lyricist who had successfully turned her hand to playwriting, he remarked:

> Clare Kummer, whose "Dearie" I have so frequently sung in my bath, to the annoyance of all, suddenly turned right round, dropped song-writing, and ripped a couple of hot ones right over the plate.
>
> (*Vanity Fair*, May 1917)

At which we might remark that Plum had – linguistically – done something remarkably similar, for it's not often that baseball vernacular is used in a theatre review, least of all by an Englishman. This example serves to demonstrate quite how much Plum enjoyed juxtaposing the demotic and the cultured, the rough with the smooth and, of course, the English and the American. Or even Old French and the American. In another piece, within the space of a few words, he refers to his status as one of the "lads of the *coulisses* [wings] and a "theatre-hound" – the first of which would have delighted Henry James, the second . . . not so much (*Vanity Fair*, September 1917). Of course, there were whole areas of fruitier, willfully offensive American slang that Plum would have considered strictly off-limits; but compared to many of his more traditionally minded colleagues, his humorist's off-kilter perspective allowed him greater latitude not simply to experiment with language but to have fun with it, all the while selling America to his British readers, while amusing his American audience at the old country's expense. A commercial as well as an artistic move, it's one that would pay dividends throughout his career.

In the vast majority of his stories from around 1915 onwards, there's usually an American angle *somewhere* whether in location, characters or themes, prompting biographer Robert McCrum to claim that "[n]o English writer of the 20th century became more adept at interpreting the two societies to each other." And as recently as 2015, the aptly named Britt Peterson of the *Boston Globe* was continuing to marvel at Plum's interest in the American idiom with its headline "P. G. Wodehouse's language is as American as it is British," quoting Katherine Connor Martin, head of American dictionaries at Oxford Dictionaries:

> "It's not an uncommon occurrence when you're working on a really characteristically American term to find one of the earliest examples is from Wodehouse."

His role as linguistic ambassador was something Plum would no doubt have been quietly proud of. But perhaps even more cheering was his contention that slang helped promote sweetness and light by breaking down social barriers between all ranks of English-speaking citizens wherever they happened to live. In a 1922 interview for the New York *Evening World*, he concluded that:

> "Slang is awfully human, and the fact that it is acceptable shows that we are all the more human than we used to be. It is a good sign and a wonderful thing, in my opinion."

Hear, hear.

Chapter 6:
Queens of Romance

He held rigid views on the art of the novel, and always maintained that an artist with a true reverence for his craft should not descend to goo-ey love stories.
Honeysuckle Cottage

[P]assionate spinsters read Ethel M. Dell. And dull men in offices read detective stories.
Dorothy L. Sayers, The Unpleasantness at the Bellona Club

There was a constant stream of requests from female readers for the 'racier' novels of the day – Elinor Glyn, Ruby M. Ayres, Ethel M. Dell. "The hot stuff," Miss Shaw giggled. Lately there had been a positive deluge of calls for the new E. M. Hull novel, *The Sons of the Sheik*, something Mr Pollock, in particular, objected to.
Kate Atkinson, Shrines of Gaiety

"Don't mind her. Let her cry. […] I have seen her and her sister cry over a book for an hour together; and they said they liked the book the better the more it made them cry."
Oliver Goldsmith, She Stoops to Conquer

In Plum's 1956 novel *French Leave*, American publisher J. Russell Clutterbuck describes the sort of book his company wouldn't touch with a bargepole:

There's this illegitimate crippled child with brutal stepfather. Stepfather whales the tar out of the unfortunate little bastard for sixteen pages with a horse whip and then hauls off and murders his mother […] Child goes mad and dies in a cornfield. Stepfather hangs himself, father of child shoots himself […] And there's a girl who gets her face burned up in a fire and a child – not the first child, another child, small-part child – who's run over by a sightseeing bus and loses both legs.

Even thinking about such plots, which often involve "a bunch of blasted sharecroppers getting all persecuted down in Alabama or somewhere" puts Russell off his lunch. So, no novels by John Steinbeck, William Faulkner or Erskine Caldwell on *his* nightstand, then.

Wodehouse wasn't overfond of them either, complaining to Hesketh Pearson in December 1947 that most contemporary American fiction seemed to be "stodgy grey stuff about life in the swamps of the Deep South." Indeed, his axis of literary doom and gloom seemed to have shifted below the Mason/Dixon, supplanting "the great Russians" like Dostoyevsky, Turgenev and Gogol who, in his estimation, had hitherto held the miserabilist crown. No, what Russell Clutterbuck prefers is something light, easy to read and "riskay but not too riskay." He'll chew your hand off for one of those and aim at selling 100,000 copies to his eager public rather than a few dozen to a bunch of fashionable literary types. Which is why, when Plum wanted to feature popular literature in his plots – which he did a lot – he homed in on two particular genres: the detective novel/thriller (which we'll examine in the following chapter); and the romance (the subject of this one) which shares the tone, scenarios and plot trajectories of many of his own stories. In fact, there are *so* many romances in his work that in 2019 the excellent Wodehouse blogger Honoria Plum organized a poll to discover his readers' favourite couples and compiled a Top 50 – which still left another 30-odd pairings out in the cold (you can find the Top 10 at the end of this chapter).

But Wodehouse was not alone in featuring popular romantic literature in his fiction. In the 'Wandering Rocks' episode of *Ulysses* James Joyce has his protagonist Leopold Bloom choose a book from the circulating library for his wife Molly. Eschewing anything serious, it's a toss-up between a pair of invented romances *Fair Tyrants* and *Sweets of Sin*; at which point Bloom, Joyce's *homme moyen sensuel*, opens the latter and reads a snatch:

> Her mouth glued on his in a voluptuous kiss while his
> hands felt for the opulent curves inside her deshabillé.
> [...]
> "You are late," he spoke hoarsely, eyeing her with a suspi-
> cious glare.
> The beautiful woman threw off her sabletrimmed wrap,
> displaying her queenly shoulders and heaving embon-
> point. An imperceptible smile played round her perfect
> lips as she turned to him calmly.

Suitably nudge-nudge wink-wink, Bloom judges the story suitable –

more suitable than he knows, since Molly is almost simultaneously in flagrante with her lover Blazes Boylan. But whereas Joyce's ear for a parodic title is only decently in tune, Wodehouse's is pitch perfect. Though a pretty decent effort, *Sweets of Sin* can't hold a candle to *A Red, Red Summer Rose, The Courtship of Lord Strathmorlick, The Woman Who Braved All, Madcap Myrtle, A Kiss at Twilight, 'Twas Once in May* and *By Honour Bound*, all written by Plum's chief *romancière* Rosie M. Banks. And there are plenty more where those came from.

In all, there are around 30 or so romance writers in Wodehouse, a tally that includes three men: the mononymous 'Swaffham', who penned *Rose-Red Lips of Vivette*; Rodney Spelvin, whose novel *The Purple Fan* is written in "the neo-decadent style"; and (ahem) Horace Wanklyn whose "powerful novels which plumbed the passionate heart of Woman and all that sort of thing" are alluded to in 1955's 'A Tithe for Charity,' the story which would mark Plum's debut in *Playboy* magazine. Notwithstanding these gentlemen, the distaff contingent dominates the market, their number including Lady Wickham (author of *Agatha's Vow, A Strong Man's Love, A Man for A' That, Meadowsweet,* and *Fetters of Fate*); Julia Ukridge (*The Heart of Adelaide*); Clara Throckmorton Stooge (*A Strong Man's Kiss*); Cora McGuffy Spottsworth (*Furnace of Sin*); Luella Periton Phipps (*The Love That Scorches)* and a good many others. All these writers, both M and F, steadfastly refuse to produce those "dim tragedies of peasant life which we return to the library after a quick glance at Page One" (as Plum put it in his 1975 introduction to *Thank You, Jeeves*) in favour of those that celebrate the complexities of mutual human attraction. In Wodehouse, that attraction is exclusively boy-meets-girl, which was of course the overwhelming predilection of his time. But in choosing to base most of his mature plots within the same traditional parameters, where – we might ask – did he seek his inspiration? After all, those pin-sharp titles, many of which are actually better than the real thing, must have come from *somewhere*.

The short answer is that there is no direct lineage to any individual writer. There has been scholarly speculation that Ms. Banks is reminiscent of the real-life author Ruby M. Ayres (as Plum himself informed Richard Usborne), but he might just as easily have been thinking of Ethel M. Dell or Edith M. Hull. All these writers were near enough Plum's exact contemporaries (Hull was born in 1880, Dell in 1881, Ayres in 1883) and enormously successful, as we'll be seeing shortly; but like-for-like comparisons ultimately prove forced and inconclusive. For it wasn't simply the particulars of the classic romance that attracted Plum, but the whole febrile atmosphere that was panting for his light, lampooning touch. Indeed, romance was a genre that often came close to doing his job for him.

His instinctive levity in such matters does not imply that Wodehouse ever reviled his source material; indeed, that would have instantly made him the profound hypocrite he wasn't. Not only was his novel *The Prince and Betty* published by Mills and Boon (to this day the last word in commercial romance), his mature plots regularly feature gooey tropes like love at first sight, twin souls, and upturned faces covered with burning kisses. While his personal library was not exactly overstocked with romance, we still witness literary agent Andrew McKinnon ticking off James Rodman in 1925's 'Honeysuckle Cottage' for dismissing Leila J. Pinckney's love stories as tripe: "No author who pulls down a steady twenty thousand pounds a year," he opines, "writes tripe." Leila will never be the sweetheart of the avant-garde nor even the chattering classes who, if they did read her books, would never dare admit it. But for all the opprobrium heaped on it, Wodehouse consistently presents romance as an iceberg looming quietly below the waterline of our collective cultural consciousness.

In 'Jeeves Exerts the Old Cerebellum' Jeeves informs Bertie that there are "a great many" writers of "very light, attractive reading" who are "neglected by the reviewers but widely read" – in which case, he implies, more fool the reviewers. The public knows best, and coming from a man who reads Spinoza without anaesthetic, this is a somewhat surprising endorsement. Romance has a large public that it services both well and efficiently: in 'Best Seller,' Miss Postlethwaite behind the bar of the Angler's Rest (perhaps reading off the book's dust jacket) insists *Rue for Remembrance* "lay[s] the soul of Woman bare as with a scalpel," and "child of faerie" Rose Maynard claims the appeal of romances lies in "their trueness to life." So whatever Plum's private opinion might have been, he often presents romance as addictively preposterous and something to celebrate. In his stories, he only gives us a few clues as to the titles he himself might have read for pleasure/research, but there were essentially two sub-genres of romance jostling for elbow-room in the crowded late Victorian/early Edwardian marketplace in which he began his professional career: the traditional love story; and what he sometimes refers to as the "sex-novel," with which we'll begin.

Most of these notorious yet massively popular productions didn't, of course, contain explicit sex-scenes; it's more that sex is acknowledged as actually existing and isn't swept under the carpet. On those occasions coupling takes place, it's usually so heavily shrouded in symbolism and innuendo or lost in ellipsis that if you blink, you'll miss it. Which meant you could get away with reading such books with only the occasional raised eyebrow. In 'The Amazing Hat Mystery,' it seems the most normal thing in the world, scarcely worth the mention, that Lady Punter should "retire to her boudoir with a digestive tablet and a sex-novel." Indeed, nearly half a century before the *Lady Chatterley* trial ushered in the so-called 'Swinging Sixties,' Wodehouse provided his readers with a succinct résumé of what was going on at the more sizzling end of the romance market in his 1914 story 'Parted Ways.' Freelance author George Marlowe is not dissimilar to himself at that time, watching trends and riding the waves of literary fashion; and as the story opens, the slightly raunchy sex-novel is "the one safe card" guaranteed to make a writer money. "Publishers' lists," the narrator tells us, are "congested with scarlet tales of Men Who Did and Women Who Shouldn't," a passing reference to the notorious 1895 novel *The Woman Who Did* by Grant Allen. An eminent psychologist, Allen's aim had been to address the many contemporary cultural issues surrounding illegitimacy, but his motives were quickly misconstrued as the book became a popular sensation. The central figure, Herminia Barton, has a child out of wedlock with a partner who quickly dies, leaving her an unrepentant single mother shunned by all but the broadest-minded in society and, ultimately, her daughter, Dolores, when she grows up. Faced with rejection, Herminia commits suicide as "a martyr to humanity," a sensational dénouement that triggered a wide-ranging societal debate concerning this "natural tragedy," and a small industry of answer novels including *The Man Who Didn't* and *The Woman Who Wouldn't*. Whether Plum had read it or not is moot, but he certainly knew *of* it. The book was a perfectly competent production but somewhat overshadowed in literary history by another novel on an identical theme that appeared the same year: Thomas Hardy's gloom-fest *Jude the Obscure* which Plum definitely *didn't* care for.

But not all sex-novels had such worthy ambitions. As he was writing 'Parted Ways,' Plum might have been reminded that *The Rosary* by rector's wife Florence L. Barclay was the fictional *cause célèbre* of 1909 and still selling healthily, a narrative that sought to hide its lasciviousness beneath a thin veneer of sobriety while all the time anticipating climaxes like this:

> [O]ut on the terrace with him she had realised, for the first time, the primal elements which go to the making of a man – a forceful determined, ruling man – creation's king. They echo of primeval forests. The roar of the lion is in them, the fierceness of the tiger; the instinct of dominant possession, which says: "Mine to have and hold, to fight for and enjoy; and I slay all comers!" She had felt it, and her own brave soul had understood it and responded to it, un-

afraid; and been ready to mate with it, if only -ah! if only –

The novel is packed with knowing insinuation, high camp and a riot of single entendres that to a modern ear (and a humorist like Wodehouse) are frankly laughable and all part of the fun.

Such productions naturally enjoyed instant notoriety: as with Beefy Bastable's *Cocktail Time*, all you had to do was get the moral majority on your case and sales would go through the roof. An edition of *The Bookman* magazine published around this time featured a fire-and-brimstone think-piece entitled 'The Fleshly School of Fiction' which ranted:

> Dissolution has set in, provoked by the agents of death which cannot thrive except where Heaven's sweet air is shut out and darkness holds rule. Yesterday, Paris almost alone spread the plague. Today it rages in London. Fashionable publishers keep it in stock; newspapers advertise it in spicy paragraphs; women's clubs and afternoon teas reek with its odours; is it not time to ask whether we want this tainted literature among us, and if not, how shall we get rid of it?

Despite such efforts at containment, the virus spread globally: *The Rosary* was translated into eight languages and became the bestselling novel of 1910 in the United States. Meanwhile, back in 'Parted Ways' we discover how the canny publishers of the racy *Rose-Red Lips of Vivette* sponsor a newspaper discussion on "The Sex Problem in Modern Fiction: Should there be a Censor?" Sixteen years later, the topic was still sufficiently current for Plum to rewrite the story as 'Best Seller,' in which the topic under debate was altered to "The Growing Menace of the Sex Motive in Fiction: Is There to be no Limit?"

Another sex novel that likely crossed Wodehouse's transom was *Three Weeks*, the notorious tale from 1907 by Elinor Glyn in which Paul Verdayne, a young English ingenu, is swept off his feet by the somewhat older and passionately exotic queen of an unnamed Russian dependency. Having chosen him as her "mate," she introduces him to every aspect of her *ars amatoria*, at which point . . .

> [H]e seized her in his arms, raining kisses upon her which, whatever they lacked in subtlety, made up for in their passion and strength. "Some day some man will kill you, I suppose, but I shall be your lover – first!"
>
> The lady gasped. She looked up at him in bewildered

surprise, as a child might do who sets a light to a whole box of matches in play. What a naughty, naughty toy to burn so quickly for such a little strike!

But Paul's young, strong arms held her close, she could not struggle or move. Then she laughed a laugh of pure glad joy.

"Beautiful, savage Paul," she whispered. "Do you love me? Tell me that?"

"Love you!" he said. "Good God! Love you! Madly, and you know it, darling Queen."

"Then," said the lady in a voice in which all the caresses of the world seemed melted, "then, sweet Paul, I shall teach you many things, and among them I shall teach you how to . . . LIVE."

And outside the black storm made the darkness fall early. And inside the half-burnt logs tumbled together, causing a cloud of golden sparks, and then the flames leapt up again and crackled in the grate.

Highly reminiscent, I'm sure you'll agree, of the passion implicit in Uncle Fred's "Ickenham system" which recommends raining down burning kisses on the upturned face of the female party, usually addressed as "my mate." Plum would use this motif on many occasions, firstly in the 1909 short story 'In Alcala' (which is about as close to a conventional romance as he ever came to writing):

Her grey eyes were wet. He could see them glisten. And then his arms were round her, and he was covering her upturned face with kisses.

Those burning kisses would remain alight until at least 1966's 'Life with Freddie,' although they had long since morphed from earnest tokens of undying love into a comedy trope.

Kissing was just about as far as Plum ever took things – but not so Glyn. Many of Paul and the princess's fleshly frolics take place on a tiger skin settee, which prompted the topical verse:

Would you like to sin
With Elinor Glyn
On a tiger skin?
Or would you prefer
To err with her

On some other fur?

This was an image that hadn't escaped Plum's attention, and seems to have rather excited him, since he refers to it at least three times in his work, making its debut (I think) in 1932's *Hot Water* during which we learn that radical novelist Blair Eggleston

> had never actually found himself alone in an incense scented studio with a scantily clad princess reclining on a tiger skin, but in such a situation he would most certainly have taken a chair as near to the door as possible and talked about the weather.

As Bertie's Aunt Dahlia notes in 'Jeeves and the Greasy Bird,' modern male novelists may construct tough personae for themselves, but show them a real woman "who doesn't come out of their fountain pen and their feet get as cold as a dachshund's nose." Blair is one such milksop, apparently, and would eschew tiger skins in favour of small talk and a fast exit. Thirty-five years later in 1967's 'A Good Cigar is a Smoke,' Plum was still using exotic animal pelts as shorthand for the popular misconception which fancies that all artists are obsessed with fornication: Gladys Wetherby's Uncle Francis imagines that painters "spend all their time having orgies in studios and painting foreign princesses sitting on leopard skins in the nude." Spots not stripes, admittedly; but the tiger returns in 1970's *The Girl in Blue* when Jerry West debunks the theory put forward by an aunt in Bournemouth that even cartoonists earn their crust "painting Russian princesses lying in the nude on tiger skins."

Glyn herself was something of a phenomenon whose influence, now largely forgotten, loomed large throughout the first four decades of the 20th century. Unhappily married, her affair with an aristo sixteen years her junior was the talk of Edwardian England and fed, it is alleged, into her fiction. By the time of the scandalous *Three Weeks*, she had abandoned her toy boy and begun a long dalliance with Lord Curzon, the former Viceroy of India, which lasted almost a decade. He had gifted her, somewhat inevitably, a tiger skin belonging to a beast which he himself had shot, but the affair foundered after Glyn read an announcement in the London *Times* of his impending nuptials with another woman. Branding him "faithless and so vile," she threw herself into work, becoming a war correspondent and one of only two women present at the signing of the Versailles Peace Treaty in 1919. Three years on, her novel *Man and Maid* would feature a maimed and cynical English war veteran, Sir Nicholas Thormonde, who nevertheless finds love with his secretary Alathea Sharp in a Rosie M. Banks-esque plot of social mobility – although it later transpires that Alathea isn't lower-class at all but a scion of a notable family who has fallen on hard times. No sex in this one, although it is strongly hinted at when, at the novel's close, the two parties kiss for the first time:

> She struggled and pretended she wanted to leave me, but I would not let her go.
> "Only when I please and at a price! I want to show you that you have a husband who in spite of a wooden leg and a glass eye, is a powerful brute!"
> "I love you, strong like that," she cooed, her eyes soft with passion again. "I am not good really, or austere, or cold."

As a nonplussed Bertie might comment: "Oh, ah!"

Hollywood was Elinor's next port of call, where her novel *The Great Moment* was being filmed with Gloria Swanson in the lead role. She quickly turned into something of a mover and shaker, hooking up with the media mogul William Randolph Hearst for a host of successful projects on the screen and in print. 1922 saw Rudolph Valentino star as Lord Bracondale in the movie of her 1906 novel *Beyond the Rocks*, and in 1927 came the short story and subsequent movie *It*, widely credited with popularizing the concept of the vivacious 'It' girl thanks to a star-making performance from the extravagantly red-headed Clara Bow.

Once again Wodehouse was ahead of the curve, with a flame-haired force of nature on his books in the person of Roberta "Bobbie" Wickham, a 24-carat "snooterer" whom Jeeves variously describes as "volatile," "frivolous," and even "dangerous" who had debuted in the 1924 short story 'Something Squishy.' It is perhaps no coincidence that her mother Lady Wickham is a successful romantic novelist, for Plum may have been reminded of Glyn's 1905 comedy *The Vicissitudes of Evangeline*, whose red-headed heroine remembers how she was once told:

> "You need not suppose, Evangeline, that you are going to have a quiet life with your colouring – the only thing one can hope for is that you will screw on your head."

Which is a nice trick if you can do it. Which of course she doesn't, for this is a wonderfully light-hearted novel whose plot contains many parallels with Wodehouse's own work.

As with Bobbie, men just can't seem to resist Evangeline's 'it-ness,' as one of her suitors reveals in a letter to a friend:

A quaint thing has happened to me! Came down here to take over the place, and to say decidedly I would not marry Miss Travers, and I find her with red hair and a skin like milk, and a pair of green eyes that look at you from a forest of black eyelashes with a thousand unsaid challenges. I should not wonder if I commit some folly. One has read of women like this in the *cinque-cento* time in Italy, but up to now I had never met one. She is not in the room ten minutes before one feels a sense of unrest, and desire for one hardly knows what – principally to touch her, I fancy.

Several of Plum's goofier males are similarly pole-axed by Bobbie, and, having a little more of the *femme fatale* and less of the unwitting *ingénue* about her than Evangeline, she takes great delight in bending them to her caprices. Here we find Bertie doing her bidding, without being quite sure *why*:

It was a lovely afternoon, replete with blue sky, beaming sun, buzzing insects and what not, an afternoon that seemed to call to one to be out in the open with God's air playing on one's face and something cool in a glass at one's side, and here was I, just to oblige Bobbie Wickham, tooling along a corridor indoors on my way to search a comparative stranger's bedroom, this involving crawling on floors and routing under beds and probably getting covered with dust and fluff.

The Glyn/Bow partnership was renewed in 1928 when the screen adaptation of *Evangeline* was released as *Red Hair*, and just like Evangeline (or "Bubbles" as she's re-christened in the movie), *la* Wickham refuses to consider her crowning glory a liability and goes on to cry havoc and break hearts whenever she appears, finally bowing out in 1960's *Jeeves in the Offing* after 36 years of chaos. It's clear that although she's a ticking time bomb and not the sort of woman his eligible males end up marrying, Plum rather enjoyed her gloriously wayward company.

Wodehouse would follow Glyn to the west coast as a screenwriter in 1930, and if he was aware of the ins and outs of her well-publicized career, as he doubtless was, he may well have invested Rosie M. Banks with some of her steely, successful qualities. It is likely no accident that in *Ring for Jeeves*, the maiden name of fabulously successful romantic novelist Rosalinda Spottsworth is also Banks, a surname shared by Evangeline Pembury's mercurial literary agent in 'Best Seller' – he of the dark romantic face and lissom figure. For while romance may be a thing of faërie, Plum acknowledges it also makes pots of money. Leila Yorke (née Elizabeth Binns) author of *For True Love Only, Heather o' the Hills, Sweet Jennie Dean* and *Cupid, the Archer* rises from being the humble sob sister on an evening paper to the châtelaine of Claines Hall in Sussex on the proceeds of her writing. Contrary to Freddie Widgeon's expectations prior to their acquaintance in *Ice in the Bedroom*, she is not some "frail little spectacled wisp of a thing with a shy smile and a general suggestion of lavender and old lace" but a large, hearty-looking woman "built on the lines of Catherine of Russia" with piercing blue eyes and the voice of a drill sergeant. With a penchant for high living and decent champagne, Leila describes herself as "as tough an egg as ever stepped out of the saucepan" for all the treacle in her "sentimental" prose.

More than once in Wodehouse, Mammon's iron fist is concealed within love's lacy finger-mitten. So although Rosie M. may be referred to as "the little woman," we are left in no doubt who wears the trousers, controls the purse-strings and is the major breadwinner in the Little household. The squishy stuff she writes is a smokescreen for a resolute, determined and successful professional on top of her game for the 43 years she remains on Plum's rep company. Glyn too enjoyed a lengthy career and was a force to be reckoned with until her death in 1943, with around 25 volumes of novels and short stories, and several non-fiction titles to her name including the four-part *Elinor Glyn System of Writing*. Nor was Plum her only devotee: Glyn also pops up in work by Evelyn Waugh, Dorothy L. Sayers, a song lyric by Lorenz Hart, an episode of period drama *Downton Abbey* and Kate Atkinson's 2022 showbiz novel *Shrines of Gaiety*.

While we're looking at the more exotic (and racier) end of popular romance, we mustn't forget Plum's familiarity with the influential and hugely popular sub-genre of the so-called 'desert' or 'desert island' romance which takes place, at least in part, in some far-flung part of the planet. It's still a popular setup today (at the time of writing Mills and Boon has 254 desert titles in its listings) but it burst onto the scene as long ago as the 1860s with *Under Two Flags* by Ouida (pen name of the English novelist Maria Louise Ramé). Plum alludes to her novels a few times in his early work, beginning in a poem he placed in the *Daily Chronicle* in 1904, whose scruffy and frankly ugly narrator notes that "A Ouida guardsman, I admit / Does not resemble me a bit." In 'Wilton's Holiday' the sartorial fastidiousness of the "Ouida guardsman" reappears, and in 1923's 'First Aid for Dora', the normally shabby Ukridge has borrowed Corky's dress clothes without their owner's permission, yet they fit "with such unwrinkled smoothness that he might have stepped straight out of one of Ouida's novels." In each of these examples, Plum might have been thinking of Bertie "Beauty" Cecil, the male lead of Ouida's *Under Two Flags*, an officer described by his batman as "uncommon particular" about his attire whether it's his military uniform, riding gear or evening dress. Tiger skins abound, as do references to the Quorn and Pytchley hunts, so beloved of Aunt Dahlia during her days in the saddle. These casual references don't in themselves argue a detailed knowledge of Ouida's work, although Plum's evident familiarity may have been prompted by seeing the novel's movie adaptation released in 1922. Her story also features an unlikely heroine called Cigarette.

As late as 1949's *The Mating Season*, Plum reveals a deeper appreciation of the desert genre when he has his regular soup queen Madeline Bassett rehearse the entire plot of Rosie M.'s *Mervyn Keene, Clubman*, hoping Bertie will see the parallels between the events in the novel and what she imagines to be his hopeless infatuation with her. It lasts three pages, so I'll viciously précis it:

- Mervyn is an officer in the Coldstream Guards, rich, handsome and "the idol of all who knew him." But there is a tragedy in his life. He loves Cynthia Grey, "the most beautiful girl in London" who is unfortunately otherwise engaged to Sir Hector Mauleverer, the explorer;
- Cynthia's "wild" younger brother Lionel commits a serious crime, for which Mervyn gallantly (and unbeknown to Cynthia) takes the rap (this is actually a direct lift from the plot of *Under Two Flags*);
- On his release from jail, Mervyn discovers Cynthia has married Mauleverer, and he flees to the South Sea Islands to become a beachcomber, "living the pace that kills, trying to forget" (incidentally, 'The Pace That Kills' was an actual pulpy romance about a couple hooked on Class A drugs, released as movies in 1928 and 1935. Had Plum seen *them?*);
- Who should turn up in this island paradise but Sir Hector and Cynthia. Desperate and by now extravagantly bearded (yet another Ouida trope), Mervyn attempts to steal one last souvenir from Cynthia's hotel room − a rose she had been wearing in her hair;
- Cynthia interrupts Mervyn's act of larceny, recognizing his voice. She tells him how, prior to his death, her brother had confessed all. This had alerted her to Mervyn's innocence, his gallantry and of course, his love;

- Enter Sir Hector, who shoots Mervyn, imagining him to be a thief – or worse;
- Mervyn dies with the rose in his hand. When the island's Governor arrives and enquires what has been stolen, Cynthia, "in a low, almost inaudible voice" replies "Only a rose."

So finishes a perfectly serviceable romance Plum could have written up in full had he wished to.

Ouida may have popularized the trend for exotic locations, but the desert romance received its most massive fillip in Plum's time courtesy of Edith M. Hull whose novel *The Sheik* [sic] was filmed in 1921 starring the dead-cert shoo-in for the role, Rudy Valentino. This is a problematic title for modern readers as the plot focuses on a headstrong young English woman, Diana Mayo, who falls in love with her abductor and serial rapist, Sheik Ahmed Ben Hassan. Back in the 1920s, this repellent theme doesn't appear to have been an obstacle to the book's success; far from it, in fact. Hull's central tenet, the redemption of a 'lost' male by the power of a woman's love, seems to have been justification enough for its readers to put any qualms aside and turn it into a bestseller.

Ahmed, who we later discover to be half English, is quite happy to continue Diana's sexual thraldom indefinitely until he 'breaks' her as he would a wayward colt (for he is also an expert horseman). On the way, he reveals himself as a devotee of the Ickenham system:

> "I am tired of holding an icicle in my arms," and sweeping her completely into his masterful grasp he covered her face with fierce, burning kisses.

The desired results arrive in pretty short order when, a little under halfway through the book, Diana rapturously declaims to herself:

> I love him! I love him! And I want his love more than anything in Heaven and earth!

Love having supplanted her initial anger, Diana rationalizes her impulsive change thus:

> She knew what her total submission meant: it was an end to all individualism, a complete self-abnegation, an absolute surrender to his wishes, his moods, and his temper. And she was content that it should be so, her love was pre-

pared to endure whatever he might put upon her. Nothing that he could do could alter that, and nothing should make her own her love. She had hidden it from him, and she would hide it from him – cost what it might. Though he did not love her, he wanted her still; she had read that in his eyes five minutes ago, and she was happy even for that.

Somewhat inevitably, Ahmed then falls in love with Diana when she is kidnapped by a rival sheik and whisked off even further into the desert. Only then does he realize he truly cares for her, launching a rescue mission in which he is badly injured. On his eventual recovery, he tells Diana he can't bear to mistreat her anymore, and that the time has come for her to return to England – alone – despite her protestations of love. At which she attempts to shoot herself, but Ahmed wrenches the gun from her hand and the book ends amid passionate protestations of mutual love.

Wodehouse gets more mileage out of *The Sheik* than we might at first suspect. In conversation with bestselling romantic novelist Raoul Saint Hubert, who happens to be The Sheik's best mate, Diana pointedly remarks how the *"preux chevalier"* only seems to exist in fiction, something Bertie Wooster might well agree with, even though it doesn't stop him using that very same epithet and trying to embrace that identical ideal in *The Code of the Woosters* and elsewhere (mind you, Ouida does introduce the phrase in *Under Two Flags* in connection with her 'Bertie' Cecil ("What a *preux chevalier!*" cried his Queen of Beauty. "You would have died in a ditch out of homage to me. Who shall say that chivalry is past!")

Other significant nods to *The Sheik* both arrive in 1924: in *Bill the Conqueror* we find Cooley Paradene's butler Roberts avidly consuming a novel entitled *Sand and Passion*, "a tale of desert love": and in the golf story 'Rodney Fails to Qualify', Jane Packard borrows Luella Periton Phipps's *The Love That Scorches* from the library and devours it late into the night, as she confides to the Oldest Member:

> "It is a very, very beautiful book. It is all about the desert and people riding on camels and a wonderful Arab chief with stern yet tender eyes and a girl called Angela and oases and dates and mirages, and all like that. There is a chapter where the Arab chief seizes the girl and clasps her in his arms and she feels his hot breath searing her face and he flings her on his horse and they ride off and all around was sand and night, and the mysterious stars […] I wish

mother would take me to Algiers next winter [...] It would do her rheumatism so much good."

This doesn't bode well for Jane's lover William Bates, who is not exactly a Sheiky kinda guy. So, necessity being the mother of invention, the O.M. advises him to propose to her while playing the sixth hole, to the left of whose fairway is an enormous, sandy bunker. Without explaining his reasoning, he adds that:

> "I have reason to believe that Jane would respond more readily to your wooing were it conducted in some vast sandy waste."

Such desert novels, the O.M. opines, only serve to "put ideas into girls' heads and [make] them dissatisfied"; and indeed, reading Ms. Periton Phipps's output serves only to put Jane in "a strange mood" until she comes to her senses at the story's close, fittingly up to her waist in the water feature on the seventh.

Realizing she was onto a good thing, Hull went on to publish further sand'n'sex escapades including *Camping in the Desert*, *The Captive of Sahara* and, somewhat inevitably, *The Sons of the Sheik* which featured Diana and Ahmed's twin offspring – and just as inevitably spawned a movie starring Valentino.

Our final globe-trotting romance arrives courtesy of the reclusive Ethel M. Dell, whose 1911 debut *The Way of an Eagle* is namechecked in Plum's 1949 novel *Uncle Dynamite* as an example of a bygone age of romance when, *Sheik*-like, men could subdue wayward women and bend them to their will. Bill Oakshott has his doubts when Uncle Fred proposes some old-school correction:

> "You will have to behave like the heroes of those novels which were so popular at one time, who went about in riding breeches and were not above giving the girl of their choice a couple with a hunting-crop on the spot where it would do most good. Ethel M. Dell. That's the name I was trying to think of. You must comport yourself like the hero of an Ethel M. Dell novel. Buy her works and study them diligently."

And the advice surprisingly bears fruit as the novel draws to its close:

> Hermione Bostock, as Bill having waggled her about,

clasped her to his bosom and showered kisses on her upturned face, felt that here was the man she had been looking for since she first read *The Way of an Eagle*.

Dell's novel begins *in medias res* out in one of the wilder sections of the
Indian frontier, as hero Nick 'The Eagle' Ratcliffe is charged by his
Brigadier – father of heroine Muriel Roscoe – to spirit his daughter
away from a border fort under ferocious siege by rebel forces. Muriel
is naturally reluctant to leave her father in such dire straits, so Nick is
forced to drug her into submission, heave her over his shoulder and carry her lifeless body ten miles over rough terrain to safety in an apparent
case of needs must:

> Light-footed and fearless, he passed through the midst of
> his enemies, marching with the sublime audacity of the
> dominant race, despising caution – yea, grinning trium-
> phant in the very face of Death.

But while Nick may be the acme of masculinity, Muriel is no pushover.
A spirited woman not unlike Diana Mayo, she is also blessed with somewhat softer susceptibilities:

> A daring sprite she had been, with a most fertile imagina-
> tion and a longing for adventure that had never been fully
> satisfied, possessing withal so tender and loving a heart that
> the very bees in the garden had been among her cherished
> friends.

A bit Madeline Bassett-y then; indeed, a certain Lord and Lady Bassett
are nominated her guardians when news of her father's death comes
through.

Fortunately, her less drippy side tends to predominate, and for most
of the novel we're in classic 'he loves her/she loves him but doesn't
know it yet' territory, as Muriel wrestles with her conflicting emotions
right down to the wire, convinced she knows her mind without actually
doing so. Nick, who has always been true in his love for her (and loses
an arm in her defence) turns out to be not just brave and masculine,
but sensitive, kind and funny too. And with only a few pages remaining,
and in a chapter titled "Surrender," Muriel finally does just that, despite
being "possessed by an insane desire to spring up and flee":

> She had fought her last battle, had made the final surren-

der. Her fear was dead. She stretched out her hands to him with unfaltering confidence.

"Take me then, Nick," she said.

Of course, that only results in a chaste kiss on the lips, while leaving us with the suggestion of something earthier.

Wodehouse was never so ambiguous, and his romantic heroines tend to know their own minds rather better than Dell's, being somewhat more proactive. But it's his Leading Romantic Males who deviate the most from the Dell template, tending with only a few exceptions towards the disinterested, confused or even downright timid. In 'The Purification of Rodney Spelvin,' the eponymous character is described as not being "one of those massive Ethel M. Dell libertines who might make things unpleasant for an intruder"; and *Bill the Conqueror*'s Bill West is also not to be classed among "Miss Ethel M. Dell's more virile heroes." Whereas in a Dell novel we're subconsciously urging the heroine to cast aside her reservations and let the hero love her, in a typical Wodehouse setup we're requiring the hero to get off his backside and do something – *anything* – to conquer his fear and lethargy. In *Money for Nothing*, the reticent John Carroll's hesitation is actually made worse by the romantic novels he seems to have read: if he does what his heart tells him to do, it's more than likely that his beloved Pat Wyvern will refuse him, saying something like "Oh, why must you spoil everything?"; and so John dares not take that risk. More of those two presently.

Back with Nick and Muriel, they resurface in Dell's 1915 sequel, *The Keeper of the Door*. By this time, they're married with a child and are considered by all and sundry to be the perfect couple. This novel proves a very different proposition to its predecessor, concerning itself not so much with war as euthanasia and the afterlife. But here once again we find a spunky heroine (Nick's niece Olga) who has to come to terms with the fact she might have murdered her best friend Violet even as she stoically resists the dubious charms of self-centred but oddly forceful surgeon Max Wyndham. In the end though, she naturally succumbs:

"Olga, you shall come to me! You shall! You shall!"
He caught her to him with the words, holding her mercilessly in a grip that was savage. She felt the hard, passionate beat of his heart against her own. And she gasped and gasped again, as one suddenly immersed in deep waters.

Plum had titled a short story with those two closing words five years earlier, serving to prove that both writers had a solid grasp of romantic clichés. Indeed, of all his possible sources for Rosie M. and her ilk, I think it's Dell's writing style that Plum is channelling most closely in the brief snatch of a Rosie novel he includes in 'Bingo and the Little Woman' when he directly quotes from *The Woman Who Braved All*:

> "What can prevail" – Millicent's eyes flashed as she faced the stern old man – "what can prevail against a pure and all-consuming love? Neither principalities nor powers, my lord, nor all the puny prohibitions of guardians and parents. I love your son, Lord Windermere, and nothing can keep us apart. Since time first began this love of ours was fated, and who are you to pit yourself against the decrees of Fate?"
>
> The earl looked at her keenly from beneath his bushy eyebrows.
>
> "Humph!" he said.

Just enough melodrama (Plum always loved a flashing eye), accompanied by five plosives that allow Millicent to spit out her contempt for Lord Windermere, whose portly figure is the major obstacle to her happiness. As in his lampoons of detective novels, Plum rarely parodies the romantic style of writing, presenting us instead with their titles, characters and plot synopses; but here we are treated to a tantalising glimpse of what might have been had he chosen to write in a different genre. And so it is we arrive at our third real-life romance writer to have 'M' as her middle initial – Ruby M. Ayres.

If her fellow M's were easier targets for Plum's satire with their penchants for melodrama and torrid prose, Ruby M was an excellent example of a more down-to-earth, jobbing *romancière*. A less flashy prose stylist than the previous two, Ayres was fabulously prolific, ending up with over 130 titles to her name, several of which were filmed. In a letter to Richard Usborne from 1955, Plum remarked that he "did have Ruby M. Ayres in mind for Rosie M. Banks. Not that I ever met her, but I wanted a name that would give a Ruby M. Ayres suggestion." Not that he necessarily admired her work: thirty years earlier, he had written to stepdaughter Leonora in high dudgeon when the editor of *Sunny* magazine proposed re-titling his *Sam the Sudden* as *Sunshine Sam* for serial publication in that heliocentric organ:

> Can you imagine such a foul title? Isn't it pure Ruby M. Ayres?

Nonetheless, Plum did see a way he could put her writing to good use, as he informed Bill Townend in July 1929:

> I've come to the conclusion that what I want for my next novel is a real Ruby M. Ayres basis – you know, the sort of plot that, treated seriously, would be a mushy love story. Then I can turn it into a comedy.

That novel was probably 1931's *Big Money*, in which Plum engineers a plot that sees just about everyone enamoured with a party they're not currently attached to: Godfrey Brent 'Biscuit' Biskerton is engaged to Ann Moon but loves Kitchie Valentine who is otherwise engaged; Berry Conway is ready with Ann's safety net should she change her mind, which is just as well because she prefers him to the Biscuit. Four central characters and two eventual marriages (plus one in the subplot between Lady Vera and 'Old Pop' Frisby) make this as much a riff on Shakespeare's comic plotting as Ruby M's; it's just that not being a *farceuse*, Ruby cuts down the cast of characters so she can foreground a single love affair/triangle and yes, treats things ever so seriously, making her hugely successful brand of romance ripe and ready for Wodehouse's 'comedification.'

Back in 1914's 'Parted Ways', Plum – who occasionally treats his readers to his personal take on literary history – remarks how very recently and abruptly, the British reading public's taste had turned on a sixpence, abandoning sex novels in favour of "good, sweet, wholesome, tender tales of the pure, simple love of a man for a maid which you could leave lying about" without fear of censure or scaring the servants. Or, of course, appearing frivolous in time of war. And it's at almost precisely this point in time that Ruby M first hit paydirt with her highly topical 1915 novel *Richard Chatterton, V. C.* [Victoria Cross] which managed to sell 50,000 copies in its first three years. The story of a slacker turned war hero who returns home injured to rescue his fiancée Sonia from the clutches of his caddish best friend, it is a classic love triangle lacking the exoticism and raciness of mesdames Ouida, Hull and Dell – which is the way Plum seemed to prefer things.

In among Ayres's other early output, 1920's *A Bachelor Husband* has the most significant number of Wodehouse parallels with its dialled-down melodrama and strong plot arc. It's once again the story of two men, one woman and a difficult choice. Marie-Celeste Chester has been in love with her adopted brother – the good-looking Christopher – since childhood. A solitary, surly type, he scarcely acknowledges her until one day he impulsively proposes. Marie is overjoyed and immediately accepts – a decision she quickly rues after the wedding when she discovers that Christopher has no intention of altering his distant behaviour towards her. The two lead separate lives (hence the novel's title) until Christopher's hulking friend Dakers, aka "Feathers" arrives on the scene, takes pity on Marie and slowly fills the vacuum left by Christopher's frequent absences, stealing his way into her heart without really meaning to. Like several of Plum's less prepossessing male romantic leads, he isn't particularly easy on the eye, but is strong, simple, honest, and above all kind. Early in their acquaintance, Feathers even performs that most Wodehousean of services when he saves Marie from drowning, administering life-saving resuscitation when she gets into difficulties in the sea. But whereas in Wodehouse the whole performance is usually a setup (usually by the male party) to inveigle his way into the female party's good graces or effect a reconciliation, here the incident occurs purely by chance and serves instead to draw Feathers and Marie closer together.

Other Wodehousean similarities include references to the poetry of Tennyson (*Maud* in this case), golf and palmistry. Ayres also creates a Knut-like character known only as Atkins or "young Atkins" whose opening words ("Awfully pleased to meet you [...] Shall we go and look on? Chris and Feathers are going to play pills [billiards]") are reminiscent of any number of Plum's Drones, members of the club he would invent the year after *A Bachelor Husband* first appeared. Ayres created a similar figure for her 1921 follow-up *Second Honeymoon*, raising the question of which writer might possibly have been influencing the other:

> Three months was a long time for Jimmy Challoner to be in love (as a rule, three days was the outside limit which he allowed himself), but this – well, this was the real thing at last – the real, romantic thing of which author chaps and playwright Johnnies wrote; the thing which sweeps a man clean off his feet and paints the world with rainbow tints.

How Wodehousean is that? The object of Jimmy's initial affections is even a chorus girl, as in so many of Plum's plots. But when all's said and done, it's in the whole, overarching package that Wodehouse and Ayres come to resemble one another: the less melodramatic (but still sloppy) language, the dialling down of the physical passion and the quotidien nature of the relationships all set them apart from those storytellers we've looked at thus far – at least, in Plum's more 'serious' encounters between his leading ladies and men.

This overlap would only last a short while, for the two writers were soon destined to drift part as Plum hit mid-season form. Until that point, around 1920 or so, the typical Wodehouse couple was almost a straight cut and paste from out of contemporary romances like Ayres's with just a few added comic touches. Take Ashe Marson and Joan Valentine from *Something Fresh*, *Uneasy Money*'s Bill Dawlish and Elizabeth Boyd, or Ann Chester and Jimmy Crocker in *Piccadilly Jim*, from 1915, 1916 and 1917 respectively. In Plum's later, less elaborate couplings, we're aware right from the start who is going to end up with whom, even if they're attached to someone else at the story's opening. For example, we know *Something Fishy*'s Stanhope Twine is never going to marry Jane Benedick because he has a comedy name and she doesn't, nor does her eventual husband Bill Hollister; and anyway, by this point in Plum's career we are assured that everything is destined to end happily for those characters he encourages us to care about. So despite Packy Franklyn being engaged to Lady Beatrice Bracken and Jane Opal to Blair Eggleston at the opening of *Hot Water*, we instantly know those partnerships will never last the course, for Blair is a modern novelist (a species Plum regularly derides) and Beatrice never smiles. Packy and Jane respectively deserve less narcissistic and jollier partners – and they get them.

Ashe and Joan, Ann and Jimmy, and Bill and Elizabeth are more troubling cases. Nothing is inevitable about their relationships, and there are quite knotty emotional obstacles to be overcome before they can pair off – not simply the opposition of a termagant aunt or uncooperative guardian that is comparatively easy to circumvent, or silly misunderstandings that can be cleared up in no time. Until a few lines from the end of her story, Joan is truly conflicted, a graduate of the school of hard knocks who has had to harden her heart against men – including Ashe; Jimmy really cuts Ann to the emotional quick when he demolishes her slim volume of poetry in print, and she has to dig deep in order to forgive him, a process not helped by his refusal to take her injury seriously; and unlike the cartoony Stanhope Twine whose loss Jane will scarcely register, Bill's Dawlish's first love Claire Fenwick turns out to be a truly unpleasant gold-digger, who nevertheless casts a powerful spell from which he must awake in order to find true happiness.

These early efforts are not so much the out-and-out comedic relationships of Plum's mature period as what we might call 'problem' relationships where he hasn't quite managed to tie up all the loose ends of his plot by the story's end. This can leave small, niggling doubts in the back of the reader's mind that work against the warm glow of the comedy, even down to Bill's evident discomfort marrying a wife who is significantly richer than him, the uncharacteristic impulsiveness of Joan's capitulation, or the anguish that Ann must still feel, even after her marriage, at being publicly shamed by her husband.

The path to happiness in Ruby M. Ayres's novels is likewise treacherous, only minus Plum's lightness. In *A Bachelor Husband*, Marie has to grow up and Chris grow a pair before they can truly come together, and it takes Feathers's tragic death to jolt them into facing up to their marital responsibilities. Marie awakes from her teenage crush on Chris, while he has an even longer journey from bachelordom to finally allowing someone to share his life and heart. Their reunion proceeds thus:

> "I've come back, Chris – if you want me."
> "If I want you!" He fell on his knees beside her, and his shaking arms closed fast about her.
> He had meant to try and explain so many times, and had planned so often in his mind what he would say to her, how he would humble himself and ask her forgiveness, but now that the time had come, there seem no need for any of it. Kisses and broken words, and the clasp of arms that had ached with loneliness and emptiness were more eloquent than the finest speech could have been.

Even mushier is the reunion that ends the long estrangement between Ayres's Jimmy Challoner and his child bride Christine at the close of *Second Honeymoon*:

> In a moment her arms were round his neck. She tried to draw his head down to her shoulder. Her sweet face was all concern and motherly tenderness as she kissed him and kissed him.
> "Don't, Jimmy – don't! Oh, I do love you – I do love you."
> She began to cry too, and they kissed and clung together like children who have quarrelled and are sorry.

This goes on for pages, but you get the idea. Now compare this with the ending of Plum's *Money for Nothing*, when John Carroll and Pat Wyvern come together in what is described as a "sacred" moment:

> "What were you thinking about me?"
> "Only that you were the most wonderful thing in the world."
> "Pat!"
> "You are, you know," said Pat, examining him gravely. "I don't know what it is about you, and I can't imagine why

I have been all these years finding it out, but you're the dearest, sweetest, most angelic . . ."
"Tell me more," said John.
He took her in his arms, and time stood still.
"Pat!" whispered John.

Plum's conclusion is a bit more adult and cool-headed – and decidedly shorter – but both his and Ayres's couples share an exhilarated sense of relief having weathered their emotional storms. Elsewhere (in *Money in the Bank*) Plum replicates Ayres's "motherly tenderness" when Anne Benedick kisses Jeff Miller back to consciousness after he's beaned with a stone tobacco jar, all the while regarding him "with the tender eyes of a mother."

What Plum's done here and elsewhere, exactly as he said he would to Bill Townend, is take Ruby M. and turn her particular brand of romance into a comedy. He couldn't satirize his already gloopy sources by making them any gloopier, so he does a 180 and actively defibrillates the language while using a battery of strategies to comedify the crucial 'coming together' moment. In *Doctor Sally*, Dr Sally Smith is actually monitoring her heart rate as she declares her love for Bill Bannister, noting it's considerably quickened. Or in *The Girl on the Boat*, when Sam Marlowe can't seal his successful proposal to Billie Bennett because his head's stuck in an uncooperative suit of armour. In 'Rodney Fails to Qualify', William and Jane pledge their love half immersed in a river, their persons festooned with eels and newts. Or again in the passage from *Money for Nothing* quoted above, in which a rogue bee crashes the scene as John is whispering sweet nothings to Pat, exploring the fleshy surface of his calf with a view to stinging him. To swat or not to swat? John decides now would not be a good time, silently concluding that "bee-stings were good for rheumatism."

Plum knew he could never compete with Ayres and her ilk; nor, with his sideways takes on *la ronde de l'amour*, did he have to. But he was clearly aware that just about all the world loves a lover, and that romance – and not necessarily sexed-up romance – sells to a surprisingly broad market. After all, even young, handsome men who should really be reading detective thrillers can encounter the elemental truth of a love story. As Sam Shotter discovers, actually being in love lowers his guard against the allure of gooey reading matter. As editor of the 'Aunt Ysobel' column in *Pyke's Home Companion* he has to wade through tons of the stuff, including Cordelia Blair's *Hearts Aflame* in which the far from flush Leslie Mordyke says to his lover "What does it matter? We have each other." The single, unattached Sam scribbles "Silly fool!" in the galley margin; but when his eventual partner Kay Derrick comes out with almost exactly the same words addressed to *him*, "he felt he had never heard anything not merely so beautiful but so thoroughly sensible, practical and inspired."

Such is the power of romance; and whether you favour their output or not, it can't be denied that the writers we've been looking at in this chapter all know their way around a gripping storyline despite being regarded by the highbrows as the Cinderellas of literature. And as Leila Yorke notes, the "inky pipsqueaks" who "do parodies of me, hoping to make me feel like a piece of cheese" have no effect on either her sales or sense of self-worth. "Love's all right," she concludes, "Makes the world go round, they say," before adding "I don't know if there's anything in it . . ."

And here as promised are Plum's Top 10 romantic relationships as voted by his readers:

10. Agnes Flack & Sidney McMurdo
    passim
9. Cuthbert Banks & Adeline Smethurst
    'The Clicking of Cuthbert'
8. George Bevan & Lady Maud Marshmoreton
    A Damsel in Distress
7. Jimmy Crocker & Ann Chester
    Piccadilly Jim
6. George Wooster & Maudie Wilberforce
    'Indian Summer of an Uncle'
5. Ronnie Fish & Sue Brown
    Summer Lightning
4. Ashe Marson & Joan Valentine
    Something Fresh
3. Bingo Little & Rosie M. Banks
    The Inimitable Jeeves
2. Madeline Bassett & Gussie Fink-Nottle
    Right Ho, Jeeves
And our winners are . . .
1. Psmith & Eve Halliday
    Leave it to Psmith

Although Eve is far from certain of her feelings until late on in their encounter, Psmith reaches his decision they are twin souls rather earlier – and not quite in his usual flippant manner. Indeed, when it comes, the moment they *both* pop the question is one of the most grown-up and touching in all of Wodehouse, with great feeling but zero melodrama, goo, gloop or treacle:

> "So you're going to be married?" said Eve.
> Psmith polished his monocle thoughtfully.
> "I think so," he said. "I think so. What do *you* think?"
> Eve regarded him steadfastly. Then she gave a little laugh.
> "Yes, I think so, too. Shall I tell you something?"
> "You could tell me nothing more wonderful than that."

And although there follows some nonsense about chicken giblets, the essential business of their wooing – and this chapter – has been satisfactorily concluded.

Chapter 7:
Whodunnit?

"Nothing in this modern life of ours," said Mr Mulliner,
"is more remarkable than the way in which the mystery novel has gripped the public. Your true enthusiast,
deprived of his favourite reading, will stop at nothing in
order to get it. He is like a victim of the drug habit when
withheld from cocaine."
Strychnine in the Soup

"I'm beginning to feel like the hero of an Edgar Wallace
novel – wondering which of you is the Strangling Terror
and which the Green-Eyed What-Not."
If I Were You

"I can always do with another corpse or two."
Jeeves in the Offing

I find now I can't read a book unless it has action.
Letter to Bill Townend, 1 August 1945

In the book world, the magicians are the
authors of literate detective stories.
Sinclair Lewis

In the Mr Mulliner story 'Strychnine in the Soup', Plum writes feelingly
of being forcibly parted from those we love:

> The subject of bereavement is one that has often been
> treated powerfully by poets […] But no poet has yet treat-
> ed of the most poignant bereavement of all – that of the
> man half-way through a detective story who finds himself
> at bedtime without the book.

Such appalling loss is experienced by Cyril Mulliner when he contrives
to leave his copy of Horace Slingsby's *Strychnine in the Soup* on the train as
he journeys up to Barkley Towers to tryst with fellow crime fanatic Amelia Bassett. How will he make it through the night? Cyril knows from
experience the exquisite torture he will face, his brain "lashing itself from

side to side like a wounded snake" as it feverishly speculates what the next plot twist might be. Will Inspector Mould escape from the underground den of the Faceless Fiend? Or will he suffer unspeakable tortures at the hands of his nemesis? An icy stream flows down the centre of Cyril's spine, the contents of his bedroom dancing before his fevered imagination. And so begins an unlikely chain of events as a copy of the book belonging to fellow crime fan Lady Bassett is stolen, passing from hand to hand until Cyril returns the tome to its rightful owner in return for her daughter's hand – permission she had hitherto withheld. At which point her ladyship reveals there is not one but *two* Faceless Fiends . . .

Although he regularly poked fun at it, Wodehouse himself had developed something of a crime addiction. One can so easily imagine him in the place of Bertie when, during a break in the frenetic action of 1938's *The Code of the Woosters*, he manages to settle down and curl up with a good mystery:

> A cheerful fire was burning in the grate, and to while away the time I pulled the armchair up and got out the mystery story I had brought with me from London. As my researches in it had already shown me, it was a particularly good one, full of crisp clues and meaty murders, and I was soon absorbed.

Bertie's preference is for a good old "goose-flesher," awash with tension and what he calls "significant passages" that render the reading experience satisfyingly immersive. Plum himself never tired of these close encounters, and indeed sneakily borrows the next part of *TCOTW*'s plot from a crime novel published the previous year by E. R. Punshon entitled *Mystery of Mr. Jessop*, in which a stolen diamond necklace is secreted on top of a tall cupboard. In Plum's version, Bertie is searching for a brown leather-covered notebook, and convinces himself that Punshon's fictional gumshoe is on to something:

> "That detective is no fool. If he says a thing is so, it is so. I have the utmost confidence in the fellow, and am prepared to follow his lead without question."

Suffice to say, life doesn't always resemble a detective novel, and a disappointed, empty-handed Bertie soon finds himself on top of his bedroom wardrobe, treed by the dog Bartholomew. By way of consolation, a few pages on in Punshon's book is a tirade against British fascist thuggery that quite clearly inspired Bertie's famous put-down of Roderick Spode, who he accuses of swanking around in footer bags looking like a perfect perisher.

Anyhow, when it came to Plum's leisure reading, crime was his go-to genre, showing even the classics a clean pair of heels when it came to his personal enjoyment. Comfortably into his 80s, he informed his friend Guy Bolton that having recently tried reading Jane Austen, who had bored him stiff, he greatly preferred the whodunnits of Patricia Wentworth. Looking at the entry for her 32 Miss Maud Silver novels in the excellent reference work *Killer Books: A Reader's Guide to Exploring the Popular World of Mystery and Suspense*, one can easily understand why he was so simpatico:

> Miss Silver is well known in the better circles of society, and she finds entree to the troubled households of the upper classes with little difficulty. In most of Miss Silver's cases there is a young couple whose romance seems ill fated because of the murder to be solved, but in Miss Silver's competent hands the case is solved, the young couple are exonerated, and all is right in this very traditional world.

Not only were Wentworth's setups reminiscent of his own, but her heroine also shared his passion for the poetry of Alfred, Lord Tennyson (see Chapter 10). In all, Plum borrowed 13 of her titles from the NYSL between 1951-55. Another of his favourites was Georgette Heyer, best known for her Regency romances but whose thrillers were graced with titles Plum himself would have been proud to invent, such as *Why Shoot a Butler?* and *A Blunt Instrument*, both of which he borrowed from the NYSL on February 23, 1954. To the end, he was forever exploring the genre, searching for new writers who would keep him guessing.

Crime and crime writing take many forms, and Wodehouse himself happily embraced all of them in his personal reading, and not a few in his writing. His debut novel *The Pothunters* had been built around a trophy heist, and Arthur Conan Doyle (whose work is examined in the following chapter) was among his earliest role models. Kidnapping, theft, blackmail, ringers and sometimes even guns would fuel many of his subsequent plots. Fast forward to the period of his greatest success and he was still chasing his crime fix. While working as a scriptwriter in Hollywood in 1930-31 and to some degree isolated from bookstores and libraries, he cannily befriended Will Cuppy, fellow humorist and author of the weekly 'Mystery and Adventure' column for the *New York Herald Tribune*, who had scores of review copies of the latest crime novels to distribute among his friends. Plum would shamelessly end his missives with suggestions for titles his friend could "shoot along," and Cuppy obligingly fenced at least two Dorothy L. Sayers novels that Plum eagerly devoured: *Strong Poison* (or possibly *The Documents in the Case*, both published in 1930) and *Five Red Herrings* (1931), gifts that prompted Plum to comment "how much better she is than almost all other mystery writers." And while his tolerance was clearly taxed by that second title ("It's a <u>lousy</u> story", he reported back to Cuppy), he remained on good terms with Sayers, with whom he regularly corresponded. Indeed, it was Sayers who revealed why it was, given that Plum was such a fan of literary crime, he had never attempted a murder mystery himself. Writing in her review column for the London *Sunday Times* in the early 1930s, she remembered:

> I once said idly to Mr. P. G. Wodehouse that, with his amazing knack of plot-spinning, he ought to be able to write a first-class detective story. His reply was to the effect that he had thought about it, but that to bring such exquisitely artificial creatures as Bertie Wooster and Jeeves into contact with real crime and real corpses would be an artistic error and throw the whole thing out of key. He was, of course, perfectly right.

As we'll see later in this chapter, Wodehouse's own work enjoyed a symbiotic relationship with that produced by the doyens of crime fiction, prompting one anonymous Crime Writers' Association member to confidently remark that Plum "cemented the idea that it was okay, and that it could be highly effective, to write a crime story comically." So we'll spend the next few pages quickly introducing a selection of these fans and friends, with whom he formed a sort of mutual admiration society.

Top of the tree is the world's bestselling author ever, Agatha Christie, who dedicated her 1969 detective novel *Hallowe'en Party* thus:

> *To P. G. Wodehouse*
> whose books and stories have
> brightened my life for many years.
> Also, to show my pleasure in his
> having been kind enough to tell
> me that he enjoys *my* books.

Which he assuredly did, an enthusiasm that survived an uncharacteristic outbreak of ill humour in 1955:

> I'm seething with fury. Sir Allen Lane of Penguin [...] told

me that Agatha Christie simply <u>loved</u> my stuff and I must write to her and tell her how much I liked hers. So with infinite sweat I wrote her a long gushing letter, and what comes back? About three lines, the sort of things you write to an unknown fan. 'So glad you have enjoyed my criminal adventures' – that sort of thing.

To add insult to injury, Christie confessed her favourite Wodehouse novel was *The Little Nugget*, a whiskery effort nearly 50 years old which Plum had clearly fallen out of love with. Nonetheless, he concluded, "one has got to go on reading her, because she is just about the only writer today who is readable."

Evidently, he had forgotten the two namechecks he received 20 years previously in Christie's 1936 Poirot yarn *Murder in Mesopotamia*. The first arrives in a description of Bill Coleman:

> As I stood on the platform hesitating and looking about me I saw a young man coming towards me. He had a round pink face, and really, in all my life, I have never seen any-one who seemed so exactly like a young man out of one of Mr. P. G. Wodehouse's books.

Coleman is a loquacious buzzer of the kind we met in Chapter 3, who at one point asks "Am I talking too much?" But beneath all his Drone-ish trappings is he all he seems? The book's narrator, Amy Leatheran, has her doubts:

> Right from the beginning I had thought Mr. Coleman's manner rather more like a P. G. Wodehouse book than like a real live young man. Had he really been playing a part all the time?

I shan't spoil the fun if you haven't read the book.

Late in life, Plum would emerge from his grump and the pair were all over each other like cats at a dog show, exchanging the occasional chatty letter touching on ill health, work routines and the iniquities of fans and publishers. In 1968, Christie sent Plum a first edition of *By the Pricking of my Thumbs*, inscribing it

> P. G. Wodehouse, Reverence, admiration and many long years of deeply enjoyed reading. No one like you! Agatha Christie

This particular volume, by the way, once belonged to the Rolling Stones' drummer Charlie Watts who could boast an impressive collection of Wodehouse first editions. Anyhoo, Christie's correspondence with Plum would continue until his death, but not before she had updated him on her considerable weight loss while recuperating from a heart attack:

> Only nuisance has been that slimmer hips has resulted in a tendency to lose my skirt when I cross a street. Have to be held together by safety pins.

She appropriately signed off what would be her final letter dated January 14, 1975, with "Goodbye for now and thanks for all the laughs." By the time of Plum's demise a month later, he had a collection of 17 Christie books in his library, and it is perhaps fitting that for a brief period during the previous year, effigies of Plum and the queen of crime were immediate neighbours in the London branch of Madame Tussauds [sic] wax museum.

In his fiction, Plum would occasionally drop Christie references that became more frequent the older he got. Mention of Hercule Poirot's "little grey cells" began as early as 1934's *Thank You, Jeeves* continuing until 1970's *The Girl in Blue*, and in *Cocktail Time* we learn how a bedridden Albert Peasmarch falls for Phoebe Wisdom as she reads him Christie stories while he convalesces. *Much Obliged, Jeeves* witnesses Bertie recommending an Agatha Christie "who-dun-it" as "always a safe bet" for leisure reading, and in *Aunts Aren't Gentlemen* he declares himself "never happier than when curled up with the latest Agatha Christie."

Next cab on the rank is another mighty global bestseller Edgar Wallace, who dedicated his 1925 releases *The Gaunt Stranger* and *A King by Night* "To My Friend P. G. Wodehouse," a compliment Plum reciprocated with the rather more formal "To Edgar Wallace" in the front of the UK edition of *Sam the Sudden* that same year. Wodehouse first mentions Wallace in his 1909 satirical novelette *The Swoop* as an intrepid newshound covering a fictional battle between the German and Russian armies for supremacy in England, who gets lost in a pea-souper fog and is unable to report on the action ("He was found two days later in an almost starving condition in Steeple Bumpstead").

So prolific was Wallace, his books would sometimes arrive at the Wodehouse household three at a time, as Plum reported in a letter to to his stepdaughter Leonora in 1924. One particular selection, which had been delivered that very morning, he pronounced "a dud and not worth reading", indicating he was either in the habit of instantly devouring Wallace's work hot from the postman or had been alerted by a damning review. He declared himself similarly disappointed with *On the Spot*, Wallace's stage drama based on the life of Al Capone, which it seems the author had sent him to peruse in advance of its opening. The play would launch the career of Charles Laughton and turn out to be Wallace's greatest theatrical success on both sides of the Atlantic, prompting Plum to sarcastically comment "So I seem to be a good picker" in a letter to novelist friend Denis Mackail.

Notwithstanding the occasional misfire, Plum appears to have greatly enjoyed Wallace's massive and varied oeuvre. In his essay 'Thrillers,' he ranked Wallace's Scotland Yard detectives the "best" in the business, and the two writers' relationship subsequently developed beyond correspondence. Wodehouse once spent the weekend *chez* Wallace and was most impressed on discovering his colleague "has a Rolls Royce for personal use and also a separate car for each of the five members of his family." He also employed two butlers, one on days, one on nights. And as Leonora revealed in an affectionate portrait of her stepfather in *Strand* magazine early in 1929:

> He writes in the afternoon, when he must on no account be disturbed. It is understood that he is thinking deep thoughts and planning great novels, but when all the smoke has cleared away it really means that he is either asleep or eating an apple and reading Edgar Wallace.

That same year, Plum's evident enthusiasm translated into a namecheck in the Jeeves and Wooster story 'A Spot of Art,' in which Lucius Pim dismisses Bertie from his presence thus:

> "And now perhaps you had better leave me. The doctor made a point of quiet and repose. Moreover, I want to go on with this story. The villain has just dropped a cobra down the heroine's chimney, and I must be at her side. It is impossible not to be thrilled by Edgar Wallace."

Unless of course you're a literary snob: in 1932's *Hot Water*, the haughty Lady Beatrice Bracken dismisses Packy Franklyn as a "Yahoo" (essentially a troglodyte) when he professes to have read Wallace's complete works – which is quite some claim, for this would prove the year of Wallace's untimely death aged 56, by which point it has been calculated that in addition to screen plays, poetry and historical non-fiction, he had managed to crank out 18 stage plays, over 170 novels and no fewer than 957 short stories. He had also recently written the screenplay for a movie that would soon see the light of day as *King Kong*.

But as one thriller writer handed in his dinner pail, so others would take his place on Plum's reading list. One dedication he would have treasured arrived courtesy of E. Phillips Oppenheim whose 1931 novel *Up the Ladder of Gold* was prefaced by:

To

My Friend

'PLUM' WODEHOUSE

Who tells me what I can scarcely believe,

that he enjoys my stories as much as I do his.

Prolific and already massively popular in Britain and the States, Oppenheim was noted for the complexity of his plots (which unlike Plum he mostly improvised), his easy-to-read-prose, and his love of a heart-warming ending which more often than not features a happy couple. You can see why Plum called him "the Old Reliable", a title he would use for one of his own novels some years later. He had cottoned on to the senior writer's work long before they met, referencing him as "E. Oppenheim le Curdler" the fictive author of the melodrama 'For Love or Honour' he wrote for the 'By the Way' column back in 1907. Plum's simple dedication to 1930's *Very Good, Jeeves* ("To E. PHILLIPS OPPEN-HEIM") arrived at a point when the two men had been dining companions, neighbours (in the south of France) and golf partners for nigh on a decade. Of his trips on the Oppenheim yacht, Plum wrote that "Opp was the perfect host" and in 1945 confessed that "I have always been devoted to Oppy."

And still they came. Somewhere along the way Plum had earned the gratitude of Leslie Charteris – creator of 'The Saint' – who would tip his hat in the front of the 1932 novel *Getaway*:

To P. G. Wodehouse who had time to say a word for the Saint stories, when he could have written them so much better himself.

Which chronology puts Plum among Simon Templar's earliest boosters, for the series only really gained traction in 1930's *Enter the Saint*, the character's second outing in book form. Essentially, Templar was Charteris's meal ticket, for he enjoyed little success with any of his other publishing ventures. By the time the character faced the final curtain over 50 years later over 100 titles had appeared, Charteris having sub-contracted the writing at around the time Roger Moore started his long-running TV portrayal of the character in 1962. In 1955, Charteris would risk Plum's ire when, without permission, one of the American magazines he had licensed to promote his own writing (*The Saint Detective Magazine*) disinterred Wodehouse's only real mystery ("and a perfectly lousy one") he had written for *Pearson's* back in 1914. We'll be examining 'The Harmonica Mystery' (aka 'The Education of Detective Oakes' and 'Death at the Excelsior') momentarily, but suffice to say, Plum was less than gruntled to find this unsuccessful experiment back in circulation and, evidently in his view, tarnishing his legacy.

Lastly, we have Anthony Berkeley's dedication "To P. G. Wodehouse" that graced the front of his 1937 yarn *Trial and Error*, in which a dying man commits a no-jury-would-convict murder of a truly unpleasant character, only to find that a wholly innocent person is suspected of the crime and he's unable to persuade the authorities of his guilt. Berkeley, of whose name I can find no trace whatever in Wodehouse, wrote under a variety of pseudonyms and was something of a literary chameleon. At the start of his career as a jobbing freelance, he wrote amusing sketches for *Punch*, and such humour as found its way into his crime novels was of a distinctly Wodehousean flavour. How about this from 1927's *Mr Priestley's Problem*?

> It appeared to him with sudden and unexpected force how remiss it was of him not to be a burglar. It was not playing the game. Here was this charming girl expecting to meet her burglar, never dreaming that she was doing anything else but meet her burglar; and there was Mr Priestley going about the place not being a burglar at all.

Even more Wodehousean (and, it has to be said, cringeworthy) was a parody Berkeley wrote in 1925 entitled 'Holmes and the Dasher', whose narrator 'Bertie Watson' describes his employer thus:

> Holmes certainly is the lad with the outsize brain; the fellow simply exudes intuition. The girl *was* a topnotcher. The way she sailed into our little sitting room reminded me of a ray of sunshine lighting up the good old Gorgonzola cheese.

It doesn't get any better, even when Berkeley cribs wholesale Bertie's "What ho!" routine with Motty Pershore from 'Jeeves and the Unbidden Guest.' As if that wasn't enough, awkward aunts feature in some of his plots (*Panic Party*, *The Piccadilly Murder*), and in *Trial and Error*, one of the lead characters is surnamed Todhunter, a possible reference to the distinctively named Hash of that ilk in *Sam the Sudden*. Perhaps an apology rather than that dedication would have been more in order.

This is not an exhaustive list of Wodehouse cross-references in criminal proceedings – others will pop up later in this chapter. But for now I will close this little canter with two more recent namechecks from massive sellers in the thriller genre, the first arriving in John Le Carré's 1993 novel, *The Night Manager*:

> "I say, Rex, you remember that personal top-secret and whatnot letter you sent me, to cover my rear end while your man Burr was staging his frolics in the West Country? For my very own file?" As usual, Padstow's lines could have been written by P. G. Wodehouse on a bad day.

Le Carré rarely lost an opportunity to plug Plum's work and proved one of his most loyal and reliable supporters until his death in 2020, remarking how he regularly picked up a Wodehouse to remind himself "what fun reading is," and elsewhere that "No library, however humble, is complete without its well-thumbed copy of *Right Ho, Jeeves*." Unfortunately Plum didn't reciprocate, judging 1965's *The Spy Who Came in From the Cold* to be so "LOUSY" he "couldn't get through it."

Wrapping up these mentions, I'll transport us to the opening lines of Ian Fleming's 1957 novel *From Russia with Love*, the fifth spy caper to feature über spy James Bond. The scene opens with an inventory of a man's personal effects as he sunbathes:

> To judge by the glittering pile, this had been, or was, a rich man. It contained the typical membership badges of the rich man's club – a money clip, made of a Mexican fifty-dollar piece and holding a substantial wad of banknotes, a well-used gold Dunhill lighter, an oval gold cigarette case with the wavy ridges and discreet turquoise button that means Fabergé, and the sort of novel a rich man pulls out of the bookcase to take into the garden – The Little Nugget – an old P. G. Wodehouse.

Coincidentally, it was the same Wodehouse title that Agatha Christie enjoyed so much, and a somewhat whimsical choice of reading matter for the Chief Executioner of SMERSH 'Red' Grant, alias Krassno Granitsky. But then, the original version of Plum's story (the 1912 *Captain* serial The Eighteen-Carat Kid') kicks off with a gunshot, a kidnapper and a private detective, marking one of Plum's few long-form attempts to muscle in on the thriller genre, albeit in the unlikely setting of a private school.

So what was it that drew Wodehouse and the *crème de la crème* of crime together, delighting in one another's writing? The short and obvious answer is a shared sense of humour. Plum didn't have to look far to find absurdity in either crime novels or thrillers, for crime is another of those genres – like romance – that regularly subverts its own seriousness, just as Plum subverts just about everything from his "cock-eyed" perspective as a humorist. Right up front on the title page, many of the best-known literary gumshoes, whether policemen, PIs or amateur sleuths, are victims of raw work at the font. In translation, Auguste Poirot is phonetically a leek (poireau), and the well-upholstered Inspector Maigret's surname is a play on the French *maigre* (thin). Then there are those with distinctive and/or preposterous handles, from Dickens's Inspector Bucket to J. K. Rowling's Cormoran Strike via Doyle's Sherlock Holmes and Sayers's Lord Peter Wimsey. And while the cases these characters investigate may be (quite literally) deadly serious, the eccentric choice of names tilts the atmosphere towards the ludic – literally so in the plots of E. R. Punshon's *Crossword Mystery* or Ngaio Marsh's *A Man Lay Dead* (both 1934). As readers, we're not compelled to engage on any emotional level with the crime victims, as they are the necessary collateral damage that allows us to join in the game of pitting our little grey cells against those of the resident sleuth. In such scenarios, humour can creep in without violating the studied seriousness of the situation; so while crime in and of itself isn't funny, its on-board solemnity is regularly subverted by, for example, Poirot's enervating self-regard, John Watson's utter literalness, Miss Marple's regular triumphs over those who patronize her, Nero Wolfe's obsession with food and beer, and so on. In *The Red House Mystery* – a rather good thriller written by Wodehouse's on/off friend (and creator of Winnie-the-Pooh) A. A. Milne – Bill Beverley finds it hard to think of Mark Ablett as an escaped murderer, since

> everything was going on just as it did yesterday, and the sun was shining […] How could you help feeling that this was not a real tragedy, but merely a jolly kind of detective game that he and Antony [Gillingham] were playing?

This playfulness is, I think, one of the things Plum found so attractive about the lighter, less forensic end of the crime genre. In *Uncle Dynamite*, he has Pongo Twistleton enhance the comic potential of Dorothy L. Sayers's debut *Whose Body?*, in which the corpse is discovered in a bathtub wearing only *pince-nez*, by the deft addition of a pair of spats. And the parodic titles he invented for thrillers in his fiction are in essence no more preposterous than many a real one. On his demise in 1975, *Patchwork of Death, Love Lies Bleeding, The Case of the Reckless Redhead*, and *The Swinger Who Swung By the Neck* could all be found in his personal library at Remsenburg, indicating that even in his later years he wasn't immune to such glorious nonsense.

To suit his satirical objectives, Wodehouse cast his net far and wide, randomly conflating detective fiction with related genres like thrillers, mysteries and even Enlightenment philosophy: in 1974's *Aunts Aren't Gentlemen* Bertie regrets interrupting Jeeves's reading of Spinoza "no doubt [...] just as Spinoza was on the point of solving the mystery of the headless body on the library floor." Starting out in 1906, and working on the principle that a writer "who curdles blood must first curdle his own," Plum had composed a short article for *Punch* imagining what it was like to be one of the more lurid crime novelists, handicapped by an overactive imagination as he goes about his everyday business:

> Took Tube. Lift-man sinister. Covered him with revolver from inside pocket. He must have noticed this, for he made no move. Got into train. Alone in carriage. On the alert for sudden attack from conductor (a sinister man). Emerged cautiously at Bank. Changed my disguise in secluded corner of subway. Took off spectacles and put on brown beard. Policeman at Mansion House crossing, I *think*, Anarchist.

The piece also contains some of Plum's earliest made-up crime titles, including *The Blood That Dripped on the Doormat* and *The Scream in the Lonely Wood*.

In 1914, Wodehouse decided he would try and be a crime writer for real, experimenting with 'The Education of Detective Oakes.' An improbable yarn complete with a German seaman, mouth organ, cat, and a victim of poisoning, it inhabits a tonal region somewhere between seriousness and parody; and while not "perfectly lousy" as Plum would later describe it (see above) it nevertheless suffers from its author's inability to commit to one perspective or the other. Here's the conundrum at the heart of the plot as described by Paul Snyder, the proprietor of a London detective agency, as he briefs the cocky young American operative he wants to bring down a peg or two:

> "In a Southampton boarding-house, in a room with a locked door, this man was stung by a cobra. To add a little mystification to the limpid simplicity of the affair, when

the door was opened there was no sign of any cobra. It couldn't have got out through the door, because the door was locked. It couldn't have got up the chimney, because there was no chimney. And it couldn't have got out of the window, because the window was too high up, and snakes can't jump. So there you have it."

Go figure. An explanation is forthcoming, not from the young gumshoe but courtesy of the deceased's elderly landlady; and while unlikely, it is no more preposterous than many another denouement in the genre. Although he managed to sell the story in both Britain and America (to *Pearson's* and *All-Story Cavalier Weekly* respectively), Plum was not sufficiently enamoured of his experiment to repeat it (although if he'd renamed the story 'Snakes Can't Jump' I reckon he might have been onto something).

It was about this time he hit on the idea of not so much writing about crime and detection as writing about writers who write *about* crime and detection, and the readers who read them. In stepping a further remove back from the story, he was creating a second layer of comic perspective in his dealings with the genre and could really let rip with his mickeytaking. In 1915's *Something Fresh* we are introduced to Ashe Marson, the novel's male lead, who works for a media combine with dozens of uncredited writers on its payroll who crank out crime by the yard:

> One of [The Mammoth Publishing Company's] many profitable ventures is a series of paper-covered tales of crime and adventure. It was here that Ashe found his niche. Those adventures of Gridley Quayle, Investigator, which are so popular with a certain section of the reading public, were his work.

That "reading public" includes Freddie Threepwood, who can be usually be found in the library of Blandings Castle engrossed in "a small paper-covered book" whose vivid red, black and yellow cover is decorated with "a tense moment in the lives of a man with a black beard, a man with a yellow beard, a man without any beard at all, and a young woman, who, at first sight, appeared to be all eyes and hair [...] Below this picture were the words, 'Hands up, you scoundrels!'" At which point we learn that Freddie "did not so much read as gulp" Ashe's story of the time Quayle took on The Secret Six. He had found nothing to pique his interest in the Classics placed before him at school or even in reading, period; but when bitten by the crime bug Freddie stays bit. "His was a dull life" we are told, "and Gridley Quayle was the only person who brought romance into it," the monthly instalments of the "Pluck Library" proving "oases" in his otherwise routine existence.

Eventually, Wodehouse World would be home to a sizeable cohort of fictional crime writers:

- In 'The Right Approach,' we meet Augustus Brattle, author of *Blood by the Bucketful* and *Death Takes the Cure*;
- Percy Gorringe moonlights as 'Rex West' in *Jeeves and the Feudal Spirit*, writing *The Mystery of the Pink Crayfish* and *Blood Will Tell*;
- *Joy in the Morning*'s 'Boko' Fittleworth is a successful producer of mystery thriller plays and "wholesome fiction for the masses";
- John Gooch of 'For Those in Peril on the Tee' authors *The Mystery of the Severed Ear* and a promised series of stories about 'Madeline Monk, Murderess';
- 'Honeysuckle Cottage' features James Rodman, who cranks out three sensational mysteries and 18 short stories annually;
- Jerry Vail, the male lead in *Pigs Have Wings* is a thriller writer;
- Rodney Spelvin, an occasional apparition in Plum's golf stories, can push out "a couple of thousand words of wholesome blood-stained fiction each morning before breakfast";
- Corky Corcoran (*Ukridge* stories *passim*) earns a crust as a tour guide of London's grisliest murders in 'The Return of Battling Billson';
- And bringing up the rear we have Horatio Slingsby, author of 'Strychnine in the Soup.'

Note that all these writers are men: Plum wouldn't create a female thriller writer until Adela (*Blackness at Night*) Cream in 1960's *Jeeves in the Offing*, despite the fact that many of his favourite authors in the genre were women.

Having created so many crime writers, it's perhaps surprising Plum was rarely tempted to write direct parodies of the pulp style, despite being perfectly capable of doing so. In 'Honeysuckle Cottage,' he includes a few intriguing lines from James Rodman's forthcoming novel *The Secret Nine*:

For an instant Lester Gage thought that he must have been mistaken. Then the noise came again, faint but unmistakable – a soft scratching on the outer panel.

His mouth set in a grim line. Silently, like a panther, he made one quick step to the desk, noiselessly opened a drawer, drew out his automatic. After that affair of the poisoned needle, he was taking no chances. Still in dead silence, he tiptoed to the door; then, flinging it suddenly open, he stood there, his weapon poised.

You get the feeling that by this golden period in his career (1925), Wodehouse could have tossed off a comic thriller as easy as breathing, complete with a consistent satiric edge he hadn't managed to sustain in 'The Education of Detective Oakes.' "The Secret Nine" was a reference to *The Nine Unknown*, a 1923 novel by Talbot Mundy, a Brit who had crossed the Pond, where his work was picked up by pulps such as *Adventure*, *Argosy* and *Cavalier* magazines. A confirmed Theosophist like Plum's elder brother Armine, Mundy's later work inclined to the esoteric, and The Secret Nine themselves were the guardians of the nine books of arcane knowledge that would create havoc were they to fall into the wrong hands. It's easy to imagine how such a plot would appeal to a writer who in *Something Fresh* had already created "the wand of death" ("the sacred ebony stick stolen from the Indian temple which is supposed to bring death to whoever possesses it"); and indeed The Secret Nine were destined to reappear in 'The Come-back of Battling Billson,' *The Mating Season, Much Obliged, Jeeves*, and in Plum's very last, unfinished novel *Sunset at Blandings* in which it is speculated that Blandings may be the organization's secret HQ.

In a chapter from his 1934 collection *Louder and Funnier* entitled 'Thrillers,' Plum lets us know quite how besotted he had become with crime writing of all kinds and levels of accomplishment. Noting how a "flood of Mystery Thrillers has engulfed the British Isles," he goes on to comment how "[t]here seems to be some virus in the human system just now which causes the best of writers to turn out thrillers" before adding that "the worst of writers […] turn them out, too." For even as Plum was cresting his mid-season form, what was already being referred to as the "Golden Age" of British crime writing was also in full swing. Listing his favourites, he includes all the authors we've already examined in this chapter, adding H. C. Bailey, creator of surgeon sleuth Reggie Fortune and sanctimonious lawyer Joshua Clunk; and Philip Macdonald, whose amateur detective Anthony Ruthven Gethryn is *so* suave and accomplished he makes Lord Peter Wimsey look like a slob. Joining these favourites were a couple of dozen others who had given over their literary talents to the dark side, including former journalists, solicitors, clerics, bank managers and academics who had blossomed into crime writers.

Wodehouse was right: everyone *was* at it. But what this article reflects even as he's chasing laughs is the perennial tension between freshness and formula in popular fiction. The detective genre was particularly conservative, and in 1929 Ronald Knox – theologian by day, crime writer and Wodehouse fan by night – drew up the "Ten Commandments" of the genre to ensure fair play in the battle of wits between writer and reader. Not to be outdone, Plum added a few recommendations of his own, starting with what in his opinion was the very worst failings of the modern crime yarn: that "ninety-six out of every hundred [thrillers] contain a heroine and a love-story"; and that said heroine "is almost never a very intelligent girl," one who will obligingly obey unsigned notes mysteriously delivered at half-past two in the morning saying 'Come at once!'

We've already encountered the problematic interface between romance and thrillers in the previous chapter, when in 'Honeysuckle Cottage' James Rodman ponders how

> [h]eroines only held up the action and tried to flirt with the hero when he should have been busy looking for clues, and then went and let the villain kidnap them by some childishly simple trick.

So troublesome heroines are most definitely out. Which should have (but seemingly didn't) kill Plum's enjoyment of Dorothy L. Sayers's later novels, in which Wimsey woos Harriet Vane glacially slowly to the accompaniment of quotes from Jacobean poets and philosophers; and also Philip Macdonald's Gethryn, who falls for young widow Lucia Lemesurier in 1924's *The Rasp* and spouts stuff like "What is it that has made me mad? It is you, you, you! You – your face, your body, all the unbelievable wonder of you!" before raining hot, burning kisses on her wrists.

Rule 2 in Plum's list concerns those baddies who fail to understand that murder is simplicity itself. You or I would most likely get a gun, fire it in the direction of the intended victim, and Bob would efficiently cease to be our uncle. But not the villain of Plum's imaginary thriller 'The Murglow Manor Mystery' who, in planning to dispose of Sir Geoffrey Tuttle, Bart., puts his professional knowledge of plumbing to imaginative use:

> "[H]e fastened a snake in the nozzle of the shower-bath
> with glue; and when Sir Geoffrey turned on the stream the
> hot water melted the glue. This released the snake, which
> dropped through one of the holes, bit the Baronet in the
> leg, and disappeared down the waste pipe."

Here, Plum was poking good-natured fun at Conan Doyle's snakey Sherlock Holmes mystery 'The Speckled Band,' as well as the widespread 'impossible crime'/'locked room' tropes that fuelled many a Golden Age crime plot (and his own 'The Education of Detective Oakes'). If villains would only keep their imaginations in check, he griped, everyone would benefit. But no: if called on to kill a fly, the typical malefactor's natural impulse would be to

> saw away the supports of the floor, tie a string across the
> doorway, and then send the fly an anonymous letter urging
> it to come at once in order to hear of something to its advantage. The idea being that it would hurry to the room,
> trip over the string, fall on the floor, tumble into the depths,
> and break its neck.

Such Heath Robinson ingenuity is usually self-defeating and is described by H. C. Bailey's sleuth Reggie Fortune in 'The Quiet Lady' as the villain's "[d]esire to show what a wonderful fellow he is. To prove his power over people's lives. Some fellows will do anything for that." Anything, that is, short of reaching for a rolled-up newspaper.

Plum's third and fourth Rules focus on the rules themselves, their proliferation and application. Crime fans and writers, as befitting those who crave reasoned exposition, tend to favour precedent and proper procedure. So at almost exactly the same time Ronald Knox's 10 cardinal directives for crime writing appeared in 1929, the American avant-garde art critic Willard Huntington Wright (who as S. S. Van Dine created the sleuth Philo Vance) upped the ante with no fewer than 20. In a wonderfully tangential way, Plum makes the point that this insistence on convention gives the writer less and less narrative space to work *inside*, ultimately leading to repetition and a yawning reader saying "What of it?" when informed there's a dead body in the library:

> He has known so many libraries, you see – such hundreds
> and hundreds of libraries, and all with corpses in them
> [...] He has grown to expect corpses in libraries.

And in the plots of myriad country house murders (which we'll start examining soon) the library *does* traditionally double as the crime scene and the rendezvous for the villain's unmasking. Indeed, in Agatha Christie's *Hallowe'en Party* which contained the dedication to Plum, the body of a young child is discovered in the library, drowned while bobbing for apples.

Now Plum was as much a sucker for a good old-fashioned murder-at-the-manor as anyone else, remarking to Will Cuppy that "there ought to be a law that all mystery stories should have an English setting" and, moreover, "ought to take place only in old English country-houses." On the other hand, the entire thesis of his 'Thrillers' article proposes that abiding by the rules makes things too easy:

> The reader knows it wasn't the hero or heroine who did the murder. He is practically sure it couldn't have been Reggie Banks, because he is a comic character and any vestige of humour in any character in a mystery story automatically rules him out as a potential criminal. It can't have been Uncle Joe, because he is explicitly stated to be kind to dogs. And he naturally rules out any hysterical governesses and brooding butlers, because their behaviour throughout has been so suspicious as to clear them from the start.

Sometimes, then, you could guess whodunnit by a simple process of elimination.

But not all writers were that predictable. More than any other aspect of Agatha Christie's writing, I feel it's her perennial ability to wrong-foot the reader that kept Plum loyal. Even at the very start of her career, she appears to have realized how easy it was to get tangled up in the abundance of 'tradition' that had already accreted in a genre that was still in its comparative infancy. Rules were made to be broken, and in her 1920 debut *The Mysterious Affair at Styles* she started as she meant to go on [SPOILER ALERT] by introducing an unfamiliar plot rhythm: putting her lead suspect in the frame, then having him ruled out, before revealing him as the murderer at the story's close. In 'Thrillers' Plum points out that in her sixth outing *The Murder of Roger Ackroyd*, she had famously cast the novel's narrator Doctor James Sheppard as the murderer, while using omission and evasion to prevent him writing anything that would prove untrue. From that point on, Plum comments, the reader has been unable to trust any character in a crime novel, and it was "very lucky for Doctor Watson that he belonged to the pre-Christie era." Indeed, only two years after Plum published his essay Christie would discombobulate the readers of *Murder on the Orient Express* [AN-OTHER SPOILER ALERT] by having no fewer than 12 murderers. Playing keep-up, he proposed his own "big sensation":

> I would not have the crime committed by anybody in the book at all.

Why not, he suggests, have the publishers, the printers or the book's dedicatee do it? "That would be something of a punch," he claims.

Unfortunately, it's in the central figure of the detective where the writer's options for change are even more limited: "[t]ry to deviate from the type," he advises, "and you only find yourself in trouble." There seems to be just three stock figures from which a writer can choose:

- The "dry" elderly fusspot who sweats the smallest stuff ("rather a bore");
- The "dull" expert who relies on specialist knowledge to get where he's going ("avoid this man"); and
- "The Effervescent," a flippant young man-about-town of independent means who despite his amateur standing and goofy mannerisms is able to show the regular plod a thing or two.

Plum's verdict on that last type? "Not a frightfully attractive young man. But spreading, I regret to say. You meet him everywhere nowadays."

Which was not only true but partly his fault, given how much cross-pollination there seems to have been between these "Tony Dalrymples" (as Plum nicknames them) and certain of his own Eggs, Beans and Crumpets. Here, he has one perfunctorily examine the victim:

> "So this is the jolly old corpse is it, Inspector? Well, well, well! Bean bashed in and a bit of no-good done to the merry old jugular, what? Tut, tut, mother won't like this at all. You're on to the fact that the merchant who messed this cove up was left-handed and parted his hair in the middle, of course?"

Among the 'Golden Age' sleuths, the most obvious debt to the Drones is Sayers's Lord Peter Wimsey, whose debut has him babbling remarkably like an early version of Bertie when that *pince-nez*-clad corpse noted earlier is discovered in the bathtub:

"I'm sure it must have been uncommonly distressin'," said Lord Peter, sympathetically, "especially comin' like that before breakfast. Hate anything tiresome happenin' before breakfast. Takes a man at such a confounded disadvantage, what?"

As an amateur detective, it is all part of Wimsey's schtick to be *thought* a silly ass, whereas Bertie actually *is* one. Although both are men-about-town, wealthy bachelors, apartment-dwellers in London's Mayfair and have gifted and devoted manservants, there's far more to Wimsey than first meets the eye. Prior to his encounter with the corpse, he instructs his man Bunter to dep for him at a rare books auction where a Folio Dante and one or two other prized collectors' items are under the hammer. Indeed, later in the novel we discover Wimsey's breadth of reading mirrors that of Wodehouse. He can even discuss the "frightfully deep-looking books" lurking on his shelves while enthusing over "clinking good love stories and detective stories":

> Lord Peter had a funny way of talking about books [...] as if the author had confided in him beforehand, and told him how the story was put together, and which bit was written first.

At the close of 1935's *Gaudy Night* it becomes clear he enjoys a similar relationship with music. So not such a silly ass, then.

The association with Bertie was one Sayers was keen, and possibly even proud, to encourage. In *Unnatural Death* from 1927, she writes of Wimsey that "His jaw slackened, giving his long narrow face a faintly foolish and hesitant look, reminiscent of the heroes of Mr. P. G. Wodehouse." And in 1933's *Murder Must Advertise* Wimsey goes undercover at a London agency such that his new colleagues describe him as being "like Bertie Wooster in horn-rims." As time went by, however, Sayers's beloved creation pivoted towards his more serious side, as he fell for the intellectual charms of Harriet Vane, accused of murdering her former lover in *Strong Poison*. At the pair's first meeting, Wimsey has never been more Woosterish:

> "You are Lord Peter Wimsey, I believe, and have come from Mr Crofts."
> "Yes. Yes. I – er – I heard the case, and all that, and – er – I thought there might be something I could do, don't you know."

"That was very good of you."

"Not at all, not at all. Dash it! I mean to say, I rather enjoy investigating things, if you know what I mean."

As the relationship slowly blossoms, so Wimsey loses the Wodehousean mannerisms to the point where post-marriage, in 1937's *Busman's Honeymoon*, the high cultural tone has become annoyingly pretentious.

But the traffic between Sayers and Wodehouse wasn't all one way. In 'Strychnine in the Soup,' Cyril Mulliner's wooing of Amelia Bassett is considerably boosted by his acquaintance with Wimsey's creator:

> From the moment he told Amelia that he had once met Dorothy Sayers, he never looked back.

Similarly in 'Trouble Down at Tudsleigh,' Wimsey is flatteringly name-checked alongside Sherlock Holmes, and the two authors' friendship blossomed to the point where Sayers invited Plum to a dinner with the Detection Club, a loose association of crime and mystery writers of which she was a founder member. So although Plum couldn't abide the fiendish but dull plot of her *Five Red Herrings* (the solution to which is buried deep within a set of Scottish railway timetables), that small hiccup seems not to have interfered with the mutual admiration that existed between two of the 20th century's ablest wielders of the written word. And in case Jeeves feels a little left out of this lovefest, here's a nod in his direction from Sayers's *Strong Poison* in which Bunter gets ahead of the game:

> "Pardon me, my Lord, the possibility had already presented itself to my mind."
>
> "It had?"
>
> "Yes, my Lord."
>
> "Do you never overlook anything, Bunter?"
>
> "I endeavour to give satisfaction, my Lord."
>
> "Well then, don't talk like Jeeves. It irritates me."

But it isn't simply Wimsey's studied oafishness and Bunter's efficiency that Sayers borrows from Wodehouse; it's the overall lightness of the tone and atmosphere of her early novels that owes him a considerable debt, combined with a shared bookishness that inevitably resulted from both authors' broad appreciation of literature. Although Sayers was not writing comedy, the comedic instinct she shares with Wodehouse is nevertheless usually present, even in the later, more serious Wimsey stories.

And it's here we can introduce another exceptional crime writer whose work not only possessed an almost identical sensibility but also mirrored Sayers's literary trajectory from the facetious to the serious.

Margery Allingham is best known for her novels featuring Albert Campion, a Bertie-esque character who first appeared in a supporting role in 1929's *The Crime at Black Dudley* where he is erroneously described as "quite inoffensive, just a silly ass." While giving a convincing impersonation of being mentally negligible, it quickly becomes apparent he is nothing of the sort, a kind of mystery man whose depths Allingham never satisfactorily reveals over the course of the 19 novels and 20 stories in which he appears. The possessor of "foolish, pale blue eyes" and a "slightly receding chin and mouth," he would pass unnoticed in the Drones Club, yet somehow ends up an eminent intelligence veteran 37 years later. His first-ever words, which include "I knew a fellow once who, when he went to bed, made a point of taking everything off first before he removed his topper" do little to dispel this aura of gormlessness; yet as the novel progresses, prior to his final disappearance through the doors of "one of the most famous and exclusive clubs in the world," Campion proves time and again that appearances can be deceptive.

Breaking out of a country house where he and his companions have been imprisoned and threatened with death by the villainous Eberhard von Faber, Campion capably takes on the role of strategist, even contriving to sound a bit like Psmith, or indeed any of Wodehouse's young male gabblers (see Chapter 3) as he directs operations:

> "While you're gathering up the wreckage I'll toddle round to find Poppa von Faber, and on my way back after the argument I'll call in for the girls, and we'll all make our final exit *en masse*. Dignity, Gentlemen, and British Boyhood's Well-known Bravery, Coolness, and Distinction are the passwords of the hour."

At which point one of his confederates demands "Do you always talk bilge?"; to which Campion replies "No [...] but I learnt the language reading advertisements." This is perhaps a sly dig at Sayers, who at the time of writing was nearing the end of her employment at Benson's advertising agency. But there's no denying the influence of both Plum and Sayers on Allingham, who had grown up in in a household full of writers and writing. As she noted in her introduction to the 1934 Campion caper *Death of a Ghost*, her lead sleuth tended to involve himself in both "grave" and more amusing, "frankly picaresque" plotlines. The latter, as the Allingham Society informs us, are written in "a blithe, easy style reminiscent of P. G. Wodehouse", and perhaps the most evident example of this lightness can be found in Campion's ninth outing, 1937's *The Case of the Late Pig*, in which he assumes the narrator's role with typical brio:

> The main thing to remember in autobiography, I have always thought, is not to let any damned modesty creep in to spoil the story. This adventure is mine, Albert Campion's, and I am fairly certain that I was pretty nearly brilliant in it in spite of the fact that I so nearly got myself and old Lugg [his valet] killed that I hear a harp quintet whenever I consider it.
> It begins with me eating in bed.

And so begins a tale that Wodehouse could very possibly have written had he been so minded. It even concludes with at least one engagement ("Happy endings and, er, all that") – although the 'Pig' of the title is two-legged and no relative of the Empress.

As the king of English comic writing throughout the 1920s and '30s, the Golden Age authors we've been looking at in this chapter would have found it almost impossible to avoid Wodehouse's gravitational pull, particularly if they were aiming to hit a more spirited and mischievous tone in their treatment of crime and detection. But it's to Agatha Christie that we must return for our most comprehensive evocation of the Wodehousean spirit, and in particular her 1925 novel *The Secret of Chimneys*, the first of five adventures to feature one of her lesser-known sleuths, Superintendent Battle, and a tale very much at odds with the more serious tone of her debut only five years before.

As in many a Wodehouse novel, the story begins in London before its cast of characters is quickly decanted into a country house ('Chimneys') whose castellan Lord Caterham is more than a little reminiscent of Lord Emsworth. "Shabbily dressed," patronized by those of an officious and pernickety tendency (including a "redoubtable" sister-in-law), eager to avoid his hereditary duties whenever feasible, and with a distinct preference for those who refuse to toe the official line, he could be Clarence's twin brother without being quite so fatheaded. Top of his list of blisters is George Lomax, a bossy Rupert Baxter-like presence who works for the government and has requisitioned Chimneys for a clandestine meeting with the presumed heir to the throne of Herzoslovakia. There are also imposters (I think I counted five in eight different disguises), not to mention a packet of stolen letters and a massive, missing diamond. Lomax's factotum, Bill Eversleigh is the very model of a Drone, aged around 25, large, ungainly, nice-but-dim and also a scratch golfer. Then we meet Lord Caterham's jolly-hockey-sticks 'it-girl' daughter Eileen 'Bundle' Brent and the young and merry widow Virginia Revel, both of them fun, forthright, independent-minded and very similar in conception to Plum's feistier single women. Superintendent Battle moves noiselessly from place to place in the manner of Jeeves, as does Hiram P. Fish, an American detective working undercover as a collector of first editions. Anthony Cade, the story's smooth male lead, is possessed of the breezy, flippant persiflage of a Wodehouse blood, and were it not for two murders and the heavy emphasis on solving crime we could be forgiven for thinking this actually *was* a P. G. Wodehouse production. There's even a happy ending that includes a marriage.

Wodehouse would comfortably outlive the Golden Age of British detective fiction, continuing to read it long after it passed from fashion. Allingham, Wallace, Sayers, and Christie were well represented among the many books he borrowed from the NYSL between 1951-55 (which included *The Secret of Chimneys*), but king of the hill with 17 loans was a writer we haven't yet encountered but who in many ways represented Plum's acme of literary excellence.

Rex Stout, like so many of his colleagues, was a Wodehouse fan with whom Plum enjoyed a warm and friendly correspondence. Describing him as "witty, wise and wonderful," Stout mourned his friend thus in 1975, the year of his own death:

> He always used the right words, and nearly always used them well. As an entertainer he was unsurpassed. While apparently being merely playful he often made acute and subtle comments about human character and behavior.

The quotation is taken from Stout's own biography, written by John McAleer, for which Plum provided an introduction with the following wholehearted endorsement:

> Nobody who claims to be a competent critic can say that Rex Stout does not write well. His narrative and dialogue could not be improved, and he passes the supreme test of being rereadable. I don't know how many times I have reread the Nero Wolfe stories, but plenty. I know exactly what is coming and how it is all going to end, but it doesn't matter. That's *writing.*

Quite the meeting of minds (and talents) then; and as with the other crime writers Plum admired, plugs were generously forthcoming in his novels. In *Much Obliged, Jeeves* a befuddled Bertie longs for a spot of re-laxation curled up with a thriller:

> I headed for the drawing-room, hoping for another quiet
> go at the Rex Stout which the swirling rush of events had
> forced me to abandon.

Unfortunately his Aunt Dahlia has beaten him to it, and, sprawled on the chaise longue with the title in her grasp, he knows he has "small chance of wresting it from her," for "[n]o one who has got his or her hooks on a Rex Stout lightly lets it go." As she registers his presence, he notes "a trace of annoyance in her demeanour" for she has just got to the part where "Nero Wolfe had come down from the orchid room and told Archie Goodwin to phone Saul Panzar [sic] and Orrie what's his name and things were starting to warm up." *The Girl in Blue* witnesses Willoughby Scrope engrossed in a Stout, and in *Aunts Aren't Gentlemen* we witness Bertie borrowing one of Nero Wolfe's regular ejaculations, "Pfui!"

The Wolfe chronicles, which comprise the bulk of Stout's output, would eventually number 33 novels and 41 shorter stories written be-tween 1934 and 1975. It's probably safe to assume that Plum would have read most if not all of them: in his personal library, there is a copy of *The Doorbell Rang* that has a number of pencil ticks against the titles of other Wolfe novels listed in the back of the book, inventory style; and he borrowed 16 Stout titles from the NYSL between 1951 and 1955. Had he read the stories in chronological order, he would have noticed how from the very first (*Fer de Lance,* named for a variety of poisonous snake that features in the plot) Wolfe's world had sprung from Stout's imagination enviably complete in just about all respects. Although the Bertie and Jeeves fictional universe had come together relatively quickly, Wolfe and his compadres had hit the ground running, with details from past cases casually strewn around that opening storyline as if the team had already been in business for years. Moreover, Wolfe's world, and the formulas and tropes that oil its wheels, are even more circumscribed than those that govern Bertie's.

For a start, the morbidly obese Wolfe only leaves his luxurious brownstone on West 35th Street NYC when absolutely necessary, del-egating the considerable leg work his cases entail to point man Archie Goodwin, who also takes on the job of compiling and narrating the stories. Aged 56 and weighing in at 272 lbs or 123 kilos ("one-seventh of a ton," we are told), Wolfe controls operations from his custom-built reinforced chair while doubling as a gourmet and an expert on rare orchids, once again employing staff to service these passions. His daily routine is strict, and for the most part inviolable. Which makes it a *very* small world, but one that repays regular visits. When cocooned in its extreme familiarity and even cosiness, the plots – despite being taut and well crafted – tend to play second fiddle to the stories' atmosphere.

It's an atmosphere that could have been tailor-made for Wodehouse, for it has elements of both the traditional English country house mystery and the American pulp thriller he seems to have adored equally. These parallel genres are brought to life in the speech patterns of the two leads which are, as with almost everything else, present and correct right at the start of the saga. Wolfe, in the words of one appreciative critic, "talks in a way that no human being on the face of the earth has ever spoken, with the possible exception of Rex Stout after he had a gin and tonic." His vocabulary may be rococo, but his grammar and syntax are consistently complex and formal to the point of fastidiousness – he refuses to say "ad" when "advertisement" will do, and in *Gambit* he sets fire to his copy of *Webster's New International Dictionary* (Unabridged, Third Edition) because it contains what he considers an inaccurate definition which "threatens the integrity of the English language." Get him on the subject of food, and this happens:

> "I have eaten *Tripe a la mode de Caen* at Pharamond's in Paris. It is superb, but no more so than Creole Tripe, which is less apt to stop the gullet without an excess of wine. I have eaten *bouillabaisse* at Marseilles, its cradle and its temple, in my youth, when I was easier to move, and it is mere belly-fodder, ballast for a stevedore, compared with its namesake at New Orleans!"

In the introduction to *Too Many Cooks*, Archie feels the need to apologize for his employer's fancy way of speaking:

> I used as few French and miscellaneous fancy words as possible in writing up this stunt of Nero Wolfe's but I couldn't keep them out altogether, on account of the kind of people involved. I am not responsible for the spelling, so don't write me about mistakes. Wolfe refused to help me out on it, and I had to go to the Heinemann School of Languages and pay a professor 30 bucks to go over it and fix it up. In most cases, during these events, when anyone said anything which for me was only a noise, I have either let it

lay – when it wasn't vital – or managed somehow to get the rough idea in the American language.

By contrast, Archie is more the blunt, wisecracking Sam Spade with a nice line in American slang, but also, as more than one critic has remarked, the occasional comedic overlay worthy of Bertie, as in the following, which very nearly works just as well in a Woosterish accent as that of the tough but clearly intelligent gumshoe:

> Durkin was all right up to the neck. When I consider how thick he was in most respects I am surprised how he could tail. I know bull terriers are dumb, but good tailing means a lot more than just hanging on, and Fred Durkin was good. I asked him once how he did it, and he said, "I just go up to the subject and ask him where he's headed for, and then if I lose him I know where to look." I suppose he knew how funny that was.

As narrators, both Bertie and Goodwin punch well above their intellectual weight, and the latter can easily hold his own with his loquacious employer when their relationship turns adversarial, as in the following exchange:

> **Wolfe**: "Your errand at White Plains was in essence a primitive business enterprise: an offer to exchange something for something else. If Mr. Anderson had only been there he would probably have seen it so. It may yet materialize; it is still worth some small effort. I believe it is getting ready to rain."
> **Archie**: "It was clouding up as I came in. Is it going to rain all over your clues?"
> **Wolfe**: "Some day, Archie, when I decide you are no longer worth tolerating, you will have to marry a woman of very modest mental capacity to get an appropriate audience for your sarcasms."

It's all banter, for neither could exist without the other: Archie needs Wolfe to keep him from getting bored, while being his employer's eyes, ears and fists outside the confines of the brownstone. Indeed as one shrewd commentator has noted, it's the chemistry between the two men that is Stout's Unique Selling Point; that and his winning ways with a sentence, which is what Plum was referring to when he italicized *writing* in that earlier quotation. And, of course, exactly what he achieved with Jeeves and Wooster.

Stout and his most famous creation are also intensely bookish. We're told Wolfe reads around 200 titles a year, and his library of about 1,200 volumes is apparently similar in size to his creator's. By no means such a catholic quoter as Wodehouse, Stout nevertheless manages to let us know he is similarly well read with references ranging from Spenser to Steinbeck, and he occasionally has Wolfe devoting considerable intellectual energy to utterly quixotic literary and historical quests. *Death of a Doxy* sees him researching the still-unsolved disappearance of two young princes at the Tower of London in 1483, and having decided beyond reasonable doubt that Sir Thomas More fitted up Richard III for the crime, removes More's philosophical works from his bookshelves by way of protest. Similarly, in Wolfe's final case – 1975's *A Family Affair* – he spends time comparing Robert Fitzgerald's 1974 translation of Homer's *Iliad* with three others in his possession. But while Archie considers his boss's habit of having three books on the go at once as "ostentatious," that spirit of enquiry and obvious erudition almost never spills over into pretentiousness, thanks mainly to Archie's down-to-earth narration. As Plum wrote:

> [Archie] brings excellent comedy into the type of narrative where comedy seldom bats better than .100 [which I take to be a low average in baseball].

It's Stout's effortless cocktail of high culture, gritty subject matter and comedy that I think most recommended him to Plum. The very idea that a writer with such abundant literary gifts should choose to work almost exclusively in a genre not generally noted for quality or lofty subject matter was one I think he found unexpected, thrillingly subversive, and perhaps even heroic, such that it's surprising he never warmed to the work of fellow Alleynian Raymond Chandler, who could produce passages like this from *Farewell, My Lovely* seemingly on tap, as detective Philip Marlowe examines a proffered photo that excites him strangely:

> It was a blonde. A blonde to make a bishop kick a hole in a stained glass window. She was wearing street clothes that looked black and white, and a hat to match and she was a little haughty, but not too much. Whatever you needed, wherever you happened to be – she had it. About thirty years old.
> I poured a fast drink and burned my throat getting it down.

"Take it away," I said. "I'll start jumping."

"Why, I got it for you. You'll want to see her, won't you?"

I looked at it again. Then I slid it under the blotter. "How about tonight at eleven?"

"Listen, this isn't just a bunch of gag lines, Mr. Marlowe."

Only, of course, it is. Even so, Plum could only rate it "good" while commenting to Bill Townend in 1945 that "it's awfully like an awful lot of other books – e.g. Dashiell Hammett and [English thriller writer] Peter Cheyney." By contrast, Stout had mixed a smooth cocktail all his own that fitted the bill just fine, a quirky lightheartedness reliably cutting through any Chandlerian *noir*. Nero Wolfe may be a deadly serious sleuth with a brain the size of a planet, but his first recorded words are "Where's the beer?", a beverage he drinks in such prodigious quantities it has him, in Archie's description, "running like a brook." When Prohibition is repealed, he has his staff organize a taste test to determine a new favourite brand as he reverts from bootleg "sewage" to legal shop-bought brew. Forty-nine brands later, he has his answer – a 3.2% lager. From that point on, Wolfe confines himself to a mere six quarts a day (that's 10 UK pints or 5.7 litres), while always intending (but never quite managing) to cut down to five for health reasons. And this from a character who, in *A Right to Die*, is planning to argue the toss with real life academic A. L. Rowse over his erroneous dating of Shakespeare's *Cymbeline*.

But while Plum was clearly a crime fanatic, it was not a genre he could ever pursue convincingly, despite there being no fewer than 90 crooks of one kind or another dotted around his fiction. Working from a base ingredient of comedy, cow creamers and popguns fitted his *modus operandi* rather better than gold bullion and Colts, and he was perhaps in awe or even a little jealous of Stout's freedom to trade in both corpses *and* humour. So it is that the sillier and more inconsequential the crimes (and the crims who commit them), the more chance they had of fitting his tried and tested formula. Brinkley Manor would always work better as a setting for such tales than the Gotham of *Psmith, Journalist*, and about the closest Plum ever got to pulpiness was this Chandlerian description of blonde bad girl Dolly Molloy from *Sam the Sudden*:

The newcomer was a girl in the middle twenties, of bold but [...] sullen good looks. She had the bright hazel eyes which seldom go with a meek and contrite heart. Her colouring was vivid, and in the light from the window her hair gleamed with a sheen that was slightly metallic.

Well, he tried it on, but it didn't suit him. Dolly and her husband Soapy, together with minor league grifters Chimp Twist and Oily Carlisle would appear intermittently between 1925 and 1972, but I will confess that with the exception of Dolly my heart tends to sink whenever they're centre stage.

The closest analogue I can find for these characters is with the far funnier small-time rogues of Damon Runyon's Broadway tales; indeed, the two writers' narrative styles have been linked in more than one scholarly commentary. This likeness is especially noticeable in the lawbreakers who perform no fewer than five of Plum's song lyrics: his very first published outing 'Put Me in My Little Cell' (from *Sergeant Brue*, 1904); 'Dear Old Prison Days' (*Oh, Lady! Lady!!*, 1918); 'Dartmoor Days' (*The Golden Moth*, 1921); 'Dear Old-Fashioned Prison of Mine' (*Sitting Pretty*, 1924); and this one, performed by Willy and Bugs in the show *Miss 1917* (er, 1917) and simply titled 'We're Crooks':

> *When I was a baby with a rattle and bib,*
> *Dear old father taught me how to crack a crib.*
> *When I was three, I learned at my mother's knee*
> *How to pick a person's pocket to pinch a ring and hock it.*
> *We're crooks, crooks,*
> *Like you read about in books.*
> *We're strong on intellect, though maybe not on looks.*
> *All your silver spoons and jewels we collect,*
> *But we've never worked in Wall Street,*
> *for we've got some self-respect.*

All good, clean fun. And not a snake or a shooter in sight.

The Story So Far:
A Writer's Writer

[Wodehouse] is the favorite writer of more writers than any other writer – I feel safe […] in asserting this.
Andrew Ferguson, Washington Examiner, December 4, 2000

Sooooo many brilliant Wodehouse lines. One of my very favourites is "It is never difficult to distinguish between a Scotsman with a grievance and a ray of sunshine."
J. K. Rowling, tweet (X?) from May 31, 2023

Though not one non-literary reader in a thousand will lift his eyes from the page to consider Wodehouse as an artist, a fellow-hack cannot fail to admire the extraordinary skill with which […] he goes about his business. Every sentence has a job to do and – in spite of the air of lunatic irresponsibility which hangs around a Wodehouse novel – does it neatly and efficiently. Bertie Wooster may live in a perpetual haze, but P. G. Wodehouse knows at any moment of the story exactly what he is aiming for."
Peter Quennell, quoted in Author! Author!

To state that Wodehouse was quite devoted to books and reading is Premier League litotes. Golf, animal husbandry, soap operas and undemanding exercise would occupy him at various times in his life, but there was really very little else he enjoyed doing other than immersing himself in words. Human society was for the most part optional; his most regular correspondents – Bill Townend and Denis Mackail – were fellow writers with whom he could discuss his craft. Ditto Guy Bolton, his frequent companion for those late-in-life afternoon strolls. Most other authors tend to have at least one hobby or vice, but words were Plum's fix from early childhood and he couldn't get enough of them.

Naturally, many other writers suffer from the same addiction: in his charming reminiscence 'I Was a Teen-Age Library User,' the prolific author John Updike fondly remembers a sympathetic librarian Miss Ruth, who let him "check out stacks of books, and she never blinked":

Stacks of what? P. G. Wodehouse is the author that comes

first to mind: the library owned close to all the master's titles, around fifty of them at that time, and they all struck me as hilarious and enchanting. They admitted me to a privileged green world of English men's clubs, London bachelor flats, country weekends, golf courses, roadsters, flappers, and many other upper-crust appurtenances fabulous to think of in wartime Berks County. A real reader, reading to escape his own life thoroughly, tends to have runs on authors.

Updike certainly had a long run with Plum. In 'Pigeon Feathers' from 1956, the central character gets so hopelessly depressed and confused even reading Wodehouse can't snap him out of it. And then there were the golf stories, which prompted Updike's own love of the game and his 1996 volume of essays *Golf Dreams* ("Wodehouse's golf stories delighted me years before I touched a club"). If you read enough of his extensive output, it's possible to detect a good deal of Wodehouse's good humour and sense of the ridiculous; so even as Plum was absorbing influences from other writers and writing, his work was happily chiming with his writing colleagues, as we began to witness in the previous chapter.

Literary influence takes many forms. Most obviously we might stumble across the occasional quote, as when we hear the cry "Pig-hoo-ey! [sic] in Terry Pratchett's *Hogfather*. But sometimes, that inspiration reveals itself in places least looked for and in ways that may be far from straightforward, only becoming clear over time. As I write, the recent death of novelist Martin Amis has prompted tributes that survey his life's work. Doubtless introduced to Plum's work by his novelist father Kingsley, who regularly cited Wodehouse among his early influences, one obituarist noted several unlikely resemblances between Martin, the Young Turk of the 1980s, and "that popular purveyor of timeless comic fertility and posh silliness," PGW:

> The clues were littered all over Amis's work. His first major novel, "Money," posed as an Englishman's wised-up attempt to "do" mid-nineteen-eighties New York, seen as a hellish but endlessly alluring island of strip clubs, pornography, and simmering racial unease. But the New York of "Money" isn't Tom Wolfe's painstakingly reported dystopia of the same era. It's an endlessly amusing, wholly invented universe, a world stripped of actual reference and filled with in-jokes and mad wordplay.

Just like Wodehouse World, Amis's Gotham is a carefully edited, self-sufficient environment created on the writer's own terms; and as with Updike's writing, that spirited Wodehousean tone, love of wordplay and comic invention is undeniably present even down among the strip clubs and pornography. When Plum's final unfinished novel *Sunset at Blandings* was published in 1977, Amis's review for the *New York Times* was by turns magnanimous, realistic, and even tender, with overtones of a debt being paid:

> Right to the end, that green world of his never began to lose its vernal brilliance.

Like son, like father: the same *New York Times* noted of Amis *père*'s debut *Lucky Jim* in 1954 that "It is funny in something approaching the Wodehouse vein" – and not simply for its wholesale filching of Gussie Fink-Nottle's prize-giving speech from *Right Ho, Jeeves* as university academic Jim Dixon drunkenly delivers his "Merrie England" lecture. Like his son, Amis also sifted valuable nuggets of writerly technique from Plum's prose:

> You must never offer the reader anything simply as funny and nothing more. Make it acceptable as information, comment, narrative, et cetera, so that if the joke flops the reader has still got something. Wodehouse understood this perfectly, even better than Shakespeare did.

Amis, K. has more than once been outed for peddling Wodehouse pastiches, as a lengthy and thoughtful 1988 article in *The New Atlantic* magazine notes. Favouring "short, brilliantly concentrated [...] sharp verbal satire and richly comic set pieces," the provenance of Amis's *Girl, 20*'s is obvious to the writer, representing "an apotheosis of the Wodehouse-style comic novel." And while there may be a distinctly *un*-Wodehousean misanthropic edge to both Amises' humour that would grow more marked (and tiresome) as time went on, Plum is always to be found nearby, gazing over their shoulders, encouraging them to lighten up.

The Waugh dynasty could boast not just two but three generations of writers, all of them Wodehouse devotees – Evelyn, Auberon, and Daisy. Critics and reviewers including Cyril Connolly and Paul Johnson had regularly compared Evelyn and Plum, often lazily and with no great understanding; but Waugh very much took this as a compliment, having made the connection himself right at the start of his career when he described his novel *Vile Bodies* as "rather like P. G. Wodehouse all about bright young people." As well as being a lifelong devotee (and a correspondent from at least 1947 to 1962), he defended Wodehouse's professional reputation vigorously on at least four occasions prior to his well-known apologia 'An Act of Homage and Reparation' broadcast on BBC radio in 1961. These included a short essay 'An Angelic Doctor: The Work of P. G. Wodehouse' from 1939 published in the *Spectator*, and a stinging response to the *Daily Mail*'s controversial 'Our Man in America' Don Iddon, who in 1953 had posed the question "Remember Wodehouse?":

> The answer from all lovers of fine writing is: Yes. We await each new book with eagerness and constantly re-read the splendid collection of his life's work.

Having namechecked Plum in his 1938 novel *Scoop*, Waugh's reviewers naturally latched on to the connection. Writing in the *New Statesman*, Desmond Shawe-Taylor noted earlier traces "of a Wodehouse strain" in Waugh's writing, and "how marked it has now become" could be observed in the following passage:

> No sound broke the peace of the evening save, in the elms that stood cumbrously on every side, the crying of the rooks and, not unlike it but nearer at hand […] a strong baritone decanting irregular snatches of sacred music. "In thy courts no more are needed, sun by day nor moon by night," sang Uncle Theodore blithely, stepping into his evening trousers.

"'Decanted'," [sic] Shawe-Taylor comments, "might be the Master himself."

The point at issue here is not so much whether these perceived similarities are accurate but that they are proposed at all. The implication that there is a recognizable, unique 'Wodehousean' style to imitate is in itself flattering, having taken Plum around two decades and a lot of hard graft before it achieved its sunniest expression – a journey I explored at the very start of my *Pelham Grenville Wodehouse* trilogy. As Plum himself had remarked in 1920, at the point when a reviewer in the London *Times* could write that an author "at times reverts to the P. G. Wodehouse manner," he had indeed arrived; in fact, as he informed Leonora, this was the key to "jolly old Fame." So it was, and so it still is; when asked why Wodehouse remains popular, most respondents pay tribute in whole or in part to his writing style.

Endorsements from fellow writers have proved an important part of keeping Wodehouse in the public eye. To those names already mentioned we should add Bill Bryson, Ruth Rendell, Douglas Adams, Kate Mosse, Kazuo Ishiguro, Philip Pullman, Salman Rushdie, J. B. Priestley, V. S. Pritchett, Neil Gaiman, Jonathan Coe, Donna Tartt, Michael Bond, Susan Hill, Bernard Cornwell, Jay McInerney, Marion Keyes, Umberto Eco, Lynne Truss, Joanne Harris, Frank McCourt, John Mortimer and even Bertolt Brecht – and this splendidly diverse gene pool seems to be continually replenishing itself as time marches on. What I'm sure unites them is not just Plum's humour and comic invention, but that they recognize someone who knew *exactly* what he was doing, making him what we might call 'A Writer's Writer.' As far back as the 1930s, poet and essayist Hilaire Belloc had dubbed Wodehouse "the best writer of English now alive," and in their rush to condemn this as hyperbole many reviewers and scholars omit to mention that it is but one sentence in a five-page piece that skilfully seeks to justify this assertion. Among the palpable hits in Belloc's argument is this:

> It is a test of power in this craft of writing that its object shall be attained by some method which the reader cannot directly perceive.

Which is so true: in his best writing, Plum alchemizes his many influences so artfully the joins don't show. Or perhaps more accurately, they don't draw attention to themselves *as* influences – unless of course he wants them to. For those requiring proof of just how good Plum is, Belloc challenges them to "attempt an imitation. You will find you cannot do it." The "simplicity and exactitude" of his writing makes it look easy – only it's not. When bestselling novelist Sebastian Faulks was invited to write a Jeeves and Bertie 'sequel' (which ended up as 2013's *Jeeves and the Wedding Bells*) he was all too aware that if he tried too hard to mimic Wodehouse, he would likely come a cropper:

> Wodehouse's prose is a glorious thing; and there's the rub. I didn't want to write too close an imitation of that distinctive music for fear of sounding flat or sharp. Nor did I want to drift into parody.

Faulks's use of "music" to describe the effect of reading Plum's prose is exactly correct, for it suggests a mystery that lies at the heart of the greatest literature which allows analysis to proceed only so far, before stopping it dead in its tracks.

Even more remarkable is the breadth of Wodehouse's literary borrowings when set against what Martin Amis rightly calls the "laughably limited" range of his literary ambitions. While everything from the Bible to romance is fuel for his humour, there's a corresponding appreciation of just about any writing that did its job well. Despite the fact that those raw American realists who opened Chapter 6 had little in common with his own writing, that didn't mean Plum's tastes defaulted to all things fluffy and Banksean. While ensuring he would never bring a blush to the cheek of anyone's maiden aunt, grittiness nevertheless had its place in the great scheme of things, as he reassured a conflicted Bill Townend in 1946:

> Ethel came back from a shopping binge yesterday bringing a book called *Night and the City* by Gerald Kersh. Do you know his work? [...] The book is terrific, and talk about coarseness! Sordid to a degree, with only one moderately decent character in it.

This he puts down to the war, which had recently ended "with a general coarsening of the public taste [...] If you ask me, I think novels are going to get dirtier and dirtier, and in another ten years anything will go."

He didn't have to wait that long. In 1949, he sent Townend a copy of Norman Mailer's sensational and much-lauded debut *The Naked and the Dead*, which ended up spending 62 weeks on the American bestseller lists. It seems he really rated it:

> I can't give you a better idea of how the literary scene has changed since the good old days than by submitting that novel to your notice. It's good, mind you – in fact, I found it absorbing – but isn't it extraordinary that you can print in a book nowadays stuff which when we were young would have been confined to fences and the walls of public lavatories?

Once again, we find Plum admiring the craft of writing, even if he wasn't particularly in tune with the content. But of those scribes we've already met, Rex Stout is perhaps the best example of a writer who ticked all Plum's boxes. Here was an intelligent, capable, creative novelist who stuck to thrillers and raised the bar in his chosen genre. The same could also be said of Plum in his own field; both men trusted their instincts, wrote only what they wanted and triumphed – even as their critics proved restive. In a letter to Stout's biographer John McAleer from 1972, Plum astutely remarked how the pioneering scholar Edmund Wilson had denied himself a great deal of pleasure by willing himself *not* to enjoy the Nero Wolfe stories: "[Wilson] was incapable," he wrote, "of recognizing good writing if the writer was working in a field of which he disapproved." To which we might add that had Plum suffered a similar prejudice, his writing would have been the poorer for it.

Fortunately, he didn't: and as we're about to see, he had had some great – and some not so great – teachers.

PART TWO: WODEHOUSE
-BEING A WRITER

Chapter 8:
Public Image Limited

I met John Buchan the other day. Nice chap, but I can't
read his stuff, can you?
Letter to Denis McKail, 10 March 1928

Do you read John Galsworthy's books? He came to lunch
yesterday – very pleasant.
Letter to Bill Townend, November 12, 1928

I never get tired of [Lord] Dunsany's stories [...] I spent
the afternoon with him once at his house down in Kent,
and he read me three of his plays – yes, *three* – one after
the other.
Letter to Bill Townend, January 11, 1929

This has been a big week for celebrities. I haven't been
able to move a step without bumping into one [...] Bernard Shaw, then H. G. Wells, and finally Kipling.
Letter to Bill Townend, May 11, 1929

Some way through his debut 'adult' novel – 1906's *Love Among the Chickens* – Wodehouse has his narrator Jeremy Garnet pose the $64,000
Question:

> It would be interesting to know to what extent the work of
> authors is influenced by their private affairs.

This massive hornet's nest, or possibly can of worms, is the conundrum
just about every writer, Wodehouse included, seems to ask themselves
at some point in their career. I'll leave Mr. Garnet, himself an author,
to elaborate:

> If life is flowing smoothly, are the novels they write in that
> period of content coloured with optimism? And if things
> are running crosswise, do they work off the resultant gloom
> on their faithful public?

In other words: what connection, if any, is there between writers and their writing? Can the *narrator* of a story be identified with the *writer* who has put their name to it? If not completely, then how much? Is there necessarily any connection *at all?*

Fifteen years later in 1921, the question would survive *LATC*'s radical rewrite, indicating Plum thought it worth a second airing. Garnet still doesn't seem able to separate his output from the turmoil in his own love life, hence the "great slabs of gloom" that intrude upon the "light-comedy effort" he's currently writing:

> A magnificent despondency became the keynote of the book. Instead of marrying, my hero and heroine had a big scene in the last chapter, at the end of which she informed him that she was already secretly wedded to another, a man with whom she had not even a sporting chance of being happy. I could see myself correcting proofs made pulpy by the tears of emotional printers.

He then broadens his musings out into the real-life literary world: "If," he speculates, "Mr. W. W. Jacobs had toothache, would he write like Hugh Walpole?" Here, he singles out two contemporary authors as alike as chalk and cheese: Jacobs – a good-humoured jobbing writer (and Wodehouse favourite) known mainly for his popular nautical tales; and Hugh Walpole – a sensitive, complex prose artist with a tendency to lapse into melodrama who we'll be meeting again shortly. Having posed the question, Garnet ruefully reflects that his current moodiness "would not do," implying he urgently needs to channel the more upbeat Jacobs if he's going to deliver what his regular readers expect from him. Unfortunately, he concludes, he is not one of those "great authors" who can simply include themselves out of their work.

Having raised this fundamental question through one of his characters, it's interesting to speculate where Wodehouse himself might have stood on this fundamental issue. To read the following passage taken from a letter to fellow scribe Bill Townend in February 1945, you might think he'd got things absolutely cut and dried in his mind:

> A thing I can never understand is why all the critics seem to assume that [Shakespeare's] plays are a reflection of his personal moods and dictated by the circumstances of his private life. You know the sort of thing I mean. They say 'Timon of Athens' is a gloomy piece of work, which means that Shakespeare must have been having a lousy time when he wrote it.' I can't see it. Do you find that your

private life affects your work? I don't. I have never written funnier stuff than during these last years, when I certainly wasn't feeling exhilarated.

Which was not just true, but nigh on miraculous.

Over the previous five years he had been thrown out of his home, parted from his wife, imprisoned in a series of Nazi internment camps, and his beloved stepdaughter Leonora had died at the tragically early age of 39. Yet while having every reason to be depressed, he busied himself writing some of his strongest comic titles, including *Joy in the Morning*, *The Mating Season* and *Full Moon*. Then there was the whole Berlin Broadcasts Business (hereafter 'BBB'), during which his good name was dragged through the mud all over the world, a yawning chasm opening up in the public consciousness between that clubbable bloke who wrote the nation's favourite light comedy and the alleged 'traitor' up to his neck in the mulligatawny. This posed an existential threat to his good name and even his entire career, so we might think *that* might just have seeped into his published writing somehow. But no, hardly at all, unless you count Bertie's "I doubt if you can ever trust an author not to make an ass of himself" from *Joy in the Morning*.

By the same token, he seems to have been able to consider other writers' work separately from what he might have thought of them as human beings. A. A. Milne was a splendid example of this principle of action, having been a friendly acquaintance of Wodehouse who then publicly turned on him re. the BBB in a letter to the *Daily Telegraph* which denounced him as one who had shirked responsibility all his life as a writer, citizen and even as a parent. Yet even this low blow didn't stop Plum enjoying Milne's novels and plays, as he informed Denis Mackail in 1945:

> I don't know if it is a proof of my saintlike nature, but I find that my personal animosity against a writer never affects my opinion of what he writes. Nobody could be more anxious than myself, for instance, that Alan Alexander Milne should trip over a loose boot lace and break his bloody neck, yet I re-read his early stuff at regular intervals with all the old enjoyment and still maintain that in *The Dover Road* he produced about the best comedy in English.

This was no isolated act of saintliness (and *The Dover Road* actually *is* rather good). Seven years later he informed the same correspondent that "[Milne] is one of the very few readable writers. I can always re-read him indefinitely." And he meant it, borrowing four Milne titles from the NYSL between 1951 and 1955 *after* he had royally roasted that author's Christopher Robin poems in *The Mating Season* and 'Rodney Has a Relapse' (both 1949). Which, though it may appear odd, was entirely consistent with his point of view that while a writer's work necessarily belonged in the public domain, his biography didn't and should be struck from the record.

It was always a fond hope, and he knew it. Wodehouse clearly appreciated that readers tend to do exactly the opposite, as they idly ponder what sort of person could possibly have written whatever it is they're reading while casually confusing one with the other. Even Frank Crowninshield, Plum's editor at New York's *Vanity Fair* (who as a literary type should have known better) fell into this trap when the two first met. Expecting the sparkling wit who wrote all those humorous columns, in walked

> a stodgy and colourless Englishman [...] self-effacing, slow-witted and matter of fact [...] I never heard him utter a clever, let alone brilliant, remark.

Although Wodehouse had his fans at the Algonquin Round Table (notably Dorothy Parker), he was never going to match those quicksilver wits in person.

However reluctantly he may have embraced the reality, Plum knew he was in effect two people: who he actually was, and who his readers imagined him to be. Until the BBB, these personae were for the most part one and the same; after the crash he spent several confused and desperate years trying to re-sync them, ultimately deciding to keep things as straightforward as possible. The public version of 'P. G. Wodehouse' had to be a jolly bloke who wrote jolly stuff. Or, in other words, pre-BBB business as usual. In May 1952, as he compiled the heavily doctored correspondence that appears in *Performing Flea* (subtitled "A Self-Portrait in Letters"), he clearly wanted the 'official' version of his life to reflect well on him, as he informed Bill Townend, the letters' original recipient:

> I want the reader to say "Dear old Wodehouse. What a charming nature he must have! Here are all the people writing nasty things about him, and he remains urbane and humorous. Bless my soul, what a delightful fellow he must be!"

During that editorial process, as I revealed at some length in Volume

3 of my *Pelham Grenville Wodehouse*, there were occasions when he could have taught Machiavelli a thing or two about reputation management. In carefully nurturing a sympathetic idea of 'Wodehouse the Man' and 'Wodehouse the Writer' as one and the same, notice how he even borrows the beloved Lord Emsworth's favourite interjection in order to make his point. What he was *actually* in the process of creating was 'Wodehouse the Myth' – how he wanted to be seen by his readers, his critics, the publishing industry and, of course, posterity.

It's a side of our man that those who haven't read his private correspondence would never suspect, that steely determination to both own and control his biography somewhat at odds with the tenor of his simple, straightforward fictional world. And in subsequent biographical volumes (1954's *Bring on the Girls*, 1956's *America, I Like You*, 1957's *Over Seventy*, and 1962's *Author! Author!*) he would burnish this 'jolly old Wodehouse' image still further. Biographer Robert McCrum calls it his "dumb brick" routine, only it isn't *quite* that. Wodehouse was as complex a human being as anyone else, so he applied the same principle to himself as he did to his fiction: what he felt didn't belong there, or didn't want his public to know, he quite simply edited out. This radically streamlined, *simplified* version of Plum was anything but dumb, frequently using the self-deprecation to be found in his non-fiction as a 'nothing-to-see-here-kindly-move-along' defensive shield raised against those who would pry into his personal life. So we might conclude, *pro tempore*, that while Wodehouse didn't take *himself* particularly seriously, his *career* was another matter entirely. Which makes Wodehouse the man and Wodehouse the writer two rather different propositions, giving the lie to those biographers (no names, no pack drill) who have wilfully confused Plum with one or other of his fictional creations. In so doing, they have obligingly fallen into the trap he set for them.

The writer's sense of self and the way it manifests itself in their life and fiction can be a complicated thing, and in the second part of this volume we're moving on from looking at the writing that influenced Wodehouse to the writers themselves, and what he learned from their careers. Being a booky kinda guy, Plum would have had plenty of intel to hand on his fellow scribes and how they had managed both their lives and creativity. A good example can be found amongst the correspondence he wrote while compiling *Performing Flea*, a period he spent engrossed in Rupert Hart-Davis's recent biography of novelist Hugh Walpole, reviewing it in a letter to Bill Townend in June 1952. With the exception of Rebecca West who he found "refreshing," not one of Walpole's many literary friends comes off well. "How seriously all these fellows took themselves," Plum wrote of the "big pots" who dominated the 'quality' end of English lit in the first decades of the 20th century: Henry James's correspondence is that of "a dull, pompous chump;" Arnold Bennett's missives "aren't much better;" Joseph Conrad was "a mess" and Somerset Maugham "silly." Had he stuck it as far as Chapter 18 – which deals with the events of 1926 – he would have found this:

> At this time too the Cazalets introduced [Walpole] to P. G. Wodehouse, "a large, simple, kindly fellow." After their second meeting, Hugh wrote: "Took to him like anything. Is that a friendship? Can't be sure yet."

They certainly appear to have given things a go. Hart-Davis relates how the pair would watch rugby at Twickenham and once made a *ménage à trois* in the House of Commons restaurant with Winston Churchill. But when Plum received his D. Litt from Oxford University in 1939, this happened:

> It was just after Hilaire Belloc had said that I was the best living English writer. It was just a gag, of course, but it worried Hugh terribly. He said to me, 'Did you see what Belloc said about you?' I said I had. 'I wonder why he said that.' 'I wonder,' I said. Long silence. 'I can't imagine why he said that,' said Hugh. I said I couldn't, either. Another long silence. 'It seems such an extraordinary thing to say!' 'Most extraordinary.' Long silence again. 'Ah, well,' said Hugh, having apparently found the solution, 'the old man's getting very old.'
>
> (*Performing Flea*)

It wasn't "just a gag" of course: that's Plum being self-effacing. But never one to forget a slight, he writes of Hart-Davis's tome:

> My God, what a book! I feel as if I had been swimming in treacle. I always knew Hugh Walpole was a bit of a louse, but I never knew he was as bad as that [...] Doesn't it appall [sic] you, the relentless way [he] forces himself on these people.

Whose number evidently included himself. Walpole's on-board effeteness seems to be Plum's major gripe; but for the purposes of our argument, it's the following criticism that carries the greatest resonance:

181

Thank God I never went in for celebrity hunting.

Because he actually did. Rather a lot.

Plum could be quite the socialite, particularly when his literary curiosity was aroused. As his fame and income grew in the 1920s, he seems to have put himself about a fair bit, as in the following anecdote from *Bring on the Girls*:

> As we took our seats at the dinner-table [John] Galsworthy immediately began to discuss the deteriorating effect of educational uniformity on the incidence and development of genius.

Nothing like a bit of light banter to break the ice, but Plum had long been fascinated by Galsworthy's serious approach to life and how it had translated into his art. The author of *The Forsyte Saga* was also a playwright whose tragedy *Justice* made several appearances in Wodehouse's theatre column for *Vanity Fair* from 1916 onwards, and when Ethel ran into Mrs Galsworthy at a garden party and snagged a dinner invite, Plum was there like a shot. There was no let-up in the earnestness of the discourse, and by the sweet course he was "punch drunk":

> Galsworthy [rapped] on the table with the end of his knife and present[ed] a new aspect of the problem. 'To what extent is genius influenced by the educational standards of parents; with special reference to the cases of Thomas Chatterton and Shakespeare?'

Plum is deep in his anecdotage here; and although it wasn't really his kind of evening, he would later invite Galsworthy to chow down at his place, so it can't have been entirely unconvivial.

Wodehouse always had his Literary Heroes, including his Premier League idols Shakespeare, Tennyson and W. S. Gilbert. Reading what he wrote about them, it's clear that in addition to appreciating their words, Plum was employing a kind of double consciousness, pondering what it was like to *be* them, not so much in a personal but a professional sense. All three had reached the top of their respective trees as playwright, poet and librettist in their lifetimes and, like him, came from comfortable rather than wealthy, well-connected backgrounds. It's also no coincidence they were all meticulous literary craftsmen, more reliant – as he might have imagined them – on perspiration than inspiration for their success. There was a lot he could learn, but not *viva voce* from Shakespeare or Tennyson, who were inconveniently dead. Gilbert, though, was still hanging on, so the young Wodehouse resourcefully wangled an invite to one of the great man's Sunday lunchtime 'at homes' in Harrow Weald, which, as we'll find out in Chapter 11, turned into a complete and utter disaster. But as one opportunity failed to knock, another presented itself. More successful was his in-person courting of another of his biggest literary heroes, Sir Arthur Conan Doyle, who also fitted the Shakespeare/Tennyson/Gilbert 'artisan made good' template.

It wasn't simply Doyle's writing that would prove useful to Plum, but the way the best-selling creator of Sherlock Holmes, Brigadier Gérard and Professor Challenger presented himself to his public, somehow preserving his personal integrity despite the many challenges faced by a successful author in a venal publishing industry. In his regular 'Under the Flail' column for *Public School Magazine* in November 1901, Plum had boasted of having a complete set of Doyle's many works, at which point he would have been devouring *The Hound of the Baskervilles*, the third of four Sherlock Holmes novels that was midway through its serialization in *Strand* magazine, where he would soon be placing a substantial percentage of his own output. Fanboy references to the ace detective pop up all over his early writing, primarily to help curry favour with his schoolboy readers, but also as a useful index of his personal enthusiasm: indeed, thanks to Marilyn MacGregor's extensive scholarship, we know there are at least 210 references to Holmes in Plum's writing, most dating from this early period.

Even by his mid-40s that loyalty was undimmed, and once more Bill Townend was the recipient of his musings:

> Don't you find as you age in the wood, as we are both doing, that the tragedy of your life is that your early heroes lose their glamour? As a lad in the twenties you worship old whoever-it-is, the successful author, and by the time you're forty you find yourself blushing hotly at the thought that you could ever have admired the bilge he writes.

> Now with Doyle I don't have that feeling. I still revere his work as much as ever. I used to think it swell, and I still think it swell [...]

> And apart from his work, I admire Doyle so much as a man. I should call him definitely a great man, and I don't imagine I'm the only one who thinks so.

In the final year of his life, in an introduction he cobbled together for a 1975 re-issue of the Sherlock Holmes novel *The Sign of Four*, Plum could still aver that "Conan Doyle was my hero. Others might revere [Thomas] Hardy or [George] Meredith. I was a Doyle man and I still am." And he was, even as he compared Doyle favourably with a pair of 'artier' prose stylists notorious for their use of long words and unnecessarily complex sentence constructions. In *Author! Author!*, he recalled the "measured way he has of talking":

> He was telling me once that when he was in America he saw an advertisement in a paper – "Conan Doyle's School of Writing. Let the Conan Doyle School of Writing teach you how to sell" or something to that effect. In other words, some crook was using his name to pull a fast one on the public. Well, what most people would have said in his place would have been "Hullo! Something fishy here." The way he put it when telling me the story was "I said to myself, 'Ha! There is villainy afoot.'"

An utterly inconsequential but telling detail Plum had squirrelled away for over twenty years.

In 'Grit', a fascinating but untypical puff piece he wrote on Doyle for *V.C. Magazine* in July 1903, we can witness quite how starstruck he was, watching a cricket match that had taken place the previous year:

> [Doyle] went on to bowl fourth change, when the score was 220 for four wickets, and the wicket playing like a billiard-table. In his third over he had clean bowled the man who had been doing what he liked with the bowling for two hours, and in another seventy minutes the side was out for 290, and he had taken five wickets for forty-four. He was captain that day. A captain who is capable of bowling like that, and yet does not try his hand till fourth change, is no ordinary man.

On that occasion, Plum had been a spectator. But on 22 May 1903, he could be found playing for Doyle's Authors XI against the Artists at Esher, during which he probably snatched the scrappy conversation on which 'Grit' is clearly based.

Despite the ad hoc nature of the encounter, Wodehouse had already done his homework, namechecking some of his subject's less familiar non-Sherlockian works including *Round the Red Lamp: Being Facts and Fancies of Medical Life,* and the boxing yarn *Rodney Stone.* Doyle, Plum informs his readers, excelled in hunting, boxing and cricket – a list of credits to which he could have added football, rifle-shooting, golf, billiards, and skiing. He was also a qualified doctor who had studied ophthalmology, medical botany and immunology, and had served in a South African field hospital during the Second Boer War at the height of his literary fame. Fiction writing was at first only an incidental adjunct to any number of other careers this Renaissance man might have pursued, which even included architecture. Sherlock Holmes only really took off when Doyle had reached his early 30s, at which point his fate as a writer was sealed; but all through his life he tried to avoid being typecast by his most famous creation, producing work in many genres including horror, romance, adventure, historical fiction and, latterly, spiritualism.

That Authors match was only the beginning of the two men's association, and Wodehouse would soon be in a better position to judge for himself what kind of chap Doyle was, sharing the crease with the older writer on at least ten occasions over the next nine years. The two would end up corresponding, with Doyle inviting the young shaver to the convivial cricketing matches he hosted at Undershaw, the house he designed and built near Hindhead in Surrey, as Plum remembered in that 1975 introduction:

> We were great friends in those days, our friendship only interrupted when I went to live in America [in 1914] [...] And after a day's cricket and a big dinner he and I would discuss literature.

For those of us raised on biographies that insist Wodehouse was next-door to a recluse, the idea that he was a schmoozer may come as a shock. Young and ambitious, he must have revelled in those cricket matches, when he would rub shoulders with, among others, J. M. Barrie (playwright and author of the Peter Pan franchise) and E. W. Hornung (Doyle's brother-in-law and creator of Raffles the bestselling amateur cracksman).

As to how Wodehouse benefitted from the Doyle connection artistically, there is little critical consensus. Noted Plum scholar Richard Usborne is the most energetic among those who try to yoke the two writers together, opening his argument strongly by noting that Stanley Featherstonehaugh Ukridge is in part modelled on James Cullingworth, the "amiable villain" in Doyle's *The Stark Munro Letters* who is perpetually just one cock-eyed scheme away from a vast fortune. A doctor by training, Cullingworth has taken over his revered father's practice, only to see it fail miserably under his stewardship, as he explains in Ukridge-like tones:

> "Munro," said he, prodding at me with his pipe, "what I
> wanted to tell you is, that I am utterly, hopelessly, and irre-
> trievably ruined [...] [T]hey've eaten me up among them
> [...] licked me clean, bones and gravy [...] Look here, lad-
> die [...] d'you see that pile of letters on the left of the ta-
> ble? [...] Those are duns. And d'you see those documents
> on the right? Well, those are County Court summonses.
> And, now, d'you see that?" he picked up a little ledger, and
> showed me three or four names scribbled on the first page.
> "That's the practice," he roared, and laughed until the
> great veins jumped out on his forehead.

Oscillating between elation and gloom, Cullingworth tirelessly connives to put his finances back on track, proposing at one stage that he travel through the jungles of Brazil as a peripatetic eye surgeon, having already bought two large hampers full of assorted spectacles ready for the journey. "It's the chance of a lifetime," he proclaims.

Unfortunately, having scored this bullseye Usborne has pretty much shot his bolt, his later parallels betraying only the sketchiest acquaintance with their Doylean analogues. Elements of Jeeves, he asserts, can be found in Professor Challenger's servant Austin from the 1913 novel *The Poison Belt*, and also in Ambrose, valet to the Regency buck Sir Charles Tregellis in *Rodney Stone*. More fundamentally, he detects a similarly between the plot arcs of Jeeves and Wooster stories and the adventures of Holmes and Watson, leading him to conclude that:

> [O]f all the authors to whom Wodehouse's debt shows it-
> self, Doyle is second only to W. S. Gilbert. And Wodehouse
> would gladly have acknowledged both.

Which he would – were these examples (Cullingworth notwithstanding) anything more than faint echoes of their originals. In fact Ukridge, Jeeves and Bertie all dance to literary rhythms far older than Doyle, to archetypal characters and plots Doyle had appropriated from his own reading. No, what I think Wodehouse gained most from his various associations with Doyle was an appreciation of the latter's downright pally relationship with his public which we might characterize as a kind of commercially minded conservatism (small 'c'). What you read was what you got, and this straightforwardness manifested itself in several related ways.

For a start, Doyle would rarely spook the horses by being too arty or straining for effect. Although far more elegant and highly polished, Plum's mid-season narrative style was similarly uncomplicated with the absolute minimum of tonal shifts. Everything can be easily understood on the first read through, and there's barely even any suspense. Nothing in the story nor its telling prompts us to beg questions of the author, or harbour nagging doubts in the back of our mind as we read. The focus is squarely on lightness and ease of comprehension, with Plum demanding nothing of his readers other than they sit back, suspend their disbelief and allow themselves, like Doyle's audience, to be entertained.

Second, Wodehouse would follow Doyle's example of giving his public what it wanted; and if that meant repeating himself, so be it. Formulas, particularly successful ones, would be no cause for shame in his scheme of things. As late as 1967, Wodehouse was writing to Anthony Powell in praise of the latter's *A Dance to the Music of Time*, a 12-volume novel sequence, confessing that

> What I like, and what I suppose everyone likes, is the feeling that one is living with a group of characters and sharing their adventures [...] I should hate to feel that I should never meet Widmerpool again.

Kenneth Widmerpool is an oddly mercurial individual who develops over the course of Powell's saga to embody many of the more unpleasant aspects of the British psyche, and has been described by author and critic John Bayley as being "as famous a character in the annals of English fiction as either Pickwick or Jeeves." Sixty years prior to Widmerpool's debut in 1951, Doyle's massive success with Holmes and Brigadier Gérard would have similarly alerted the young Wodehouse to the advantages of evolving a set of recurring characters: not only did they become part of an ersatz 'family' in the reader's imagination, the act of placing them in a familiar setting obviated the need for the writer to create a new fictional 'world' with every outing. This economy would allow him to service his market more frequently while growing his audience's loyalty.

Wodehouse would struggle to emulate Doyle's triumph until Bertie and Lord Emsworth both sprang from his imagination in the *annus mirabilis* of 1915; but unlike Holmes's creator, he never considered them a millstone round his neck, keeping them on his rep company until the end of his life. Possibly better than Doyle, he identified with the reader's love of familiarity: indeed, no-one seems to have been happier than Plum following the news of Holmes's imminent resurrection, which he celebrated as a song lyric for *Punch*:

When Sherlock left his native Strand, such groans were
seldom heard;
With sobs the Public's frame was rent: with
tears its eye was blurred.
But the optimists reflected
That he might be resurrected:
It formed our only theme of conversation.
We asked each other, Would he be? And if so,
How and where?
We went about our duties with a less dejected air.
And they say that a suggestion
Of a Parliamentary question
Was received with marked approval by the nation.
And Sherlock, Sherlock, he's in town again,
Sir Conan has discovered him, and offers to explain.
The explanation may be thin,
But bless you! we don't care a pin,
If he'll but give us back our Sherlock.

Once again, these are the sentiments of a fan; and no, he didn't give
two hoots that the explanation of how Holmes cheated death at the
Reichenbach falls was unconvincing. He was just glad to have him back,
no questions asked.

Third, and I reckon most important, was Doyle's public image and
the way it seamlessly connected to his writing, as Plum spelled out at the
opening of the 'Grit' article:

> [T]here can be no doubt that, however much such a feel-
> ing may be censured by the superior person, *the public likes
> a man to resemble his books.* [italics mine]

It was an ideal Doyle appeared to fulfil in spades. Notice how Wodehouse implicitly disparages the pretensions of a "superior" reader, who
would presumably favour a more complex, ambiguous, 'clever' relationship between the writer's public and private personae. Not him,
though. And even if there *were* more to Doyle than met the eye, virtually
none of the great man's friends and colleagues seemed able to detect
it, Plum included: "He's so solid," he wrote. Early biographer Hesketh
Pearson, who approached a good many of those friends for comment,
never tires of using such terms as "simplicity," "innocence," "solidity,"
"trusting," "ingenuous," and "reverent" to describe his subject, while
patronisingly stressing the lack of sophistication in Doyle's thought and

opinions. Somewhat acquainted with Pearson, Plum had read the book and described it as "very interesting" to Bill Townend, so it's possible he agreed with this assessment. For all the enduring enigma that is Sherlock Holmes, his creator could still come over as a straight shooter, which, taken together with his talents and interests both literary and otherwise, contributed to Plum's assessment of him as "definitely a great man." Not a Hugh Walpole then, for (to quote Pearson again) "he had nothing of the artist about him," an opinion corroborated by Anthony Hope, author of 1894 bestselling adventure *The Prisoner of Zenda* who envied Doyle for writing "good books, yet looked as if he had never heard of such a thing in his life."

So it seems Doyle couldn't help writing the way he did, because that's who he *was* – apparently. His son Adrian would later dismiss Pearson's portrait as "a stranger's personal and quite unauthoritative opinions" that had been foisted on his father, but it's proved a compelling image that has since passed over into received wisdom. There appears to have been an *integrity* between the man, his work and his public profile that Wodehouse would have had ample opportunity to witness up close and personally. Perhaps most attractively, Doyle lacked the airs of graces that regularly accompanied literary success, undesirable character traits that would prove a rich seam of humour in Wodehouse's fictional *littérateurs*. Neither man could abide pretension, and in the person of the novelist, playwright, and professional Manxman Sir Thomas Henry Hall Caine CH KBE, they each found a lightning rod for everything they disliked in their profession.

From the very beginning of his career, Wodehouse seems to have taken against those of his colleagues who made a big thing of curating their own lives on and off the page: Ernest Hemingway was one he mentions occasionally (in *The Mating Season* and elsewhere) as one who had cast himself as a tough guy who "like[d] living dangerously" and took considerable pains to bolster that image. Caine was an earlier example of this self-mythologizing tendency, and in August 1897, Doyle politely but firmly berated him in the letters pages of the *Daily Chronicle* for what he considered to be regular breaches of professional etiquette. This would have been billed as a clash of the titans, had Doyle not honourably withheld his name to obviate that very possibility, enclosing his card to be forwarded to Caine should he choose to reply. Caine was massively popular at the time; his novel *The Christian* (likely the subject of Doyle's missive) would be the first commercial book ever to enjoy audited sales of one million copies. He would later have an airport named after him. But in serving his sizeable international public, Caine would regularly stoke anticipation for forthcoming publications by granting interviews and producing press articles that invariably stressed how he had sweated blood during their gestation.

Nowadays, of course, it's unusual if writers *don't* participate in the promotion of their books, a duty that's often written into their publishing contracts: Q&As, book signings, blogs and appearances at literary festivals all take up time that might be better spent writing. But although this type of activity was far less prevalent in the 1890s, Doyle's admonishment would have appeared somewhat other-worldly even then:

> I do think it unworthy of the dignity of our common profession that one should pick up paper after paper and read Mr. Caine's own comments on the gigantic task and the colossal work which he has just brought to a conclusion, with minute descriptions of its various phases and of the different difficulties which have been overcome. Surely [...] it is for others to say these things, and there is something ludicrous and offensive about them when they are self-stated. Each successive book of Mr. Hall Caine's has been self-heralded in the same fashion. All these wire-pullings and personalities tend to degrade literature, and it is high time that every self-respecting man should protest against them.

"To achieve large sales with dignity," Professor John Sutherland tells us, "[was] the dual prize in fiction throughout most of the [19th] century," naming Sir Walter Scott and William Makepeace Thackeray (another Wodehouse favourite) as writers who had managed to pull this off. Like them, Doyle viewed literature as a principled profession, much like his own medical calling, with its own set of unwritten rules and what he calls "honourable traditions." Which made Caine's self-promotion vulgar and even caddish, an attempt to rig the game by steering readers in the direction of what to think. Better to let his work speak for itself; and although neither Doyle nor Wodehouse was wholly immune to publicizing their own wares (Plum managed to get himself fired from his regular column in *Tit-Bits* for plugging his 1907 novel *Not George Washington*), they never tried to grease up to their public on the industrial scale Caine attempted.

In his 1924 autobiographical work *Memories and Adventures*, Doyle devotes just two of the book's 32 chapters exclusively to his fiction, and even in those spends as much time critiquing his own writing as bigging it up. His star turn Holmes "admits of no light or shade" and is at root no better than "a calculating machine," while Watson "never shows one gleam of humour or makes one single joke." Later that year, he would contribute to a literary symposium in his beloved *Strand* magazine titled 'How Our Novelists Write Their Books' that was similarly matter-of-fact and almost completely unrevealing. Immediately below Doyle's column is a contribution on the same theme by one P. G. Wodehouse, which is funnier but equally unforthcoming: writing, he claims, is responsible for "the hideous, lined face and bald head which appear in the photograph accompanying these words" and he confesses to terrible problems with plots before they eventually disentangle themselves, apparently without his help. He then generously plugs his friend Bill Townend's "sea-stories" before ending on the bombshell "I always work on the typewriter. I have never tried dictation."

No 'hold the front page' eye-openers there; in fact, I've only been able to track down around 30 or so interviews Plum gave in his entire lifetime, several of which appear not to be interviews at all but cut-and-paste jobs constructed by enterprising sub-editors from syndicated quotes. And, of course, in violent contrast to Caine and his ilk, Plum's strategy when asked was to give away as little of himself as possible. Even in those occasional prefaces and self-penned articles that touch on his writing, he is sufficiently self-deprecating to make a present-day press agent want to scream. My favourite example is the well-known introduction to *Summer Lightning*, in which he complains of a certain critic who had snarkily commented that *Money for Nothing* contained "all the old Wodehouse characters under different names." To which he responded:

> With my superior intelligence, I have outgeneralled the man this time by putting in all the old Wodehouse characters under the same names. Pretty silly it will make him feel, I rather fancy.

Which elegantly turns the critic's argument on its head, as when Plum upended Sean O'Casey's barbed insistence that he (Plum) was "English literature's performing flea" by commandeering it for the title of his 1953 collection of correspondence.

Some of his fictional writers are not so backwards in coming forwards, however, and prove more than happy to climb aboard the marketing merry-go-round. In 1970's *The Girl in Blue*, actress Dame Flora Faye, who has recently published her theatrical memoirs, summarizes a ghastly literary lunch from which she has just returned which had nothing to do with literature and everything with profile and promotion. Jimmy Fothergill, evidently a booky sort chasing a knighthood "and not wanting to miss a trick" was predictably present, but the star of the show was Emma Lucille Agee "who wrote that dirty novel that's been selling millions in America. Her publishers got up the lunch as part of the campaign for inflicting it on England." Dame Flora continues:

> "The Agee woman told us for three quarters of an hour how she came to write her beastly book, when a simple apology was all that was required."

Mee-ow! As I have noted elsewhere, Plum loathed the discussion of literature in public and seemed to view it as a sort of betrayal when publishers actively encouraged it. In 'Best Seller,' poor old Egbert Mulliner, an assistant editor on *The Weekly Booklover* has reached the end of his tether and is taking a rest cure at Burwash Bay, since "[t]he strain of interviewing female novelists takes toll of the physique of all but the very hardiest." The narrator continues:

> For six months, week in and week out, Egbert Mulliner had been listening to female novelists talking about Art and their Ideals. He had seen them in cosy corners in their boudoirs, had watched them being kind to dogs and happiest when among their flowers. And one morning the proprietor of *The Booklover*, finding the young man sitting at his desk with little flecks of foam about his mouth and muttering over and over again in a dull, toneless voice the words 'Aurelia McGoggin, she draws inspiration from the scent of white lilies!' had taken him straight off to a specialist.

Fortunately, Egbert gets his mojo back and returns to what he does best, probing the "art and aims" of celebrity novelists. Here he is in full flight with his former fiancée Evangeline Pembury, who has written the Best Seller of the story's title:

> "Are you fond of dogs, Miss Pembury?" he asked.
> "I adore them," said Evangeline.
> "I should like, a little later, if I may," said Egbert, "to secure a snapshot of you being kind to a dog. Our readers appreciate these human touches, you understand."
> "Oh, quite," said Evangeline. "I will send out for a dog. I love dogs – and flowers."
> "You are happiest among your flowers, no doubt?"

"On the whole, yes."

"You sometimes think they are the souls of little children who have died in their innocence?"

"Frequently."

And so on, as Plum makes hay with the kind of literary tittle-tattle still familiar to us today.

Not that male authors were immune to this kind of proprietary small talk, as Caine was so ably proving. In 1901, a cash-in biography entitled *Hall Caine: The Man and the Novelist* appeared whose author, C. Fred Kenyon, so strenuously denies Caine's involvement in the book it arouses an instinctive suspicion of what Doyle had termed "wire-pulling." Its Preface even concludes with a personal letter to the author from Caine, in which he states:

> If your view of my life and my books is to have any value for the public, it must stand as your own, without any criticism or endorsement from me.

. . . even as he's endorsing it by writing an open letter clearly intended for publication. This breathtaking lack of self-awareness (or abject cynicism) is immediately topped by Kenyon's cringeworthy panegyric:

> The keynote of Hall Caine's character, both as a man and as a novelist, is sincerity, and the deepest thing in him is love of humanity. He is dominated by the ambition to get out of the realm of thought all that is best and wisest, and from his heart a stream of love for suffering, tortured humanity is constantly flowing. Heart and brain alike are ever at work for the good of mankind. "I have a real sense of joy in the thought that I am at least in the midst of the full stream of life, not in an eddy or backwater," he said to me one summer day, as we lay among the ferns of Greeba. He loves to feel that he is striving with the complex forces of these impetuous days of a new century; loves to feel that he is being carried along by the River of Life, for ever battling with the torrent, and always stretching out eager hands to help those who are weaker than himself. This, I repeat, is the deepest thing in Hall Caine, both as a man and as a writer, and the critics who find other interpretations of either know both imperfectly.

Pass the sick bag, Alice. Wodehouse may not have known Caine personally, but even at the age of 24 he was already predicting the inevitable
endgame of passing off advertorial as biography. In a 1906 *Punch* article entitled 'The Book-Hawkers,' he had imagined a dystopian future
in which the famous writers of his day are forced to flog their books
mountebank-style from market barrows in the Strand, the London thor-
oughfare that was home to several large publishing concerns and the
Globe newspaper where he was working at the time. Most of his featured
writers, with the exception of Henry James, seem to have successfully
adapted to their new role. And bless my soul, who should we meet but
'Old Pop' Kipling plugging his recently published *A History of England*, a
textbook aimed at children:

> "Instruction with amusement! We blend 'em. We blend
> 'em! Give the kiddy our last, and see him take in English
> history till he swells. Do you want, best-beloved, to think
> 'scruciatingly imperially? This is the place for you. Here
> we are! Here we *are!!*"

He's joined on the stump by George Bernard Shaw, H. G. Wells, H.
Rider Haggard, and Anthony Hope, each with his own characteristic
line in sales patter. But first to market is Hall Caine himself:

> "Here you are! Here you are! Buy! Buy! Buy! All genuine
> Manx, and genius in every syllable. We are the old firm.
> Here you are, lady. *The Eternal City*. All about the great city
> of Rome, of which you have doubtless heard."

Doyle is notably absent from this skit. But Caine has no shame, boasting that "This is no new job for me. Been doing my own booming for
years!" Which he had, never missing an opportunity to proclaim his
towering genius to anyone who'd listen. In a 1904 piece for *The Books of
Today and the Books of To-morrow*, Plum had asked his readers what was
wrong with the following statement:

> We hear that Mr. Hall Caine is busily engaged upon another book.

The answer? To refer to a Caine novel as merely a 'book' was to demean
its magnificence: "Colossal masterpiece" was both preferable and more
accurate. Three years later, in a limerick entitled 'Injured Innocence',
Plum once again takes aim, no doubt prompted by Caine's public attempts to justify his boosterism:

> A WRITER of drama named Caine
> Writes notes to the press to explain
> That 'Boom' is a word
> Of which he's not heard.
> For his is a soul above gain.

Caine's *faux* modesty, as well as his ambition, knew no bounds – an assessment of the writer Plum shared with, among others, Doyle, G. K. Chesterton, Thomas Hardy, and Oscar Wilde. But this very un-British brand of exhibitionism would also bleed into Caine's writing style in the form of an ingratiating sentimentality that makes his books a challenging read for anyone with even the slightest sense of the ridiculous.

At the start of his wildly bestselling 1902 novel *The Eternal City*, on a bitter winter's night, a young Italian ragamuffin (who speaks remarkably good English) has by chance stumbled into the home of a Soho teacher clutching only a dead squirrel (?!). His nationality established, he is then interrogated by the three-year-old daughter of the household, described as a "little daughter of Eve";

> "Oo a boy?"
> The boy smiled again and assented.
> "Oo me brodder?"
> The boy's smile paled perceptibly.
> "Oo lub me?"
> The tide in the boy's eyes was rising rapidly.
> "Oo lub me eber and eber?"
> The tears were gathering fast, when the doctor, smoothing the boy's dark curls again, said:
> "You have a little sister of your own far away in the Campagna Romana – yes?"
> "No, sir."
> "Perhaps it's a brother?"
> "I . . . I have nobody," said the boy, and his voice broke on the last word with a thud.

I can't be sure, but this is either intended seriously or it's some incredibly arch humour. As things turn out, the young orphan is the son of the Pope – just one of many unlikely twists and turns in this superfatted melodrama. Or how about this from 1897's *The Christian*, in which the heroine, Glory Quayle, takes leave of her home on the Isle of Man, possibly never to return:

> "The dear little island! I never thought it was so beautiful! Perhaps I might have been happy even there, if I had tried. Now, if I had only had somebody for company! How silly of me! I've been five years wishing and praying to get away, and now! [...] It *is* lovely, though, isn't it? Just like a bird on the water! And when you've been born in a place . . . the dear little island! And the old folks, too! How lonely they'll be, after all! I wonder if I shall ever . . . I'll go below. The wind's freshening, and this water in the wake is making my eyes . . . Good-bye, little birdie! I'll come back – I'll . . . Yes, never fear, I'll –"

Subtle it wasn't, yet it sold by the truckload, spurring Caine on to further heights of ick in the very opposite of a virtuous circle. Still he longed for status and respectability, appending an "Author's Note" to the novel in which he assured his readers he had remained "true to the principles of art" and was "following the precedent of great writers" by interlacing fact with fiction, casting himself as the humble "mould" through which "the metal has passed from the fires kept burning round about." On that showing alone, you can tell why Plum and Doyle had it in for him.

To the unassuming, diffident Wodehouse, there must have been something very needy about writers who instinctively chose to turn the spotlight on themselves as well as their writing. And not only that; melodrama of Caine's intensity also betrayed an almost desperate sort of over-eagerness to ingratiate himself with his readers, as if he could not trust them to enjoy his stories without this heightened febrility. Put plainly, he seemed addicted to over-stimulating his readers' emotions, a sort of Charles Dickens on steroids, which in Plum's book wasn't necessarily a good thing. Indeed, his relationship with the mighty Victorian writer was tellingly ambivalent and seems to have foundered on the very same rocks that made him loathe Caine.

A favourite among Wodehouse's schoolboy peers, Dickens's novelistic debut *Pickwick Papers* is singled out for special mention in Plum's 'A Shocking Affair,' and in *The Pothunters* we find the following lavish – if possibly equivocal – praise for *Great Expectations*:

> "I'm in the middle of a rather special book. Ever read *Great Expectations*? Dickens, you know."
> "I know. Haven't read it, though. Always rather funk starting on a classic, somehow. Good?"
> "My dear chap! Good's not the word."

But although Dickens's massive popularity made him almost untouchable, subversion would occasionally creep into Plum's thinking, intensifying the older and tetchier he got.

Nominally the editor of the 1934 anthology *A Century of Humour*, Wodehouse had nodded through a short piece of Dickens juvenilia ('Sentiment'), but by 1949's *The Mating Season* we witness Catsmeat Potter-Pirbright warning Bertie to avoid sentimentalism at all costs – "Never get Dickensy" is a rule he has failed to heed, and suffered the consequences. In 1954, Plum enquired of fellow novelist Denis Mackail, "Do you hate Dickens's stuff? I can't read it" – which may account for the complete absence of the writer's work from his personal library in Remsenburg (although he did have a copy of Edgar Johnson's 1952 biography). The following month he relented slightly and gave *Bleak House* a "last chance," and although it wasn't "as lousy as I had expected" he continued to marvel why Dickens seemed incapable of "ever draw[ing] a straight character." By way of illustration, he offers his correspondent (once again Denis Mackail) some misremembered lines of "whimsical comedy" involving Mr and Mrs Badger, Professor Dingo and Captain Swozzer (actually Swosser) that add nothing to the plot but seem to have intensely annoyed him. "Fine if the Badgers were the only comic characters, but there are at least a million others, even worse freaks," he fulminates. He quite likes the philanthropic Cheeryble brothers, however; yet on one occasion he directly refers to them (in 1970's *The Girl in Blue*), he places them in *Oliver Twist* rather than *Nicholas Nickleby* – a mistake his editors didn't spot.

Unfortunately, the more Dickens sold, the more he seems to have convinced himself that reducing his adult readers to floods of tears was the way forward. This habit would climax with the death of the hideously saccharine Little Nell from 1841's *The Old Curiosity Shop* who hears celestial music as her end approaches, the narrator further upping the ante by remarking "[s]o shall we know the angels in their majesty, after death." At which point Francis, Lord Jeffrey, founder of the sternly cerebral *Edinburgh Review* broke down and was discovered weeping with his head buried in his arms on his library desk; and Member of Parliament Daniel O'Connell began violently sobbing and threw his copy out of the window of the train he was travelling in. And these gentlemen were not alone; such was Dickens's popularity a period of national mourning seems to have been declared for a fictional character.

The granite-hearted Wodehouse was not so easily gulled; rather than being caught blubbing, he would have applauded the *bon mot* attributed to Oscar Wilde that "[o]ne would need to have a heart of stone to read the death of Little Nell without bursting into tears . . . of laughter." There's little doubt that Plum considered the soliciting of raw emotion a somewhat cheap shot; turning on the waterworks was simply a function of writerly technique readers could spot a mile off even as their eyes moistened. Lord Jeffrey was well aware he had been "a great goose to have given way so; but I could not help it," because Dickens knew how to play his readers like finely tuned musical instruments – as did any romantic novelist worth their salt. In 'No Wedding Bells for Bingo' Mortimer Little is introduced to the romances of Rosie M. Banks, and when Bertie, impersonating Ms. Banks, asks old Morty what he makes of the novels, the usually scratchy old buster replies:

> "Mr. Wooster, I am not ashamed to say that the tears came into my eyes. […] It amazes me that a man as young as you can have been able to plumb human nature so surely to its depths; to play with so unerring a hand on the quivering heartstrings of your reader; to write novels so true, so human, so moving, so vital!"
> "Oh, it's just a knack," I said.

And in Plum's view, that's *all* it was, a facsimile of real emotion wheeled out on demand and cynically marketed as the real thing.

There are consequently very few heartrending tears in Wodehouse, and when they do appear they quickly evaporate. In *The Adventures of Sally*, tears exist to be fought against or summarily dismissed, so when the wet and weedy Gerald Foster (author of the tellingly titled plays *The Primrose Way* and *The Wild Rose*) parades his troubles before Sally Nicholas, she gives him wonderfully short shrift:

> A tear rolled down his cheek. His intoxication had reached the maudlin stage. "Sally . . . S-Sally . . . I'm very miserable." […]
> "Go to bed, Gerald," she said. "You'll feel better in the morning." […]
> "May not be alive in the morning," he said solemnly. "Good mind to end it all. End it all!" […]
> Sally was not in the mood for melodrama.

Nor was Plum, even as he repeatedly milked its comic potential for all it was worth. In *Indiscretions of Archie*, a lung-busting performance of the lachrymal 'Mother's Knee' proves positively Pavolvian, as hard-assed union boss Aloysius Connolly obligingly turns into a spot of grease on hearing the song performed, calling off a labour dispute – just as the conniving Archie knew he would – when its lyrics recall the dear old matriarch he left back in dear old Ireland thirty years before.

But Dickens and Caine were not the only sentimentalists the youthful Plum had in his cross hairs. Topping even Caine's sales and egomania was Mary Mackay (pen-name Marie Corelli) with whose work and career Plum also made regular sport – remember the school library skit in Chapter 2? Her 1903 biography *Marie Corelli: The Writer and the Woman* (co-authored by Plum's editor at *The Captain* R. S. Warren Bell) makes for interesting reading, if only because it appears to have been written with a good deal of self-flattering input from its subject. Claiming noble Italian ancestry, Marie began her career as a musician; but aged 30, her debut novel *A Romance of Two Worlds* began a vertiginous rise through the ranks of bestselling writers to the point, it is claimed in more than one place, she was Queen Victoria's favourite novelist and regularly exceeded the sales of Doyle, Wells and Kipling combined. The printing history of her 1895 tome *The Sorrows of Satan* would seem to support this assertion, reaching ten 'editions' in its first year, 32 by its second and 66 by the time of her death, three decades after it first appeared. A Faustian tale of no great originality, it contains immortal passages such as this, courtesy of the book's conflicted narrator Geoffrey Tempest (see what she did there?):

> Why should the wicked flourish like a green bay-tree? I have often thought about it. Now however I believe I could help to solve the problem out of my own personal experience. But . . . such an experience! Who will credit it? Who will believe that anything so strange and terrific ever chanced to the lot of a mortal man? No one. Yet it is true; truer than much so-called truth.

The breathless stridency rarely lets up as we learn of the travails of a penniless writer, sorely tempted by a mysterious Count of wealth and taste named Lucio Rimânez, who everyone but Geoffrey (who clearly hasn't read his Marlowe) can tell is the earthly incarnation of Satan. Suddenly acquiring untold wealth, Geoffrey mixes in high society and crosses paths with the massively successful female writer Mavis Clare, a "rival in art" of whose fame he is insanely jealous. Clare is, somewhat inevitably, a thinly disguised Corelli, giving her creator a chance to settle some old scores and make pointed, self-interested observations on the state of a literary market that despises her books even as they fly off the shelves.

Wodehouse may well have borne Mavis/Marie in mind when creating his own army of romantic novelists, for some of the parallels are

really quite striking. When, Jeeves remarks that Rosie M. Banks is one
of the "great many" authors who are "neglected by the reviewers yet
widely read," he is echoing Mavis's confession that she is "not a press
favourite and I never get good reviews." Yet, as with Rosie M., this snobbish disparagement hasn't harmed her sales, a conundrum that encourages Tempest to buy a copy of her latest to see what all the fuss is about.
He too, it appears, is labouring under the colossal misapprehension that
'popular' axiomatically equates with 'rubbish.' But then . . .

> I had not read many sentences before my heart sank with
> a heavy sense of fear and – jealousy! – the slow fire of
> an insidious envy began to smoulder in my mind. What
> power had so gifted this author – this mere woman – that
> she should dare to write better than I! And that she should
> force me, by the magic of her pen to mentally acknowl-
> edge, albeit with wrath and shame, my own inferiority!
> Clearness of thought, brilliancy of style, beauty of diction,
> all these were hers, united to consummate ease of expres-
> sion and artistic skill.

This shameless self-promotion goes on and on, paragraph after paragraph, in the course of which Corelli remembers to butter up her readers:

> [T]he great masses of the public in all nations are always
> led by some instinctive sense of right, that moves them to
> reject the false and unworthy, and select the true.

Not so her critics, who she took care to trash at every available opportunity. In her biography, she even included an illustration of her Yorkshire
terrier Czar snacking on a sheaf of critical reviews, the picture cap-
tioned "What Becomes of the Press Cuttings." However, despite his en-
slavement to Clare's artistry, Tempest joins her detractors in the fourth
estate and pens a damning assessment of her novel *Differences* which, for
all the jealous misogyny that fuels it, has no effect whatever. And then,
much against his better judgment, he actually gets to meet the source of
his angry confusion.

Mavis resides in Lily Cottage, a chocolate-boxy rural dwelling that
could easily double for Honeysuckle Cottage, the eponymous setting for
Plum's 1925 tale of the power of romantic fiction. Both retreats prove
to be small oases of love and calm in a naughty world, their tranquil
aura promoting feelings of calm and benevolence even among those
who swear they will never succumb. Far from finding the "unsexed"

bluestocking of his prejudice, Tempest is introduced to a young, impossibly attractive "butterfly thing" playing with her dog Tricksy and falls in love at first sight. However, like Plum's Leila J. Pinckney, Mavis is not some gauzy refugee from a romance, but – it is regularly emphasized – a hard-working, self-made woman who has risen by her own merit. She sublimates her ill-treatment at the hands of the critics by maintaining a flock of turtle-doves, each bird named after the title of a publication in which she has been poorly reviewed, real-life publications that Corelli lists exhaustively, almost as if she has been keeping a list. In her study hang likenesses of Shakespeare, Shelley, Byron, and Keats along with aspirational quotations from these and other literary greats, at which point she has the immortal crust to remark that "as a rule, literary people take themselves far too seriously."

Immediately on making his acquaintance, she sees straight through Rimânez, her beauty, clear sight and obvious goodness breaking the spell he has cast over Tempest and presumably saving her fellow writer from a grisly sojourn in Hell. Such is the redemptive power of Mavis's personality and her writing, Corelli portrays her as the angel to the Count's devil, prompting Tempest's "cruel" and "shallow" wife Sibyl to remark:

> "I see now how perfectly she has won her public – it is by the absolute conviction she has herself of the theories of life she tries to instil. […] [She is] a woman who finds life beautiful, and God existent, [who] has secured an enviable fame and the honour of thousands, allied to a serene content."

Had Plum read this, which I bet he had done, it would only have confirmed his suspicions that Corelli, like Caine, was a monstrous humbug. In between eruptions of incredulous laughter he would have noted the irony that in her lengthy anatomization of the English publishing industry, there were several points they could agree on.

Unfortunately, any fellow feeling had been dispelled by the time he read and reviewed her 1905 publication *Free Opinions Freely Expressed*, in which Corelli stepped out from behind her fiction to deliver lectures on no fewer than 27 subjects close to her heart. In a piece entitled 'WHAT I THINK', subtitled "Rude Opinions, Crudely Expressed" by 'Carrie Morelli', Plum nails the book's style and content in a series of contentious remarks, including:

> THE TRUE test of merit in a book is whether it sells. I

sell. So does the author of the 'Deadwood Dick' series of penny novelettes.

THE UNSEEN rulers of human destiny are, on the whole, very kindly Fates. They are at liberty to make what use they please of this testimonial.

THEY SAY that Bacon wrote Shakespeare. Soon they will discover a cryptogram in the Waverley Novels to prove that George the Fourth wrote them. Where will this stop? There are people who believe that I am Hall Caine.

Certainly in Plum's mind, the two writers were not dissimilar in that they represented the very antithesis of the kind of public figure he would eventually engineer for himself. Where they were pompous and overbearing, he would be self-deprecating, gentling undermining any seriousness with humour; he would not strain for effect, except of course for comic purposes; he would have no message nor agenda, nor direct his readers what to think except in jest; and above all, he would not desperately thrust himself on his public, courting and even craving their approval unless ironically. Even as he took a leaf out of Caine's biography by writing an open letter for inclusion at the end of *Performing Flea*, it's a contrivance that rings truer than anything Caine ever wrote about himself:

> I sometimes wonder if I really am a writer. When I look at the sixty-odd books in the shelf with my name of them, and reflect that ten million of them have been sold, it amazes me that I can have done it. I don't know anything, and I seem incapable of learning […] I feel I've been fooling the public for fifty years.

As a writer of frothy comedies that could oh-so-easily be dismissed as trifles by unsympathetic and careless critics, Plum sometimes gave house room to doubts as to the worth of his work, an argument he would further explore – and not entirely light-heartedly – in chapters 5, 7 and 20 of 1957's *Over Seventy*. But what Wodehouse *did* share with Caine and Corelli was a steely determination to succeed, a healthy contempt for those who considered success a dirty word – and a deep love of the subject of this book's next chapter, William Shakespeare.

The possessor of a distinctive domed forehead reminiscent of Shakespeare's, Caine would trim his hair and beard in such a way that it would more closely resemble the Bard's – and if people still failed to notice the likeness he was only too happy to point it out to them, or have his biographer do it:

> His head is the head of a poet, a thinker, a prophet. It is
> suggestive of most of the portraits – ideal and otherwise –
> of Shakespeare; there is the same noble forehead, and the
> same large, passionate eyes.

Not to be outdone, Corelli even went as far as moving to Stratford-on-Avon in 1898, immediately involving herself in the preservation of the town's Elizabethan heritage, as her biography gushingly informs us:

> That she is not merely a lover of Shakespeare, but a Shake-
> speare enthusiast, is known to all her friends; she would
> see the day come, if possible, and help to speed its com-
> ing, when the whole town of Stratford-on-Avon shall be a
> Shakespeare memorial. She would exclude steam-launch-
> es and all similar misplaced modernities from the peaceful
> Avon; she would have every new building that is erected in
> the birthplace of Shakespeare constructed in accordance
> with the architecture of the Master's day; she would sacred-
> ly and lovingly guard every old building and the form of all
> Stratford's old streets; she would have the storehouse, that
> exists there, of never explored sixteenth-century records,
> thoroughly ransacked and reported upon, as it should be,
> by competent and national authorities, and given an ade-
> quate place and publicity. We should hear little more then,
> we venture to assert, of Baconian theories.

For all that PR babble, Corelli regularly put her money where her mouth was and ended up making a valuable contribution to the preservation of Stratford's Shakespearean heritage. And that final sentence at least contains something she and Wodehouse – those polar literary opposites – could wish for.

Chapter 9:
Shakespeare

Shakespeare's stuff is different from mine, but that is not to say that it is inferior.
Kind Words for Shakespeare

[T]he works of P. G. Wodehouse are practically a dictionary [of Shakespeare quotations] in themselves.
Jane Armstrong, compiler of The Arden Dictionary of Shakespeare Quotations

"Oh, I know *Hamlet*. Aunt Agatha once made me take her son Thos to it at the Old Vic. Not a bad show, I thought, though a bit highbrow."
Much Obliged, Jeeves

"I once went to Valparaiso as a stewardess on a fruit boat, and the only book on board was *The Plays of William Shakespeare*, belonging to the chief engineer. By the time the voyage was over, I knew them by heart. I suppose that's why I quote him a good deal."
The Old Reliable

"That's Shakespeare, isn't it?"
"I shouldn't wonder. Most of the good gags are."
Full Moon

In 1899, aged 18, Pelham Grenville Wodehouse cheekily signed off a letter to schoolfriend Eric George as "P. G. Wodehouse-Shakespeare" after being praised as the "lorryit" [sic] of Dulwich College. The association would stand the test of time, for over the next 75 years, William Shakespeare and Plum would prove inseparable in both life and art. His well-thumbed *Complete Works* was one of only two books Wodehouse took with him into Nazi internment in 1940; and his "brother-pen" (as he calls Shakespeare in *Something Fresh*) is quoted or referenced no fewer than 1,200 times in his novels and stories, from first to last.

While many writers cosy up to The Bard to bask in his reflected glory, it's plain Wodehouse's attachment wasn't simply cultural window-dressing, and the ways his writing cavorts with his predecessor's legacy while gleefully poking fun at it is an object lesson in how to creatively annex another writer's work to the greater glory of both. Since the mid-18th century, the Man from Stratford had been revered, even worshipped; but from Plum's comedic perspective, Shakespeare was a jobbing playwright who faced the same creative issues common to all writers time out of mind – including himself. So it is that in all Plum's writing about his illustrious antecedent, there is a palpable sense he is on a mission to rescue Shakespeare from Olympus and make him one of us again, narrowing the gap between 'Shakespeare the Literary Deity' and 'Shakespeare the Honest Scrivener' that generations of well-meaning but over-zealous fans had helped open up.

One of his earliest forays can be found in an uncredited 1907 piece for *Punch*, in which he re-imagines *Hamlet* condensed for an American audience with a very short attention span. Here's the whole thing in a little over 200 words, anticipating *West Side Story* (which would do a similar job on *Romeo and Juliet*) by exactly half a century:

Scene—*Battlements at Elsinore. Enter* Jas. P. Hamlet, *son of the Danish President, and* Horatio *and* Marcellus (*of the Elsinore football-team*).
Hamlet. Say, fellers, about this yer spirut. [*Enter* Ghost]
Ghost. Say, Hamlet.
H. Sure?
G. I'm your pop. Your step-pop murdered me.
H. You don't say?
G. Sure. Poured poison in my ear. I was easy fruit. Say, Hamlet, it's up to you.
H. Sure. [*Exit* Ghost]

Scene—*The Palace. Enter* Hamlet, *with* Rosencrantz *and* Guildenstern (*sophomores of the Elsinore University*).
Hamlet. Say, fellers.
R and G. Huh.
H. Guess we'll have some theatricals here. Go and corral some all-wool stars.
R. and G. Sure. [*Exeunt R. and G*]
H. Guess I'll make step-pop sit up, the pie-faced mut.

Scene—*The Palace. The Players begin their play.*
The Danish President. Say, Hamlet, got a book of the words with you? What's this piece about, anyway?
Hamlet. You'll see quick enough.
The President (as play proceeds). Holy Cat! Some gazebo

must have been giving these yaps the wise word. This is all about me and the late President. Yes, there I go pouring poison in his ear.

H. Like the play, pop?

The President. Vurry bright, Hamlet, vurry bright. Beats Vaudeville all the way.

H. (in a sinister manner). Sure.

Scene—*The Palace. Enter the President, his wife, Hamlet, Rosencrantz, Guildenstern, Laertes, and all the characters who are left alive after preceding Act.*

Hamlet. And now for a bully old rough-house. (*Stabs President, and poisons President's wife.*) That's the sort of man *I* am.

R. and G. (giving College yell). Rah! Rah! Elsinore! Rah! Rah! Rah!

H. (to Laertes). Care to fence with poisoned rapiers?

L. Sure. [*They fence*]

H. Got you there. [*Wounds him*]

L. Had you then. [*Wounds him*] My notice is up. [*Dies*]

H. Me for the golden shore. [*Dies*]

R and G. Rah! Rah! Elsinore! Rah! Rah! Rah!

Curtain.

Shakespeare's version clocks in at around four hours. Plum's? Less than two minutes.

The rehabilitation of his illustrious predecessor, which would occupy Wodehouse for over 40 years, began in earnest in a 1915 article for the American *Vanity Fair* magazine, 'What Really Happened to Hamlet,' containing the germ of the idea he would elaborate in 'All About Shakespeare' for the same publication in April the following year. Content from both these pieces would be further refashioned as 'An Outline of Shakespeare' in the 1932 compilation *Louder and Funnier*. Then there's 'The Wodehouse-Shakespeare Controversy: Latest' and 'Kind Words for Shakespeare,' *Punch* columns from 1956 that were re-worked in both *America, I Like You* (1956) and *Over Seventy* (1957). Plum certainly got some decent mileage from this material, but never managed to knock it into any kind of organised shape. So for the first part of this chapter, I propose to reconstruct Plum's fractured take on Shakespeare's biography using material culled from all seven of these pieces.

Wodehouse's account (which contains a surprising amount of accurate information) begins by informing us that while Shakespeare's birth-day is traditionally celebrated on April 23, he wasn't actually baptized until the 26 April 1564. It's hardly the greatest start to a biography if you don't know when your subject was born; but The Bard's early life is full of similar disobliging lacunae, including his actual name. Several different versions of Shakespeare's signature have been identified on official documentation of the period. But do they belong to *our* Shakespeare? Plum quickly gets on the case:

> [W]hen I say Shakespeare, do not run away with the idea that I am not perfectly aware that it may have been Shakspere or even Shikspur.

Or Sakspere, Schakosper, Saxper, Schaftspere, Shakstaf and Shasspere. It's a tad ironic that the god of English Literature couldn't sign his own name with any consistency. Or perhaps Plum paused to reflect that like his own father Ernest Wodehouse, John Shakespeare suffered a seismic financial reverse that left his son's formal education at Stratford Grammar School incomplete. If so, it wouldn't be the last biographical coincidence that bound the writers together.

As well as not knowing who he was, we don't have much of a clue what Shakespeare looked like, other than that uncanny resemblance to Hall Caine (see previous chapter):

> [T]here are sixteen portraits of him in the book of reference to which I owe so grateful a debt, and except that they are all solid on the fact that he never shaved, each is absolutely different from the others.

Here, Plum's research errs on the side of caution. Between 1856 and 1900, no fewer than sixty 'true likenesses' of Shakespeare were offered to London's National Portrait Gallery, and the painted bust on the north side of the chancel in Holy Trinity Church, Stratford-on-Avon, where Shakespeare was buried in 1616, has been described as "the kind of monument that might be constructed for a self-satisfied pork butcher," and by Mark Twain as having the "deep, deep, subtle, subtle expression of a bladder." None of which stops Plum referring to 'Soapy' Molloy's "fine, high forehead, rather like Shakespeare's" in *Money in the Bank*, *Ice in the Bedroom* and *Pearls, Girls and Monty Bodkin*.

Having left grammar school, Shakespeare "seems to have had the idea that there was a good living to be made out of stealing rabbits from the preserves of the local squires." In *Joy in the Morning* rabbits have turned to ducks, while many biographers opt for deer. 'Shakespeare: Deer Rustler' is a story popularized (but probably not originated) by Nicholas Rowe, who in 1709 published an edition of Shakespeare's plays prefaced by an 8,300-word "Life." Rowe based much of his narrative on reminiscences from the celebrated actor Thomas Betterton, who travelled to Warwickshire with the express purpose of milking the more elderly locals of any anecdotes they might have picked up from remaining members of the Shakespeare family. Except he probably didn't bother to go, prompting a later Shakespeare editor, Edmond Malone, to state unequivocally in 1790 that out of the eleven "facts" in Rowe's piece, eight were simply not true. Including the rustling, which was, in his opinion, "an unfounded calumny."

It's at this point that Plum markedly deviates from his sources, contending that game and/or livestock were the young Shakespeare's gateway drug to plots:

> [I]t was only when approaching years of discretion that it suddenly occurred to him that a man could do much better for himself by stealing plots. In the year 1591 he began to write plays, and from then onward anybody who had a good play put it in a steel box and sat on the lid when he saw Shakespeare coming.

And yes – once more it's true. Of Shakespeare's 38 canonical plays, only three can be said to have no direct source (*Love's Labour's Lost*, *The Merry Wives of Windsor* and *The Tempest*). Which means that Shakespeare must have – technically – stolen the rest. On this point, you'd think Plum would be quick to understand and slow to condemn; after all, thinking up things for his characters to do was very much *his* constant bugbear. For *Barmy in Wonderland*, he even bought plot and dialogue from his friend George S. Kaufman; and Ethel, Leonora, and Bill Townend were all regularly tapped for ideas. But before we start to examine this issue from a Shakespearean perspective, we must somehow transport our man from rural Warwickshire to London, so he can properly embark on his life of literary larceny.

In the so-called "lost years" which lasted from his marriage to Anne Hathaway in 1582 until 1591, Shakespeare biographers claim he earned a crust as:

- A legal clerk.
- A schoolmaster in the north of England.
- A ligger/musician in the households of Catholic families.

- An actor/play doctor/special FX man specializing in stage blood.
- A valet horse parking attendant at 'The Theatre' in Shoreditch (there was only one permanent theatre in London during this period, hence its definite article).

Plum inclines to that final one, painting a touching tableau of a young stage-door Johnny trying to get the ear of James Burbage, The Theatre's owner:

> There seems to be no doubt that Shakespeare had the usual struggles of the beginner who tries to break into the play-writing business. Tradition says that he started in a modest way by holding horses at the doors, and a moving historical picture might be painted of the future king of the English stage, trying to read Burbage the opening scene of a comedy while the latter flitted past on his way to the Mermaid Tavern [...] and at the same time endeavouring to elude the attentions of a peevish mustang who was trying to bite him in the back of the neck.

This is a story Plum had pilfered from an outrageous piece of historical embroidery in Samuel Johnson's Preface to his 1765 edition of Shakespeare's plays. According to the good Doctor, the would-be playwright, on the lam from the authorities in Stratford, cooled his heels in East London doing menial jobs. Still he managed to distinguish himself; so attentive was he to his patrons' horses that "in a short time every man as he alighted called for Will Shakespeare, and scarcely any other waiter was trusted with a horse while Will Shakespeare could be had. This was the first dawn of better fortune." *That's* how he got Burbage's attention, and the rest is history. Really? No, of course not, Johnson hoping – not for the first or last time – his stentorian tone would somehow turn wild speculation into facts.

Back in Wodehouse's version of the story, once the young renegade had caught the manager's eye he was away to the races:

> Shakespeare's first play, according to the authorities, was entitled "The Contention of York and Lancaster (2, 3 Henry VI)." One is forced to admit that as a title it could be improved, but the Encyclopaedia Britannica says that was it, so there can be no mistake.

So *that's* the source of Plum's intel. And yes, what we now call *Henry VI, Part 2 is* generally thought to have been Shakespeare's first performed play, so successful it begat a prequel and a sequel.

At which point Plum moves swiftly on to a subject that was rarely far from his thoughts: just who *did* write the plays normally attributed to Shakespeare? It was a story that passed through several iterations at Plum's hands between 1915 and 1957, beginning with the possibility that Shakespeare's first big break at The Theatre was as a script doctor, or what Plum calls a "theatrical fixer." It's a theory still very much in vogue in modern scholarship, with computer-generated lexical, metrical and stylistic tests 'proving' that Shakespeare had a hand in plays written by other people, and vice versa. But Plum was ahead of all of them, citing one such title – *Hamlet* by Francis Bacon – as a good example of how Shakespeare improved a dodgy original by adding humour, alienating the original author and copping the writer's credit.

Wodehouse himself had been a sort-of fixer in London's theatreland, where he had worked backstage as an on-call lyricist in musical comedy, so he knew whereof he spake. But the fast-talking, spiky, been-there-done-it all William 'Bill' Shakespeare he creates for these articles owes a greater debt to Broadway than the West End. We're now in the realm of pure Wodehousean fantasy as Bill explains precisely where Bacon, the philosophical essayist and Chancellor of the Royal Exchequer, is getting it all wrong with his story of the dithering Dane:

> "What you want at the final curtain is to have the whole crowd jump on one another and everybody kill everybody else. We'll have the King poison the wine and Laertes poisons the sword and drops it and Hamlet picks it up in mistake for his own and plugs Laertes, and then the Queen drinks the wine and Hamlet sticks the King with the poisoned sword. Then you'll have got something."

Which is of course the version of *Hamlet* posterity has handed down to us. Bacon may consider it "a little improbable," but then he isn't in touch with "what the public wants." Further Shakespearean 'improvements' that stuck include making Hamlet *pretend* to be mad (Bill's manager tells Bacon that "[t]he matinée girl doesn't like loonies"); making Ophelia mad instead ("[a]n audience doesn't mind a crazy girl"); inserting a three-way comedy routine featuring Hamlet, Rosencrantz and Guildenstern ("[i]t'll go well on Boat Race night"); and finally, he lengthens the 'To be or not to be' soliloquy:

"How's this for one? "Or to take arms against a sea of troubles." I thought of that this minute, just like a flash."

When Bacon correctly points out that taking arms against a sea is a mixed metaphor and Shakespeare disagrees, the mighty philosopher/politician throws his toys out of the pram and returns to his day job never to darken a theatre again. The fixer's name gets top billing and that's the way history remembers things.

Yes, Wodehouse was joshing, but in a way, 'improving' an original is precisely what Shakespeare built his career on. Take that very same *Hamlet*, whose roots lie in Scandinavian legend, first taking recognizable shape in Saxo Grammaticus's 13th-century *Gesta Danorum*. From that, a stage version known as the *Ur-Hamlet* appeared by 1589, in which Shakespeare might just have had a hand, itself probably influenced by the story's inclusion in François de Belleforest's *Histoires Tragiques*. This long and complex ancestry culminates in Shakespeare's triumphant re-telling, which was written sometime between 1599 and 1602. Rather than go all through that genealogical rannygazoo (and those last few lines are a brutally edited version of the play's *actual* literary lineage), Plum kept things simple by annexing the theory that Bacon wrote everything Bardic and made hay with it right through to 1965's *Galahad at Blandings* when Gally Threepwood comments that "There's nothing low or degrading about an alias. Look at Lord Bacon. Went about calling himself Shakespeare."

What this long-running controversy really boils down to is the Baconistas' snobbish belief that a glover's son from the English Midlands didn't – indeed couldn't – be possessed of the necessary mental equipment to be a great poet. To have written what he did, Shakespeare would have to have been a well-educated aristocrat like Bacon or those other pretenders Sir Walter Raleigh, or the Earls of Oxford or Essex. Plum, the son of a middle-ranking colonial magistrate, would almost definitely have sided with his brother-pen on this issue, alluding to the literary spat Shakespeare had with a rival playwright only a few months after he gave up the valet-parking gig to write full time:

Occasionally someone would call him Shakescene or Johannes Factotum and say he had a tiger's heart wrapped in a player's hide.

That rival was Robert Greene, one of the so-called "University Wits" and the first writer ever to have a pop at Shakespeare for plagiarism. The passage Plum is paraphrasing occurs in Greene's *A Groatsworth of*

Wit published in 1592:

> [T]here is an upstart crow beautified with our feathers,
> that with his tiger's heart wrapped in a player's hide sup-
> poses he is as well able to bombast out a blank verse as
> the best of you; and, being an absolute Johannes Factotum
> [Jack of all trades], is in his own conceit the only Shake-
> scene in a country.

Yes, he's definitely fingering Shakespeare, the "tiger's heart" a lift from
Henry VI, Part 3. But then Shakespeare took his revenge 16 years later
when he nicked bits of Greene's play *Pandosto* when writing *The Winter's
Tale* – by which time Greene was long since dead and couldn't complain.

Amid all the jokes about Shakespeare being a plot-nicker, Wodehouse is tacitly acknowledging two truths that are often overlooked in
large swathes of modern Bardic criticism: that originality in art was not
as prized in Shakespeare's time as it is in our own; and that the artist
is primarily a craftsman rather that a conduit for their muse. Which
means Shakespeare really *was* a fixer, and he did indeed 'collaborate'
with other writers with or without their co-operation. However, what
still sets Shakey apart from his fellow scribes is genius, and like Plum he
ended his career a wealthy man. Indeed, a further link between these
self-made successes is their practical experience of working in the theatre at the business end of production.

Shakespeare, in addition to his portfolio career as a land and property speculator, grain-broker, tithe-buyer and loan shark, also part-owned
and ran a hugely successful theatrical company, the Lord Chamberlain's
Men. As early as 1594/5, having just turned thirty and only about four
or five years into his playwriting career, he was already in the management game. While majoring in writing, he would also be scanning box
office receipts in much the same way Plum would have done during his
time working on Broadway and in the West End, never losing sight of
the fact that what he wrote and how he wrote it needed to translate into
bums on seats. Both men would have been all too aware that in the aptly
named show*business*, you're only as good as your last show. Writing to
Bill Townend, he remarked:

> What a wretched thing failure in the theatre is. There isn't
> a dramatist from Shakespeare downwards who hasn't had
> the most ghastly flops, but one never gets over that feeling
> of pollution you get when you are associated with a bad
> failure.

Wodehouse clearly understood the travails of a hard-working drama-turge, emphasizing the high turnover of material in the fiercely compet-itive world of London theatre in the 1590s and early 1600s. In 1594-5, the Admiral's Men (perhaps the hardest working men in showbusiness at the time, and rivals of Shakespeare's company) put on a 49-week rep-ertory season at the Rose Theatre, acting six days a week and staging a total of 38 different plays, 21 of which were new. That's a lot of plays, and a punishing schedule Plum knew only too well. In 1917 he had six, arguably seven shows at various stages in production on Broadway even as he continued to publish novels, short stories and journalism. He and Shakespeare had both been through the mill:

> Shakespeare […] would dash off *Macbeth* on Sunday night for production on Monday, and on Tuesday morning at six o'clock round would come Burbage in a great state of excitement.
>
> "Good heavens, William, why aren't you up and work-ing? Don't you know we've got to give 'em something to-night?"
>
> "What about *Macbeth*?", Shakespeare would ask sleepily.
>
> "*Macbeth* finished its long and successful run last night, and it you haven't got something to follow we'll have to close the theatre."
>
> So Shakespeare would heave himself out of bed, dig down into the box where he kept other people's plots, and by lunchtime he would hand Burbage the script of *Othello*. And Burbage would skim through and say it was rotten but it would have to do.

The put-upon writer was a theme Plum explored autobiographically in his theatre reviews for *Vanity Fair* between January 1915 and May 1918, written as he was putting together the books and lyrics for his own productions. The title of one piece, 'The Agonies of Writing a Musical Comedy (Which Shows Why Librettists Pick at the Coverlet)' from March 1917 says it all. Indeed, on this evidence the two men could have been brothers.

And it's at this point, with Shakespeare at the peak of his popular-ity, that Wodehouse abruptly abandons his biography. It's all been a bit of fun, and one gets the impression that for Plum, the question of whether "Shakespeare" (however spelt) was an individual, "syndicate" or "limited company" consisting of "Sir Francis Bacon, Sir Walter Ra-leigh, the Earl of Essex, Queen Elizabeth, Mr Gordon Selfridge, and the second girl from the end in the front row of the chorus of the Merry Widow No. 1 Touring Company" was a mere bagatelle. The plays were the thing, giving us our cue to begin looking at those 246 different Shakespeare references which he borrowed a total of 1,192 times in his novels, stories and other shorter pieces (a total that doesn't count incidental phrases and stage directions unattributable to particular plays, such as "alar(u)ms and excursions," "confused noise without," and "i' faith" that "many a time and oft" pepper Plum's prose). Here's the stats: (and by the way, this amazing feat of scholarship has been compiled by Diego Seguí, aided and abetted by the team behind that incomparable Wodehouse resource madameulalie.org. My sincerest thanks to everyone concerned for the chance to share their findings).

- These attributable references are drawn from 28 of the 38 currently acknowledged Shakespeare plays, the Sonnets and even the seldom-read poem *The Passionate Pilgrim*, whose attribution continues to be questioned. This bolsters the case that Plum read far and wide throughout the canon, and that he didn't confine his Shakespeare sourcing to *Bartlett's Familiar Quotations* (although there is considerable overlap). The plays he didn't quote from are: *The Comedy of Errors, Coriolanus, Cymbeline, Henry VI, Part 1, Henry VI, Part 2, Love's Labour's Lost* (ironically, his self-professed favourite), *Pericles, Titus Andronicus,* and *The Two Gentlemen of Verona* (there's also *The Two Noble Kinsmen*, but this wasn't widely admitted to the canon until comparatively recently).
- Plum's top five Shakespeare plays by total number of references are: *Hamlet* (265 occurrences of 52 different references); *Macbeth* (206/32); *Julius Caesar* (137/27); *Othello* (95/10), and *Romeo and Juliet* (66/10). These are all tragedies, which may seem odd for a comic writer, and we'll discover why Plum was disproportionately drawn to Shakespeare's gloomier works later in this chapter.
- The top five Wodehouse novels containing the most Shakespearean references are: *Joy in the Morning* (1946) with 43; *Ring For Jeeves* (1953) 33; *Jeeves and the Feudal Spirit* (1954) 32; *Uncle Dynamite* (1948) 30; *The Mating Season* (1949) 28. Notice how all these novels were published after Plum's wartime internment, suggesting once again that he made good use of the micro-library he was allowed to take with him into captivity.
- Plum's top five most regularly borrowed references are as

214

follows (with the salient phrases emboldened where appropriate):

At #5 with 21, it's Lady Macbeth, baiting her husband about her proposal of regicide, which he's decidedly chary about:

> "Wouldst thou have that
> Which thou esteem'st the ornament of life,
> And live a coward in thine own esteem,
> **Letting I dare not wait upon I would,**
> **Like the poor cat i'th'adage?**"

Example: [Bertie] "Yes, I recall the Sipperley case. He couldn't bring himself to the scratch. A marked coldness of the feet, was there not? I recollect you saying he was letting – what was it? – letting something do something. Cats entered into it, if I am not mistaken."
[Jeeves] "Letting 'I dare not' wait upon 'I would,' sir."
"That's right. But how about the cats?"
"Like the poor cat i' the adage, sir."
"Exactly. It beats me how you think up these things."
(Right Ho, Jeeves)

At #4 with 27, we hear Hamlet's father, about to reveal how he was murdered by Claudius:

> "I could a tale unfold, whose lightest word
> Would harrow up thy soul, freeze thy young blood,
> Make thy two eyes, like stars, start from their spheres,
> Thy knotted and combinèd locks to part,
> And each particular hair to stand on end,
> **Like quills upon the fretful porpentine.**"

Example: "I am not a weak man, Jeeves, but when I think of what will happen if Stilton cops me while I am draped in that uniform, it makes my knotted and combined locks . . . what was that gag of yours?"
"Part, sir, and each particular hair –"
"Stand on end, wasn't it?"
"Yes, sir. Like quills upon the fretful porpentine."
"That's right. And that brings me back to it. What the

dickens is a porpentine?"
"A porcupine, sir."
"Oh, a *porcupine*? Why didn't you say that at first? It's been worrying me all day."

(Joy in the Morning)

In at #3 with 28, we have Mark Antony taking down Brutus and Cassius at Julius Caesar's funeral:

"Ambition should be made of sterner stuff."

Example: On the stage and in motion-pictures one frequently sees victims of drink keel over in a state of complete unconsciousness after a single glass, but Ukridge was surely of sterner stuff.

('Buttercup Day')

At #2, with 30, is Hamlet's famous mixed metaphor:

> Whether 'tis nobler in the mind to suffer
> The slings and arrows of outrageous fortune,
> **Or to take arms against a sea of troubles**,
> And by opposing end them?

Example: [Jeeves] "There is a method by means of which Mrs. Travers can be extricated from her sea of troubles. Shakespeare."
[Bertie] I didn't know why he was addressing me as Shakespeare, but I motioned him to continue.

(Jeeves and the Feudal Spirit)

And at the top of the heap, with 40 appearances, Lady Macbeth is still goading her husband, prior to his murder of King Duncan:

> "Yet do I fear thy nature,
> It is too full o'**th'milk of human kindness**
> To catch the nearest way."

Example: A pain in the neck to his sister Constance, his sister Julia, his sister Dora and all his other sisters, [Lord Emsworth] was universally esteemed in less austere quar-

ters, for his heart was of gold and his soul overflowing with
the milk of human kindness.

(Pigs Have Wings)

So much for the stats. Now it's time to look at precisely *how* Plum used
what he borrowed.

Back in Wodehouse's schooldays, it's clear that Shakespeare had already taken up residence in his consciousness, worming his way into
his leisure activities as well as his classroom studies (for the record, *King
Lear* and *The Merchant of Venice* were his two set texts). W. S. Gilbert
had written a rather pedestrian (for him) skit on *Hamlet* in 1874, and in
1900, the College lads dusted off *Rosencrantz and Guildenstern*, with the
18-year-old Plum cast (or possibly self-cast) as the second of Hamlet's
playmates. The in-house *Alleynian* magazine gave him a decent notice
(possibly written by Wodehouse himself), singling out his character's
biggest scene which involved an extemporized dance and some by-play
with a revolver. This was to prove the first time Wodehouse monkeyed
around with Shakespeare in public; then two years later in his debut
novel (1902's *The Pothunters*) there would follow eight Bardic references,
all short phrases he left uncredited, knowing his readers would most
likely recognize them. These included the debut of one that would remain in his repertoire until 1965:

> "She pined in thought,
> And with a green and yellow melancholy
> She sat like **Patience on a monument**
> Smiling at grief. Was not this love indeed?"
>
> *(Twelfth Night)*

Viola's word-picture of her hypothetical 'sister' pining away illustrates
a crucial aspect of Plum's affection for Shakespeare: he seemed to love
phrases that conjured up bizarre images in his imagination, or else
sounded ridiculous. It's a tangential way of looking at Shakespeare
Plum suddenly experiences in a letter to Bill Townend from 1932 when,
mid-way through paraphrasing the action of *Thank You, Jeeves*, he breaks
off and remarks:

> Golly, what rot it sounds when one writes it down! […]
> Come, come, Wodehouse, is *this* the best you can do in
> the way of carrying on the great tradition of English Lit-
> erature? Still […] I bet the plot of Hamlet seemed just as
> lousy when Shakespeare was trying to tell it to Ben Jonson

in the Mermaid Tavern. ("Well, Ben, see what I mean, the central character is this guy, see, who's in love with this girl, see, but her old man doesn't think he's on the level, see, so he tells her – wait a minute, I better start again at the beginning. Well, so this guy's in college, see, and he's come home because his mother's gone and married his uncle, see, and he sees a ghost, see. So this guy turns out to be the guy's father . . .")

So described, *Hamlet* would never have made it on stage. But it was to become Plum's go-to play whenever he wanted to point up either the solemn greatness or comic ridiculousness of Shakespeare's art. Viewed from this twin perspective, not only was Shakespeare a great artist, but also a charlatan with a massive brass neck who got away with bamboozling generations of playgoers with a load of nonsense disguised as profundity.

Take Bertie's famous quote from *Joy in the Morning*: "It's like Shakespeare. Sounds well, but doesn't mean anything". Reading through the Jeeves and Wooster canon, it becomes apparent that Bertie is quite the Shakespeare sceptic, refusing to believe that The Bard is literature's last word. In *Thank You, Jeeves*, Viola is once again cited as a source of perplexity:

> "And what is worrying her is that he does not tell his love, but lets concealment like . . . like what, Jeeves?"
> "A worm i' the bud, sir."
> "Feed on his something . . ."
> "Damask cheek, sir."
> "Damask? You're sure?" [...] But it doesn't seem to mean anything."
> "An archaic adjective, sir. I fancy it is intended to signify a healthy complexion."

Were it merely Bertie suffering this confusion, we could put it down to his mental negligibility. But it appears Plum, writing in his own person, echoed these sentiments:

> [T]his, I think, [is] a peculiarity in Shakespeare's work which has escaped the notice of many critics – to wit, the fact that while his stuff sounds all right, it generally doesn't mean anything. There can be little doubt that, when he was pushed for time, William Shakespeare just shoved

down anything and trusted to the charity of the audience to pull him through.

('Kind Words for Shakespeare')

This is such literary heresy, Plum feels the need to justify his controversial but wholly tongue-in-cheek stance by citing some of The Bard's more egregious vocabulary.

Consider the word 'abroach', which Shakespeare uses correctly in *Romeo and Juliet* ("Who set this ancient quarrel new abroach?"), but which whizzes over the top of Burbage's head: "It's something girls wear," explains The Bard, "Made of diamonds and fastened with a pin." Burbage doesn't get the joke and persists in his claim that "it doesn't seem to make sense," a charge airily dismissed by the playwright:

> "Oh, it's all in the acting . . . You just speak the line and nobody'll notice anything."

And this isn't an isolated instance of Shakespeare playing fast and loose with exotic language nobody understands. Plum goes on to list a further eight incredibly esoteric (and odd-sounding) verbal examples he claims to have found in Shakespeare. A little research reveals that six of them check out perfectly:

- 'wanion' (which appears just once, in *Pericles*, meaning 'curse')
- 'geck' (twice, in *Twelfth Night* and *Cymbeline*, meaning 'butt' [of a joke] or 'victim')
- 'cullion' (six times, in *Hamlet, Henry VI, Part 1, Henry IV, Part 2, Henry V, King Lear* and *The Taming of the Shrew*, meaning 'a scurvy fellow')
- 'punto' (twice, in *The Merry Wives of Windsor* and *Romeo and Juliet*, meaning a 'hit' [in fencing])
- 'frampold' (once, in *The Merry Wives of Windsor*, meaning 'quarrelsome'), and
- 'rawly' (once, in *Henry V*, meaning 'without provision').

Then there's two he either misremembers or found in a non-standard edition:

- 'loggat' (actually 'loggets' in *Hamlet* – seemingly, from the context, a game played with small pieces of wood) and
- 'egma' (possibly a misprint of 'enigma').

Given that this short lexicographical canter was first published in 1956, it's tempting to picture Wodehouse passing the long winter evenings of his prison camp confinement in 1940-41 poring over every last detail of the lesser-known *Cymbeline* or *Pericles*, squirrelling away words that amused him for possible use in some future work. He even used to sleep with his Shakespeare – if we are to believe the following passage from his unreliable 'autobiography' *Performing Flea*:

> Getting the pillow just the right height was always a difficulty. Some men used suitcases for bolsters, but I found that I obtained the best results with a sweater, a cardigan, a pair of trousers, a Red Cross parcel and the Complete Works of William Shakespeare. Shakespeare, who wrote not for an age but for all time, produced exactly the right amount of stuff to make him an ideal foundation on which to build.

This uncommon level of intimacy may have allowed Shakespeare to seep into Plum's consciousness during the night hours in the same way his other prison camp reading, a copy of Tennyson's poems, helped stave off hunger pangs when rations grew short (see Chapter 10).

A further aspect of Shakespearean convention that Plum regularly punctures is the dramatic soliloquy. After all, it's really not a healthy sign if you're having a conversation out loud with someone who isn't there:

> Someone was approaching, or rather I should have said that two persons were approaching, for if there had been only one person approaching, he would hardly have been talking to himself. Though, of course, you do get that sort of thing in Shakespeare.
>
> ('A Good Cigar is a Smoke')

It's a habit that particularly annoys Lord Uffenham in *Money in the Bank*:

> "Young man, you talk too bloody much [...] That mouth of yours. Does it shut? It does. Then shut it, blast yer. Lord-love-a-duck, anyone would think you were one of those ghastly fellows in Shakespeare that do soliloquies."

And the king of the soliloquy is, once again, Hamlet. He can't resist – which is just as well or there'd be long intervals of silence on stage while he thought things through in his head without articulating them. But then again, he is an actor in a drama and normal rules of social etiquette don't apply. So soliloquize he does, allowing Plum to quote from "To be or not to be" 73 times.

And now, as we face the final curtain, to briefly answer that earlier question: why is it Plum quotes more from Shakespeare's tragedies than his comedies? Quite simply, it's because tragedies are funnier; or perhaps more accurately, have the potential to be funnier, being tragic. The more Shakespeare piles on the agony, the more effectively Plum can counterpoint his humour against that background of pain and suffering. Take the following quotation from *Uncle Fred in the Springtime* on the delights of beer:

> The Ovens home-brewed is a liquid Pollyanna, for ever pointing out the bright side and indicating silver linings. It slips its little hand in yours, and whispers "Cheer up!" If King Lear had had a tankard of it handy, we should have had far less of that "Blow, winds, and crack your cheeks!" stuff.

Lear's titanic sufferings and descent into madness could so easily have been avoided by the simple expedient of buying him a pint. His tragedy is not so much his misjudged abdication and the treachery of his daughters, but the fact the blasted heath on which he is wandering half naked is lacking a pub where he might restore his tissues and cheer up. As Plum ably demonstrates, within every tragedy is a farce just waiting to escape – it's simply a question of playing with the perspective, as the narrator of *The Adventures of Sally* makes clear:

> There are few situations in life which do not hold equal potentialities for both tragedy and farce.

In *Pigs Have Wings*, Plum once again uses beer as his touchstone while riffing on Aristotle's well-known definition of tragedy in literature. On this occasion, our tragic hero is George Cyril Wellbeloved, Lord Emsworth's former pig man, who may indeed be said to have "plumbed the depths," being barred from drinking beer by his new employer, Sir Gregory Parsloe-Parsloe. "There is no agony," we are told, "like the agony of the man who wants a couple of quick ones and cannot get them." And although George Cyril is not exactly King Lear ("it would [...] be inaccurate to describe him as running the gamut of emotions, for he had but one emotion"), the beer ban is a tragedy *for him*. It's a point made by the narrator of 'The Coming of Cedric,' in which he notes that in the cosy bar parlour of the Angler's Rest where Mr. Mulliner holds court, "[t]ragedy, to us, has come to mean merely the occasional flatness of a bottle of beer." It's all a question of scale, and Plum relished the opportunity to shrink the pitiless suffering rained down on humanity by vengeful Shakespearean gods to minor annoyances that can easily be fixed.

For all his good-natured joshing, however, Wodehouse remained completely in awe of Shakespeare, who taught him not only a great deal about stagecraft, but a host of transferable skills that greatly inspired his approach to novel and story writing. These performative influences don't quite belong here and will be dealt with in the next volume in this series. For now though, it's important to acknowledge the depth of Plum's attachment to his hero in a short passage that cuts through all the clowning of this chapter.

Matthew Arnold was a fellow Shakespeare fan whose 1849 sonnet 'Shakespeare' features on at least six occasions in Plum's writing when singling out a character for especial praise. Here, Arnold is directly addressing his fellow poet:

> Others abide our question. Thou art free.
> We ask and ask: Thou smilest and art still,
> Out-topping knowledge. For the loftiest hill
> That to the stars uncrowns his majesty,
> Planting his steadfast footsteps in the sea,
> Making the Heaven of Heavens his dwelling-place,
> Spares but the cloudy border of his base
> To the foil'd searching of mortality:
> And thou, who didst the stars and sunbeams know,
> Self-school'd, self-scann'd, self-honour'd, self-secure,
> Didst walk on Earth unguess'd at. Better so!
> All pains the immortal spirit must endure,
> All weakness that impairs, all griefs that bow,
> Find their sole voice in that victorious brow.

As Plum so correctly comments in *Over Seventy*, "when a level-headed man like Matthew Arnold lets himself go like that it means something" (while claiming Arnold wrote it about him). But seriously, so it is here: the main take-away from the poem is that, yes, Shakespeare was a genius whose greatness is unquestionable: but he was also an auto-didact ("Self-school'd, self-scann'd, self-honour'd, self-secure"), and was somehow even the wiser for that ("Better so!") Even the most intelligent of us bumble our way through life, lost in the "cloudy border" at the "base" of knowledge's mountain. Shakespeare, by contrast, could see the mountain from top to bottom and beyond to the sun and the stars. Moreover, he speaks to and for all of us, taking the whole of human life for his subject.

Bertie makes use of the poem in both *Thank You, Jeeves* and here in *Stiff Upper Lip, Jeeves* when praising, with some emotion, his omnicompetent employee:

> "Jeeves," I said, and if my voice shook, what of it? We Woosters are but human, "you stand alone. Others abide our question, but you don't, as the fellow said."

An inventory of Jeeves's seemingly bottomless resources of knowledge and skills would include a great deal he wouldn't have learned at school; so we must conclude that like Shakespeare, his degree arrived courtesy of the University of Life. As Bertie tells us more than once, he is both friend and mentor while remaining a complete enigma: a man wholly himself, comfortable with what and who he is. Our lack of a detailed biography only serves to intensify that air of mystery – and the same goes for Shakespeare, to whom repeatedly Bertie links him.

Of all the adjectives pertaining to the Bard in Arnold's poem, the one that strikes me most forcefully in a Wodehousean context is "self-secure," which, among other things, I take to mean something like 'happy in his own skin.' I wonder if this was an image Wodehouse himself admired and even perhaps aspired to. To paraphrase a comment from *Over Seventy*, from the very start of his career Plum 'knew he was good' – all he had to do was make the world sit up and share his self-belief. Not by boasting in the empty manner of Hall Caine, but by proving himself. It's perhaps significant that in 1907's *The White Feather*, published when he was 26, he paints a sympathetic portrait of one such well-balanced, modest, and self-contented man, Joe Bevan, who was once the Light Weight and Middle Weight World Boxing Champion but is now perfectly happy to train the pugilists of tomorrow within the humble purlieus of the Blue Boar Inn near Wrykyn.

We are first introduced when Joe breaks up a fight in which the schoolboy R. D. Sheen is being bettered by Albert, a local thug. Albert then sets on Joe, who swats his punch away "without fuss" simply by "touch[ing] the back of [Albert's] wrist gently with the palm of his right hand." Once advised who he's up against, Albert beats a tactical retreat, at which point Joe turns his attention to Sheen:

> "Beware," said Mr Bevan oracularly, "of entrance to a

quarrel; but, being in, bear't that th' opposed may beware of thee. Always counter back when you guard. When a man shows you his right like that, always push out your hand straight. The straight left rules the boxing world."

And with those "oracular" but uncredited words from Polonius, Shakespeare once more enters the scene. For as well as a boxer, Joe was once a repertory actor, who doesn't just know his *Hamlet*, but seems to have incorporated some of the play's pithier sayings into his personal philosophy.

> "Always keep going on. Never give in. You know what Shakespeare says about the one who first cries, 'Hold, enough!' Do you read Shakespeare, sir?"
> "Yes," said Sheen.
> "Ah, now *he* knew his business" said Mr Bevan enthusiastically. "*There* was ring-craft, as you may say. *He* wasn't a novice."

Sheen marvels that a mere boxer can also have an appreciation of high culture. But to Joe, Shakespeare *isn't* high culture; he's a manual for everyday living. "I've always read Shakespeare," he says, "and I always shall read him" as much for profit as pleasure, we are led to think.

And that, just possibly, is what Wodehouse thought too.

Chapter 10:
Tennyson

"Bertie, do you read Tennyson?"
"Not if I can help."
Right Ho, Jeeves

No man with any pretence to a cultivated mind will publicly admit that he is not acquainted with every important
poem of Tennyson.
W. S. Gilbert, 'Unappreciated Shakespeare'

There was a young fellow called Artie
Who was always the life of the party

This subsequently became *The Idylls of the King.*
Over Seventy

You are […] a great favourite with the young ladies.
Henry Hallam to Alfred, Lord Tennyson (1845)

In Wodehouse World – as in our own – poetry is very often used as a
prelude to seduction. And the poems of Alfred, Lord Tennyson seem
particularly well-suited to this, as Keggs the butler informs us in 1910's
'The Good Angel':

"[Y]oung ladies is often took by Tennyson, hespecially in
the summer time."

And he has the evidence to prove it: his former employer Lord Stock-
leigh's daughter, Lady Angelica Fendall, is particularly partial to having
Tennyson's long narrative poem 'The Princess' read aloud to her, eloping with one of her *lecteurs* and marrying him in a registry office two days
after her father forbids the liaison. "With certain types of 'igh-spirited
young lady hopposition is useless," Keggs aspirates, particularly those
"hinclined to be romantic."

And so it proves. In 1922's *The Girl on the Boat* Tennyson scores a second time. This time, it's his mighty epic *Idylls of the King* that is beloved
of American heiress Billie Bennett, and you can bet that Sam Marlowe
loses no time in borrowing a copy to hasten his wooing. Noticing he is

carrying a book about his person, Billie asks what it is:

> "It's a volume of Tennyson."
> "Are you fond of Tennyson?"
> "I worship him," said Sam reverently. "Those" – he glanced at his cuff – "those 'Idylls of the King'! I do not like to think what an ocean voyage would be if I had not my Tennyson with me."
> "We must read him together. He is my favourite poet!"
> "We will! There is something about Tennyson . . ."
> "Yes, isn't there! I've felt that myself so often!"
> "Some poets are whales at epics and all that sort of thing, while others call it a day when they've written something that runs to a couple of verses; but where Tennyson had the bulge was that his long game was just as good as his short."

Whether massive epics or brief sonnets, Tennyson is the goods. Despite the inept golf references that indicate Sam hasn't the first clue what he's talking about, the shipboard romance blossoms. As he reads a passage from *Maud*, Billie "was drooping toward him. Her face was very sweet and tender, her eyes misty. He slid an arm about her waist. She raised her lips to his." At which point, he haltingly pops the question.

In 1935 it's game, set and match to Tennyson when a similar scenario re-appears in 'Trouble Down at Tudsleigh.' Freddie Widgeon, that serial Wodehousean loser in love, having fallen hook, line and sinker for April Carroway, suddenly remembers that "when it comes to wooing, it's simply half the battle to get a line on the adored object's favourite literature." First, though, he has to find out "what this bilge was" he's heard her reciting out loud to her younger sister. It proves the work of an instant, and Freddie biffs off to buy a *Collected Works of Tennyson* so that he can "mug it up and decant a line or two in her presence" hoping to achieve the desired result "[b]efore you can say "What ho!" Unfortunately, the hapless Freddie plays his hand a little too early, certainly before his knowledge of Tennyson has reached a critical mass:

> "You don't mean to say you read Tennyson, Mr Widgeon?"
> "Me?" said Freddie. "Tennyson? Read Tennyson? Me read Tennyson? Well, well, well! Bless my soul! Why, I know him by heart – some of him."
> "So do I. 'Break, break, break, on your cold grey stones, oh Sea . . .'"
> "Quite. Or take the 'Lady of Shalott'."

"I hold it truth with him who sings . . .'"

"So do I, absolutely. And then again, there's 'The Lady of Shalott.' Dashed extraordinary that you should like Tennyson too."

"I think he's wonderful."

"What a lad! That 'Lady of Shalott'! Some spin on the ball there."

April is able to quote freely from 'In Memoriam' and 'Break, break, break,' and probably has many another Tennysonian nifty up her sleeve while Freddie seems fixated on the single poem he thought might do the trick. Things don't quite go according to plan, and after the smoke clears he later tells one of his Crumpet friends that he got off lightly: the bilge he had to mug up "might quite easily have been Shelley or even Browning." Still and all, if Freddie had bothered to read a little further in Tennyson's oeuvre, he might have come across the aphorism that perfectly defines his approach to love:

> 'Tis better to have loved and lost
> Than never to have loved at all.
>
> (*In Memoriam*, xxvii)

Beyond an aphrodisiac, Plum managed to find other uses for Tennyson, so much so that he comes a likely fourth after the Bible, Shakespeare, and Gilbert & Sullivan in the great quotation handicap with lines and allusions liberally strewn from his second novel (1903's *A Prefect's Uncle*) through to his last (1977's *Sunset at Blandings*). *The Poems and Plays of Tennyson* was one of only two titles he managed to hastily pack before being carted off into internment by German forces in 1940, and when his personal library was catalogued after his death it was discovered he'd somehow ended up with three copies. Also present were Harold Nicolson's 1923 study *Tennyson*, whose front leaf Wodehouse signed in 1935 (the same year he wrote 'Trouble Down at Tudsleigh'); and the memoir/biography *Alfred Tennyson by his Grandson Charles Tennyson*, which dates from 1949.

So Plum knew his Tennyson. But beyond pointing out the range and frequency of his borrowings, literary criticism has offered virtually no analysis of *why* he might have been so drawn to his predecessor's work – something I'm going to address in the next few pages. What *has* been remarked on, but with no great rigour, are the following lines he wrote to regular collaborator Guy Bolton on 24 November 1948:

> I'm afraid I have got one of those second rate minds, be-
> cause, while I realize that Shelley is in the Shakespeare and
> Milton class, I much prefer Tennyson, who isn't.

This is odd. Surely Shelley's impassioned idealism was "the sort of stuff
that long-haired blighters read to other long-haired blighters in English
suburban drawing rooms?" (*Piccadilly Jim*). Plum did admit that 'The
Revolt of Islam' was "like being beaten over the head with a sandbag"
but then claims to have always liked 'Ozymandias' and even 'Epipsy-
chidion,' a poem packed to the gills with the kind of overwrought emotion not usually to his taste. To think he might even consider rating
this style of verse over Tennyson's opens up a fault line through Plum's
aesthetics it's important we explore.

We might begin by asking whether his assessment of Tennyson's
poetry as enjoyably second-rate speaks more about Tennyson or Wodehouse himself. When Plum wrote those words, Tennyson's stock had
long been trading at an all-time low, along with many of his high Victorian contemporaries like Robert Browning, Matthew Arnold, and
Dante Gabriel Rossetti. "It's so absurd, the way people sneer at him
nowadays," April Carroway complains in 'Trouble Down at Tudsleigh,'
reflecting a critical attitude that regularly finds favour in our own time.
To a modern ear, Tennyson is by turns long-winded, stuffy and termi-
nally bourgeois, or else gloomy, grumbly and self-pitying. W. H. Auden
once patronized Tennyson as the "stupidest" of all the English poets,
adding that: "There was little about melancholia he didn't know; there
was little else that he did." And yes, he is guilty on all these charges.
But take the trouble, as Plum did, to explore his voluminous output (the
spine of my edition is a good 8 cm wide), and it quickly becomes apparent there's far more to him than that.

In 1936, the poet and critic T. S. Eliot tried to use his influential position among the *literati* to rescue his predecessor's blighted reputation.
In an essay on 'In Memoriam', the sequence of poems many consider
Tennyson's masterpiece, he berates us in his best schoolmasterly way for
his having to explain something that should be obvious to anyone with
half a brain:

> Tennyson is a great poet, for reasons that are perfectly
> clear. He has three qualities which are seldom found to-
> gether except in the greatest poets: abundance, variety and
> complete competence.

Well that's us (and Auden) told. But in our defence, as we'll see in a moment, it's very easy to get Tennyson all wrong, and Eliot (mostly) doesn't, praising his versification as "masterly" and possessed of "the greatest lyrical resourcefulness that a poet has ever shown." Which hints at one of the main reasons he is so frequently undervalued: Tennyson was *technically* so good, he made the writing of poetry look easy. So easy, in fact, that many critics have persuaded themselves that his work is merely proficient rather than inspired – a view Eliot clearly had no time for.

Did Plum fall into this trap of confusing "complete competence" with the second rate, a journeyman with a genius? It would be most ironic if he had, for he too is a regular victim of the identical (and ludicrous) prejudice that demands 'true' art be elusive, abstruse, and just plain difficult, wrested from jealous Muses at great personal cost to the artist. On the other hand, as a master craftsman himself, it's easy to see what attracted him to Tennyson, for both men have much that unites them:

- a broad, vibrant and at times idiosyncratic vocabulary;
- strict discipline in both rhyme and rhythm (as in Plum's song lyrics and comic poetry);
- a love of narrative drama, particularly the kind with romantic themes; and
- an uncanny knack for choosing subjects that chime with a popular audience.

To which we might add their way of expressing themselves as transparently as possible so as not to burden their readers with constant re-reading. Hence the use of Tennyson's poetry for the purposes of seduction: first time through the poem in question, both parties will be singing off the same hymn sheet. In *Uneasy Money*, Bill Dawlish is "greatly addicted" to *Maud* because, one suspects, not being the sharpest knife in the drawer, he can actually understand what Tennyson's on about; and, moreover, its subject of "wistful yearning" sums up his own predicament as he transitions from one girlfriend to another. Here's the poem's best-known bit:

> Come into the garden, Maud,
> For the black bat, night, has flown,
> Come into the garden, Maud,
> I am here at the gate alone;
> And the woodbine spices are wafted abroad,
> And the musk of the rose is blown […]

She is coming, my own, my sweet;
Were it ever so airy a tread,
My heart would hear her and beat,
Were it earth in an earthy bed;
My dust would hear her and beat,
Had I lain for a century dead,
Would start and tremble under her feet,
And blossom in purple and red.

Yes, it's now clichéd by being quoted to hell, but that doesn't take away from the passage's technical excellence. The febrile tone is perfectly judged, and absolutely in keeping with the psychology of the lovestruck narrator whose pent-up erotic desperation you can almost feel. Moreover, that image of the narrator's dust reconstituting itself is just a little too Edgar Allan Poe to be comfortable, throwing forward to that writer's later period of madness. Clever, and anything but simple to do *right*, Tennyson always knew how to keep *just* this side of melodrama – yet another talent he and Plum shared.

The poem's other barrier to acceptance by the culturati was its massive popularity. In *A Damsel in Distress* Plum hints at its broad appeal by having Albert the page boy recite an extract in broad Cockernee, correcting himself even as he murders it:

'Wiv blekest morss the flower—ports
Was—I mean were—crusted one and orl;
Ther rusted niles fell from the knorts
That 'eld the pear to the garden—worll.

But Albert needn't have encountered the poem on the printed page. So rhythmically precise is the scansion, Michael William Balfe didn't have much work to do when he set a short extract of *Maud* to music shortly after its publication in 1855, lending the poem a new lease of life as a Victorian parlour-room standard to be sung with pianoforte accompaniment. Plum, no mean songsmith himself, would have admired how easily Tennyson's verse could transition to lyric; and indeed, the song makes a guest appearance in *Love Among the Chickens*, murdered in the bath by Jeremy Garnet's upstairs neighbour:

"Come," resumed the young gentleman persuasively, "into the garden, Maud, for ther black batter nah-eet hath-er-florn."

And here it comes again, in 'Reginald's Record Knock,' where it can either be recited or sung by the amateur Lothario should the need ever arise:

> Westaway happened to be of a romantic and sentimental nature [...] At country houses, when they lingered on the terrace after dinner to watch the moonlight flooding the quiet garden, it was Westaway and his colleagues who lingered longest. Westaway knew Tennyson's "Maud" by heart.

Ready and waiting, one presumes, to be recited or sung should a prospective Maud present herself.

From his childhood onwards, Wodehouse would have found it difficult to avoid Tennyson, who died when he (Plum) was 11. As the poet's biographer Peter Levi notes, "[t]o the ordinary, literary, though not necessarily sharp or intellectual [...] he was like a god," cutting across barriers of age and class in a way few poets have ever managed. As a consequence, few middle-class households (or school libraries) would have been without one or other of The Author's Edition, the Cabinet Edition, the Miniature Edition, the Illustrated Edition, the Original Editions, the Eversley edition, *Selections From* or, ultimately, The Collected Edition, for Tennyson grew to be a publishing phenomenon, even something of an industry. With such a massive audience reach, it's no wonder movie mogul Ivor Llewellyn is profoundly disappointed when, in *The Luck of the Bodkins*, he discovers that Ambrose Tennyson, who is working for him as a scriptwriter, is not *the* Tennyson.

In several aspects, the real Tennyson's life and career trajectory intertwine with Wodehouse's. Both were born into families that had once been minor nobility, subsequently rising through their literary endeavours to being members of the high Establishment – and rich ones at that. Again like Wodehouse, Tennyson had never considered any other career except writing, being described by William Makepeace Thackeray as a man who "reads all sorts of things, swallows them and digests them like a great poetical boa-constrictor as he is." Exactly the same could be said of Plum, and both men, degree-less in their youth, ended up with honorary doctorates from the University of Oxford while captivated by so-called 'light reading' that might have been thought beneath them. The two have been described as hopelessly naïve, remote and distant from the world (Tennyson admitted he was "not a public man in character") and were inclined to shun literary society whenever possible. It is more than likely that as a schoolboy, Plum would have read or even conned Tennyson's best-known 55 lines, 'The Charge of the Light Brigade', commemorating the disastrous British cavalry offensive at the battle of Balaclava in 1854. He regularly alludes to the poem in, among other titles, *Something Fresh, Leave it to Psmith, Summer Moonshine,* Jeeves and the Song of Songs' (UK version) and even his Hollywood satires *Laughing Gas* and 'The Rise of Minna Nordstrom' in which the eponymous heroine has conned the poem as an audition standby. In *The Luck Stone*, he makes Ram, the teenage orator we met earlier, recite it by heart as his party piece. Along with Thomas Hood's 'Ben Battle' and Longfellow's 'The Wreck of the Hesperus,' the poem was a staple of the schoolboy repertoire.

Created Poet Laureate on William Wordsworth's death in 1850, Tennyson would write poetry marking significant national occasions for the next 40 years. Completed, according to Tennyson's posthumously published *A Memoir*, "in a few minutes" after reading a war report in the London *Times*, 'The Charge of the Light Brigade' is still familiar and widely quoted, long after the events that prompted it have grown fogged in the memory. Here's three of the best-known passages:

> Half a league, half a league,
> Half a league onward,
> All in the valley of Death
> Rode the six hundred.
> [...]
> Theirs not to make reply,
> Theirs not to reason why,
> Theirs but to do and die.
> [...]
> Cannon to right of them,
> Cannon to left of them,
> Cannon in front of them
> Volleyed and thundered.

And we mustn't forget the payoff "Someone had blundered," which has long since entered the language, and which is the only bit of the poem Bertie manages to remember when performing it out loud for his parents' friends:

> I always remember that bit [...] feeling just as those Light
> Brigade fellows must have felt.
>
> (*Jeeves and the Feudal Spirit*)

Once again, the joke's on Bertie, as the regular rhythm and repetitions help most people remember the words – but not him. It takes a particularly high level of bone-headedness not to retain such a poetic *tour de force*.

Tennyson begins the poem midway through the charge, hooking us immediately, the repeated dactyls (what Bertie calls "tum tiddles") of "half a league" artfully echoing the horses' gallop as if we're right in there among the cavalry. The rhythmic onslaught is heightened by the anaphora of "cannon," whose hard opening consonant and heavy emphasis on the first syllable suggest the breech explosions as the deadly guns are fired on all sides. Tennyson instinctively pulls out all the technical stops as he points up the towering folly of that "wild charge" in which half the "six hundred" and a similar number of horses were either killed or cut to ribbons. When the smoke had cleared, the French general Marshal Pierre Bosquet memorably stated: *"C'est magnifique, mais ce n'est pas la guerre"* ("It's magnificent, but it isn't war"), nor was it. Tennyson in his role as Laureate deftly steers his poem towards commemoration rather than an ill-advised attempt to celebrate this colossal error of military judgment. In the closing lines, even as he instructs us to "Honour the Light Brigade," the mood is angled towards puzzlement rather than patriotism, forcing us to ponder whether "[all] the world wondered" in admiration or sheer stupefaction.

In this and other pieces, Tennyson proved he could write accomplished, memorable verse quickly and to order. Even into his 80s, that craftsman's ability never left him, scribbling down the poem that is often considered his swan song while travelling home on the Isle of Wight ferry – a journey of around 40 minutes. Entitled 'Crossing the Bar,' its modest beauty is captivating. Here are the first two stanzas:

> Sunset and evening star,
> And one clear call for me!
> And may there be no moaning of the bar,
> When I put out to sea,
>
> But such a tide as moving seems asleep,
> Too full for sound and foam,
> When that which drew from out the boundless deep
> Turns again home.

The 'bar' at the entrance to a river or port becomes the moment separating life and death, and the simplicity of the metaphor sees the poem regularly pressed into service as an epitaph. Like 'Maud,' it has also been set to music on several occasions, Tennyson once again capturing a private mood that easily and directly resonates with his readership. Even these short examples serve to illustrate how completely poetry 'inhabited' him, such that many could see, even from a young age, that he had an uncanny ability, in the words of his early biographer Alec Waugh in 1892, to "[catch] the spirit of the people and crystallize it in literature."

This demotic instinct is also, I suspect, what first recommended Tennyson to Wodehouse's literary sensibility. Here's a trio of his borrowings, starting with this old chestnut from 'Lady Clara Vere de Vere':

> Kind hearts are more than coronets,
> And simple faith than Norman blood.

This neat epigram can be found in, among others, 'The Début of Battling Billson', *Jill the Reckless*, *Thank You, Jeeves* and *Uncle Fred in the Springtime*, and is regularly wheeled out when Plum addresses the theme of snobbery.

For when friends part brass rags, there's this, from 'Merlin and Vivien,' put to good use in 'The Shadow Passes,' *Ice in the Bedroom* and *Stiff Upper Lip, Jeeves* as Jeeves ponders the swings and roundabouts of Gussie Fink-Nottle's relationship with Madeline Bassett at Brinkley Court:

> "The poet Tennyson speaks of the little rift within the lute
> that by and by will make the music mute and ever widening slowly silence all."

And so it proves when Gussie ends up eloping not with Madeline but the cook.

Then there's this vaudeville-style joke from *Cocktail Time*, contrived from 'Locksley Hall':

> 'My name, as I have already told you, is Wisdom.'
> 'How did you get in?' asked Mr Saxby with a show of interest.
> 'I was shown in.'
> 'And stayed in. I see Tennyson was right. Knowledge comes, but Wisdom lingers.'

Nothing is entirely sacred to Wodehouse, as when Aunt Dahlia uses *The Collected Works of Tennyson* as a handy projectile to lob at Bertie in *Right Ho, Jeeves* – from which we can see that Tennyson can add heft to just about any occasion. But Plum's appreciation of his fellow poet travelled far deeper into his writer's consciousness than aphoristic quotation. And to examine that process at work, we can begin by returning to Eliot's praise of the poet's "complete competence."

When reading, what Wodehouse valued over just about anything else was *integrity* – a conviction that the writer was in full control of whatever he or she was writing. As the narrator remarks in *Uncle Dynamite*, "[y]our true artist will always give of his best," and if he falls short in this ambition or simply disregards it, any relationship he might build with his audience is destined to be short-lived, for the reader will sense that something isn't ringing true. In Plum's view, the writer should never write down to his readers, nor should he make life difficult for them. They are not to be treated as a therapy block for the writer's private neuroses, or lab rats for his pet aesthetic theories. Irrespective of the genre in which he's writing, he should bend every sinew to steer them through the sense of his work while keeping them alert and entertained. In short, he should "take trouble":

> My books may not be the sort of books the cognoscenti feel justified in blowing the 12s 6d. on, but I do work at them. When in due course Charon ferries me across the Styx and everyone is telling everyone else what a rotten writer I was, I hope at least one voice will be heard piping up, "But he did take trouble."

This passage is taken from *Over Seventy*, and later in that sort-of autobiography published late in life, Plum wrote (for once, quite seriously) that "[a]nyone who reads a novel of mine can be assured that it will be as coherent as I can make it." "Coherence" was the fruit of all the trouble he took, and while I have absolutely no proof of this, I think at the heart of Wodehouse's lifelong adoration of Tennyson was the feeling that the Victorian laureate would have agreed with him – which he actually did, writing that art is "toil cooperant to an end" (*In Memoriam*, CXXVIII), a shared endeavour between those who create and consume it. "Art for Art's sake," the cry of the aesthete, was not a creed he would have recognized.

Tennyson was indeed an inveterate tinkerer, reviser and revisitor who always tried to give of his best. Like Plum, not wanting to feel that he had "picked a lemon in the garden of literature," Tennyson would "write every sentence ten times [...] or in many cases twenty times," even as poetry poured out of him at breathtaking speed. He would return to poems many decades on, write sequels or sit on verses for years if they didn't feel right. In the early days of his career, he left a nine-year gap between publications until he had a collection of verse he was satisfied with – a collection that, when it did finally appear in 1842, would make his name, vindicating his punctilious quality control. In short, he was "up on [his] toes" the whole time. And even if Plum didn't actually learn this mindset from Tennyson, he would be likely to cleave toward a fellow writer who appeared to believe in the same values he did.

From there, it was but a short step to admiring the poetry this mindset produced. In addition to what the critic Margaret A. Lourie calls the "crafted, controlled quality" of Tennyson's work, the 18-year-old Wodehouse also seized on the poet's vivid pictural writing, here pressed into service to describe a mountainside covered in flowers, like some kind of technicolor waterfall:

> I think some of the descriptions of nature in T. are absolutely whacking. Eg in the 'Voyage of Maeldune,' "The whole isle-side flashing down from the peak without ever a tree." Heck mon, it's just beutiful! [sic]

Writing to his schoolfriend Eric George, Plum – clearly already a fan – had dug out a somewhat obscure late work from around 1880 in which Tennyson borrows the framework from an ancient Irish myth of an Odysseus-like adventurer sailing between a series of islands, each with its own peculiarities. This gives the poet a broad canvas on which to demonstrate his descriptive skills, as in the lines that follow on from Plum's quotation:

> Swept like a torrent of gems from the
>   sky to the blue of the sea;
> And we roll'd upon capes of crocus
>   and vaunted our kith and our kin,
> And we wallow'd in beds of lilies, and
>   chanted the triumph of Finn,
> Till each like a golden image was
>   pollen'd from head to feet
> And each was as dry as a cricket,
>   with thirst in the middle-day heat.
> Blossom and blossom, and promise of
>   blossom, but never a fruit!
> And we hated the Flowering Isle, as
>   we hated the isle that was mute,
> And we tore up the flowers by the million

and flung them in bight and bay,
And we left but a naked rock, and in
anger we sail'd away.

It feels somewhat churlish extracting individual aspects of Tennyson's style for inspection, so brilliantly does he fuse them together. Excelling not just in one department, but in the total package, the combination of those dramatic pictorial images, the adventure plot and that exuberant, rollicking rhythm proved both irresistible and memorable to Plum, namechecking the poem (while slightly misremembering its title) over a decade later in *The Prince and Betty*. Tennyson did indeed "take trouble" – such that Plum nursed a lifelong suspicion of those who didn't follow the same way of working.

Chief among these was Robert Browning, Tennyson's contemporary and friend, who considered Tennyson's obsessive revising "insane" and symptomatic of "mental infirmity." Not so Plum, who was less than impressed whenever Browning lapsed into prolixity or pretension, a sure sign the poet had forgotten that people might actually be reading his work. Or didn't forget but carried on regardless. In that schoolboy letter to Eric George, Plum remarks:

> I read some Browning today. I still like Tennyson better, though.

As indeed he would for the rest of his life. Not that he dismissed Browning out of hand – that would have been neither fair nor consistent, since the styles and geniuses of the two poets overlapped considerably (in their respective 'dramatic monologues,' for example). Nevertheless, Plum was inclined to over-egg Browning's shortcomings in the interests of humour, sometimes casting him as a sort of 'anti-Tennyson,' as in the 1902 story 'The Babe and the Dragon.' MacArthur ("The Babe" – a sporting schoolboy with no great love of poetry) and Miss Florence Beezley ("The Dragon" – a snobby Cambridge bluestocking who is "intensely learned") come to blows over the dining table:

> "Do you read Browning, Mr. MacArthur?"
> "No, not much."
> "Ah!" This in a tone of pity not untinged with scorn.

With a view to shaming her fellow diner, Miss Beezley then reels off the titles of several Browning favourites MacArthur hasn't bothered to read, including one of the poet's notoriously densest works, 'Sordello'.

At 5,975 lines, even the poem's author was aware it wasn't his most reader-friendly effort:

> My own faults of expression were many [...] [and] I lately gave time and pains to turn my work into what the many might – instead of what the few must – like.

Revision wouldn't have been necessary for Miss Beezley, who is clearly one of "the few"; the Babe, however, likens the poet's output to "higher algebra." At the pair's next encounter, Miss Beezley won't let the subject lie, noting that "few of Tennyson's works show the poetic faculty which Browning displays in 'Sordello.'" Well, no, they don't, if you equate "poetic faculty" with difficulty. And Plum evidently didn't. In 'Reginald's Record Knock,' the romantically inclined Westaway can be viewed with both awe and pity when it's revealed he can read Browning "without gas."

It's all good-natured joshing, for while they are nowhere near as prevalent as Tennyson's, Browning quotes do tend to litter Plum's stories – and not just ones he nicked from *Bartlett's*. 'How They Brought the Good News from Ghent to Aix' is a regular favourite, but by a long neck the winner is the following passage from 'Pippa Passes':

> The lark's on the wing;
> The snail's on the thorn;
> God's in His heaven –
> All's right with the world!

It's a sentiment that adorns *Hot Water, The Mating Season, The Girl in Blue, Cocktail Time, Leave it to Psmith, Something Fresh* and many a Jeeves and Wooster yarn, summing up the ethos of Wodehouse World in a nutshell. Indeed, Cooley Paradene from *Bill the Conqueror* is quite the Browning fanatic, shelling out thousands at auction to bag first editions of the poet's early work:

> At the sale of the Mortimer collection I was lucky enough to secure quite cheap – only eight thousand dollars – Browning's own copy of *Pauline* (Saunders and Ottley, 1833), also Browning's own copy of *Paracelsus* (E. Wilson, 1835) and of *Strafford* (Longmans, 1837).

Apart from the slight mis-spelling of 'Otley', all these references check out, although once again it's impossible to tell whether Plum is writing from a deep knowledge and love of Browning's poetry, or quoting from an auction catalogue he stumbled across in a dentist's waiting room. I wasn't able to find any Browning on the shelves of Plum's library, making any firm conclusions problematic; but what we can say is that if push came to shove, Tennyson would always be the clear winner, for success, to Plum, was ultimately about enjoyment, and if that made him a guilty pleasure then too bad.

So yes, Tennyson was possessed of the kind of artistic integrity Plum prized. But what of the poetry itself? Here it is we find ourselves in vaguer territory, for by and large, any comments Wodehouse made about art tended to focus on craft and technique rather than possible meaning; to do otherwise would risk sounding pretentious. On the subject of Shelley, for example, he makes a beeline for the arch-Romantic's "lousy" prose, peppered with laboured "double adjectives"; or how in his best-known poem, 'To a Skylark', the rhyming leaves something to be desired:

> Will Allsop's face lit up, as that of the poet Shelley [...] must have done when he suddenly realized that "blithe spirit" rhymes with "near it," not that it does.
>
> <div align="right">(<i>Galahad at Blandings</i>)</div>

And here's your proof in the poem's opening lines:

> Hail to thee, blithe Spirit!
> Bird thou never wert,
> That from Heaven, or near it,
> Pourest thy full heart.

Note also how "wert"/"heart" doesn't quite work either. To Wodehouse the conservative (small 'c') disciplinarian, this was just sloppy writing – and disrespectful of the reader. One gets the feeling that on this score, his tongue was not always firmly inserted into his cheek, as he fingers Robert Burns for the same crime in one of his early pieces for the American *Vanity Fair* magazine:

> [I]n a moment of inspiration, [he] rhymed "Loch Lomond" with "before ye," and set a standard which will make modern poets thankful that they took to *vers libre*.

By contrast, Tennyson's verse hits the rhyme *precisely* almost every time – despite employing a wide variety of sometimes tricky verse constructions. Eliot, as we've seen, had remarked on his "lyrical resourcefulness," and Peter Levi also notes "his complete mastery of his hearers, his perfect mastery of his metre," which he attributes to Tennyson's belief that "he knew the classical length or sound value of every English word." This "classical" sense of "fixed and immutable" principles of rhyme and rhythm helps in no small way make him "so readable," even in his longest works. The reader doesn't have their attention regularly distracted by irregularities in sound or measure – a principle Wodehouse was to carry over into his own comic verse and even his prose. All part of the service, he might have said, which is why he has been so consistently praised as a master stylist: efficient, elegant and sophisticated yet at the same time utterly *readable*.

There is a further wrinkle to this facet of Tennyson's genius that chimed with Wodehouse – one I touched on earlier – which can start us on a run into deeper evidence of why he was so drawn to his work. In *The Penguin Book of English Song*, an anthology of song lyrics that began their lives as poems, Tennyson can boast no fewer than 32 entries, bested only by A. E. Housman and Thomas Hardy. Benjamin Britten, Edward Elgar, Ralph Vaughan Williams and Frederick Delius are among dozens of composers who heard the dramatic potential in his verse – its ability to be sung and *performed*. It's probably no coincidence that Tennyson himself greatly enjoyed reading his work out loud, sometimes getting quite carried away as he put his heart and soul into the delivery. Shortly after the publication of *Maud*, he was down in the dumps after reviewers had given it a rough ride, and while staying with the Brownings in London was prevailed upon by Elizabeth Barrett Browning, herself an accomplished poet, to read from it, knowing it would offer him some relief. It did the trick, and the picture of the ungainly, extravagantly bearded Poet Laureate standing with tears streaming down his face as he recited evidently presented an arresting and memorable spectacle.

In the 1950s, academics conceptualized this progression from page to performance as "performativity;" but being the root of all drama, it was of course a 'thing' long before being given a fancy name – and Plum, with his marked theatrical bent, was particularly susceptible to it in his own work, and that of others. And even though Tennyson didn't start writing plays until the twilight of his career, thumbnail sketches such as 'Ulysses,' 'St Simeon Stylites,' 'Tithonus,' and 'Tiresias' or else discrete elements within his longer-form poems all share this same predisposition to double as verse dramas. Freddie Widgeon's favourite 'The Lady of Shalott' is, at under 200 lines, a play script in miniature complete with a mysterious back story that we are encouraged to trick out for ourselves. As with Plum's best work, Tennyson gently grabs us right from the start before immersing us in his narrative:

> On either side the river lie
> Long fields of barley and of rye,
> That clothe the wold and meet the sky;
> And thro' the field the road runs by
> To many-tower'd Camelot;
> And up and down the people go,
> Gazing where the lilies blow
> Round an island there below,
> The island of Shalott.
>
> Willows whiten, aspens quiver,
> Little breezes dusk and shiver
> Thro' the wave that runs for ever
> By the island in the river
> Flowing down to Camelot.
> Four grey walls, and four grey towers,
> Overlook a space of flowers,
> And the silent isle imbowers
> The Lady of Shalott.

This is from the later (and greatly improved) 1842 version of the poem which preserves the original's ballad stanza with its AAAABCCCB rhyme scheme (and yes, it has been set to music – rather beautifully – by the Canadian musician Loreena McKennitt). The plot is simple and haunting: the Lady of Shalott is cursed to live alone on a river island hard by King Arthur's castle of Camelot, slowly creating a tapestry from images she sees in her weaver's mirror. This private realm of art, at one remove from the real world, is no substitute for life, and the Lady complains she is "half sick of shadows." Then comes the fateful day when Sir Lancelot rides by, an impossibly romantic figure clad in ornate armour. Truly a vision, she is compelled to look at him directly – at which point her mirror immediately "crack[s] from side to side" (a line Plum borrows in *The Code of the Woosters* and *Summer Moonshine*). Exclaiming that "[t]he curse is come upon me" she then finds a boat, writes her name on its prow, and languidly drifts downstream towards Camelot and her death. And that's it.

There are so many ways this simple tale could be re-cast as a play, it's difficult to know where to begin. But while Wodehouse would have appreciated the dramatic consciousness that animates the narrative, he would also have been alert to what he repeatedly called the "atmosphere" of the piece, the imaginative ethos that defines its setting. It was Plum's abiding conviction that if writers got their atmospheres wrong, their work simply wouldn't ring true, and the atmosphere that Tennyson was so adept at creating – according to essayist and playwright J. B. Priestley in his 1960 publication *Literature and Western Man* – arose out of the previous generation of Romantic poets, and in particular Keats. Tennyson, says Priestley, alchemized his source material into something "warmed and softened [...] dreamy and passive, strangely feminine," crafting some "luxuriant, listless and melancholy dreamland" that would entertain – and sell.

This isn't a traditional way of thinking about Tennyson, yet it's not one the poet would necessarily have been unhappy with. Nor would Plum, and placed in this context, it's possible to picture the two writers each using Romanticism as the base ingredient for his own, very different atmospheres. Whereas slightly crazed or even doomed love is Tennyson's thing, the unreality of young love is Plum's, permeating the vast majority his plots and, indeed the whole of Wodehouse World. Both are idealized to a considerable extent, so it's not that surprising to find both writers drawing on the same perennially popular source material, namely the lore and legends of King Arthur and the Knights of the Round Table (from which 'The Lady of Shallot' had been Tennyson's first-ever borrowing).

From its shadowy medieval origins in England, France and Italy, the matter of Arthurian England steadily grew in volume until it found its supreme expression in Sir Thomas Malory's *Le Morte d'Arthur*, first printed in 1485, which wove many disparate tales into a stable narrative. Tennyson drew on Malory throughout his career, culminating in his 10,166-line romantic blockbuster *Idylls of the King*, published in sections between 1859 and 1885, which may well have served as Plum's introduction to all things Arthurian. The scholar Jay Ruud certainly thinks so, ingeniously noting parallels between Plum's 1912 story 'Sir Agravaine' and Tennyson's 'Tale of Sir Gareth' in his 2015 article 'Camelot and the World of P. G. Wodehouse.' If indeed that is the case, it's possible to claim that Tennyson radically influenced the romantic predispositions of that most *preux* of *preux chevaliers*, Bertie Wooster.

Bertie, at least in his own mind, is a 20th-century equivalent of Sir Galahad, modelling his behaviour towards women on that of his illustrious predecessor, rarely missing the opportunity to style himself as a good old-fashioned courtly lover boy. In *The Code of the Woosters*, he casually informs us that his chivalric ancestors came over with William the Conqueror in 1066, boasting in *Thank You, Jeeves* that they "did dashed well at the Battle of Crécy" in 1346. In 'A Spot of Art,' he describes himself as "the parfait gentle knight" (a mangled quote from the most Arthurian of Geoffrey Chaucer's *Canterbury Tales*) and doesn't cease these chivalrous allusions until the end of his innings in 1974's *Aunts Aren't Gentlemen*, during which, confessing his unhappiness to his Aunt Dahlia about his engagement to Vanessa Cook, she asks him how he came to be in such a mess:

> "I proposed to her a year ago, and she turned me down, and just now she blew in and said she had changed her mind and would marry me. Came as a nasty shock."
> "You should have told her to go and boil her head."
> "I couldn't."
> "Why couldn't you?"
> "Not *preux*."
> "Not what?"
> "*Preux* . . . You've heard of a *preux chevalier*? It is my aim to be one."

To which his sage relative matter-of-factly responds: "Oh, well, if you go about being *preux*, you must expect to get into trouble." And this trouble is, of course, an open-mouthed gift horse to a farceur like Plum, for Bertie, being the gallant ("preux") knight, can refuse a woman nothing, no matter how ridiculous the consequences.

Take Bertie's attachment to Madeline Bassett: although he variously describes her as "[t]he last thing [...] one would want about the home" and "as mushy a character as ever broke biscuit," he feels honour and duty bound to accept that she has chosen him as her husband, as he tells us in *Much Obliged, Jeeves*:

> If a girl thinks you're in love with her and says she will marry you, you can't very well voice a preference for being dead in a ditch. Not, I mean, if you want to regard yourself as a preux chevalier, as the expression is, which is always my aim.

And so being a man who ne'er the word of "No" woman heard speak, Bertie *does* resemble the lovelorn knights of high medieval and Tennysonian romance, with the glaring disparity that that he's not exactly enamoured of his ladies, who are not remote and unattainable but seemingly quite the reverse. And while the chivalric code would send some artists into poetic raptures, Plum instinctively targets its humorous Achilles heel, turning it inside out to get his laughs. For it's not just Bertie who cleaves to these knightly ideals of service: Uncle Fred, Jeeves, many of the Drones and even Psmith are motivated by many of the same impulses. And then, of course, there's Galahad Threepwood, named for the worthiest of all Arthur's knights, but who in Wodehouse World is an unrepentant roué who has at one time or another been thrown out of every club and restaurant in London's West End. Hovering around the age of 60, he is still ready, able, and willing to help the lovelorn – though rarely using the Arthurian playbook.

But what unquestionably unites Wodehouse and Tennyson can be best be summed up in a brief visit to 1832's 'The Palace of Art,' a straightforward allegory on the creative process that is, at least thematically, a sort of companion piece to 'The Lady of Shallot.' The poem's opening line "I built my soul a lordly-pleasure house" echoes Coleridge's Romantic classic 'Kubla Khan,' whose narrator longs to do much the same thing – to live in an enchanted world of high art. Unfortunately, it's an ambition that comes with a significant downside: Art, for all the joy it may bring its creator, is essentially a solitary pursuit, encouraging the artist's soul to inhabit what the poem's narrator calls "[t]he abysmal deeps of Personality." A connection with the rest of humanity is lost, which is not just bad for the artist's art, but their spiritual health:

> "I sit as God holding no form of creed,
> But contemplating all."

Or in the case of the Lady of Shallot, contemplating the world at one remove through a mirror. Ironically, the late Victorian movement of high Aestheticism which embraced this self-regarding philosophy of "art for art's sake" claimed Tennyson's work for one of its central inspirations, which was to badly misconstrue the Laureate's ambition to connect with his audience, and *not* to sit on an "intellectual throne" where "[n]o voice breaks through the stillness."

So it is that the central figure of Tennyson's poem, lonely and "[s]truck through with pangs of hell" in her self-imposed exile, forsakes her lofty castle and instead goes to live in a modest "cottage in the vale" where she can get back down to earth and repent of her folly. Only not completely; one day, she hints, she might return once she's been through rehab, for, like any addict, she can never be entirely free from the lure of her intoxicant. Art, or, rather, *the wrong sort of Art*, can be a dangerous drug, luring the writer away from humanity towards the world of illusion. From Wodehouse's less than serious perspective, that impulse leads not to psychological issues but to pretension, his sizeable host of ghastly poets from Ralston McTodd and Rodney Spelvin to Aubrey Barstowe and Percy Gorringe ample testimony to his loathing of arty affectation in all its forms, as we'll explore in Chapter 12.

Which brings us neatly back to our opening comparison between the respective merits of Tennyson and Shelley, and Plum's youthful praise of 'The Voyage of Maeldune.' Peter Levi makes the telling comment that

> [o]ne is somehow restrained by its unpretentiousness from calling it a great poem, but how extremely memorable it is.

And right there is the 'trap' that Plum fell into when he suspected Tennyson of being "second rate." 'The Voyage of Maeldune' *is* easy, perhaps a bit *too* easy to like. It wears its riches on its surface – Tennyson doing here what he does best: translating abstract thought into simple, lucid language that resonates in the reader's imagination. In so doing, to return to the beginning of my argument, he tricks the unwary or prejudiced (or a 67-year-old humorist temporarily off his guard) into two erroneous lines of thought: that approachability equates to shallowness; and that this kind of stuff is easy to produce. Although poetry was a sort of reflex to Tennyson, just as humour was to Wodehouse, both men carefully crafted those protean impulses into high-quality finished work they would be confident their readers could understand and enjoy without having to work too hard.

And that, Levi diagnoses, is the curse of which so-called "middlebrow" art is the eternal victim: can something simple or "extremely memorable" ever be considered "great"? The ridiculous prejudice that insists it can't continues to blight the reputations not just of Tennyson but of a long roll-call of the world's more approachable artists including W. S. Gilbert, the subject of the following chapter. The work of these artists may not be to your taste, but that shouldn't take away from the fact that they are all accomplished craftsmen who enjoy a broad appeal. Of course, *bad* art should be shown the door, as Plum, borrowing Tennyson's 'Lady Clara Vere de Vere' insisted in his 1905 poem 'Cacoethes Scribendi' which pilloried titled lady authors whose work was reviewed irrespective of its quality at the expense of better, but less socially exalted writers:

> No book can be, it seems to me,
> Worth reading if it is not good:
> Grammar is more than coronets,
> And simple style than Norman blood.

"Grammar" and "simple style" are Plum's gold standards in this poem, the only principles that make writing "worth reading." Nothing else truly matters. Which makes Tennyson's work equally sustaining as that of more weighty poets – literally so, as Wodehouse wrote in the *Encounter* magazine versions of his Berlin broadcasts, on those occasions when the bread ran out in his internment camp at Huy:

> I found [...] that Tennyson's early poems make quite good eating, as do Shakespeare's sonnets, especially if you have some cheese to go with them. And when the canteen opened, we could sometimes get cheese [...] Wrap this up in a page of Shakespeare's Sonnets or 'When Claribel low lieth,' and add some wooden matches, and you had something which, while not perhaps a gala dinner with coloured balloons and squeakers, was at any rate something.

Not one of Tennyson's masterpieces, 'Claribel' could be sacrificed for the greater good, in a rare case of art nourishing both the soul *and* the body.

Chapter 11:
W. S. Gilbert

> When I was your age, my two idols were W. S. Gilbert,
> the Savoy opera man, and Conan Doyle, [the former] a
> sort of remote godlike character to me. (I did meet him
> once. A mutual friend took me to lunch at his (Gilbert's)
> house and I killed one of G's best stories by laughing in
> the wrong place!)
> **Letter to a fan, 1964**

> I lost an English literature prize at school because I com-
> pared W. S. Gilbert to his advantage with Shakespeare.
> **Letter to a fan, 1974**

> Wodehouse's theatrical achievement [...] was no less than
> to pick up the lyrical torch lit by W. S. Gilbert and use it
> to light the way to the modern musical.
> **Barry Day (ed.), The Complete Lyrics
> of P. G. Wodehouse**

To paraphrase Bertie Wooster's metaphor in 'Aunt Agatha Takes the Count': there was the 13-year-old P. G. Wodehouse, heedlessly picking daisies on the railway, when the down-express caught him right in the small of the back.

Writing several decades later, Plum describes how that life-changing collision took place in 1895 at the Crystal Palace, a gigantic cathedral of iron and glass erected on a prominent hill in southeast London, conveniently situated two miles from Dulwich College, where he had recently started school. He still remembered how this Damascene encounter had made him "absolutely drunk with ecstasy. I thought it the finest thing that could possibly be done." Specifically, *it* was a production of William Schwenck Gilbert and Arthur Sullivan's *Patience*, the sixth of the partnership's hugely popular Savoy Operas, written in the year of Plum's birth, 1881. And from that moment on until the end of his life, Pelham Grenville Wodehouse was hooked on musical theatre.

References to *Patience* pop up in one form or another nearly 40 times in his writings, the final occasion in 1963's *Stiff Upper Lip, Jeeves*, written almost 70 years after we think (opinions vary) he first saw the show. By contrast, Bertie Wooster proves rather more resistant to its charms:

> "Oh, yes, now I recollect. My Aunt Agatha made me take her son Thos to it once. Not at all a bad little show, I thought, though a little highbrow."

Which of course it isn't, being a withering takedown of arty pretension. But while Bertie may have entirely missed the point, it was the start of something big for his creator – Plum's well-known remark that his novels were essentially musical comedies without the music indicating quite how significant the epiphany would later prove to be.

Once bitten, Plum soaked up whatever merchandise he could get his hands on, the eminent Wodehouse scholar Norman Murphy betting that:

> [i]f he hadn't seen every G&S show by the time he left Dulwich [in July 1900, aged 18], then I reckon he would indeed have bought the printed editions and compilations of the operettas.

In many respects both musically and theatrically, the musical comedy Wodehouse would later write was a lineal descendent of these operettas, and Gilbert and Sullivan's 14 collaborations were the top of the heap. As a youngster, Plum would not have been teased or bullied for his devotion, for G&S enjoyed widespread popularity in English 'public' schools until well within living memory.

Wodehouse would exploit this partiality in his early schoolboy novels, helping create a like-minded freemasonry among those of his young readers who 'got' the G & S references he regularly inserted. In 1903's *A Prefect's Uncle*, there are no fewer than seven mentions, including two apiece from *Patience* and *The Gondoliers*, and one each from *H.M.S. Pinafore*, *Trial by Jury* and *The Mikado*. *Tales of St. Austin's* contains a further seven, *The Gold Bat* four and so on. The habit would continue into his mature work. Even the partnership's final, arguably most obscure operetta *The Grand Duke* is liberally referenced, supplying what seems to have been Plum's favourite quote of all (which also appear in *The Gondoliers*): "[n]othing is more annoying than to feel that you're not equal to the intellectual pressure of the conversation." Direct quotes or paraphrases of these words can be found in no fewer than 29 separate titles, the last being *Bachelors Anonymous* published two years before he died. All of which makes Plum and Gilbert lifelong soul-mates. And before we go any further, I should acknowledge that all the stats in this chapter arrive courtesy of Arthur Robinson, who has made his amazing body of Gilbertian research freely available on the madameulalie.org website.

As the wordsmith of the G & S partnership, Gilbert inevitably received the lion's share of Wodehouse's attention. "England's greatest librettist," as he called him in *A Prefect's Uncle*, was born in Central London in 1836 (coincidentally just yards away from where Plum would later work at the *Globe* newspaper), to solidly middle-class parents. It's claimed by biographers that the young Gilbert didn't really get on with either of them. In later life, his sense of personal affront on a constant hair trigger, he could practically pick a quarrel in an empty room despite being perfectly clubbable when he needed to be. His professional relationships with Sullivan and his long-term business partner Richard D'Oyly Carte constitute long litanies of fallings-out and reconciliations, anger and apologies, rendering large sections of his life story tediously predictable. But it was this onboard prickliness that also helped make his humour so provocative. Mixed in with mischief, idealism and a satirical streak a mile wide, it would end up defining his best work – and, suitably modified, prove a massive influence on Plum's own comic writing.

With a series of pantomimes, burlesques and prose comedies to his name in the 1860s, the pre-Sullivan Gilbert would become one of the most successful dramatists in London, having no fewer than seven openings in a variety of genres in 1871 alone. In addition to his bankability, his hands-on approach to staging and insistence on attending rehearsals made him something of a one-man band. Not only did he write to order, produce, direct and even on occasion act, his work was almost universally acknowledged to be of a uniformly high quality, so partnership with the ostensibly more highbrow composer/conductor Arthur Sullivan was more a marriage of equals than it might have appeared at first glance. Their second collaboration, 1875's *Trial by Jury*, was a simple, one-act, through-sung drama that brilliantly showcased the two men's compatibility, the London *Times* commenting that the words and music seemed to have "proceeded simultaneously from one and the same brain." Although the thinnest of plots, the breach of promise case on which the operetta hinges would prove useful to Plum in several of his own stories including *The Girl on the Boat*, 'The Code of the Mulliners,' *Piccadilly Jim*, 'No Wedding Bells for Him,' and *A Man of Means*.

Most of the ingredients of G&S's future successes were present and correct from the off, including an undertow of topical satire that would grow more pointed over time. The figure of fun in *Trial by Jury* is the judge himself, a self-seeking money-grabber who has committed an identical 'crime' of desertion to the one he's currently trying, throwing over his intended when she was no longer any social or financial use to him. His shameless scramble up the greasy pole to his present eminence is skilfully sketched, and he is under no illusions about his lack of probity, judicial ability, or the chicanery he has used in getting to the top:

> Though all my law be fudge,
> Yet I'll never, never budge,
> But I'll live and die a Judge!
>
> It is patent to the mob,
> That my being made a nob
> Was effected by a job.

The operetta's precipitate resolution arrives when the judge impulsively decides to marry the pretty young plaintiff, the case collapses and all ends happily for everyone concerned. There would be 12 more Gilbert and Sullivan collaborations over the next 21 years, most of them fabulously successful, both in Britain and America; and although both men had many more strings to their collective bows, it is the Savoy Operas – staples of am-dram companies all over the world for almost 150 years – that keep their reputations alive and kicking well into the 21st century.

At which point we return to the 18-year-old Plum, who right at the start of his own writing career inscribed the following lines from *Iolanthe* on the opening page of his 'Money Received for Literary Work' ledger:

> Though never nurtured in the lap
> Of luxury, yet I admonish you,
> I am an intellectual chap,
> And think of things that would astonish you.

Plum, who already "knew [he] was good" despite being unknown, might well have identified with the singer of those lines – Private Willis of the Grenadiers – who, at least in his own mind, is far more able and intelligent than his lowly rank suggests. Or perhaps he was more of a 'Jack Point,' the *nom de plume* he chose for signing off his monthly 'Under the Flail' column for *Public School Magazine* which ran from December 1900 to March 1902. Jack Point is Gilbert's 'Strolling Jester' from *The Yeomen of the Guard*, an interesting choice of alter ego for the young Wodehouse as he launched his career in London's glittering theatreland, the West End. The comedian, who remarks that "there is humour in all things" can also "trick you into learning with a laugh," for he takes care to always insert "[a] grain or two of truth among the chaff!"

> When they're offered to the world in merry guise,
> Unpleasant truths are swallowed with a will -

For he who'd make his fellow-creatures wise
Should always gild the philosophic pill!

Unlike Gilbert, whose idea of gilding was the equivalent of a punch in the face, Plum would demonstrate far greater subtlety in the ways he introduced satire into his writings, such that several commentators have denied it's there at all. Yet it is, and Gilbert would have been one of the most important reasons why.

Wodehouse's early career would shadow Gilbert's at many points, entering the literary fray some 40 years after his hero. Both men began as jobbing freelance journalists in their 20s, writing anything for anyone who would pay them – Gilbert was even a war correspondent for a time. They would crank out theatre reviews and poetry for the very same London magazines, including *Fun*, where Gilbert's massively popular *Bab Ballads* had their home. These topical satires, collected in two volumes in 1869 and 1873, read well even now: here's a few lines from one that is perhaps inspired by his own experience – 'The Played-Out Humorist':

Quixotic is his enterprise, and hopeless his adventure is,
Who seeks for jocularities that haven't yet been said.
The world has joked incessantly for over fifty centuries,
And every joke that's possible has long ago been made.
I started as a humorist with lots of mental fizziness,
But humour is a drug which it's the fashion to abuse;
For my stock-in-trade, my fixtures, and the goodwill of the business
No reasonable offer I am likely to refuse.

Wodehouse was one of many humorous copy writers who imitated Gilbert's patented verse style, and his poems are sometimes indistinguishable in style – and quality – from his mentor's. Take 'The Road to Success,' a Plum lyric that can be sung to the tune of Bunthorne's song 'If you're anxious for to shine in the high aesthetic line' from *Patience*:

If you're anxious to outdistance
In the struggle for existence
Every rival on the scene,
You must imitate your Dowie,
And try hard to find out how he
Grew a beard at seventeen.

And everyone will say,
As you walk your prosperous way,

"If this young man can grow a beard
(Which has never occurred to me),
Why, what a most particularly gifted sort of youth
This sort of youth must be."

As editor of the daily 'By the Way' column in the *Globe* newspaper, true yet unlikely stories were Plum's bread and butter, and Gilbert's influence is never far away from his poetry when bringing them to life. In this one we learn of John Alexander Dowie, a Scotsman who made huge amounts of money in America by shaving his head and growing a long white beard in the manner of an Old Testament prophet. As he later recalled, "People used to think me about twenty-five, and I soon got the salary of a man of twenty-five, when I was seventeen."

Many, if not the majority, of the poems Plum wrote while working as a journalist aspire to the condition of song lyrics, as their titles sometimes suggest: 'Songs on the Situation,' 'Songs of the Moment,' 'Suffragette Songs,' 'The Barber's Love Song,' and 'The Bachelor's Song' might all have been set to music had a composer or theatre manager spotted their potential. As he wrote in 'Sing It!,' "I am prepared to supply lyrics at reasonable rates to all who may need them in their profession," before showcasing three 'songs' that could benefit a family doctor, a literary editor and a cricket umpire, the last of these reminiscent of Gilbert's lyric 'When I First Put This Uniform On,' once again from *Patience*:

When I first put this white coat on,
I vowed I would act on the square,
And always be guided
In what I decided
By what was right and fair.
If I ever had any doubt
As to whether a man was out,
No fieldsman should make me
Nervous, or shake me,
However loud he might shout.
This point I'd decided upon
When I first put my white coat on.

If everyone, even the great and the good in musical theatre, was enjoying success by ripping off Gilbert, why shouldn't Plum? In an article he wrote for *Punch* in October 1906 entitled 'The Cooks and the Gaiety Broth,' he imagines a writers' meeting at London's Gaiety Theatre, in which he namechecks members of that theatre's real-life creative team as they float ideas for their next show, *The New Aladdin*, which had actually opened the month before the piece was published:

> *Mr. Tanner.* My idea is – something Gilbertian.
> *Mr. Risque.* Well, you've got it, haven't you? Your stout fairy who nestles in a buttercup is copied from *Iolanthe*; your genie who has to talk in rhyme comes from *The Fairy's Dilemma*; your chorus of policemen from *The Pirates of Penzance*; and your policeman lost in London from *Peter Forth* in *The Bab Ballads*. One would think that that was enough Gilbert for one piece.

Was this imagined conversation a job résumé thinly disguised as satire? Unfortunately for Plum, the piece was printed unsigned, so the identity of the writer who seemed to know so much about the milieu of the stage musical (and the works of W. S. Gilbert) would have remained a mystery. One year on from writing this piece, Plum would actually be working at the Gaiety – but that time was not yet.

So keen was he to set out his stall as what he would sometimes call a "lyrist," he even created a returning character (and perhaps ironic alias), Henry William-Jones, who longs to break into the big time by writing librettos for grand opera, but whose work mimics Gilbert's more populist operettas. Published in *Punch*, the last of three such articles from September 1904 follows the trial (by jury) of a millionairess accused of shoplifting a handkerchief, for whom a gallant shop assistant, Algernon Hildebrand Plopp, has gallantly volunteered to take the fall. The couple declare their love for one another on the witness stand, and overcome by sentiment the judge drops the case; at which point the Counsel for the Defence delivers these waspish lines:

> But mark, this lovely girl,
> Whose charms, I own, bewitch one,
> Is only daughter to an Earl,
> And (by the way) a rich one.
> His Lordship's fortune, so I hear,
> Is twenty thousand pounds a year.
> Such being her papa
> (So runs the law of Britain),
> Not theft, but Kleptomania
> Must her offence be written.
> And thus, it's needless to explain,
> She leaves the Court without a stain.

The punishment, to paraphrase *The Mikado*, most definitely *doesn't* fit the crime – and by this point it is almost impossible to tell where Gilbert leaves off and Wodehouse begins. Plum doesn't simply inhabit his mentor's style; he also embraces his outspoken brand of satire, stating that a woman of lowlier status would have been frogmarched straight to jail, whereas the titled offender's crime is excused on the grounds that she could not help herself helping herself.

Wodehouse's quiet subversion chimed with Gilbert's more outspoken version on those occasions when snobbery is held up to ridicule, and lovers woo one another across the class divide. Two such victims are the lowly Able Seaman Ralph Rackstraw and Josephine Corcoran, the daughter of the ship's captain in *H.M.S. Pinafore*:

> Ralph: Josephine, I am a British sailor and I love you!
>
> Josephine: Sir, the audacity! (Aside.) *Oh, my heart, my beating heart!* (Aloud.) This unwarrantable presumption on the part of a common sailor! (Aside.) *Common! Oh, the irony of the word!* (Crossing, aloud.) Oh, sir, you forget the disparity in our ranks.

At the same time, Little Buttercup – a sort of peripatetic corner store for the sailors at anchor, has eyes for Josephine's father:

> Who is poor Little Buttercup that she should expect his glance to fall on one so lowly! And yet if he knew – if he only knew!

Naturally, both couples are united at the end of the operetta as they would in any Wodehouse plot, the Captain informing the First Lord of the Admiralty that "love levels all ranks."

But although something of an armchair iconoclast, Wodehouse would rarely taunt his audience as openly and confrontationally as Gilbert seemed to delight in doing. Despite his wide popularity, the latter's waspishness was held against him in certain quarters, and when he toned it down (as in, say, *The Yeomen of the Guard*) his biographer Jane W. Stedman informs us that a wave of palpable relief could be felt throughout the Establishment. What really got Gilbert's goat was injustice, a distaste no doubt nurtured during his brief career as a barrister in the early 1860s. Plum would also regularly sift his characters not by who, but what sort of person they are, usually reserving his censure for those who ought to know better but don't.

Meanwhile, back in 1904, Wodehouse's naked ambition to break into musical theatre paid off when his lyric 'Put Me In My Little Cell' belatedly found its way into the West End production of *Sergeant Brue*, which was already some way into its eventual run of 200 performances. It was an immediate hit and encores were demanded, prompting an uncharacteristically excited Plum to write "This is fame" and "I have Arrived" in his private *Money Received* ledger. Over on Broadway, where the show opened on April 24, 1905, the song was feted as the evening's best number – or as the *New York Times* had it: "the funniest thing in this very funny show," its trio of performers "recalled and recalled 'till they's [sic] come out no more'." It was a similar story on tour, and the song was recorded with Americanized lyrics for phonographic release in a version by Billy Murray, a pop idol of his day. An astute reviewer on the *Syracuse Herald* noted with delight the "mock-serious stage business and quaint dance" sparked by the lyric, praising the actors for "their clever interpretation of its whimsicalities," indicating that Plum, first time out of the traps, had produced a lyric that not just sang well, but could *play* well live on stage – his words suggesting how the actors might busy themselves while singing them. The strong, immediate central conceit, along with the regular rhymes and rhythms that herald Gilbert's influence, are all present, and there are also hints of traditional British music-hall in there somewhere, accented by the tune provided by Frederick Rosse. Not a bad start for the 23-year-old stage-door Johnny.

Wodehouse would end up writing hundreds of songs (and often the libretti) for almost 40 musical comedies between 1905 and 1934, applying the same high artistic standards he set himself for his prose works. In this professionalism, he once more shadowed his idol. Plum could not have known that in 1876, Gilbert had written to the comedian John S. Clarke that "I never scamp my work, & whatever I do is the best of the kind that I *can* do," but as a fanboy he might well have sought out the regular interviews Gilbert gave to newspapers and magazines, or the biographies that cashed in on his fame. In these publications, he would have learned of the older man's fastidious approach to his craft. One interviewer, writing for *Cassell's Magazine* in 1900, had been loaned one of Gilbert's notebooks in which he found ample evidence of the writer's "painstaking" care:

> As one turns the pages one finds the idea of the plot freshly begun, altered, varied, and added to some twenty or thirty times, roughly written in jottings, and growing in scope of idea and action, gathering characters, incidents, and whimsical notions and speeches and suggestions for lyrics,

as well as details of scenes and costumes, at each fresh writing; while the pages are dotted with clever and characteristic sketches of the personalities of the piece, as they suggest themselves to the author's fancy. Some hundreds of pages are filled with these jottings, through which one can trace the piece growing and taking shape.

Similarly, in an article titled 'Real Life Conversations' for *Pall Mall Magazine*, Gilbert remarks on the necessary "neatness," "finish" and "rational proceeding" that is the hallmark of good work.

Now compare Wodehouse's rigorously righteous way of working as revealed in his letters and in Chapter 20 of the autobiographical *Over Seventy*, and it's clear that both writers were craftsmen who toiled long and hard to get things *right*. In the draft of a speech probably written in the 1870s, Gilbert stated that although dramatic composition did not require "the highest order of intellect," it did demand "shrewdness of observation, a nimble brain, a faculty for expressing oneself concisely, a sense of balance, both in the construction of plots & in the construction of sentences." Which is uncannily similar to what playwright Wally Mason comes out with in Plum's 1921 theatre novel *Jill the Reckless*:

> "I don't say musical comedy is a very lofty form of art, but still there's a certain amount of science about it."

Add to that both men's astonishing work ethic and their reliable instincts of what would work on stage or page, and that does indeed constitute a "science." Which made them both, quite simply, *professionals*.

Even as Wodehouse awaited a follow-up to his first hit song, Gilbert's career in the theatre would remind the ambitious young shaver that starving in a dingy garret was not the only model an aspiring dramatist need follow. As Plum noted in *Not George Washington*, working in the theatre was one of the best and quickest ways to get yourself "money and a name automatically," and this had certainly been true in Gilbert's case. Most magazine interviews of the period somewhere mentioned the ageing Savoyard's sumptuous mansion 'Grim's Dyke' on the outskirts of London (now a hotel) and his taste for the good things in life. And it was amid those lush surroundings in August 1905 that the two men (Plum aged 23, Gilbert 68) met for the first and only time – which, as Wodehouse later remembered, did not go well when he killed one of his idol's best after-dinner stories stone dead by laughing in the wrong place. The resulting mortification did not prevent him hanging on Gilbert's every word and scribbling down five and a half pages of foolscap notes during the encounter, however, every day being a college day at this early stage of his career.

Wodehouse now started musing out loud about the craft of lyric writing and the nature of comedy in his daily pieces for the *Globe* newspaper. In October 1905 he noted that "the essence of Gilbertian humour is that the speaker should seem to be unconscious that he is saying anything funny." Clearly, this was a lesson well learned, for it would become the kernel of much of Plum's own schtick and one of the keynotes of Bertie Wooster's narrative person and writing style. Then, the following month, Wodehouse complained how even the most carelessly dashed-off lyrics still managed to get the applause:

> Nothing is more extraordinary in our modern life than the patience with which audiences receive the baldest, tritest lines [in songs] which do not even scan. The same materials are used over and over again, the sentiment is ludicrous, and yet, to use the technical phrase, they go. Another mysterious thing is that it is hard, we believe, to write a popular song. Perhaps these examples before us are really the work of sleepless nights, and have been polished with great care. Perhaps the authors spent a day on that beautiful couplet, "Lad and lass shelter together 'neath a tree, hoping that the rainstorms ended soon will be." These things are a great mystery.

On this occasion, Plum had a personal axe to grind; the slapdash lyric he quotes was taken from a song parachuted into the hugely successful musical *The Catch of the Season* in preference to one of his own. But his remarks also serve to highlight another important similarity between himself and Gilbert – their shared appreciation that humour would never be taken seriously if comic writers persisted in palming off shoddy goods, no matter how much audiences might lap them up. Wouldn't it be preferable if humour's lowlier status moved those writers to indignation, spurring them on to higher things? As Plum would comment at the peak of his songwriting success in 1917, this lack of artistic ambition was holding musical comedy back:

> [E]ven a metropolitan audience likes its lyrics as much as possible in the language of every-day. That is one of the thousand reasons why new Gilberts do not arise. Gilbert had the advantage of being a genius, but he had the additional advantage of writing for a public which permitted

him to use his full vocabulary, and even to drop into foreign languages, even Latin and a little Greek when he felt like it. (I allude to that song in *The Grand Duke*.)

"That song" (which he clearly expects us to be familiar with) opens Act II, and does indeed embrace slang and classical erudition:

> In the period Socratic every dining-room was Attic
> (Which suggests an architecture of a topsy-turvy kind),
> There they'd satisfy their thirst on a recherché cold ἀριστόν
> Which is what they called their lunch – and so may you if you're inclined.
> As they gradually got on, they'd τρέπέσθάί πρός τό πόντόν
> (Which is Attic for a steady and a conscientious drink).
> But they mixed their wine with water – which I'm sure they didn't oughter -
> And we modern Saxons know a trick worth two of that, I think!
> Then came rather risky dances (under certain circumstances)
> Which would shock that worthy gentleman, the Licenser of Plays,
> Corybantian maniac kick – Dionysiac or Bacchic –
> And the Dithyrambic revels of those undecorous days.

Back in Chapter 4, I proposed a direct lineage between the comic songs of Aristophanes and those of Gilbert. Well, here you have it on a plate garnished with watercress. In the more buttoned-up Victorian era, Gilbert can only hint at what his "undecorous" Ancient Greek predecessor could get away with in his plays, but the similarity in form and approach is remarkable given the two and a half millennia that separate their work. It's quite the linguistic and cultural tour de force. Yet for all its erudition, the song ultimately mocks learned pretension as its singer, Ludwig 'the Leading Comedian' helpfully informs us in a sung aside:

> Periphrastic methods spurning,
> To this audience discerning
> I admit this show of learning
> Is the fruit of steady "cram"!

Regularly making fun of high culture unites Gilbert, Aristophanes, and Plum, all of whom pull the neat trick of beefing up their comedy by associating it with high culture, while undermining that culture by making it comedy's victim.

But while Wodehouse and Gilbert occasionally demonstrated impatience with their chosen genre and what they both sometimes perceived as the low cultural expectations of their audiences, I would argue that Plum was more comfortable with his lot as comic writer than Gilbert, who, with his irritable nature and borderline paranoia, grew convinced that comic operetta was painting him into a corner, his success forcing him to continue working in a genre that would (or could) never allow his genius to fire on all cylinders. Hence his occasional forays into serious drama and even tragedy, no doubt to prove to the critics, his public and himself that he could do highbrow stuff if he set his mind to it, and that a 'dramatist' (his preferred designation for one of his calling) was just as deserving of being considered an artist as painters and composers. Even his ennoblement in 1907 – making him the first dramatist to be so honoured in Britain – could not satisfy Sir William Gilbert that he belonged in the top drawer, particularly since Sir Arthur Sullivan had received *his* gong 24 years previously. In his darker moods, he was merely "an idle singer of an idle day" – as he described himself at a dinner celebrating his elevation – or when he grumbled to his early biographer Edith A. Browne that he was merely trading on "the easy trivialities of the Savoy libretti."

Plum ponders this piece of musical history in *Jill the Reckless* by inserting a set speech from Otis Pilkington, a musical comedy writer with ideas above his station (he wears tortoiseshell-rimmed glasses and refers to his 12 chorus girls as his "ensemble"):

> "We feel that the time has come when the public is beginning to demand something better than what it has been accustomed to. People are getting tired of the brainless trash and jingly tunes which have been given them by men like Wallace Mason and George Bevan. They want a certain polish. It was just the same in Gilbert and Sullivan's day. They started writing at a time when the musical stage had reached a terrible depth of inanity. The theatre was given over to burlesques of the most idiotic description. The public was waiting eagerly to welcome something of a higher class. It is just the same today. But the managers will not see it."

Both Pilkington (the librettist) and Roland Trevis (his composer) consider their collaboration as being on a par with anything their celebrated predecessors ever came up with – and perhaps even better. In a cringe-making mutual love-fest, Pilkington claims his partner's music has "all Sullivan's melody with a newness of rhythm peculiarly its own"

while Trevis praises his co-writer for "avoid[ing] Gilbert's mistake of being too fanciful" (we'll examine what he means by that later in this chapter). But Pilkington's grasp of theatrical history is somewhat incomplete,
failing to point out that prior to Sullivan's arrival on the scene, Gilbert
had made his name writing the very burlesques (send-ups of existing
plays and operas) he (Pilkington) so despises. Gilbert knew what he was
getting into, yet still did his best to raise the bar in a genre that regularly
insisted on plumbing that "terrible depth of inanity." Indeed, he was
praised for succeeding in titles such as 1866's *Dulcamara*, and *Robert the
Devil* two years later. Despite the plaudits and popularity (that latter play
toured for three years in the provinces) he still felt the need to insert an
apology immediately prior to the curtain of his final burlesque, 1869's
The Pretty Druidess:

> Forgive our rhymes;
> Forgive the jokes you've heard five thousand times;
> Forgive each breakdown, cellar-flap and clog [on-trend
> dance styles],
> Our low-bred songs – our slangy dialogue;
> And, above all – oh, ye with double barrel –
> Forgive the scantiness of our apparel!

Although there's a fair bit of ironic self-deprecation going on here, the
play would close after less than two months, probably confirming Gilbert's worst suspicions about theatre audiences, who evidently preferred
their humour coarser than he was prepared to make it.

Back in *Jill the Reckless*, Wodehouse makes the theatre manager, not
the audience, the drag on standards, although the ghastly Mr. Goble
would claim he's merely the slave of his paying customers, never losing money by giving them what they want. On seeing the run-through
of Pilkington and Trevis's *The Rose of America* he complains that "It's
all wrong! It don't add up right! You'll have to rewrite it from end to
end!", citing a preposterous speech "about life being like a water-mel-
on" as Exhibit 'A'. The "you" he's addressing here is not the writers, but
the 'fixer' – who just happens to be the very same Wally Mason whom
Pilkington earlier slagged off for his "brainless trash." And Plum gives
Wally a similar back story to Pilkington; he too had experienced a rush
of blood to the head in which he longed to raise standards in the theatre
and truly challenge himself as a writer, as he tells Jill Mariner:

> "I've been writing musical comedies for the last few years,
> and after you've done that for a while your soul rises up

within you and says, "Come, come my lad" You can do better than this!" That's what mine said, and I believed it. Subsequent events have proved that Sidney the Soul was pulling my leg!"

Wally has already learned – and acted on – the lesson that Pilkington will never learn, and that Gilbert was never truly comfortable with; namely, that the audience and its money holds all the cards. The trouble with Gilbert was that his version of Sidney the Soul (what we might call his 'artistic conscience') never really stopped tugging at his leg, whereas Plum's equivalent seldom troubled him. Wodehouse very quickly came to terms with being a popular, populist writer, and that this was far from the worst fate that could have befallen him. Unlike Gilbert, he was perfectly happy to take his patrons' money guilt-free, on condition he felt he was giving of his best.

In 1905, where we left his career a few pages back, Plum would soon be employed not as the star writer but a backroom fixer just like Wally Mason, first at the Aldwych Theatre and then at the Gaiety, re-writing encores, doctoring lyrics and coming up with new songs as required, all the while continuing to polish up his act. In an unsigned article for the London *Evening Standard* on May 2, 1906, titled 'On Lyric Writing,' he helpfully shares some of the gleanings he has so far collected, which I'll briefly summarize:

- "There are no second chances on the stage" – the theatre-goer has just one chance to get what you mean, so keep everything, including your language, as simple and transparent as possible.
- Assume very little prior knowledge on the part of your audience, so think very carefully before introducing allusions or references of whatever kind, particularly when they are the fulcrum of a joke.
- Don't be afraid of suggesting your punchline in advance, allowing your audience to anticipate it before joyfully confirming their suspicions in the final line of the refrain.

Note how Plum's focus is almost exclusively on his audience and how it 'takes in' what he has written. Later the same year ('Launching a Popular Song'), he could be once again caught dissecting his craft:

- Make your lyrical ideas instantly memorable.
- Pace your set pieces and big numbers so they don't arrive

too thick and fast; give your audience some breathing (and
thinking) room.

All these principles he could, and probably did, learn from studying
Gilbert, in whose best works they are all sedulously applied. Even so,
he tells us in February 1907, any budding lyricist "has to endure being
constantly reproached for not being Mr. Gilbert, while having all his
most Gilbertian work refused." Well, not quite. Working on *The Beauty
of Bath*, Plum had already enjoyed another copper-bottomed hit – 'Oh!
Mr Chamberlain' – that bent the second of his rules out of shape by
featuring a currently popular politician, yet always got the laughs; and
he would soon produce another topical lyric, 'The Glow-Worm,' that
was singled out for praise in several reviews of *My Darling*, a show that
debuted in March the same year.

But any artist can only get so far by aping their heroes; and while
it's clear that Wodehouse absolutely adored Gilbert's work, there are
significant points at which their sensibilities diverged. While both he
and Gilbert loved a happy ending with couplings galore, the latter never
really 'did' intimate in his operettas. For a significant majority of the
time, the atmosphere on stage is full-on and public rather than nuanced
and private, and even in a genre as contrived as romantic comedy, Wodehouse's lovers can strike us as somehow more authentic than Gilbert's
equivalents. It's as if they are actually in love rather than singing *about*
being in love, a distinction Bertie alludes to in 'Scoring Off Jeeves':

> [T]here's no reticence about Bingo. He always reminds me
> of the hero of a musical comedy who takes the centre of
> the stage, gathers the boys round him in a circle, and tells
> them all about his love at the top of his voice.

While there is tenderness to be found in Gilbert (Phoebe's song 'Were I
Thy Bride' from *The Yeomen of the Guard* is a fine example, as is *Patience*'s
'Sad Is That Woman's Lot'), this sort of sentimentalism is somewhat
tokenistic, for he wasn't big on sincerity either. That wasn't in the deal,
for Gilbert's overwhelming sense of satire and fun could rarely resist the
impulse to undermine things, rendering them utterly ridiculous.

Gilbert's broad brush was occasionally too broad for Plum, who, as
he found his own voice, tended to dial down his predecessor's surreal
craziness, abrupt tonal reversals, outspokenness and occasional coarse-
ness in order to produce work that was more refined, and with a broad-
er emotional palette. *Qua* Roland Trevis in *Jill the Reckless*, Wodehouse
would abandon some of the more "fanciful" aspects of Gilbert's craft.

Take, for example, the latter's well-known and unsparing use of the so-called "lozenge" device, or his frequent recourse to "Topsy-Turvey-dom" to generate his plotlines, habits that grew out of an early Bab ballad ('My Dream') from 1870:

> The other night, from cares exempt,
> I slept – and what d'you think I dreamt?
> I dreamt that somehow I had come
> To dwell in Topsy-Turveydom!
> Where vice is virtue – virtue, vice:
> Where nice is nasty – nasty, nice
> Where right is wrong and wrong is right –
> Where white is black and black is white.

Babies are born wise and grow more stupid as they get older; magistrates are mostly robbers; policemen jail the innocent; historians write fantasy – and so on. Gilbert would give houseroom to these kinds of switcheroos for the entire run of the Savoy Operas. Indeed Sullivan, who preferred a more realistic approach driven by genuine emotion, grew heartily tired of his partner's repeated attempts to sell him plots where reality can be suddenly and violently turned on its head by magic potions (*The Sorcerer*), a surreal legislature (*The Mikado*) or *deus ex machina* revelations (passim). Wodehouse, who also enjoyed subverting reality, tended to draw the line at these implausible wrenchings, only really experimenting with this sort of ruse twice: in 1936's *Laughing Gas* when the Hollywood child star Joey Cooley exchanges souls with English toff Reggie Havershot while they are both under ether at the dentist; and more plausibly in 1931's *If I Were You*, when Lord Droitwich loses his title to a barber, Syd Price, due to a mix-up in the nursery. Neither novel represents Wodehouse anywhere near the top of his game, and for all the thousands of critical column inches that try to persuade us that Plum created an out-and-out fantasy world, he really wasn't comfortable with the more improbable aspects of topsyturveydom, preferring to generate plots that arise *out of* his charac-ters, rather than parachuting ideas *on top of* a set of chess pieces (Gilbert famously built himself a miniature stage complete with model scenery and blocks of wood representing the actors to help him plan the onstage business of each production). So while Gilbert inverts reality, Plum sends it gloriously askew, the former's comedy arising out of his presentation of weirdness as the most normal thing in the world, while the latter revels in deviant behaviour for what it is – potty – using reality as his yardstick.

After 1907, things went pretty quiet on the lyric-writing front, just as things seemed to be looking up. Wodehouse's 'New and Original Revue'

Nuts and Wine would tank in the West End in 1914, perhaps hastening his decision to leave England for a while. He had already learned from Gilbert and Sullivan that British and American tastes in musical theatre were to a great degree compatible, and that writers could run parallel careers in both countries. *H.M.S. Pinafore* and *The Mikado* had both been massive hits across the Pond and were regularly staged by both professional and amateur companies (during Plum's extended sojourn from 1914 to 1919, *Pinafore* was revived on Broadway in 1914, 1915 and 1918 – that last year a bumper G&S Fest that also featured *Iolanthe, The Pirates of Penzance, Patience* and *The Mikado*). But that was to prove a sort of last hurrah: as the Edwardian era drew to a close it was clear that the times they were a-changin': the G&S partnership had produced its final collaboration in 1896; Sullivan had handed in his dinner pail in 1900 aged just 58, and Gilbert, ostensibly 'retired,' would follow in 1911. Work stamped with the 'Gilbert' imprint no longer enjoyed the dominant influence it once had as the public's taste gently slid across from operetta to musical comedy – a process that had begun back in the early 1890s.

By the time Plum published *Jill the Reckless* in 1921, the transition was long since done and dusted – if we can believe Phil Brown, who has recently auditioned for Otis Pilkington, as he describes his experience to chorus girl Nelly Bryant:

> "He said it [*The Rose of America*] was an effort to restore the Gilbert and Sullivan tradition. Say, who are these Gilbert and Sullivan guys anyway? They get written up in the papers all the time and I never met any one who's run across them. If you want my opinion, that show's . . . a comic opera!"
>
> "For heaven's sake!" Nelly had the musical comedy performer's horror of the older-established form of entertainment. "Why, comic opera died in year one!"
>
> "Well, these guys are going to dig it up."

If Phil is right, and *The Rose of America* is a "citron" (lemon), those who were still 'writing up' G&S must have been inveterate nostalgists. And so it was that in a scripted interview for the *New York Times* in 1915, while Wodehouse had praised Gilbert as "a humorist of first rank" and "an originator" who got "a new angle on things," he clearly implied it was time to move on to something fresh – while never quite leaving the best of Gilbert behind.

Which is exactly what happened, and continues to happen. A century on from Plum's musings, Gilbert and Sullivan's legacy remains in robust health, at least in their home country. So far this year (August

2023) this writer has seen five London productions with a sixth on its way, ranging from a lavish big-budget *Pinafore* to a radical all-male *Mikado* set on a school camping trip. Both were superb. As for how Plum built on Gilbert's legacy from 1915 onwards and became a Broadway legend is a story for another day and will be dealt with in my next volume. For now though, I'll break off by remarking that even at the age of 92, Gilbert was still Plum's go-to guy when he was looking for authentic Scottish-inflected gibberish to grace a new preface to *The Golf Omnibus*, tracking it down in an obscure poem from 1868, 'The Ghost, the Gallant, the Gael, and the Goblin':

> These are the men whose drives fly far, like bullets from a rifle,
> Who when they do a hole in par regard it as a trifle.
> Of such as these the bard has said: "*Hech thrawfu' raltie rorkie, wi' thecht ta' croonie clapperhead and fash wi' unco' pawkie.*"

And to conclude, here's a non-too scientific yet curiously interesting experiment. First, I'm going to quote a 1957 review in *The Times*, which examined "the continued vitality of the Savoy operas" as follows:

> [T]hey were never really contemporary in their idiom [...] Gilbert's [world], from the first moment was obviously not the audience's world, [it was] an artificial world, with a neatly controlled and shapely precision which has not gone out of fashion – because it was never in fashion in the sense of using the fleeting conventions and ways of thought of contemporary human society [...] The neat articulation of incredibilities in Gilbert's plots is perfectly matched by his language [...] His dialogue, with its primly mocking formality, satisfies both the ear and the intelligence. His verses show an unequalled and very delicate gift for creating a comic effect by the contrast between poetic form and prosaic thought and wording [...] How deliciously [his lines] prick the bubble of sentiment. Gilbert had many imitators, but no equals, at this sort of thing [...] Light, and even trifling, though [the operas] may seem upon grave consideration, they yet have the shapeliness and elegance that can make a trifle into a work of art.

Now: read that again substituting 'Wodehouse' for 'Gilbert' – and it *still* makes perfect sense.

Chapter 12:
T. S. Eliot and the Modernists

[Wodehouse is] awfully able. Far abler than any
of these highbrows.
Arnold Bennett

She wrote this novel and it was well received by the intelligentsia, who notoriously enjoy the most frightful bilge.
Jeeves and the Feudal Spirit

James had to read to her. And poetry at that. And not the
jolly, wholesome sort of poetry the boys are turning out
nowadays, either – good, honest stuff about sin and gas-
works and decaying corpses, but the old-fashioned kind
with rhymes in it, dealing almost exclusively with love.
Honeysuckle Cottage

Across the pale parabola of joy.
Leave it to Psmith

In 1933, T. S. Eliot wrote a poem about a famous pig.

'Mr. Pugstyles' celebrates a glorious animal that "takes the gold
medals / At all the stock shows and our grand county fair" despite the
best efforts of "schemers, contrivers and plotters" who own inferior
"underbred swine." Christopher Ricks and Jim McCue, the diligent
scholars behind the 2015 complete edition of Eliot's poetry, find echoes
therein of Dickens, Shelley, Housman and 18th-century broadsheet political verse. But not, oddly, P. G. Wodehouse, whose own portly porker
Empress of Blandings had made her debut six years prior to Eliot's
composition in the short story 'Pig Hoo-o-o-o-ey'.

It's a small but significant oversight, for it's widely known Eliot was
a dedicated Wodehouse fan. Christopher Sykes tells us how the great
poet's admiration existed "just this side of idolatry," Eliot having a comprehensive collection of Wodehouse publications which he loaned very
rarely, and then only to friends he could trust. Peter Ackroyd, Eliot's
biographer, also reveals that the poet regularly immersed himself in
Wodehouse for much-needed relaxation. And there's more:

• In his poem 'Bustopher Jones: The Cat About Town' (from

Old Possum's Book of Practical Cats) Eliot playfully name-checks Wodehouse's Drones Club and his debut novel *The Pothunters*.

- As a director and editor at Faber & Faber, he is likely to have overseen the publication of Plum's book of essays *Louder and Funnier* in 1932.
- Both writers were children of the 1880s, born seven years apart (Wodehouse 1881 in England, Eliot 1888 in America). They lived for long periods in one another's countries; they were privately educated with a classics-heavy bias; both had toiled in London banks – Plum for two years, Eliot for seven – and shared a taste for boxing, music halls and pulpy detective fiction.
- Both men knew their literature inside out, and vigorously eschewed personal or confessional styles of writing that probed the psyche.

But while the two writers might have had much in common, Wodehouse was not as enamoured of Eliot's work as Eliot was of his, frequently deflating the pretensions of literary modernism of which his brilliant colleague was often a reluctant figurehead.

In *Jeeves and the Feudal Spirit*, Plum makes light work of his coeval's daunting reputation for high seriousness when Lady Florence Craye demands of Bertie Wooster:

"What have you been reading lately?" [...]
"I am in the process of plugging away at a thing called 'The Mystery of the Pink Crayfish'" [...]
"How can you fritter away your time like that, when you might be reading T. S. Eliot?"

Although Plum's playful criticism of Eliot never descends to outright ridicule, there's clearly some guilt by association going on here. The humourless Florence, steeped to the gills in serious purpose, is keen to "mould" Bertie into a civilized human being (or as she phrases it, to "foster the latent potentialities of your budding mind") by weaning him onto a diet of quality literature, which in her view *The Mystery of the Pink Crayfish* most definitely isn't. She too has some form publishing arty stuff, being the author of the experimental novel *Spindrift*, which has enjoyed no little success, popular with "the boys with the bulging foreheads out Bloomsbury way," but which Jeeves dismisses as a "somewhat immature production lacking in significant form."

Which would be Wodehouse's criticism too. His biggest beef (1 of 4) with verse of Eliot's kidney was its haughty disdain for rhythmic and formal integrity. In other words, you could bung down any old nonsense that didn't rhyme or scan properly, call it *vers libre* or blank verse, and it would be hailed as a masterpiece by the literary fashionistas and mint you a fortune. Plum had been taking pot-shots at slatternly versifying since the early days of modernism: in 1916's 'The Aunt and the Sluggard' Rockmetteller Todd trousers $100 for a 28-word poem called simply 'Be!', which allows the poet "to stay in bed until four in the afternoon for over a month":

Be!
Be!
The past is dead.
Tomorrow is not born.
Be today!
Today!
Be with every nerve,
With every muscle,
With every drop of your red blood!
Be!

And that's yer lot. As an incredulous Bertie Wooster puts it, "American editors fight for the stuff," which stylistically resembles the more exhortatory forms of Vorticism that Eliot briefly flirted with, notably in his 'Rhapsody on a Windy Night,' printed in the movement's house journal BLAST in 1914. But really, there was little new under the sun, and the analogue of both men's verses is likely to have been either Walt Whitman (1819-92, sometimes known as "the father of free verse") or even Henry Wadsworth Longfellow's 'A Psalm of Life' from 1838:

Trust no Future, howe'er pleasant!
Let the dead Past bury its dead!
Act—act in the glorious Present!

And Longfellow will be along again momentarily.

1914 was the year Eliot emigrated from America to England, while at almost exactly the same time Wodehouse could be found travelling in the opposite direction for what turned out to be a five-year sojourn in the States. Bertie would soon follow him to the Big Apple, and in 1916's 'Leave It To Jeeves' we find him rubbing a fraternal shoulder with the bohemian artists "who lived with the gas turned down mostly around Washington Square" and loving it. His creator, by contrast, was rather more sceptical of this hippy enclave, at least if the lyrics to the song 'Greenwich Village' are anything to go by:

> Way down in Greenwich Village
> There's something, 'twould appear,
> Demoralizing in the atmosphere.
> Quite ordinary people,
> Who come to live down here,
> Get changed to perfect nuts within a year.
> They learn to eat spaghetti
> (That's hard enough, as you know)
> They leave off frocks
> And wear Greek smocks
> And study Guido Bruno.
> For there's something in the air
> Down here in Greenwich Village
> That makes a fellow feel he doesn't care:
> And as soon as he is in it, he
> Gets hold of an affinity
> Who's long on modern
> Art but short on hair.

Guido Bruno was a tonsorially challenged and roguish entrepreneur who ran the 'Garret on Washington Square,' where for an admission fee tourists could observe "genuine Bohemian" artists at work in their native habitat. Modernism, in Plum's view, had already become something of a racket.

A second feature of Modernist poetry that irked Wodehouse was its default setting of romantic pessimism, that "something [...] [d]emoralizing in the atmosphere" he had referred to in his lyric. This kind of *weltschmerz* was usually more aesthetic than clinical, and in 1927's *The Small Bachelor* we are allowed to eavesdrop on the world première of aspiring poet Officer Garroway's latest work – the decidedly downbeat 'Streets' – as he reads it aloud to his mentor Hamilton Beamish:

> "Streets!
> Grim, relentless, sordid streets!
> Miles of poignant streets,
> East, west, north,
> And stretching starkly south:
> Sad, hopeless, dismal, cheerless, chilling
> Streets!"

That opening reads uncannily like Eliot's 'Preludes,' in which the poet evocatively describes the dark, damp, grimy streetscape of London. By the end of his tribute, the policeman poet has switched to channelling the *grand ennui* of 'The Hollow Men' which had appeared only weeks prior to *The Small Bachelor* in Eliot's first-ever volume of collected verse. By this stage, the world is not simply going to hell in a handcart but has reached its destination:

> "Men who once were men,
> Women that once were women,
> Children like tiny apes,
> And dogs that snarl and snap and growl and hate."

Garroway's note-perfect parody argues that Wodehouse was familiar with Eliot's collection. Indeed, by this stage TSE was the poster boy of literary Modernism on both sides of the Atlantic after his breakthrough 'The Waste Land' had exploded onto the cultural scene in 1922, just as Wodehouse was writing *Leave it to Psmith*. It is in this novel – surely not uncoincidentally – we are introduced to "celebrity" Canadian poet Ralston McTodd, the sullen, temperamental and gloomy-looking "singer of Saskatoon." And in 1927's 'Came the Dawn,' Plum once more skewers the doom-laden atmosphere of Eliot's masterpiece in 'Darkling (A Threnody)' from the pen of Lancelot Mulliner:

> Black branches,
> Like a corpse's withered hands,
> Waving against the blacker sky:
> Chill winds,
> Bitter like the tang of half-remembered sins;
> Bats wheeling mournfully through the air
> And on the ground
> Worms,
> Toads,
> Frogs,
> And nameless creeping things;
> And all around
> Desolation,
> Doom,
> Dyspepsia,
> And Despair.

In Wodehouse's take, Modernism perversely chose to wallow in ugliness and negativity, as typified by McTodd's slim volume *Songs of Squalor*. That same year Plum came up with three further ominous parody titles – *Sewers of the Soul*, *Grey Mildew*, and *The Stench of Life* – all written by Wilmot Royce, the pen-name of Felicia Blakeney's mother in 'Chester Forgets Himself.' Others of that ilk include Stultitia Bodwin of 'Best Seller' and *Hot Water*'s Blair Eggleston, both of whom have produced volumes entitled *Offal*.

Talking of tripes, dyspepsia was also a metaphor Wodehouse linked to Modernism, an ailment that sours the sufferer's mood in a number of his novels and stories. Which makes Modernism not so much a heroic challenge to the fragmented reality of the 20th century but a by-product of acid reflux, heartburn and excessive burping that a regime of liver salts would quickly put right. His tissues restored, the writer could then return to creating cheerful stuff. As Hamilton Beamish tells Garroway:

> What's wrong with you […] can be set right with calomel. My dear Garroway, it surely must be obvious to you that this poem of yours is all wrong. It is absurd for you to pretend that you do not see a number of pleasant and attractive people on your beat. The streets of New York are full of the most delightful persons … The trouble is that you have been looking on them with a bilious eye."
> "But I thought you told me to be stark and poignant, Mr. Beamish."
> "Nothing of the kind. You must have misunderstood me. Starkness is quite out of place in poetry. A poem should be a thing of beauty and charm and sentiment and have as its theme the sweetest and divinest of all human emotions – love."

But Garroway was right; Beamish's aesthetic *had* done a 180; having fallen in love with May Stubbs while Garroway was busy writing the poem, his gloom had lifted, to be replaced by an all-enveloping sweetness and light.

As late as *Ring for Jeeves* from 1953, Wodehouse was still insisting that poets didn't *actually* want to write relentlessly miserable material but were forced to do so by mercenary editors exploiting what they supposed was the zeitgeist. Former bohemian poet Rosalinda Spottsworth has been one such victim:

> Although in her vers libre days in Greenwich Village she had gone in almost exclusively for starkness and squalor,

even then she had been at heart a sentimentalist. Left to herself, she would have turned out stuff full of moons, Junes, loves, doves, blisses, and kisses. It was simply that the editors of the poetry magazines seemed to prefer rat-ridden tenements, the smell of cooking cabbages, and despair, and a girl had to eat.

Fellow travellers in this cabal of gloom were Tolstoy, Dostoevsky and 19th-century continental philosophers like the "fundamentally unsound" Friedrich Nietzsche, Baruch Spinoza (a favourite of Jeeves whose idea of fun was watching spiders fight to the death), and Arthur Schopenhauer, with whose philosophy Eliot was enduringly fascinated. Here's the disconsolate Millicent Threepwood playing Job's comforter to a similarly dejected Sue Brown in *Summer Lightning* (my emboldened passage is a direct quote from Schopenhauer):

> "Schopenhauer says that all the suffering in the world can't be mere chance. Must be meant. He says life's a mixture of suffering and boredom. You've got to have one or the other. His stuff's full of snappy cracks like that. You'd enjoy it […] [He] says suicide's absolutely O.K. […] Schopenhauer says **we are like lambs in a field, disporting themselves under the eye of the butcher, who chooses first one and then another for his prey**."

Fortunately, things don't continue so gloomy after both women's romances have been sorted out. Which makes love and calomel surefire antidotes to an attack of Modernism.

Which brings us to Plum's third sticking point: Modernism's stubborn refusal to yield sense; or, in straining after innovative ways of seeing the world, resorting to outrageous novelty to fulfil its literary ambitions. Writing to Bill Townend, he commented:

> The reader has to do all the work. The writer just shoves down something that seems to have no meaning whatever, and it is up to you to puzzle out what is between the lines.

Surely, he reasoned, it was the writer's job to *make* things make sense, even down to the individual metaphors they use. Failure to do so, on whatever pretence, represented a dereliction of duty. Take this joyously bathetic shocker from Percy Gorringe's poem 'Caliban at Sunset,' as featured in 1954's *Jeeves and the Feudal Spirit*:

> "And he,
> This man who stood beside me,
> Gaped like some dull, half-witted animal
> And said,
> 'I say,
> Doesn't that sunset remind you
> Of a slice
> Of underdone roast beef?'"

Here, Plum simply *must* have been channelling the notorious opening lines of Eliot's 1915 poem 'The Love Song of J. Alfred Prufrock,' which is also set at twilight time:

> Let us go then, you and I,
> When the evening is spread out against the sky
> Like a patient etherized upon a table.

Plum was so chuffed with his roast beef image that he wheeled it out on three further occasions. It's *sort* of right (Bertie describes the sunset as "[v]ery fruity [...] the whole horizon was aflame with glorious technicolour") and yet it is also wilfully, gloriously queasy, as Eliot had intended his own metaphor to be. Or take Ralston McTodd's notorious "Across the pale parabola of joy." What does that even mean? Wodehouse scholar Neil Midkiff manfully wrestles with its significance on the *Madame Eulalie* website yet can't quite resolve it into sense. But he does point out that it is unusually cheerful for a modernist writer, and – horror of horrors – is written in regular iambic pentameter. Ralston must have been having a brief respite from his dyspepsia.

Plum wasn't at all puzzled by the unhelpful tropes of modernism: he absolutely got the theory but didn't seem to think it any big deal. As early as June 1914 in his *Vanity Fair* column 'The Literature of the Future' he brutally simplifies Futurism, one of modernism's early, minor offshoots. He begins with the avant-garde's assertion that a new, more convoluted reality had dawned, urging artists to completely re-invent how they addressed it:

> In these complex, hustling days, if authors are to be true
> to life, they must put far more into their descriptions of
> every-day life and action than they have dreamed of doing
> hitherto [...] It is the old principle of the Irish Stew.

Which, minus the Irish Stew, is almost exactly what Eliot would write seven years later in a highfalutin' essay on Baudelaire:

> We can only say that it appears likely that poets in our civilization, as it exists at present, must be difficult [...] The poet must become more and more comprehensive.

Plum relished a challenge, and with his jobbing writer's hat squarely on his head sets out to craft a Futurist story, one that "is going to make me very rich." And here it is in its totality, a riff on the five-word statement 'Jones crossed Thirty-third Street':

> Jones . . . Zunk . . . Whoosh . . . Wow . . . Now . . . Ah . . . Clangclangclangclang . . . Wow . . . Whew . . . Woof . . . Kindly look where . . . Brrrrrrrrrrr . . . Where do I . . . Ardent gaze . . . Affinity? . . . Whoosh . . . Wow . . . Wuxtry . . . Brrrrrrrrrrr . . . Brown's Balsam for the Bilious . . . Wha-a-a-a-aaaa . . . printing-machine . . . Yipe-yipe-yipe . . . moving pictures . . . Whoosh . . . Oo . . . Affinity . . . Burning-stare . . . Clangclangclangclang . . . Hi-yi-yi . . . Whfff. . .

Jones's adventure (as well as a popular intestinal disorder) is all present and correct, albeit scarcely recognizable without the gloss Plum provides at its end, craftily anticipating the seven pages of footnotes Eliot would helpfully append to 'The Waste Land' to help its readers puzzle it out. The passage also predates the sonic clang that would open the 'Sirens' section of James Joyce's *Ulysses* published eight years later:

> When first he saw. Alas!
> Full tup. Full throb.
> Warbling. Ah, lure! Alluring.
> Martha! Come!
> Clapclop. Clipclap. Clappyclap.

By contrast with this associative gallimaufry, Plum claims *his* jumble of words is not the mess it might first appear; rather, it is "a new *improved* Irish Stew," a "compressed soup tablet of literature" that contains all human life in it *somewhere*. Which is precisely what many of the literary modernists were aiming to do: represent reality not in linear, sequential sentences but in exploded 4D planes that at least tried to embrace an experience in its totality. It's a technique that could work for you too, as Wodehouse tells us in his best imitation of a snake-oil salesman:

It is ridiculously easy. Try it yourself. Anybody can see the whole picture.

"A child can do it," he says, "And, what is worse, nearly every child *is* doing it." An alternative is to simply recast some perfectly good rhyming stuff like Longfellow's 'The Village Blacksmith,' as he suggests in 'The Alarming Spread of Poetry' from 1916:

> Under the spreading chestnut-tree
>   The village smithy stands.
> The smith a brawny man is he
> With large and sinewy hands.

Which then becomes:

> In life I was the village smith.
> I worked all day
> But
> I retained the delicacy of my complexion
> Because
> I worked in the shade of the chestnut-tree
> Instead of in the sun.

So while Plum clearly understood some of the underlying principles of modernism very early in its evolution, there was no way he was buying into it.

The poetic parodies we've looked at so far have been broad-brush burlesques; but his most pitch-perfect parody of a modernist lyric, even down to the title, is the opening of Percy Gorringe's 'Caliban at Sunset,' immediately prior to the appearance of the underdone roast beef (q.v.):

> I stood with a man
> Watching the sun go down.
> The air was full of murmurous summer scents
> And a brave breeze sang like a bugle
> From a sky that smouldered in the west,
> A sky of crimson, amethyst and gold and sepia
> And blue as blue were the eyes of Helen
> When she sat
> Gazing from some high tower in Ilium
> Upon the Grecian tents darkling below.

Had Wodehouse not been cursed with an all-conquering sense of the ridiculous that quivers just below the surface of these lines, he could have earned a crust as a serious poet. Tonally reminiscent of Eliot's later, more mature blank verse, they come complete with that air of calm, contemplative intellectualism and the occasional alliteration, onomatopoeia and repetition that let us know we're dealing with a poetic sensibility. But cleverest of all is the technical mastery of the emotion-free language Eliot often banged on about, words purged of sentiment but not atmosphere. But while he could never have written *Four Quartets* in a year of Sundays, Wodehouse skilfully demonstrates that he could tune his eye, ear and brain to the same poetic frequency. Which is not as easy as it looks when writing a poem whose subject is *actually* the boneheadedness of Stilton Cheesewright.

As we've witnessed time and again through this book, Plum never thought of himself as an Artist with a capital 'A'. Rather, he was a craftsman, a commercial writer who needed to publish regularly to keep his audience onside and his cashflow healthy. Bertie tellingly refers to the readers of his chronicles as paying "customers"; and it's significant that when he wants to take the rise out of high culture's humourless pretension (his fourth and final annoyance), Plum juxtaposes it – to its detriment – with commercial prose such as advertising copy. 'Darkling (A Threnody),' Lancelot Mulliner's "mere *morceau*" we examined earlier, was actually the poet's tin-eared response to a commission for a slogan promoting Briggs's Breakfast Pickles, his "Promethean fire" reluctantly pressganged into the service of Mammon:

> "The thing," he said, "is symbolic. It essays to depict the state of mind of a man who has not yet tried Briggs's Breakfast Pickles."

Although Lancelot's effort is utterly risible, he still takes it incredibly seriously, insisting it be "printed in hand-set type on deep cream-coloured paper [...] bound in limp leather, preferably of a violet shade, in a limited edition, confined to one hundred and five copies." And he's not alone: Ralston McTodd's verse ("not light summer reading") is similarly published in "a slim volume [...] in squashy mauve"; and then there's Rodney Spelvin who occasionally manages to squeeze out a "slim volume of verse bound in squashy mauve leather." These exiguous talents are presented as neither gifted nor enlightening but are blessed with a rather over-generous opinion of themselves. In 'Rodney Fails to Qualify', Spelvin complains that

"Only last week a man, a coarse editor, asked me what my sonnet, 'Wine of Desire,' meant." He laughed indulgently. "I gave him answer, 'twas a sonnet, not a mining prospectus."

Which, with added preciosity, matches Eliot's unhelpful rejoinder when a group of students asked him what "Lady, three white leopards sat under a juniper tree" (from his poem 'Ash Wednesday') was all about. His reply? "It means, Three white leopards sat under a juniper tree."

But within the warm embrace of Wodehouse World, there is still hope for some of these unfortunates. In 'Rodney Has a Relapse,' Spelvin stops being a precious ass and morphs into a thriller writer who pushes out "a couple of thousand words of wholesome blood-stained fiction each morning before breakfast;" and although Percy Gorringe ends up producing a dramatized version of *Spindrift* (which tanks after three performances), he too moonlights as a purveyor of blood and gore, writing as Rex West. Lancelot Mulliner's future lies in silent movies rather than literature, but at $10K a week, he won't be too disappointed with that.

But for all their differences, there is one mighty big resemblance between Eliot and Wodehouse neither of them was likely to have been aware of, and which brings this book right back to where it started. In his seminal essay 'Tradition and the Individual Talent' from 1919, Eliot addresses the struggle of the poet for relevance; how they can fit their work, both aesthetically and historically, into the continuum of Great Literature. "[I]f you want it," he opines, "you must obtain it by great labour," "it" being the "historical sense" that acknowledges not only "the pastness of the past, but [...] its presence." If you haven't found a solution to this problem by the age of 25, he confidently states, your oeuvre is destined for the dumpster. Fortunately he had; three years later 'The Waste Land' would conduct a spectacular ram raid on the world's literary cultures, parading some of its spoils in those seven pages of footnotes appended to it. If historical significance wouldn't materialize in his poetry because modern society was simply too confused and confusing for the artist to create meaning, he would make his own by quoting or alluding to cultural milestones for all he was worth. So by borrowing a lot of stuff from different periods in literary history and weaving it all together, he would try to create a historical context for his own poem to sit *inside* even as he was writing it. Like Plum, he mercilessly pillaged the Bible and Shakespeare, but also a range of writers our man never really bothered with, including Dante, Spenser, Marvell, Goldsmith, Verlaine, Baudelaire, and the *Upanishads*.

Did he succeed? The jury's out and always will be; but the fourth line from the end of *The Waste Land* reads, "These fragments I have shored against my ruins" – which mischievously (or despairingly) leaves the whole thing hanging in the air, or perhaps even canvassing the reader's opinion on his strategy's effectiveness. What we do know is that in the very same year (by publication), that other mighty modernist James Joyce was using exactly the same process of fragmented quotation and allusion in *Ulysses* to create as comprehensive a picture as possible of an ordinary day in Dublin, to snatch that day from history and therefore give it a heightened significance as art.

But what has all this got to do with Wodehouse? On the surface, very little. Yes, he may have been born the same year as Joyce and Pablo Picasso, but surely his sensibility was diametrically different from these Modern giants? Not according to Stephen Medcalf's 2010 essay 'The Innocence of P. G. Wodehouse,' in which he claims that Plum's writing leads us down "stylistic paths through the same insecurity that the modernists exposed." Having dropped this thought-provoking bombshell, Medcalf lapses into incomprehensibility, but at least in this respect he is absolutely correct: that Plum put his literary knowledge to work just as originally and brilliantly as Eliot and Joyce. For to be able to write in a variety of styles, or to think of literature as a kind of smörgåsbord from which to pick and choose, is often viewed as a somewhat modern, even post-modern take on the act of writing, as cultural commentator Lev Grossman acknowledged in a 2011 article for *Time* magazine:

> [Wodehouse] was a comic writer in an age of serious aesthetes: he was of the generation of James Joyce and Virginia Woolf, and the toweringly serious works of his famous coevals have gone a long way towards obscuring Wodehouse's enormous gifts as a stylist.

Again, right on the money. But Wodehouse's "stylist" m.o. was fundamentally different from his modernist contemporaries, having no social, historical or aesthetic axes to grind as he elegantly shoe-horned those hundreds of literary borrowings into his work. Not for him the modernist neurosis that feared for culture's future. His literary cornucopia wasn't filled with Eliot's "fragments" drained of their meaning or even the bits of old junk Yeats kept in the rag and bone shop of his heart (see Chapter 1) but prime cuts ripe and ready for use as *entertainment*. As writer and literary scholar John Bayley has written, Wodehouse's "lordship of language" contains "more true Shakesperean buoyancy [...] than Joyce" for all the latter's playful linguistic experimentation. Indeed, Plum didn't need to experiment with language, being perfectly happy with the traditions handed down to him. Academic Laura Mooneyham wrote in 1994 that his was "a recombinatory genius" that takes the ability of literature to survive cultural cataclysms for granted, even as he undermines its seriousness. And as this book goes to press at the close of 2023, Charles Moore opined in the *Spectator*:

> His work's modernity, making such innovative use of the main literary traditions of the West, would have been unimaginable in the nineteenth century […] Samuel Johnson famously complained of the seventeenth-century Metaphysical Poets that, in their work, "the most heterogeneous ideas are yoked by violence together." But what Wodehouse saw, as Johnson perhaps did not, was that such yokings can be funny.

Which truth – shock, horror – qualifies Plum for membership of the Modernists' Club.

Would he have been happy to read this? Possibly, provided any enhancement of his literary respectability didn't lower his stock as an entertainer. He might even have been quietly chuffed that these endorsements represent a poke in the eye for those benighted souls who lazily (or snobbishly) dismiss his work as fluff. So for one last time here's proof of how elegantly he thieves from cultural history, in a single sentence from *Jeeves in the Offing*:

> In a matter of seconds by Shrewsbury clock, as Aunt Dahlia would have said, I could see that she was going to come out with one of those schemes or plans of hers that not only stagger humanity and turn the moon to blood but lead to some unfortunate male – who on the present occasion would, I strongly suspected, be me – getting immersed in what Shakespeare calls a sea of troubles, if it was Shakespeare.

Which indeed it was, taken from Hamlet's famous soliloquy in Act 3 Scene 1. But did you also notice the "Shrewsbury clock," courtesy of Sir John Falstaff in Act 5, Scene 4 of *Henry IV, Part 1*? Or, for that matter, the reference to the Book of Joel, chapter 2, verse 31?

> The sun shall be turned into darkness, and the moon into blood, before the great and terrible day of the Lord come.

Or even that quote from Transvaal President Paul Kruger at the start of the Second Boer War in 1899:

> The Republics are determined, if they must belong to
> Great Britain, that a price will have to be paid which will
> stagger humanity.

A rich tapestry indeed: four cultural trophies spanning over two millennia and three continents seamlessly woven into a single sentence. And as we witnessed in the Shakespeare chapter, Plum liked to repeat his favourite quotes time and again in the manner of the oral storytellers of antiquity. Harking back to Homer, who, as he smote his bloomin' lyre (see Chapter 1 again) would call on his sizeable library of familiar phrases and epithets when performing the *Iliad*, so Plum presents us with many of *his* favourite sayings, which either has us frantically Googling or patting ourselves on the back for having recalled them unaided. We might even quote them in our own writing or conversation, handing on the cultural baton as in a relay – one of the many ways art survives and thrives into Eliot's "time future."

So unlike his sweatier or more culturally anxious contemporaries, Plum proves how playing with literature and/or cultural artefacts of any kind can actually be FUN. And if you think I'm overstating the case by placing him up there with Joyce and Eliot in the imaginative ways he addresses his literary heritage, here's a compendium of the real-life writers who have thus far found their way into this book, conveniently arranged in alphabetical order of surname (except for a few mononymous authors):

Douglas Adams, George Ade, Aeschylus, Gustave Aimard, W. H. Ainsworth, Grant Allen, Margery Allingham, Kingsley Amis, Martin Amis, F. Anstey, Archimedes, Aristophanes, Matthew Arnold, Kate Atkinson, John Aubrey, Ruby M. Ayres, Francis Bacon, H. C. Bailey, R. M. Ballantyne, Florence L. Barclay, Francis Beaumont, J. M. Barrie, Harold Begbie, Hilaire Belloc, Arnold Bennett, E. F. Benson, Anthony Berkeley, Walter Besant, Ambrose Bierce, Bjørnstjerne Bjørnson, Michael Bond, J. S. Borlase, Bertolt Brecht, Charles Brookfield, Robert Browning, Bill Bryson, John Buchan, Edmund Burke, Robert Burns, Lord Byron, Hall Caine, Erskine Caldwell, Thomas Carlyle, Lewis Carroll, Raymond Chandler, Leslie Charteris, Geoffrey Chaucer, Anton Chekhov, G. K. Chesterton, Peter Cheyney, Agatha Christie, Jonathan Coe, Wilkie Collins, Joseph Conrad, James Fenimore Cooper, Bernard Cornwell, Marie Corelli, Crates, Cratinus, Thomas de Quincey, Ethel M. Dell, Charles Dickens, Denis Diderot, Benjamin Disraeli, Isaac

Disraeli, Arthur Conan Doyle, John Dryden, Alexandre Dumas (*père*), Lord Dunsany, Mignon G. Eberhart, Umberto Eco, T. S. Eliot, Eupolis, Frederick W. Farrar, William Faulkner, W. H. Fitchett, F. Scott Fitzgerald, Gustave Flaubert, Dick Francis, Neil Gaiman, John Galsworthy, W. S. Gilbert, George Gissing, Elinor Glyn, George Grossmith, H. Rider Haggard, Richard Hakluyt, Henry Hamilton, Dashiell Hammett, Thomas Hardy, Joanne Harris, Joel Chandler Harris, Bret Harte, Ernest Hemingway, Bracebridge Hemyng, William Ernest Henley, G. A. Henty, Hermippus, Hesiod, Georgette Heyer, Susan Hill, Oliver Wendell Holmes, Homer, Anthony Hope, Horace, Thomas Horde, E. W. Hornung, Thomas Hughes, Edith M. Hull, Vicente Blasco Ibáñez, Kazuo Ishiguro, W. W. Jacobs, Henry James, Gertrude Jekyll, Jerome K. Jerome, Dr. Samuel Johnson, Ben Jonson, James Joyce, Juvenal, Marion Keyes, Charles Kingsley, Rudyard Kipling, Ronald Knox, Andrew Lang, Ring Lardner, Philip Larkin, John Le Carré, Mikhail Lermontoff, Sinclair Lewis, Livy, Jack London, Henry Wadsworth Longfellow, George Horace Lorimer, Thomas Macaulay, Philip Macdonald, Magnes, Bernard Malamud, Christopher Marlowe, Nicholas Marryat, Ngaio Marsh, Philip Massinger, William Somerset Maugham, Frank McCourt, Jay McInerney, H. Seton Merriman, A. A. Milne, John Milton, John Mortimer, Kate Mosse, Talbot Mundy, Vladimir Nabokov, Ovid, Edith Nesbit, Friedrich Nietzsche, Sean O'Casey, E. Phillips Oppenheim, George Orwell, Ossian, Ouida, Barry Pain, James Payn, Hesketh Pearson, Max Pemberton, Plautus, Pliny the Elder, Alexander Pope, Ezra Pound, Terry Pratchett, J. B. Priestley, V. S. Pritchett, Philip Pullman, E. R. Punshon, Sir Arthur Quiller-Couch, Talbot Baines Reed, Thomas Mayne Reid, Ruth Rendell, Samuel Richardson, Frederick Earl Roberts, Bertram Fletcher Robinson, Dante Gabriel Rossetti, J. K. Rowling, Salman Rushdie, John Ruskin, Saki, Dorothy L. Sayers, Arthur Schopenhauer, Sir Walter Scott, Sir Charles Sedley, W. C. Sellar, William Shakespeare, Tom Sharpe, George Bernard Shaw, Percy Bysshe Shelley, John Steinbeck, Robert Louis Stevenson, Rex Stout, R. S. Surtees, Frederick Swainson, Jonathan Swift, Booth Tarkington, Donna Tartt, Philip Meadows Taylor, Alfred Lord Tennyson, Terence, William Makepeace Thackeray, Thucydides, Leo Tolstoy, Bill Townend, Anthony Trollope, Lynne Truss, Mark Twain, John Updike, S. S. Van Dine, Virgil, Edgar Wallace, Hugh Walpole, Mrs Humphrey Ward, R. S. Warren Bell, Auberon Waugh, Daisy Waugh, Evelyn Waugh, J. E. C. Welldon, H. G. Wells, Patricia Wentworth, Rebecca West, Walt Whitman, Oscar Wilde, Geoffrey Willans, Edmund Wilson, Virginia Woolf, William Wordsworth, Willard Huntington Wright, R. J. Yeatman, William Butler Yeats and Edward Young.

I make that 235. Which total doesn't include Eudora Welty, A. E. Housman, Sir Compton Mackenzie, or M. R. James, who were also Wodehouse advocates and/or friends I wasn't able to crowbar into the argument. Respectively a Harvard lecturer and lyrical novelist of America's Deep South; a renowned classicist and elegiac poet; the polymathic Scottish author of comic novels *Whisky Galore* and *Monarch of the Glen*, and a medievalist who wrote some of the scariest-ever ghost stories, these were not only brilliant writers who knew their stuff but were possessed of widely different sensibilities. There's also those mighty *menschen* W. H. Auden and C. S. Lewis, the latter writing to his brother Warnie in 1939 that *Right Ho, Jeeves* was "one of the funniest books I've ever read." As a schoolboy, he had joyfully devoured the Psmith canon; and in his reconstruction of an evening's conversation with the Inklings (a loose association of Oxford writers whose number included J. R. R. Tolkien), biographer Humphrey Carpenter attributes the following observation to Lewis on the subject of literary snobs:

> For a start, they may be proved entirely wrong by history: the book that they scorn today may be a classic for the intelligentsia of the twenty-third century. Very odd things may happen: our age may be known not as the age of Eliot and Pound and Lawrence but as the age of Buchan and Wodehouse, and perhaps Tolkien.

From Nobel winners to pulp fiction writers, an enormous number of his fellow scribes have taken Wodehouse to their hearts – and still do.

Which prompts one final and not altogether serious conundrum, namely: could Wodehouse and Eliot ever have been friends? I reckon they could. For all the gentle fun Plum pokes at 'advanced' poetry, he would have recognized – and possibly admired – the fact that Eliot, cerebral to his socks, had managed to become that rare thing: a world-famous, serious poet whose work had been immortalized in a slogan for Esso petrol ('Time future contained in time past'). Not to mention that *Old Possum's Book of Practical Cats* – a set of poems intended as a bagatelle for his godchildren – was re-imagined as a stage musical that has to date grossed over $3.5 billion. That alone would have given them plenty to chat about while Plum signed Eliot's prized copies of his work.

And, of course, Eliot *did* write that poem about a famous pig, once advising his close friend Frank Morley that "[T]he way to pick a good pig" is to choose ones that look like Rudyard Kipling's cousin Stanley Baldwin, which are invariably "better than ones that look like Winston [Churchill]; get one of Stanley's pigs."

Lord Emsworth, whose love of poets was not great, would surely have made an exception in this case.

* * * * * * *

And that's about it for this book, which, as I noted at its start, is far from the whole story of the myriad influences that went to make up Wodehouse's entertaining and enduring writing style. Its companion volume *Showbiz Wodehouse* will start being written just as soon as I can scale the Everest of reading necessary to research it.

Till then, Pip Pip.

Appendix A:
Wodehouse's School Set Texts

The place was stiff with dead literature.
Under the Flail

Pelham Grenville Wodehouse arrived at Dulwich College on May 2, 1894, in the Midsummer Term and was placed on the 'Classical' side in the Upper Third B of the Junior School. The following term, he entered the Senior School where he remained until July 1900. During those "six years of unbroken bliss" (age 12½ to 18½), he would study a range of disciplines, and what follows is an inventory of the syllabuses set between the Upper Third B (1894) and VI Form (1899-1900) which will serve to flesh out some of the general comments I make in Chapter 4.

In terms of the texts themselves, there are a couple of caveats. First, Dulwich only published academic timetables in the Michaelmas (Autumn) and Midsummer terms; what the boys read in Lent (Winter) term may or may not be covered by these records, and it isn't a given they studied all the titles listed. As Plum describes in his 1900 article 'Work,' changes to the syllabus could be utterly random and capricious. Certainly at my school, timetabling suitably knowledgeable masters with the many different set texts didn't always work out, so certain books, even though they were included on the curriculum, quietly fell by the wayside. Also, as the academic year wore on, we tended to get a bit behind, with much the same outcome.

In compiling what follows I have correlated (with invaluable guidance from Dulwich's Keeper of the Archive Calista Lucy) the various termly syllabuses ("Form Work") with separate lists detailing Wodehouse's exam positions, allowing us to determine which form he was in when he sat them. This revealed that he unexpectedly shifted form twice in mid-year (in 1895 from Lower IV to Lower V, and 1896 from Lower V to Upper V), which meant he would have missed studying some of the titles we might otherwise assume he had read, or studied additional titles we reckon he hadn't. This may explain why my results are occasionally at variance with the work of previous Wodehouse scholars. Immediately prior to leaving the Dulwich Archive, I discovered a handwritten sheet of paper tucked into the back of one volume on which an anonymous researcher had completed the exact same exercise I had just finished. Thankfully, our findings were identical, so here they are:

JUNIOR SCHOOL

Classical Upper Third B, Midsummer Term 1894, age 12

LATIN & GREEK:	Virgil *Aeneid* 5 (part); Livy, part of Hannibalian War; Greek Grammar; Morice's Stories
ENGLISH SUBJECTS:	English History William III to Victoria
DIVINITY:	Acts of the Apostles 1-15

SENIOR SCHOOL

Classical Lower IV, Michaelmas Term 1894 – Lent Term 1895, age 12-13

GREEK:	Colson's Greek Reader 3-5
LATIN:	Ovid *Fasti* (selections); Livy *History of Rome* Book 27 1-14
HIST & ENG:	Fyffe's Greek History Primer
DIVINITY:	Acts of the Apostles Chapters 1-14

Classical Lower V, Midsummer Term 1895 – Michaelmas Term 1895, age 13-14

GREEK:	Thucydides *History of the Peloponnesian War* Book 2 1-75 (excl. Speeches); Aristophanes *Vespae* ('The Wasps') 950 to end; Aeschylus *Prometheus Vinctus* 1-327; Euripides *Heraclidae* 1-866 (omitting choric parts); Thucydides 3 1-100 (omitting speeches)
LATIN:	Livy *History of Rome* Book 3 51-end and Book 4 1-45; Virgil *Aeneid* 3 and 8; Horace *Odes* 3
HIST & ENG:	Greek History; Milton *Paradise Lost* 2 and 3
DIVINITY:	Lectures and Essays on the Parables of the Bible

Classical Upper V, Lent Term 1896 – Midsummer Term 1896, age 14

GREEK:	Thucydides 5 (part); Homer *Odyssey* 12
LATIN:	Virgil *Aeneid* 9; Horace *Epodes* and *Odes* 2
HIST & ENG:	Cox's Athenian Empire
DIVINITY:	St. Mark 1-5

Classical Remove, Michaelmas Term 1896 – Midsummer Term 1898, age 14-16

GREEK: Thucydides *History of the Peloponnesian War* Book 4 and 8; Homer *Iliad* Books 2-4, 19-22 and *Odyssey* Books 5-9; Aeschylus *Agamemnon*; Sophocles *Philoctetes;* Demosthenes various inc. *3rd Philippics*; Euripides *Orestes*; Lysias *Selected Speeches*; Aristophanes *Ranae* ('The Frogs')

LATIN: Tacitus *Annals* Books 3, 4 1-35; Virgil *Georgics* Books 1 and 3-4; Plautus *Rudens; Horace Epistles* and *Ars Poetica;* Livy *History of Rome* Book 5; Cicero *pro Sulla*; Virgil *Aeneid* Books 3,4,5 1-400; 6; Cicero *Verrine* Book 4; Plautus *Menaechmi* (part); Tacitus *Histories* Book 1; Propertius V [misprint?]

HIST & ENG: History of Early Roman Empire; Roman History 133-63 BC; Milton *Paradise Lost* Books 11 and 12; Early Greek History; Introduction to Homer; Greek Literature Primer, Creighton's Age of Elizabeth; Shakspere [sic] *King Lear*

DIVINITY: Era of the Protestant Revolution; Acts of the Apostles 13-28

Classical VI, Michaelmas Term 1898 – Midsummer Term 1900, age 16-18

GREEK: Thucydides *History of the Peloponnesian War* Book 3; Aristophanes *Clouds*; *The Wasps* (in part); Sophocles *Oedipus Coloneus*; Aeschylus *Prometheus Vinctus* and *Seven Against Thebes*; Theocritus, Bion and Moscius *Select Idylls*; Plato *Republic* Book 3 and *Apology*; Sophocles *Electra*; Demosthenes *De Falsa Legatione*; Aristophanes *Pax*; Aristotle *Athenaion Politicia*; Pindar *Pythian Odes*; Aeschylus *Agamemnon*; Plato *Republic* Book 4; Aristophanes *Knights* (part)

LATIN: Juvenal *Satires* Books 1-8; Tacitus *Annals* Books 14-15; Cicero *Pro Sestio* and *Pro Plancio* (beginning); Lucretius *De Rerum Naturae* Book 3; Cicero *Selected Letters* (Watson) Part 4;

	Persius *Satires* Books 1-3; Virgil *Aeneid* Book 8 (part); Critical papers on advanced grammar; Juvenal *Satires* 10-16; Cicero *De Oratore* 1 and *Philippics* 2 and 5; Catullus (selections); Vergil [sic] *Aeneid* Book 1; Lucan *Pharsalia* Book 1
HIST & ENG:	Early Roman History; Justin McCarthy *A Short History of our Own Times*; General Papers on English Literature; Greek History; Shakespeare [sic] *Merchant of Venice* [sic]; French Revolution; Tennyson *The Princess*; English History outlines; special period 1756-1789; essays on literary subjects
DIVINITY:	Life of St. Francis of Assisi; St Paul *Epistles*; The captivity of the Jews; Divinity essays; the Gospel of St. Matthew

Appendix B:
Wodehouse's Personal Library

Plum's personal library was, as you might imagine from reading this book, extensive. At the time of writing (August 2023), it has three homes:

- Dulwich College – to whom Lady Wodehouse donated a large selection of Plum's personal copies of his own works. These are now shelved in a permanent exhibit along with Plum's desk, on which can be found, among others, a small book rack containing two volumes of *Pick of Punch*, *The Saturday Evening Post Treasury* and J. I. Rodale's *The Synonym Finder* (Special Deluxe Edition). The original bequest has since been added to.
- The British Library, London – to which Wodehouse's family has loaned a massive archive of letters, manuscripts and ephemera, grouped into 548 separate "collections" (these are listed at https://searcharchives.bl.uk/)
- The family home of Plum's step-grandson (Sir Edward Cazalet) in East Sussex.

This last repository is a fascinating treasure trove, shipped over from

Plum's home in Remsenburg, NY, to England around ten years after his death in 1975. An inventory was compiled in 2018 and divided into two lists, of which only the second need concern us here.

At 35 single-spaced pages, it is unfortunately too long to be included in this book, but the first thing to note is that it is very much a 'working' library rather than a collection. These books have been read, some almost to destruction, and/or are second-hand copies that Plum acquired from who knows where. A few are loans he never returned. Their publication dates span many years, and are semi-randomly arranged on 53 shelves, each numbered. As noted elsewhere, detective, thriller and mystery titles predominate but the rest are almost completely random: Of the writers featured in this book, Barry Pain is top of the heap with 21 titles, followed by Patricia Wentworth (20); Agatha Christie (17); Anthony Powell (15); A. A. Milne (10); Evelyn Waugh (10); F. Anstey (9); Edgar Wallace (9); Jerome K. Jerome (8); W. W. Jacobs (8); George Ade (8) and Ngaio Marsh (6).

Of the writers not mentioned or quickly passed over, Henry Cecil scores highest with 16 titles; James Branch Cabell (15); F. Scott Fitzgerald (14, including critical works and biographies); Leo Tolstoy (13); William Caine (10); John O'Hara (9); Ed McBain (9); Colette (7); Noel Coward (7); E. M. Forster (6); J. B. Priestley (5); Erle Stanley Gardner (5); Edmund Wilson (5); William Hope Hodgson (5); Aldous Huxley (4); Julian Symons (4); William Somerset Maugham (4) and Christopher Isherwood (4).

Plum's friends and collaborators are well represented: there are 7 Bill Townend titles, 9 Denis Mackails and 2 by Ian Hay.

A few points to note: among these books are several signed by his daughter Leonora, which indicates some of her personal library may well have got mixed up with Plum's. Colette may seem an untypical Wodehouse choice, but all is made clear in the new Preface he wrote for *French Leave* in 1974:

> I was living near Cannes and trying to learn French by going to the local Berlitz school and reading the novels of Colette.

Next comes F. Scott Fitzgerald. A near neighbour on Great Neck in 1918, Plum actually met him on a train in 1923 when Fitzgerald was riding high with *The Beautiful and the Damned*. As he wrote to Leonora (who must have expressed an interest in this new literary superstar):

> He seems quite normal, and is a very nice chap indeed.

You would like him. The only thing is, he does go into New York with a scrubby chin, looking perfectly foul. I suppose he gets a shave when he arrives there, but it doesn't show him at his best in Great Neck. I would like to see more of him.

Unfortunately, the friendship never blossomed, and in later life Plum wasn't hugely complimentary:

[W]hy do they worship Scott Fitzgerald over here? *The Great Gatsby* was good, but his short stories, the things he made his name on, are AWFUL.

By that stage, in 1951, Fitzgerald was ten years dead.

Then there are those 13 Tolstoys, which include a biography, selected non-fiction, a collection of letters, two copies of *Anna Karenina* and three of *War and Peace*. Given that Plum never lost an opportunity to poke fun at the Great Russians and their industrial-grade doom and gloom, this level of interest is surprising – although once again, Leonora might have been the culprit. The fantasy writer James Branch Cabell is another outlier, although his 1904 debut *The Eagle's Shadow* has been described as "a country house farce of the P. G. Wodehouse sort, but less funny and more deep." By contrast William Caine and Henry Cecil – both men of the law turned crime novelists – were right up Plum's alley. Of Noel Coward there will be more in my next volume, which will also touch on the numerous other theatre books dotted around the shelves.

Further Wodehouse enthusiasms include cultivated East Coast wit, with ten and four titles respectively from loyal fans **James Thurber** and **Ogden Nash**, as well as five by New York savant **Robert Benchley**. But the treasures among these books must be two first editions by the mighty wit **S. J. Perelman**, *The Road to Miltown* (1957) and *Chicken Inspector No. 23* (1966), respectively inscribed "To P. G. Wodehouse, with friendship and admiration" and "To P. G. Wodehouse for friendship and admiration" (see Appendix C for more on both Benchley and Perelman). Then we have cats, represented by *Best Cat Stories, Cats and People, A Quorum of Cats,* and *The Complete Cat*; around sixty titles concerning the theories and practices of spiritualism, a long-term Wodehouse interest I write about at length in Volume 2, Chapter 8 of my trilogy *Pelham Grenville Wodehouse*; a sizeable section on cricket, residing mainly on shelves 38-40 and cosying up to Leonard Coppett's *A Thinking Man's Guide to Baseball*; and finally, on shelves 18 and 19 of what is known as the "womb" section of the archive, there are copies of the following:

- Scott Meredith, *Writing to Sell* (X2)
- Gordon Taylor, *Creative Writing in English*
- William Strunk Jnr, *The Elements of Style*
- Alan Casty, *Let's Make it Clear*
- George Kirgo, *How to Write 10 Different Bestsellers* and
- Walter Kerr, *How Not to Write a Play*

Now what can he possibly have needed *those* for?

Appendix C:
Wodehouse's New York Society
Library Borrowings

(My grateful thanks to Tad Boehmer of Michigan State University for allowing me to use his extensive research in what follows.)

Wherever he was, and at whatever stage in his life, Wodehouse needed access to books. Passing seventy, from March 1951 to the start of April 1955 he borrowed 818 books from the New York Society Library, a convenient 600-yard stroll from his and Ethel's apartment at 1000 Park Avenue on the Upper East Side. Broken down, this figure represents 354 titles in 9 months of 1951, 132 in 1952, 172 in 1953, 103 in 1954 and 57 in three months of 1955, at which point the couple moved full-time to their home in Remsenburg on the south shore of Long Island. It's a remarkable total; and while we must remember that they may not all have been for him – and that he may not have read all of them – his borrowings are a fascinating record of what he thought he *might* have liked to read. Indeed, the list provides us with yet more evidence of what a catholic consumer of literature Plum was.

Many of the authors who feature in this book are on the list: Agatha Christie (4 titles borrowed), Edgar Wallace (7), George Ade (4), Hilaire Belloc (4), Barry Pain (8), Anthony Berkeley (5), Patricia Wentworth (13), Arthur Conan Doyle (4), Rudyard Kipling (1), A. A. Milne (4), E. Phillips Oppenheim (7), F. Anstey (3) and Rex Stout (with 16, his most borrowed author). The titles he selected no doubt represented lacunae in his personal collection.

In terms of genre, Plum's choices stretch far and wide, though crime titles tend to predominate. Of those murder mystery writers we haven't yet come across in this book, we find that throughout 1953 he binged on ten works by **G. D. H. Cole,** an English political theorist, historian and economist who also wrote thrillers on the side between 1925 to 1948, most in collaboration with his wife Margaret. *Off With Her Head!* and *The Corpse in the Constable's Garden* are mainstream Golden Age romps, their titles broadly indicative of their tone and contents. Interestingly, Plum had worked up a plot idea for a stage play in 1948 to be called *The Long Arm* which, as things turned out, shared a central premise with the Coles' 1941 novel *Counterpoint Murder* and therefore had to be dropped. **Elizabeth Daly** is also well represented with six titles; her regular gumshoe Henry Gamadge was a bookish author, bibliophile, and amateur detective with a line in wry humour apparently beloved of Agatha Christie. Other notables include **David Dodge** (6 titles); **Mary Fitt**, the pen name of classicist Kathleen Freeman (7); the prolific **Anthony Gilbert**, real name Lucy Beatrice Mallison (7); **Michael Innes**, aka J.I.M. Stewart, an Oxford academic whose work which includes *A Comedy of Terrors* has been described as "an over-civilized joke with a frivolity which makes it a literary conversation piece with detection taking place on the side" (4); **Ngaio Marsh**, one of the acknowledged queens of crime whose love of theatre frequently spilled over into her plots (5); and **R. A. J. Walling,** author of *The Corpse with the Floating Foot* and many other *The Corpse with . . .* titles (9). At the (even) more ridiculous end of the genre, Plum borrowed five volumes of **Early Durr Biggers**'s tales, including two that feature his most famous creation Charlie Chan. We should also mention **Howard Haycraft**, who was among the mystery genre's earliest historians and chroniclers (5).

New York metropolitan humour is also a genre of note. Algonquin Round Table regular **Robert Benchley** (8) who arrived at (US) *Vanity Fair* soon after Plum had left, is top of the heap for borrowings. He and Plum were regular acquaintances (at least according to *Bring on the Girls* in which he pops up several times). Then there's **Franklin P. Adams** (6), a writer who talent-spotted **George S. Kaufman** (4) and Dorothy Parker (Wodehouse's successor as *Vanity Fair*'s theatre critic) in his influential column 'The Conning Tower.' It's rarely remarked that Plum's many *Vanity Fair* articles published between 1914-19 helped set the tone for the sophisticated cultural reporting apotheosized in *The New Yorker* from 1925 onwards, and prominent among that magazine's contributors were short story specialist **Sally Benson** (3) who would script the Judy Garland vehicle *Meet Me in St Louis*; humorist **Will Cuppy** (4) who we've already met in his role as crime reviewer; **Arthur Kober** (3) creator of husband hunter Bella Gross (and sometime husband of Lillian Hellman); **Frank Sullivan** (4) whose 'Mr Arbuthnot The Cliché Expert' was something of an institution; **James Thurber**, whose cartoons and short stories were regulars in the magazine; **E. B. White** (4), author of *Stuart Little* and *Charlotte's Web*; and the renowned **S. J. Perelman** (4), the sort-of surreal humorist and one of Plum's many literary admirers. The feeling was mutual, Wodehouse inscribing a copy of 1966's *Plum Pie* "To S. J. (The Top) Perelman / With awe and homage / from / P. G. Wodehouse." English humour is a bit thin on the ground, but **Edward Verrall Lucas** (8) and **A. P. Herbert** (7) appear to be favourites.

After all these, it becomes a highly serendipitous list. Notables include the short stories of **Stacy Aumonier** (4), **Max Beerbohm** (creator of *Zuleika Dobson*, 3) and no fewer than 10 titles from among the fiction and non-fiction of **Arnold Bennett**, whose *How to be a Writer* Plum quoted to Bill Townend when his friend was experiencing some sort of existential crisis. The theatre is represented by dramatists **Noël Coward** (4), **J. B. Priestley** (3), **Jerome Weidman** (4), **John Van Druten** (4) and American critics **John Mason Brown** (4) and **George Jean Nathan** (4). And apart from 5 novels by **Dornford Yates** (real name Cecil William Mercer), four of whose titles are either omitted or illegible, that's about it.

INDEX TO *PLUM'S LITERARY HEROES*
including Wodehouse characters

P.G. WODEHOUSE: WORKS CITED

ALSO BY PAUL KENT

Pelham Grenville Wodehouse: "This is Jolly Old Fame"
Pelham Grenville Wodehouse: "Mid-Season Form"
Pelham Grenville Wodehouse: "The Happiness in the World"

The What Ho! Series

What Ho! P. G. Wodehouse on Food
What Ho! P. G. Wodehouse on Love
What Ho! P. G. Wodehouse on Money
What Ho! P. G. Wodehouse on Sport
What Ho! P. G. Wodehouse on Class
What Ho! P. G. Wodehouse on Cats & Dogs
What Ho! P. G. Wodehouse on Hollywood
What Ho! P. G. Wodehouse on Fashion
What Ho! P. G. Wodehouse on Childhood
What Ho! P. G. Wodehouse on Faith

A title on P. G. Wodehouse and the Theatre is forthcoming